CONSOLE CONFESSIONS

THE GREAT MUSIC PRODUCERS IN THEIR OWN WORDS

Edited by Anthony Savona

Backbeat Books
San Francisco

Published by Backbeat Books
600 Harrison Street, San Francisco, CA 94107
www.backbeatbooks.com
email: books@musicplayer.com

An imprint of the Music Player Network
Publishers of *Guitar Player*, *Bass Player*, *Keyboard*, *EQ*, and other magazines
United Entertainment Media, Inc.
A CMP Information company

CMP
United Business Media

Distributed to the book trade in the US and Canada by
Publishers Group West, 1700 Fourth Street, Berkeley, CA 94710

Distributed to the music trade in the US and Canada by
Hal Leonard Publishing, P.O. Box 13819, Milwaukee, WI 53213

Cover design by Doug Gordon
Interior photos by Edward Colver

Library of Congress Cataloging-in-Publication Data

Console Confessions : The Great Music Producers in Their Own Words / edited by Anthony Savona.
p. cm.
Includes index.
ISBN-13: 978-0-87930-860-5
ISBN-10: 0-87930-860-5 (alk. paper)
1. Sound recordings—Production and direction. 2. Sound recording executives and producers—Interviews. I. Savona, Anthony.

ML3790.c715 2005
781.49—dc22

2005013809

Printed in the United States of America

05 06 07 08 09   5 4 3 2 1

Contents

Section III: Technical

Section IV: Surround Sound

Introduction

My Life in Recording

A story about a vicarious reality

Did I ever tell you how I helped create Phil Spector's legendary "Wall of Sound"?

No?

How about how I miked Frank Sinatra's orchestra?

Really?

Well, I must have told you about getting Michael Jackson's vocals down during the recording of *Thriller*?

Oh, right. I didn't do any of those things. That was Larry Levine, Al Schmitt, and Bruce Swedien, respectively. You'll have to forgive my confusion, although once you've pored through this collection you'll understand my mistake.

How could I think, even for a second, that I could've taken part in such important moments in recording history? I mean, despite my 12 years or so of working on *EQ* magazine, I have never professionally pushed a fader. Sure, I've tweaked knobs, punched buttons, and, yes, glided a fader or two through countless demonstrations of the latest and greatest consoles, recorders, and other gear, but I've never worked in a studio before — project or otherwise.

I joined *EQ* magazine straight out of college — St. Johns University in Queens, NY, to be exact, where they offered audio recording as part of the Communications program. I took that course, which helped me with the concepts I would soon face editing *EQ*, but I never pretended for a second that it qualified as a true studio experience.

The thing of it is, I feel as though I've worked behind the board on dozens of projects. From simple songwriting sessions all the way up to some of the biggest records ever released.

The reason for this was the impetus behind compiling this collection of the first-person stories from *EQ* magazine. This book contains the hows, whens, and whys about professional recording from the biggest names in the business. And these stories are not filtered through a journalist's questions — they come right from the source itself. If you've wondered what it would be like to share a session with the likes of Phil Ramone and Eddie Kramer, pull up a chair and start reading.

For me, it was an incredible gift to be able to play a part in these stories reaching print. I, and the *EQ* staff, were always amazed by the generosity of the studio pros we approached to write stories for us. We were nearly always met with an enthusiastic response. Despite being in an industry where careers are built on trade secrets, these pros were willing to pass on what they had learned, what they had experienced, to our readers.

Looking through these stories today, I see quite a few dead-on predictions about the industry — and probably just as many that didn't materialize. In these pages, you'll see the birth of digital recording — and the beginning of the transition to hard disk recording.

Many of the articles devote some space to the analog-digital debate, which has pretty much been settled by now, although there are still some engineers out there willing to put up a fight. But, for the most part, the majority of the concerns the original analog defenders were concerned about have been taken care of in digital recording by newer technology.

And speaking of technology, in retrospect, Alesis ADATs may not have turned out to be the long-term workhorses we thought they were, but there was no question that their arrival was revolutionary — sparking the project studio revolution — and those articles from that time period will give glowing reports on their abilities.

Through these articles it's clear to see that it's not about the tools, but the hand that uses them. The gear references have all been left intact, though many of the models have been discontinued or pushed to the side in favor of newer time-saving, cost-effective methods. Whatever gear was used, the reasoning behind each choice is also given, and that doesn't change with time. The techniques used a decade ago still work today — even if the methodology of doing it has changed.

If you are a long-time reader of *EQ*, then these pages will spark some memories and remind you of some of the great tips these stories originally gave. If you're a younger engineer, or if you're just discovering these stories, I hope you enjoy your one-on-one time with the best in the business.

– Anthony Savona

SECTION I

HISTORY

It's easy to argue that, in a book that collects stories from the past decade or so, everything in it is history. That may be true, but the stories in this section were considered history *at the time we ran them.*

These stories are among my favorites. I find it amazing what these recording pioneers were able to accomplish with the technology at hand, and the length of time the fruits of their labor still inspire, entertain, and touch us.

So go back in time to the days when it was only a matter of hours between recording a song and hearing it on the radio, and see how today's techniques were born.

Home Alone

"Gene Autry is not going to get up on his horse and play a goddamn synthesizer."

By Les Paul

Originally appeared in August 1991

Everyone is talking about this home studio phenomenon as if it's something new. Well, I had my first home studio back in the '30s, and let me tell you, it was the hard way to go. Everybody told me I was crazy as hell.

My original goal was to get around all the nonsense of making records back in those days — unions, rules, regulations. So the solution was building my own studio — an idea my business manager laughed at. In fact, Bing Crosby was the only person who believed in me. He drove me up and down Sunset Boulevard looking for a place to build it until, finally, I lost heart. I said, "Why do I want to do this? Why should I be a crusader?" So Bing turned the car around and we ended the search. When we got home, my friends said, "Why not build it right here in the house, Les?" And we did it.

No one was convinced that it was a good idea even then. One day I got a call from my manager. He said, "Your honeymoon's over, Les. You're extinct. RCA's studio lights are lit all night long — no one needs your home studio any more."

He wasn't the last to talk extinction at me. I had to spend 18 hours arguing with Gibson back in 1966 when they told me the solid body electric guitar was extinct. My point has always been that the proof is in the pudding — the electric guitar and the home studio were anything but extinct. They were the future, and I was sure of it.

You should have seen what went on in my house. Gene Autry, Bing Crosby, the Andrews Sisters, Art Tatum — you name it, they all came into my backyard to record. I recorded Mary Ford while she was making spaghetti in the kitchen, and Capitol Records soon found out that there was something happening in my kitchen that wasn't happening in their studios. There was something happening in my living room — Billy May with his feet on my coffee table at four in the morning — that couldn't happen in their fancy rooms.

Today there are a zillion home studios. But the interesting thing is that the people who have them aren't necessarily qualified. Everybody's got their toys, but that doesn't mean they can do the job.

There were people like Ricky Nelson who put a studio in their homes, but a studio wasn't the answer. For Ricky, the music was the answer. Now Bon Jovi has the finest equipment money can buy, but will he ever be actually qualified to use it? Some people...they can't even find the switch to turn the stuff on. But they go build the studio anyway and find some Joe Schmo contractor who builds it incorrectly and then they get an engineer to run it. And when something goes wrong they have to call Boston or L.A. or Salt Lake City and fly someone in to fix the goddamn thing.

Me, I'm in there on the floor fixing it myself. When the last machine I bought came off the Mayflower moving van I said, "We're going to take it apart and clean it." They said to me, "Les, it's brand new." I said, "I know." So we took this enormous multitrack thing apart and laid it out all over the floor. It didn't need cleaning. But let me tell you, I know every part of that machine. If something goes wrong and someone says to me, "It's the capstan," or whatever, I can look over my glasses at him and say, "No, you're wrong."

There's another point about all this equipment I really want to make: It might be hardware, but it ain't inspiration.

The other night Bob Dylan comes up to me and asks me, "What kind of guitar are you playing? An old one?" I say, "Yeah, if 1980 is old." No matter what guitar I play I get my sound. It's the same with recording studios. No matter what kind of walls there are, what kind of acoustics — even if they're cutting with a nail — I'll get my sound. EQs, patchbays, enormous amounts of toys...throw it all out. The sound comes from you.

My son and I are now doing 125 sides for Capitol, remastering a lot of released and unreleased tracks. And they are quiet — dead quiet — even though they're 50 years old. And we're doing it in analog. My son says, "Why go analog when you can go digital?" And I say, "Because I like analog." Digital makes a lot of corrections. You get Apogee filters in there and they manage to correct the problems, but it's brittle and hard. There's no hum and no hiss, but it relinquishes nothing. It gives you what you think is the hard truth, but it's not. It's the machine's error.

Of course, having the right studio can't hurt. We started a year and three months ago building a studio of tomorrow. There are only four or five others even entertaining the concept of what we're working on. The control room is the studio. Everybody's in the same room, the same way I made records back in 1928.

Today, if Billy Joel wants to hear the recording, he has to take his earphones off and walk 50 feet, through two doors, to the control room. And then the engineer has to get up so he can sit in the sweet spot because of nearfield monitoring.

Let me just say that the nearfield concept is radically wrong. People say to me, "Les, we're not going back to old speakers that are going to blow your head off." I say, "Well, no one said it's going to do that." Look, everybody has his opinion, his own way of doing things. That's why you make your own studio. You make yours your way, I'll make mine my way.

My way is totally different. In fact, this studio is exactly similar to the tradition of recording in your living room that I started out in Hollywood.

There was a clarinet player in my house the other day. I went downstairs and found him playing in the oven. I said, "What the hell are you doing?" He said, "It sounds good." I said, "Okay."

Just watch a violin player. They're always scratching on the thing, walking around, figuring things out. They're looking for the spot where it sounds good, and they don't even know that they're doing it. They're like ants scuttling all over the place. That's what I want my studio to be: the place where it just sounds good.

What kind of gear do I have in there? It doesn't matter. Because it's not the gear that makes the talent. You can go down to Trader Horn and buy a heap of garbage and put it in your house and have a studio that'll work. Now everybody has what we had years ago, but there are obstacles, and those obstacles are going to rear their ugly heads.

Just remember that building a studio is a positive experience. You just have to do it for the right reasons. And audio gear is a good thing. You just have to buy it for the right reasons.

Here's what I mean: The other day I squeezed a beer can and it crushed like paper. Twenty years ago, you'd be hard pressed to put a dent in a beer can with two hands. The cans today still hold the liquid, but they're not nearly as good. And the equipment you buy today is not a Sherman tank. It's delicate. It's made so that when it finally goes to hell you throw it right into the dumpster.

The guy who builds a car has to make sure that the wipers collapse at the same time as the rest of the car collapses. Why make a great wiper and a lousy steering wheel? Today's engineers make objects that destroy themselves evenly. But that doesn't mean that new gear isn't necessarily better for the job. A lot of new things are faster, smaller and smarter. So you mix the old and the new together to get what you want.

The only rule is that there are no rules in recording.

It takes special talent to be an audio engineer. And sadly, 99 percent of the people — and the hair is going to go up on the back of their necks when I say this — have the toys, but that doesn't make building their own studios a wise idea. You have a buddy who knows electronics, so all of a sudden he's a producer.

Let me put it this way. If I go to the bathroom and sit down and read this whole magazine cover to cover, I haven't learned a hell of a lot because everything is going to change by tomorrow. Keeping up is impossible. By the time you go to buy an R-DAT you read about somewhere it's no longer being made. It's in the surplus bin. They're striking it from the line. And I say — "For what?" What's really going to be the improvement 50 years down the line?

I like to use this analogy. You got an automobile. It's got four wheels. And after all these years, it's still a box with four wheels that putters some guy down the street. What is recording equipment? It gets your sound on tape. What's a guitar? The same. You slip a pickup in it and go.

Guitar Player magazine called me 15 years ago and predicted that the guitar would be extinct in a decade. I said, "The bunch of you are in la-la land. Gene Autry is not going to get up on his horse and play a goddamn synthesizer." The synthesizer today is still like a United Airlines dinner. You get off the plane and say, "What did I eat?" It looked like an egg, but what the hell was it?

But you know, I have four synthesizers here so these younger guys can go crazy. They say, "I've gotta have a synth," so I say, "Plug it in and do your thing."

You may be thinking that I'm against technology, but I'm not. You might even think I'm against home studios, but I'm all for them. I'm just saying that they can be dangerous things.

You see all these gifted musicians who all of a sudden say, "Christ, if I buy a Synclavier I never have to leave the house." And then they disappear for a year. People put themselves in the nuthouse this way. And half the time the music comes out sounding like neither fish nor fowl.

You know, a synthesizer piano shouldn't bend notes like a guitar. I heard Ray Charles do this and it really turned me off; he left what made him in the first place. I think this technology can sidetrack a musician. Ray could play the worst piano in the world and it would sound better than a synthesizer.

It all comes down to your natural gift. I don't care if you're an atheist or not, you're naturally gifted from God. Everyone has one gift or another. The question is where.

There's many a person who plays the guitar who should be a sewer digger, and there's no shame in digging sewers. There's many a doctor who's a butcher. A lot of people walk down the street with one foot in the curb, because loving something doesn't make you gifted at it. If you're not gifted with rhythm, can you go down to Sam Ash and buy it? If I bump into something, I can hum it in five-part harmony, but should I be a dentist?

If you're gifted in electronics and pick up real fast on it — if you have the gift for finding the solution to a problem — then you've got what it takes to be a recording engineer. It's a natural thing; it's genius. That's what you need to make it in the studio. You need energy, perseverance, talent, and luck. And if you've got it, you'll make it.

The Story Behind the Story

At the time this story was published, Les was promoting a Capitol 4-CD boxed set called *Les Paul: The Legend and the Legacy,* which included rare outtakes, tracks, and photos.

This is a beautiful thing. We're all differently touched. We all have something to offer. Maybe you're great with the electronics but you can't play, or vice-versa. Or you can sing but God help you with an instrument. Do what you're good at, because no piece of machinery can make you something you ain't.

There's an unwritten law I figured out. Look at your hand. You got five fingers. Name me five piano players, guitar players — whatever. If you can name me more I'll kiss your ass in Macy's window.

"But Les," you say, "there's four million guitar players just in goddamn Newark! It doesn't make sense, what you said." But it does make sense, because one guy can keep time but he can't play. Another has good rhythm but no sense of melody. You know what I mean. There are very few that play from the heart. What makes a great mixing engineer? It's the same thing. Go ahead — just find me five.

Nobody knows more than me that it's not easy to mix after you have all your music together. This is a big, dangerous thing. You have all these electronic toys and you want to use them. I say, if you don't need it, don't put it in. But you get tempted. You've got it; you want to use it.

Guys go absolutely nuts with these toys. I was talking to my son about recording the other day. "Son," I said, "if it takes you more than an hour to finish this thing, you're screwed up." If I spend 12 hours making an album, something's wrong. Somebody asks me, "How long is it going to take you to do this tune?" I say 20 minutes.

Nobody believes me about this. They come over with their cameras and they say do a number for us right on the spot. I say, "OK, I'll do it and I'll write it in a half hour." So they say, "We'll tell you to stop when we have to reload the cameras," and I say, "Get your shit together now because I'm not stopping."

The point is that recording is a matter of inspiration. It's also a constant search. In a way, it's like reading the Bible. I sit there listening to the preacher, waiting to hear the answer to that one line — and I don't even know what I've been looking for until I hear him say it. The same thing happens in the studio. You're always looking. You've just got to have your antenna up. If it isn't up, the signal's going to go right by you. See you in church — or in the studio.

Phil Spector

An EQ exclusive memoir by the man who engineered the legendary wall of sound

By Larry Levine

Originally appeared in February/March 1991

Phil Spector first came to Gold Star Studios in L.A. in the late '50s to work with Stan Ross, the studio's owner and my cousin, on several projects, including the Teddy Bears and the Paris Sisters. Then, in 1962, he flew in from New York to record "He's a Rebel" in a big hurry because he was racing the release of Vicki Carr's version at Liberty Records. Stan was vacationing in Hawaii, though, and Phil was forced to use me instead. Later, with "Zip-a-Dee-Doo-Dah," I was to become his regular engineer.

I had met him earlier when he was working with Stan and I didn't like him at first. (Most people didn't.) I thought he had this aura about him that said "spoiled brat." But by this time I knew of his reputation and was in awe. I remember the "Zip" session well: We were setting up, trying to record for three or four hours and all of my pots were real hot — all my meters were pinning at the top and I knew I wasn't going to be able to record like that. Phil was really working us hard and I didn't know what to do to make him back off.

I finally decided that there was nothing else I could do, so I just turned all the pots fully off, all twelve of them. Phil looked at me like I was crazy and started screaming at me that he had just about had it and how could I do that. I told him that there was no way that I was going to get that on tape. I started bringing the pots back up one at a time, first the basses, then the drums, guitars, and so on. I had 11 of the pots turned up and had mixed them pretty gently to where they were when Phil yells, "That's it! That's the sound. Let's record." I told him that I didn't have Billy Strange's mic open yet. (Billy was playing lead guitar.) Phil said, "Don't turn it on!" So we recorded it that way and the guitar sound on the tape is what bled through the other microphones. The room was small so you could hear it, but it didn't have the presence that a microphone can give.

It was my single greatest experience with a record and from there on in, I was Phil's engineer. I was so excited about "Zip-a-Dee-Doo-Dah" that I would take people into the control room and tell them, "If you tell me there's a chance, just a chance, that it won't make the Top Ten — I'll eat the tape right in front of you." They'd look at me like I was crazy because nobody could predict with that kind of certainty what would happen to a record after it was released, but I never did have to open that bottle of ketchup.

Letting the Good Tapes Roll

The good times were the great times. If things were going good, Phil would do stand-up comedy in the control room. Sometimes he would do as much as 25 minutes' worth. He used to love to use me as the butt of his jokes, but I didn't mind because I knew that was the role I was playing.

The sessions were a lot of work, though, and you could never relax. When you played things back you had to play them back as a record. It was very tiring and there were times when we would argue over it. The Christmas album was particularly exhausting. After we finished, I had to tell Phil I couldn't do it anymore. Our separation lasted about three months. Phil was working back in New York and Sonny Bono came to me and said that Phil really wanted to work with me again. By that time I missed making great records, so I was happy to have him come back to Gold Star. Of course, Phil and I worked well together, but there was something special about Gold Star itself.

When I first arrived there in 1952, it wasn't anything like the place that Phil Spector would help make famous. I started hanging around there in the evenings because there wasn't much else happening. At first I just did gopher stuff, but when business increased and they needed someone else to work the board, Stan and Dave Gold gave me my big chance.

It was great fun in those days (even at $25 a week). We were doing basically demos at that point. No one was doing sessions except larger studios. We were working with songwriters or publishers who would come into the studio, sit at the piano, and have their song recorded onto disc. You would count to three, point at the guy in the studio, and drop the stylus onto the disk. And that was it.

We had one tape recorder then, a Brush and a wire recorder, and a console that Dave had built. The console was very basic — six or seven inputs and an amplifier. It wasn't state-of-the-art because at that time there was no art. And although Gold Star Studios would soon become famous for its incredible echo, at this time we had a long way to go.

In fact, to get our first echo we used the hallway that ran from the main reception room to the main control room. The singer would stand in the doorway of the studio — half in and half out — and sing. We'd put a microphone at the other end of the hall and try to capture some semblance of echo. The technique didn't work too well and it was a pain trying to keep everybody from walking down the hallway. For our next attempt, we built this little attic above the hallway. It was a three feet by 30 feet by three-feet-deep box. We painted it with slate to harden up the surface to make it reflect better. It's amazing we didn't kill ourselves with the fumes. Unfortunately, despite our efforts, it sounded like shit and we were back to the hallway.

The Boom-Boom Room

In 1960, shortly before Phil arrived, we really started living! Dave redesigned the studio and we had gotten an Ampex 350 mono deck and a 351 2-track. We also had a new console built by Dave and Bill Putnam that had 12 inputs and three outputs. This console had a divider, so as you increased the echo send, you decreased the send to the fader, which was the way we thought echo should be. Echo was to make things sound farther away, not to create the effect.

Dave had designed two chambers that were angled, so that they were two geometric shapes that would fit side by side. These were the chambers that Phil Spector would make famous. Inside the chambers, we put a little 8-inch speaker and an RCA flat ribbon microphone to capture the echo and bring it into the board.

The control room at Gold Star was perhaps the best-sounding room I've ever heard. We had these great Altec D3 monitors. Phil would always have the music blasting. I didn't mind one bit. Whenever anybody new came into the room, Phil would want to impress them so he'd turn it up yet another notch. I knew all they'd be able to hear would be a mess of noise because nobody can get their ears set to that level so quickly. (Around the studio, Stan and Dave and the other guys started to refer to their levels by a "Larry." Most guys would go half a "Larry." You could never get past three-quarters of a "Larry.")

Phil-anthropist

Phil always knew what he wanted and, although he never put his hands on the board, he could have worked it if he wanted to. I never lied to him about what I was doing because he always knew what was happening. I saw guys try to bullshit him but it never worked. Phil trusted me on the console so that he was free to do whatever he was going to do — but he was always aware.

I remember during the recording of "And Then He Kissed Me," I was trying to get more level because Phil wanted things louder and louder. What I decided to do was to send the original to two tracks and double up the level of sound. Later, I would just keep one of the tracks and use the other track for voices and strings. What had happened was that the echo also got doubled. It was okay when I had both tracks, but when I erased the other track I was left with essentially twice the echo that I had originally put on.

I didn't admit it was an accident, though Phil knew how it had happened. But he liked what he heard. He listened and understood exactly how it had happened. He had that kind of knack.

Everything that was created during those sessions was done by Phil. Nobody else should get any credit for the "wall of sound." (The phrase was coined by some disc jockey or reviewer in response to Phil's revolutionary rhythm section.)

Scaling the Wall

Here's how we built the wall: We'd fill up the studio with 20 to 25 people. The room was very small and there would hardly be room enough for the musicians to move around one another. The room was filled with musicians playing their hearts out and we'd fill every available space on that tape with it. There were other aspects to the sound, which were very much part of the physical structure of Gold Star itself, but this was the basic building block of Phil's "wall."

Retro-Spectored

Phil Spector's band, studio crew, and stars recall the heyday of the wall

Phil Ramone, Producer/Engineer

"Phil had his own way of doing things. The record industry was dominated by rules and he broke almost every one of them. At that time arrangers drove the business, but not with Phil. He would take the song from the arrangement and carry it to where it would work.

"I hear his influence today, particularly in rap music with its layering, sampling, and big orchestral drops. People aren't even conscious of where it came from. If Phil got back into recording today, he could walk all over the dance market."

Hal Blaine, Drummer

"We would always play Friday nights at Gold Star Studios. It was always a tremendous party. The biggest joke was that there was a sign on the door that said 'Closed Session'—meaning that no one should enter—but Phil grabbed everybody that poked their head in and made them play a percussive instrument. Everybody from musicians like Brian Wilson of the Beach Boys to other producers who came down to see what Phil was doing. Everybody would play. There was magic when we worked with Phil.

"He would pack us all in the studio for the wall of sound effect. General recording sessions have four rhythm tracks, but Phil used two or three basses alone. He had four or five percussionists, although I was the only one who played drums, and four or five guitarists as well as horn and string sections. It was always huge and always a party.

"I worked with him years later on a Leonard Cohen album. It was still a big party and Phil still made any onlookers, which in this case included Cher, Bob Dylan, and poet Alan Ginsberg, perform."

Sonny Bono, Percussion

West Coast Promotion for Phillies Records

"Phil was the Wagner of pop music—larger than life, grandiose. He brought a whole new way of thinking to recording. Rather than thinking about an entire album, Phil focused 100 percent of his energy into a single song. He wrote it and produced it. Then he crammed the studio full of musicians and pushed all the sound up into the distortion range.

"The first time I saw it, I thought, What the hell is going on here. He was breaking every rule. And to my knowledge, Phil invented the technique called bouncing. He got two 2-track recording machines and bounced the various instruments back and forth, which enabled him to squeeze even more sound onto the tape. Nobody had ever done that before. Call it clever, call it genius, it was unique."

Darlene Love, Singer

"Although I had worked with other producers, Phil was the first one who had produced a number one hit. He was different in that most producers wouldn't teach you the song that you were performing—most of the songs were sung by the songwriter—but Phil would sit down with you and tell you exactly what he wanted. He would sit with me at the piano at Gold Star Studios and go through the entire song with me.

"The big wall of sound sessions were great—you could actually see Phil's genius. He only had three tracks to work with, whereas today you have 64. He put an amazing amount on those three tracks. Plus he had an incredible ear. Today you can push a button and hear only the instrument that you want to hear. Phil couldn't do that, but he didn't have to. He could hear anything—everything—he was looking for, no matter how many instruments were on the tape. He could pick out anything, from a guitar lick to a single note.

"The wall of sound, however, is more than just musical sound, it is the sound of all the people who created it. It is built with all of our hearts and souls."

Steve Douglas, Saxophonist

"Phil's sessions were special because all he recorded were hits. The music was different, unique. Phil was the first guy to go into the studio with an unfinished tune. Generally it was all written out before you went into the session, but Phil would start with the written arrangement then move off of it. He would do two things at once; he would work the sound and the arrangement.

"Everything was loud. Phil would keep the playback volume shatteringly loud. I remember the recording of 'Zip-a-Dee-Doo-Dah,' Billy Strange's guitar was so loud that Phil turned off his microphone—so what you hear on the single is the sound that bled through everybody else's microphone.

"Phil had a very calculated, workmanlike approach to a record. He put a lot of care into every song. He would work the band hard, some grumbled but most didn't—we all wanted to work with him. There was a high level of camaraderie."

Bill Medley, Singer, member of the Righteous Brothers

"What most impressed me about Phil is that he knew what a hit song was. I once asked him why he owned a record company. He replied, 'Because I know what the public wants and I can give it to them.'

"Phil could also recognize a hit voice—he was the first to utilize my baritone abilities. It is always good to work with a producer who knows what he wants, except when what he wants goes against your style. Phil knew what we could do and used our singing abilities to their fullest potential.

"He was the genius of that time—and he still has a lot to say."

Stan Ross, Engineer/Co-Owner of Gold Star Studios

"Gold Star was a special place. My partner, Dave Gold, designed the equipment, the studio, and the echo chambers. The control room didn't have sit-back seats, they were more like four foot stools. They made for better communication between artist and engineer.

"We built the chambers in 1950 for the purpose of giving a nice echo on horns and other instruments. They became very successful and, although our studios were relatively small, the echo made the rooms sound three times larger than their actual size.

"The electronic echo that is used today doesn't compare to acoustic echo."

Shelly Yakus, Engineer
"Every record that Phil Spector produced was more than a record—it was an event. These events changed the perception of what records should be. They heightened the awareness of what you could do with a record.

"Other people in the industry heard what he was doing and knew that whatever they did after that would have to be just as good or better. He made the industry go further than it had and raised the standard for making records.

"Phil showed us we could do it."

Compiled by Anthony Savona

I used to feel sorry for the guitar players because they played the entire session. Phil would start off by saying, "Let me hear the guitars." The acoustic guitars were always first. He'd have them play off of a lead sheet and have them try different things. Then he would add the piano, then the basses, then the horns, and then back to the guitars. That's the way he'd build what he heard in his head, and only Phil knew what that was.

There were times that I had guys with microphones that weren't even plugged in. I'd tell Phil that he could send them home because I didn't have any more open inputs. But Phil would say, "This is the sound. They stay." And he was right. There was a presence on the tape. Whether it was body absorption or whatever, they were a part of what was making the sound happen. That's something that today's electronic musician can learn. The human body adds something to the sound.

We'd always experiment, just trying out different things to see what worked. I never used EQ until I needed it to bring out an effect. What we had then was very basic anyway. We had curves of 3, 5, and 10 kHz, and they could be moved up or down in increments of 3 dB. We used balance, or a different mic, more than we did EQ.

Making Tracks

The thing Phil hated most was that Motown was always able to get a certain sound out of their drums that he could never get. They even nailed the drums to the floor so they'd never lose it. In our room, the drums' sound changed according to what key the song was in. If the guitars were playing open strings, then there was more level coming out of the guitar itself, which meant that the mics were not as loud, which meant I didn't get as much leakage from the drums into the guitar mics. If they were playing with closed strings, the opposite would happen. Everything always sounded different, but I think that was great because there were more different sounds in the wall than just the one you could identify.

Part of Phil's genius is his ability to surround the vocals with this incredible rhythm track and not let them be swallowed by it. We only had three tracks: The orchestra went on

Rebuilding the "Wall"

The making (or remaking) of Back to Mono, *the Phil Spector box set*

Phil Spector's *Back to Mono* (Abkco Records) box set was more than a nostalgia trip for Spector and engineer Larry Levine. The collection was the result of a careful blend of new digital technology and vintage sound equipment.

All of the analog-to-digital transfers, sequencing, and equalizing of the original masters were done at Frankford/Wayne Mastering Labs in New York. According to the facility's mastering engineer, Tom Steele, the majority of the work involved transferring the original masters to Sony PCM 1630 digital. Keeping with Spector's "Back to Mono" theme, all of the remastering was done in good-old hi-fi monaural.

To preserve the authenticity of the recordings (some over 30 years old), an Ampex 351 tape machine, the model the original material was recorded on, was used for playback during the transfer process. A "vintage" machine to say the least, the 351 was hard to find, and locating mono heads for it was even harder. Steele dusted off some other vintage gear for the project including several Pultec and Fairchild compressor/limiters. Most of the 25- to 30-year-old masters, also a bit dusty, were originally recorded in either full-track mono or 2-track mono on Ampex tape. According to Steele, they were all still in remarkably good condition.

Steele also says that Larry Levine's presence was the key to the process. "He was both the recording engineer and the mastering engineer for Phil Spector back then, and it was really a big advantage that he was playing the same role again," Steele explains. "He knew the tapes and their producer intimately."

Levine also helped Spector adapt his expectations to the era of digital audio. For example, in most cases, Spector didn't like the sound that resulted from the transfer to digital. "When you equalize in digital the sound stays too clean and you don't hear any changes," Levine says. "We

the first, the strings on another, and the vocals on the third. It would be easy to lose the vocals inside the wall of sound, but Phil never did. I never worked with anyone else who had that ability.

He had a unique way of working. When I had to mix something down, Phil would leave the room and I'd be left alone to mix. When I had something I liked, I'd call Phil back and he would critique it. Then he'd leave and I'd start mixing again. There were two great things about working this way. One was I didn't have him looking over my shoulder the whole time, and the other was there was always a fresh ear listening.

For the Record

When "Mountain High, River Deep" failed to do well in the United States, Phil took it pretty hard. He sort of rubbed people the wrong way and I know a lot of people who wanted him to fall flat. I mean, I love Phil — but our relationship didn't start out as love. Everyone who worked with Phil liked him, but there were plenty of people in the industry who were thrilled at seeing his string of hits end. It left all of us with a bad taste. I was leaving to go to A&M Records at the start of the following year anyway, so with everything put together I guess Phil decided it was time to close up shop.

We worked together after that. We did some songs with the Checkmates and the Ronettes over at A&M Records. Later, in 1979, we recorded with the Ramones back at Gold Star. That was the last original recording we ever did together. (Gold Star closed in 1984, after 33 and a third years of operation.) It wasn't a good time for Phil and we'd be there all night and it wasn't any fun — for Phil, the

Ramones, or for me. Phil and I got into a big dragged out argument one night and the following evening I had a heart attack. I was smoking and drinking a lot of coffee at the time, so I don't really know if the fight had anything to do with the attack, but I know Phil felt guilty even though we never spoke of it.

After that, he really withdrew into himself and I'm really sorry for any part I played in making him pull further into himself than he already had. We didn't speak again until 1986, when he began inviting me and some other people to his house to watch championship fights on his big screen TV, and I didn't really work with him again until the making of the *Back to Mono* box set.

had to take the digital back to analog and put it through a tube amp to soften the sound. And then we went back to digital with it."

Though the clash between old and new was problematic at times, the results were more than positive. "I think with today's equipment you can hear more of the textures of the 'wall of sound' than you could back then," claims Levine.

Interestingly, improving the sound of the original recordings wasn't one of their goals. "We just wanted to re-create the music the way it was recorded," adds Steele. "We went in thinking that the old stuff was great to begin with. From what we've heard back about the box set already, it looks like we were right."

—Jon Ruzan

Back on (One) Track

It was great to work with him again — better than old times. He was a different person and it was great to get back to the music. I couldn't believe how great it sounded. It was almost as exciting as when we originally recorded them.

Mono's sound content held up amazingly; those singles have as much depth as if they were recorded in stereo. The one basic advantage of mono is that it maintains the integrity of the sound. The sound that you put on the tape will be the sound you come back to whether it's been a day, a week, a month, or 30 years.

Phil would like everyone to go back to mono because, as a producer, he can put it together as the listener is going to hear it, just as the producer intended. He believes that mono can create a texture that will remain and not change depending on where people are sitting. I understand his philosophy, but I don't believe it's necessary to go to that extreme.

Phil changed the industry with more than just his music. He created a little record company [Phillies] that could make things happen and he was also the first producer to put an engineer's name on the label. He had a highly developed social conscience and insisted that the people who contributed be acknowledged. You would never have heard of me or Jack Nitzsche, who was Phil's arranger, if Phil hadn't done that. I still believe that because Phil gave credit to others, it diluted some of the things that are more creditable to him than to Jack or myself. We were tools in his hands and practically everything that came out of those sessions came out of Phil's head. I don't think that a mixer or engineer can create a hit. It's the producer or songwriter who creates the hit; the most an engineer can do is call attention to it.

I still hear some of Phil's techniques today. It's not really all that surprising; anybody who made good records has left his influence. Bruce Springsteen has credited Phil for influencing him. It's not necessarily copying, but contemporary artists are taking Phil's techniques and enlarging on them — which is what should be done.

The problem, I think, with all artists is that they outrace technology. A truly creative person can't just keep repeating himself. They need to go somewhere the technology doesn't allow them to go and so they get frustrated. That's what happened to Phil with "Mountain High, River Deep." The technology wasn't there to let him go as far, or as high, or as deep, as he wanted.

Phil is talking about going back into the studio and recording, and if he wants me to go in with him I will, because I know that it's not going to be in the same way that groups are recorded today. You can overkill with technology. But there's also so much you can do. I'd love to be involved with Phil's projects today and see what kind of hits he could put out — mono or otherwise.

My Hendrix Experience

With a smoking Strat and a radical sound, Jimi Hendrix changed the face of music forever

By Eddie Kramer

Originally appeared in November 1992

The late '60s/early '70s was an amazing period in the history of rock 'n' roll. Many of the artists recording at that time were creating standards and expectations that still have to be met today. I was fortunate enough to work with a number of these legends, including the Who, Eric Clapton, the Kinks, the Beatles, Led Zeppelin, the Rolling Stones, and, of course, Jimi Hendrix.

I vividly remember the day I met Jimi. It was 1967 and Gerry Stickles, the Experience's road manager, came struggling up the stairs to Olympic Studios with a huge 4x12 Marshall amp on his back. Through a deeply reddened face he bellowed, "Where do you want me to put this?" I was pretty taken aback, seeing all these large Marshall amps come in.

Jimi arrived shortly thereafter. He was very quiet and shy. I liked him immediately. And, although quiet, he was very demanding. It's not often you hear these characteristics combined, but he knew exactly what he wanted in the studio.

Chas Chandler, Jimi's producer, was the one who actually made the decision to come to Olympic Studios in London. Olympic was, at the time, the newest studio and was probably the best in all of Europe. Traffic and Small Faces had recorded there.

It was also the most advanced studio at that time, although we only had four tracks to work with. The Americans had eight tracks, but we had better consoles and rooms. American rooms were typically pretty dead, acoustically; ours, however, were alive.

Making Tracks

The basics of how I got Jimi down on tape are as follows: I would fill the four basic tracks with stereo drums on two of the channels, the bass on the third, and Jimi's rhythm guitar on the fourth. From there, Chandler and I would mix this down to two tracks on another 4-track recorder, giving us two more tracks on which to put whatever we wanted, which usually included Jimi's lead guitar and vocals, as well as backing vocals and some additional percussion.

I came up with this method of recording Hendrix because he had been used to the 8-track studios of America and he liked hearing the basic tracks across on all four tracks. Doing it this way made him feel much more comfortable and at ease in Olympic.

Of course, there is much more to Jimi than just these basics. Jimi and I shared a love of the weird and bizarre. Jimi liked to be pushed creatively, and I used to take so many chances with his sound — he loved that. Whenever I did something wild and strange in the studio, it was an inspiration to him. And consequently, whenever he did something unusual in the studio, it was an inspiration to me. It was all pretty subconscious. We never knew exactly what was going to come out when we rolled tape. It was all new and fresh.

Jimi was vastly different from his contemporaries. His whole approach to recording was different to me. He was in his own little world of sounds. Basically, he created the sound in the amp and I just took it and ran with it — expanded upon it. With the Beatles and many of the other groups, much of the sound was created in the control room. Jimi was so wrapped up in his guitar and his sound, that whatever he produced from there was part and parcel of him. So when he plugged in and did something wild with the guitar — whether he would scrape a string or make a rumbling kind of motorcycle sound — he would be creating that so his style would be radically different from anybody else's. And his contemporaries realized this. They all used to come in and watch, whether it was the Stones or whoever else was around. They would just hang out and watch in amazement.

I remember how different it was recording the Beatles' single "All You Need Is Love." They came in and said (in their Northern accent), "We've got to do this television thing and John says he's got something." So we set up a place for John to sit in the control room and we wired up the talkback mic in such a way that he could sing into it while Paul, George, Ringo, and George Martin (who played keyboards) set up in the studio. We would run tape continuously for an hour, with John singing next to me the whole time. When they got a take they liked, they said, "OK, that one," and that was it. It was pretty amazing, but also completely different from my sessions with Hendrix.

Case in point: I remember in particular the June '68 recording of "If Six Was Nine," which appeared on the *Axis: Bold as Love* LP. Olympic Studios often recorded classical sessions, so they had built special platforms to hold all the members. We had pulled one of these platforms forward and put Mitch Mitchell's drums on it. We also put a mic above and below the platform in order to record a foot-stomping track. Jimi was the "stomping leader." Graham Nash and Gary Leeds of the Walker Brothers had stopped by and were recruited to walk.

I compressed the foot stomps so much that you can hear the compression kick in and out. To add even more to the song, at the end of the tune Jimi played a recorder that he had purchased for two shillings from a street vendor.

Purple Phaze

Another technique I used with Jimi was phasing. He had come to me wanting to produce an underwater sound he had heard in his dreams. He often described sounds to me and I was able to produce them, but this one proved to be a bit of a challenge. I had been experimenting

Life of a Lady

Over 20 years ago, Jimi Hendrix decided to build his own personal studio. He is on record as saying that he wanted it to be the best studio in the world. Hendrix knew what he wanted—something new, something designed for rock, a place in which he could be comfortable and inspired. Eddie Kramer was the key person when it came to materializing Jimi's dream, and he was given the job of overseeing the studio. Now, 20 years later, it has become commonplace for musicians to have their own personal studios, but Jimi led the way in this endeavor, as he did in music.

Electric Lady Studios is proud to have helped a number of famous rock 'n' roll musicians over the years. A few of the classics include: Jimi's *Rainbow Bridge,* Stevie Wonder's *Songs in the Key of Life,* and parts of *Led Zeppelin II.* Additionally, Led Zeppelin recorded and mixed *Houses of the Holy* and *Physical Graffiti,* and mixed the soundtrack to *The Song Remains the Same,* at the Electric Lady. The Rolling Stones are said to have recorded *Exile on Main Street* there, as well. AC/DC did *Black in Black* and Foreigner recorded *Foreigner 4.* David Bowie gave us "Fame" and, with John Lennon, recorded "Across the Universe." Kiss recorded and mixed at least seven albums at the "Lady," and Iron Maiden mixed five albums here.

Today, Electric Lady Studios is still making platinum and gold records for artists such as Prince, Mariah Carey, C&C Music Factory, Lou Reed, Anthrax, Warrior Soul, and David Sanborn. The present staff continues to make Jimi's studio a place he would be proud of.

Much has changed over the years and much has been retained. A person familiar with the original studio would recognize, on the hall walls, the original Lance Jost murals that Jimi commissioned as well as the collages in the washrooms. Studio A acoustically looks and sounds very much as it did 20 years ago. The control rooms have gradually changed as the technology improved. Today Studio A features one of the two original Rupert Neve-designed Focusrite consoles.

Studio B has evolved the most. Seven years ago it was rebuilt, swapping the studio side with the control room side to provide enough space for ever-bigger consoles. New in this room is a custom 80-input SSL G Series console with Ultimation. Along one wall sit the Studer analog machines and a Sony PCM 3348. Both Studio A and Studio B feature George Augsperger-designed monitors powered entirely with Manley tube amps.

Studio C, on the top floor, likewise features SSL with Ultimation. It also has TAD components in the monitors and a pair of Studer multitracks. This room is a favorite of many top New York music makers, owing partly to the proximity of the monitors and the tight low end, and partly to its seclusion and privacy.

The microphone and effects list is too long to list here. Older classic EQs from Neve and Pultec are standard, as are UREI LA2's and 1176's. There are also newer Focusrite EQs and a variety of Lexicons and Eventides. Lately ELS has been featuring the Manley tube mics and EQs. And history continues to be made...

— Craig "Hutch" Hutchison, Chief of Maintenance, Electric Lady Studios

The Kramer Chronicles

If you were to make a list of the greatest legends in rock 'n' roll, you would undoubtedly include Jimi Hendrix, the Beatles, the Rolling Stones, Eric Clapton, Led Zeppelin, and David Bowie. One of the amazing things about this list is that it matches a major portion of Eddie Kramer's client list. So who is this man who helped shape the sounds that shaped music history?

In the mid-1960s, the South African native went to work for Pye Studios in England, which was a very unusual studio at the time in that it was outfitted with American equipment. "I learned a tremendous amount there," says Kramer. "It showed me how you could integrate European equipment with American equipment."

Pye Mobile, a division of Pye Studios, was where Kramer honed the on-location recording skills that would later capture the legendary Woodstock Festival. "Bob Auger, who is still around today and perhaps one of the best classical engineers in England, ran both divisions of Pye," explains Kramer. "I used to go out with him and record huge 100-piece orchestras on a 3-track, ½-inch machine with three microphones. It was all pretty amazing."

From there, Kramer opened his own demo studio, went to work for Regent Studios, and then to Olympic Studios, where he worked with a veritable Who's Who of rock 'n' roll that included the Beatles, the Rolling Stones, Traffic and Jimi Hendrix, among many others.

A year-and-a-half later, Eddie left England to work in New York City's newly opened Record Plant. It was there that he continued to work with Hendrix as well as with other artists, including Joe Cocker and N.R.B.Q.

After a year-long stint as an independent engineer for the likes of Led Zeppelin and Johnny Winter, Kramer was hired as director of engineering for Hendrix's Electric Lady Studios. He engineered all the Hendrix albums made during his lifetime. After Hendrix's death in 1970, Eddie compiled Jimi's posthumous recordings and created four albums.

For the next five years, Kramer would stay on at Electric Lady and record a variety of talent that included David Bowie, Led Zeppelin, Dionne Warwick, Lena Horne, and Dion & the Belmonts. It was at this time that Kramer started his own company, Remarkable Productions, Inc., for which he produced artists like Carly Simon and Sha Na Na.

In 1975 he left Electric Lady to become an independent producer/engineer, working with Kiss, Peter Frampton, Foghat, Santana, the Rolling Stones, Ace Frehley, and many others. Over the last ten years he has engineered and produced many successful artists, including Anthrax and Triumph, and he is constantly seeking up-and-coming bands as well as established artists to work with.

In addition to his musical duties, Kramer has just finished, together with rock historian John McDermott, the quintessential Jimi Hendrix book entitled *Hendrix: Setting the Record Straight* (Warner). This book not only describes Jimi's life and music, but also discusses the ways Jimi changed the recording business that have endured to this day.

—Anthony Savona

with phasing and its possible uses for Hendrix, and when I played the results for him he yelled, "That's it! That's the sound I've been hearing in my dreams."

We first used phasing on "Bold as Love." I phased Mitch's drum roll (that rushed from left to right), then I panned the drum sound through the speakers, canceling the phase mere seconds before Hendrix's guitar re-entered the recording — also enveloped in phased sound. This was one of the first times phasing had ever been recorded in stereo.

Jimi and I communicated very well. Later in Jimi's career, however, it would be harder to keep him focused in the studio. His life at that point was filled with pressures — from legal troubles to touring problems. To keep him focused, I found myself continually challenging him in the studio — keeping things interesting for both him and me.

I also knew how to make Jimi feel comfortable in the studio. From the outset, he had strong reservations about his vocal ability — he never really liked the sound of his voice. To help him overcome this discomfort, I would put partitions all around him when he placed the lead vocal overdubs. Jimi also asked that the lights be dimmed, so they were. After we recorded the track he would poke his head around the screen and ask, "How was that? Was that OK? Was it all right?" And I would tell him it was fine because, when it came to his singing voice, Jimi needed all the confidence he could get.

(Move Over Rover) Jimi Takes Over

After the recording of *Electric Ladyland* in 1968, Jimi had been given a band to produce, named Eire Apparent, and he asked me to be his engineer. We always worked well together, and Jimi had always helped produce his own recordings, so I accepted.

But Jimi was at a point in his life where he wanted to be in control of everything — and it started to creep into my area of the board. Not that I didn't like that when I was working on one of his projects, where we would share the console. On certain pieces I would say to him, "You grab the vocal and do the pan on the echo," and I would grab the rest of the console. But with the Eire Apparent sessions he wanted to take control of the whole process, and I was annoyed at that. I think he was just expanding his horizons, but he was trying to take over my gig.

We had a parting of the ways because of this project. I didn't even finish it. I put my foot down — as a producer on his albums it was fine because we shared everything. On Eire Apparent, I felt as though my job was being usurped. That was the year I became an independent engineer.

Boxey Lady

The separation didn't last long. Jimi and I didn't work together again until the building of Electric Lady Studios in 1969. We got together by chance — Jim Marron, manager of the soon-to-be-built studio, invited me down to the site where the studio was to be built — unbeknownst to Jimi. I had known Marron through visits to the Scene Club and he asked me to come down and look at the site, being completely unaware of my relationship with Hendrix.

Jimi and I, however, were happy to put the Eire Apparent incident behind us and work together again. I was brought on as chief engineer for Electric Lady Studios and was deeply involved in its design and construction.

John Storyk and Bob Hanson were brought in on the project, Storyk as architect and Hanson as acoustician. Storyk had originally designed Electric Lady as a nightclub, a plan he had to scrap when it was decided that the facility would be a full-fledged studio. He was really pissed off about that. He had never designed a studio before. (He has since become one of the foremost studio designers in the country.)

My role was to play devil's advocate. I would say, "Hey guys, I want it live. I want wood here and carpet there and I think the control room should be this big," and so on. I tried to incorporate some of the design elements I had been aware of in both Europe and America. It was not a huge studio by any stretch of the imagination, but it did have a 16-foot ceiling at one point that dropped down to about 12 feet. American studios were largely boxes — pretty dead. So I incorporated part of Olympic Studios, which is a fairly live studio, into the design. I kept insisting that we make it as live as possible. After the studio was constructed, we stood there and clapped our hands and said, "Yeah, sounds good — there's a little bit of flutter." So we built these large heavy screens in order to absorb the flutter and separate the studio into two halves. In one half there was all wood, in the other, carpet. We were very lucky because, in those days, acoustics were pretty much 50 percent luck and guesswork, and the rest was created. It must have worked out well — acoustically the studio is still the same and still sounding great.

Philosophically, the studio was completely different from anything that had ever been done before. It was a studio that was built specifically for the artist. Plus, it was built with moods in mind. We had installed theater lighting and white carpet on the walls — so that you could wash the walls in color. It was meant to be womb-like and comfortable, a "groovy place to work."

In comparison, Olympic and the Record Plant were boxes. They were all multitrack, the Record Plant being 16-track and Olympic 8-track, but the Lady was 24-track. We had the first 24-input console that actually had 24 busses. It was a Datamix (which was sold at a Hendrix memorabilia auction earlier this year). We also had one of the first 24-track tape machines, as well — an Ampex MM1000.

Working Woodstock

While I was working on the construction of Electric Lady, I was asked to head to Bethel, NY, to record the Woodstock Music and Art Fair. I agreed and was looking forward to capturing Jimi live (I love to record live). I remember driving up there at about five in the morning. We had to walk a mile to get to the gate from where we had parked the car. I especially remember the sun coming up from behind the stage, which was still in the process of being built. Despite this idyllic scene, I was about to become involved in a nightmare — an absolute, horrendous nightmare.

What Would Jimi Think?

A hands-on test of the Amek Hendrix console

When I first learned that Amek named a console the Hendrix, I expected to see a tie-dyed board with grass sticking out of it. I'm basically opposed to using names on consoles. That being said, I recently had the chance to put this console to the test and see if it was truly worthy of Jimi's name.

For the purposes of the test, I used the Hendrix console at the new Artisan Recorders Red Truck, a 36-foot trailer that houses the 40-input Hendrix automated console. Peter Yanilos, owner of Artisan, tells me that, although the truck is pretty new, it has already been used to record Gloria Estefan and Whitney Houston.

Operation. Coming down the line, the tape section has ±20 dB of gain with a detent, which is a lot. That's great. I like the idea of the detent. Pretty cool. The EQ section is very good for a console of this price range. It seems to be fairly smooth. I like the fact that the frequencies overlap and that you can pull different sounds in the upper mids. There is an effective broad-to-sharp bandwidth control and a bell curve button that is impressive on the high end—very smooth.

In the mid range, if you really want to get nuts (which some people like to do), you can have a fine old time tweaking and ducking and creating a range of special effects—very wild. The board is extremely responsive, and easy to get at.

It did take some getting used to how the numbers are written in. In the lower mid frequencies, there is a duplication of 50 Hz through 1 kHz, which, although in the same range, sounds different. This is because the "Q" point of the mids is different from the "Q" range of the highs and lows. They don't tell you that. Some form of ID is necessary to differentiate between them.

Sonically, the EQ/mic line section is the heart and soul of this console. I think that it is a fairly comprehensive, far-reaching EQ. It can get you into trouble if you don't know what you are doing (by going over something very quickly), but, on the other hand, if you have some experience and you want to go for some crazy tweaking, you can duplicate yourself up the wazoo. One has to be careful not to accidentally push the little Insert button, which does have an LED. So does the EQ On button. The Phase button, which is grey on a grey background, is very hard to see. (An LED here would have been helpful—failing that, a bright color would suffice.)

The bus monitor or tape return switch has a nice master-on/off feature. Fader reverse is good to have on an economically priced console. I think that the layout of the two sets of pan pots is well thought out, this being an area in which I particularly like to work. The action is smooth, and I like the detent in the middle. Plus the knob itself has a molded pointer to indicate where you are at, so I can do fast panning. The VCA Out switch, which is a master fader, is another excellent feature.

The mute switches feel very good. I don't mind the fact that when you activate the switches a red light comes on. (There is supposedly a link inside that enables one to reverse the process so that the light will be on in the off position.)

What I would like is a Master Mute switch and some group muting outside of the automation. Two to four groups would be wonderful.

The feel of the faders is not great. It's a little light with not quite enough resistance. They work well, though. I like the feel of the stereo bus faders. It feels like there's some heft to them—a bit more professional.

One thing I did notice when I got into the mic pregain control: When I was up all the way (or close to it) for a low-level acoustic guitar—the pot itself gave a strange amount of gain at 3/4 way around—it all of a sudden went nuclear! It's not very linear. Whether it was that particular pot or would also have happened with the other mic pots I don't know.

One of the other things I found was that the control monitor pot (which one uses a million times a day) cuts out on the right side toward the end of its travel counterclockwise, and leaves you with a tiny bit of volume on the left. Once again, it's not linear. And the actual feeling of the pot itself is stiff. One possible explanation for nonlinearity of the monitor pot is because of the console's film mode, which allows 4-track film monitoring and requires a four-gang pot that feels different from standard audio pots. As for the stiffness of the pot, I don't know if this is on all Hendrix consoles, but it could be that this unit's pot is binding on the metal plate itself.

Layout. One of the first things I noticed about the console was that, for its size, its facilities are very compact. Cramming them all into a module that small was a pretty neat piece of engineering, although from an operator's standpoint, it does make it a little tricky; you've got to have dainty fingers to get in and out of those bus assignments up at the top. I think it's a good idea to have busses 1–24, but only 12 buttons with a change-over switch. Very economical.

The control part of the console is very well laid out. Unfortunately, I did not have a chance to use the integrated computer equipped with Supertrue, which I'm told adds a new dimension to the console. The keyboard, by virtue of the size constraints of the center panel, is laid out alphabetically and not in the traditional keyboard manner.

Looking at the console from a sitting position, as we come down the strip, you cannot see beyond the middle row of EQs. Many of the numbers get lost on the way up so you have to get up out of your chair to see what's really happening. That's one of the disadvantages you find with any angled console. So as you come down the line after the bus selection (which is pretty much hidden), the auxes really require standing up to see.

Another visual problem is that there are no LED indicators for the mic and line switches. Other LED functions that should be included are the four auxes to monitor or channel and the stereo assign on the monitor. The stereo assign is important because there are two of them, and it's kind of confusing. You have one stereo bus here and you also have the stereo bus up top for the big fader and have no idea whether it's on or off. (Short of using LEDs, the whole situation would be helped immensely by using different-colored buttons.)

The lack of a writing strip for the monitor gain selection is probably the primary glaring omission. A ½-inch strip above the monitor pots to write what track you're on would make our job much easier.

We had to put a ½-inch piece of sticky tape across a whole bunch of buttons—which is not very convenient.

Conclusions. The overall look of the console is remarkably sleek. It has a very substantial feel (weighing 1,200 pounds). It does not wobble or move and it feels extremely solid. It has some ergonomic problems, but, in a console this compact, inexpensive, and with this many functions, it is almost expected.

All in all, the console is a very good value for the money. It has many of the same functions of a larger, more expensive console, but it packages them in a small, economical body. It is exactly geared toward the small studio on a tight budget that wants to get a good sound but can't afford a Neve, SSL, or Focusrite. It's a great place to start.

There is apparently a motorized-fader version of the Mozart console in the works and I'm told that they will eventually be offered as an option for the Hendrix. This will be a great addition to an already worthy console.

— *Eddie Kramer*

The PA system was still being built as the show started. We were in the back of this tractor trailer with two Scully 8-track machines balanced precariously on an orange crate. It was a 12-input console that had these horribly noisy switches for selecting the track bus, which I had to switch in between songs. We had a stack of Shure mixers on top of the console to give us enough inputs. There was only one monitor, an old Altec 604. It was madness!

The communication between the tractor trailer and the stage was equally horrendous. The stage was circular, with one band performing on one half and another band setting up on the other. It was on wheels, so the idea was to have it turn to change bands — unfortunately, the wheels broke off after the very first band performed. I had to keep running up on stage in between acts and make sure that the mics were set correctly. Then I had to run down to the truck and make sure everything was running properly.

On top of all this, only seven of our tracks were usable because the eighth had a 60-cycle pulse on it for the purpose of the movie that was being filmed (SMPTE timecode hadn't been invented yet). With all of this and the wind and the rain, it was amazing that we got anything down on tape. What's even more amazing is that it ended up sounding as good as it does.

Back on Track

The next time I would record Jimi would be when Electric Lady opened in mid-1970. It was different working with Jimi at Electric Lady from working with him at a hired studio. For one thing, he was on time at Electric Lady. He loved the studio. He was so enthralled with the idea that he had a place of his own — it was his pride and joy.

It was a treat just watching him in the studio because his whole demeanor changed. He was like a kid in a candy store, the way he fussed over everything. He loved that room.

The year before Electric Lady opened, Jimi had a particularly rough year. He would go into the studio and jam and get stuff down on tape, but it lacked focus and had no direction. Electric Lady helped him regain focus. I think my presence also helped. In the studio, he could relax and know that I would take care of everything.

One of the best sessions Jimi had during his short time at Electric Lady was the recording of "Dolly Dagger" in July and August of 1970. Actually, he had cut the song twice: once at the Record Plant in November of '69 and again here at Electric Lady. We cut the basic tracks in one evening, but spent three or four days overdubbing guitars and finishing the background vocals. Jimi would do a solo one night and it would amaze everybody listening — except Jimi, who would call it a piece of shit the next day and redo it. The only thing was, he would do it better! I had nine or ten solos to choose from and they were all incredible. I let him continue playing because I knew I would be able to mix together the best ones, keying them in and out of the mix to savor the highlights of each.

Ultimately, "Dolly Dagger" was a complex track with many layers of sound. Hendrix's lead guitar floated through the entire song and locked it together. We recorded his guitar in stereo, combining direct feeds from both his guitar and amplifier. Since both Jimi and bassist Billy Cox were playing basically the same riff, it locked the rhythm in. We applied the same technique to Cox's bass, and later overdubbed a fuzz bass to capture just the right effect. When we were cutting the basic track, Jimi put a lead vocal down at the same time he was recording his lead guitar to get into the mood of the vocal.

This set continued for a long time, breaking into different songs that included Jimi's "Pali Gap" and the Spencer Davis Group's "Gimme Some Loving." It was an amazing set that brought Jimi's confidence back to him.

Jimi recorded furiously during those months, but he had to leave on a tour shortly after the "Dolly Dagger" session. He would never get to record at Electric Lady again.

Jimi died on September 18, 1970, while in London. It's a shame that Jimi died before he could use his studio to its full potential — and before he himself could reach his own. I think that had he lived he would have surprised us all in terms of the expansion of his music. He had a very inquisitive mind and he never stopped searching for new sounds.

Back Tracks

One final comment: When I listen today, on compact disc, to the stuff we did back then, I'm disappointed. Transferring all that we did to digital — I don't feel good about it, quite frankly. First of all, they didn't call in the people who originally did the work to help out with the remastering. I know the guys who are doing the transferring are doing the best they can, but it's not the same. If Phil Ramone did a record 15 years ago, why don't they call him up and say, "Would you please supervise this for us, just to make sure that it is going to sound pretty much like the original?"

I'm not a big fan of digital. I think it has its place, but I also think it's very cold. What I have done on some occasions is combine the technologies: I use an analog machine for the drums, bass, and guitar tracks, then transfer them to a 48-track Sony digital tape machine to keep them in pristine condition. When you mix, you lock the two back up again; this way you don't lose anything and the voices sound pretty good. Many times the budget won't allow for this procedure, in which case you would have to use two analog machines — which is fine with me. By the time the bloody thing gets to CD or cassette and people are playing it on their car stereos, you're not going to hear that extra little bit of hiss. People get so hyper about hiss — that's bullshit, analog still sounds great.

Much of the music that has influenced people for years was recorded on analog equipment. Jimi alone is responsible for many of the sounds heard today. Artists like Prince and Living Colour cite Hendrix as a major presence in their musical lives. I hate to hear that sound tampered with.

Of course, Jimi was influential in more than just his sound. He was a trailblazer in the record business and in the recording studio as well. And as a legacy, he has left an unforgettable sound, millions of fans, and, of course, his Electric Lady.

Dowd on Dowd

The story of Atlantic Records and the emergence of the multitrack age

By Tom Dowd

Originally appeared in October 1993

I joined Atlantic Records in the late 1940s when it was still a fledgling experimental organization. I began as a consultant and soon thereafter joined on as a full-time employee. The original Atlantic recording studio was located above Patsy's Restaurant on West 54th Street in Manhattan. The shipping room was on the fourth floor and the studio was on the fifth. The building itself was a woodframe affair and the floors were craggy and squeaked. Nonetheless, Ahmet (Ertegun) and Jerry (Wexler) were sticklers for clean sound and I was determined to get it.

The studio was actually the company's offices by day, and desks were pushed out of the way by night to accommodate recording sessions. Soon the offices were moved a block away and I was able to quit moving furniture and build an echo chamber in the room where the accounting offices had once been.

Then again, the equipment in those days wasn't much more sophisticated than the room. The mixing console was a portable piece of RCA radio equipment that consisted of an RCA OP-6 and OP-7. The OP-6 was a four-position mixer and the OP-7 was designed for remote radio broadcasts. Tape had not been introduced as a viable recording medium until 1950, so most records were cut directly to disc on a cutting lathe. Some recordings were made on tape's predecessor, the wire recorder, but it was an extremely unstable and unreliable medium with relatively poor fidelity. Atlantic recorded direct to disc until 1951. Before the introduction of the Neumanns, I was using RCA 77 BX's, RCA 44 BX's, Western Electric 639A's and C's, a Western Electric "Salt Shaker," and a pair of Emory Cooke mics made by M.W. Kellogg and Company.

And Along Came Stereo

It was Emory Cooke who first introduced stereo at an AES Convention in 1953 at the Hotel New Yorker. He demonstrated the new technology with a recording of a train coming down a track and the Queen Mary blowing her foghorn; it nearly scared everybody to death. He was a brilliant man. He also owned a little cutter head, which is what Atlantic was mastering with in those days. He was the one who introduced me to stereo, and I duplicated his system.

In 1951 we acquired an Ampex 400 that was a portable tape recorder that traveled at 7 ½ and 15 ips and was naturally mono, since that was the only thing Ampex made. Ampex was still holding the line in mono. But I had this Magnacord and we did some jazz on that device — Wilbur De Paris, Lenny Tristano, those types of guys.

The pattern for the integration of stereo into the recording business was established this way: First came the Ampex 350 stereo machines with two small, 7 ½-inch rack amplifiers with their own inputs and outputs and record and erase heads. Unfortunately, you couldn't overdub or bounce track-to-track on 2-track machines, and the engineers were screaming that the signal-to-noise was not tolerable because mono machines were 10 or 15 dB quieter. The next innovation was to take three tracks and put them on a ½-inch tape so that they would shut the engineers up by being wider, having greater separation between tracks. Three tracks on ½-inch were better than two tracks on ¼-inch, geometrically speaking.

Then the tape manufacturers started becoming sensitive — predominantly 3M and then, trailing, Ampex. They started using new formulas and making better tapes. All of a sudden, the next evolution — perhaps a year later — was the 4-track ½-inch tape machine. By 1957 or '58 they were running that way. The next year, various studios were reviewing different engineering criteria to determine whether to go 3- or 4-track.

Believe it or not, the early Ampex multiple-track machines were not constructed with overdubbing in mind. Ampex was more interested in getting three tracks — and in some cases, four — onto a ½-inch tape. The company never thought anybody would bounce one track to another track, so the repro heads and recording heads were not always wired in the same polarity. Therefore, when you bounced, and if you opened up two faders, there was cancellation instead of addition. But the only place you could hear that was in mono. When you played the tape in stereo everything sounded fine except to a trained ear, but if you put it in mono, one of the tracks had to disappear or suffer some loss, depending on the amplitude.

In fact, this was a problem on some early Beatles albums. I spoke to George Martin about it and he was not aware of it. They were servicing the radio stations with stereo product and when some of the albums were played in mono, you'd hear a voice or an instrument drop out and then suddenly come blaring back in again — it was very embarrassing. But by the late 1950s, the machines being turned out were wired in phase as overdubbing became commonplace. The decks at EMI's Abbey Road must have been quite old by the time the Beatles used them.

The studios were first employing the 3-track by putting the rhythm on one track, the horns and strings or background singers on the second track, and the principal vocal on the third. If they went to 4-track, it was more or less the same; you'd put the rhythm instruments on one track, the strings and horns on one track, the lead vocal on a third, and the background singers and solos on the fourth. You were mixing down predominantly to mono because stereo hadn't been introduced to the public in the form of a disc. (It was originally introduced, believe it or not, in the form of open-reel 7 ½-inch tapes.)

Atlantic Overflow

Back at Atlantic, we were outgrowing our studio space. There were times when we couldn't record in our own studio because of the size of the orchestration; so if we did have to, I would lug the 2-track machine down to the New York Capitol Studio or Coastal Recording, and the engineer in residence would be doing the mono and I'd be doing the 2-track on the floor of the studio. We would release the stereo version of the mono album on Livingston Audio Tape and you could get a 10- or a 12-inch album on ¼-inch tape. Can you imagine releasing a master tape on 2-track today? You know how many bootlegs you'd have overnight? But that practice was prevalent in the 1950s.

There were stereo recordings being made at the time with excellent fidelity and true stereo spreads, but they weren't generally recorded on 3- or 4-track machines. The Capitol California stuff was impeccable. Capitol had wonderful rooms for recording; they were just about the size of a basketball court. So when you put an orchestra in there you could visually set it up much the way you're accustomed to seeing an orchestra. When they'd mic it, they would more or less record it from the same traditional viewpoint. And the material was orchestrated live and played live. Today, you recorded this one day, that the next, and paste it all together until it becomes a monolith instead of a stereo program.

An Unforgettable Moment

Al Schmitt, who is a dear friend, was chuckling about going into Capitol last year and recording Natalie Cole with a 35-piece date where all the engineers were saying, "How do you do a 35-piece orchestra? We don't have that many mics and this and that." Al said he just stood there and giggled. He told them, "You put up two or three mics on the strings, you put two in front of the brass, one in front of the reeds, put a mic on everybody in the rhythm section and let me at the console." The younger school of engineers has never been exposed to that, so they're not accustomed to it. They're so accustomed to putting a mic on everything and then cranking everything, they don't realize that the arranger and the room are what contribute to the sounds.

But while Capitol was recording full orchestras direct to stereo tape and the major recording studios were all going 3- or 4-track, back at Atlantic we were exploring a different course. All the studios were going through this tortuous process of deciding whether to go to 3-track or 4-track and worrying about signal-to-noise. We, too, had a concern for signal-to-noise, but I kept scratching my head trying to figure out how Les Paul was doing some of the things he was doing, because I knew you couldn't copy two-to-two or one-to-one and not degenerate after the third or fourth generation. Yet listening to his records and analyzing them I realized he had four to five guitar parts, several vocal parts with bass parts, and everything else, and I could not for the life of me figure out how he was doing it until I got wind of this 8-track phenomenon.

I said to Atlantic, "Look, there's no use going 2-track, 3-track, or 4-track. We've been stereo since 1952 and all of the stuff we recorded in our own studio is stored in stereo."

Every one of the records we had made between 1952 and 1955 had been recorded live to 2-track. So I said, "We ought to look into this 8-track proposition," and they said, "How much will it cost?" I described it to them and they said, "Well, what will it do for us?" I said, "We can remix our records, or we can correct errors, or we can leave parts out and then add them once we know what we want to add." And they said, "All right, go for it, Dowd." So I ordered an 8-track machine.

Now this was very cute — the only problem was that when I ordered the 8-track machine in 1957, there were no consoles out there that could accommodate it. So I had to sit down and design and build a console for a machine I hadn't seen yet. I breadboarded the thing for a while, using trial and error. Finally I said, "Okay, I know what I want," ordered the parts, and put the doggone thing together. When the machine arrived, we plugged it into the console, put a bunch of musicians in the studio, hit the Record button, and said, "Let's go!" And we were off into another world.

It was, in fact, another world. Atlantic was growing financially, as well as artistically and technically, and we built a whole new studio. We had such success on 56th Street with the 8-track that we found ourselves doing bigger and bigger production dates at Capitol on 46th Street or in Coastal on 40th Street, where the rooms were bigger. The reason I went there was that they let me operate their console; at Capitol, they wouldn't.

Building a Better Studio

By then, even though we had eight tracks, we were still handcuffed to two tracks in any big studio we went to. We kept saying, "This is stupid! Why don't we build a big studio?" And that's how 11 West 60th Street came about. The studio was 32 feet deep, 44 feet wide, and 15 feet high. "Up on the Roof," "On Broadway," "Save the Last Dance for Me," and "Stand By Me" were all done in that room.

How did we do it then? Depending on the complexity of the sessions, when we were doing things like "Up on the Roof" we usually had up to 16 strings, plus six rhythm, background singers, and so on. What I would normally do would be to put the guitars on a track, the bass on a track, the drums on a track, and the piano and organ on a track — that would account for four tracks. I'd take the lead vocal on a fifth track, the background vocals on the sixth track, and put horns and strings on tracks seven and eight. When we would remix, we'd repan and reassign them. With the leakage in rooms like that, it's not a hard thing to re-create, because the strings would be leaking into this mic or that, and the guitars would be leaking, and the drums would be all over the place; We weren't using crannies and niches and things like that; we had all these people on the floor live. And their dynamics were what you had to live with.

Going South

While New York was bustling with activity, we were also recording and using facilities in various other parts of the country. We started breaking ground with Criteria Recording in

Miami back in the 1950s because there were different record conventions held in Miami annually — the NARM, for instance. The different companies would come to these conventions with samples of their year's projected releases. Atlantic was still a small company and the principals would come down and I would be charged with preparing a tape of two or three excerpts from the new Drifters album, the new Coasters album, and the new MJQ album, none of which was to exceed 30 seconds. And we would have about ten albums to play, which would take about 30 minutes, with a little introduction to each artist, and I would always prepare these on stereo tape.

We did not ship amplifiers, speakers, and equipment down there because — the God's honest truth — we couldn't afford it. So I would get a hold of Mac Emerman, who I knew had a professional pool of equipment down there, and I'd say, "Mac, can you ship me two speakers and a stereo McIntosh amplifier and a stereo Ampex? I'd make my tape, put test tones on the front of it, go down there, and tickle his machine up. I'd set it up in a little ballroom and play the stuff, and then we'd give the equipment back to Mac.

When Mac heard I had an 8-track, he came up to New York to see what the heck I was doing, and he also started getting inquisitive about the console. He said, "Man, we need to get this 8-track nonsense and we need a better console and this and that." He and Jeep Harned were thick as thieves and I had explained to Jeep the problems I had in the design of my console. He and Mac sat down and breadboarded a new console, the groundbreaker for MCI to get into the multitrack console business.

At this time, Atlantic's emphasis on recording had shifted in many strange ways: Ahmet was doing London and Los Angeles with an occasional stop in New York, Jerry was sticking predominantly to the blues aspect, and Ahmet's brother Nesuhi was strictly doing the jazz. I was dispatched once or twice down to Memphis to persuade Stax Records, which had a distribution deal with Atlantic, to move a little faster, and I got them out of mono into stereo, and out of stereo into multitrack. Booker T. & the MG's and Wilson Pickett, to name a few examples, were recorded in an old movie theater live and direct to tape.

The same thing happened in Muscle Shoals, another Atlantic recording haunt, because Jerry Wexler started going there and was saying, "Hey, we keep recording on this old-fashioned equipment." So I said, "All right, we can do this and that," and we ended up kind of influencing the South. Nashville was into 3- and 4-track because of the major studios. But the smaller guys such as Muscle Shoals, or any of the outfits in Memphis — the Mitchell Studio, the Stax Studio, Fame, or even the Elvis Presley Studio — were mono or 2-track at best. Then a guy named John Fry down there started and went to multitrack and then to 8-track while the rest of them were still yawning, except for Stax.

All of a sudden, I was commuting about ten or twelve times a year to Memphis and five or six times a year to Muscle Shoals. I was going into Macon three or four times a year. I was seldom in New York. I'd be on the road; come home; listen to something; do this, that and the other thing; and go back out again.

I was wearing different hats on all these missions; sometimes I was needed for updating facilities, or for engineering, suggesting arrangement changes or conducting — you name it. Whatever had to be done, had to be done. Jerry bought a house in Florida and he'd always liked Criteria.

We started entertaining more and more things in Criteria. Toward the late '60s and by the early '70s we put in our own rhythm section and started bringing our artists down there rather than having us go all over the map.

Stuck in the '70s

By 1970, I was in residence at Criteria. I was still flying into Memphis, and still flying into Muscle Shoals. But by then my scope had broadened because once in a while Ahmet would flash me into London or out to Los Angeles, and I was bringing home different bits of things that would make me say, "Oops, what do I do with this, I've either got to add horns or go to New York to put the strings on." I was running around like a librarian holding ten things to do under my arm, not knowing what I was going to do first. Ultimately when it would come time to remix, I'd come back down to Miami and do it.

The next step was that we then put in a 16-track console in my Florida home. Because I had still been technically up to date, we came up with a 16-track console that was about 20 inches wide; they were ¾-inch centers instead of those monstrous things you see today. We got two EMT echo chambers and hung them in my garage, and I had some Koss electrostatic earphones, and I would come home and have tapes arriving on the doorstep. In the morning it would be something from Muscle Shoals or Memphis, or something I had brought home from London or Los Angeles. I'd take a night and a day and rest. After taking a dip in the pool and blot up some fresh air, I'd figure, "Well, let me listen to this and see what the hell I have," and I'd start mixing. And maybe a day or two later, I'd send an album up to New York and they'd say, "Hey, just great, but just change this cut, or mix this one down to sound like a single instead of stereo," etc.

So we were using Criteria to record and my home to remix in. If I couldn't remix at home, though, because it needed two machines, I'd do it at Criteria. I mean it got to be a pretty wicked operation.

Eric & the Dominos

It was during this period that Derek & the Dominos was created. Actual recording time on that project was only ten days. We'd arrive at the studio at about one and two o'clock in the afternoon and come out somewhere between one and three o'clock in the morning. They were ten- to 12-hour days.

We recorded in Criteria Studio B on a very early customized MCI 16-channel console. At the time, the Ampex MM-1000 was the popular 16-channel ATR, but that's not what we used. Ampex got into a very bad habit where its machines didn't track at a uniform speed from beginning of reel to end of reel. That happened even on the ¼-inch machines, and that's how MCI got into the tape machine business. It started out reworking Ampex tape decks so that they would travel at the same velocity at the very beginning of the tape as they would at the very end. So one of the machines we had at Criteria was an MCI, the other a 3M.

The thing that made the album a pleasure to do was that, unlike anything else I had done with Eric (Clapton), when this album was recorded, everybody went to very small amplifiers. I didn't have to worry about double stacks of Marshalls and insane combinations like that. Eric used a Fender Champ, and the biggest amp he used was a Princeton. When Duane (Allman) came in, he was using a Fender Deluxe or a small Vox. Carl Radle was using an Ampeg piggyback with a 15-inch speaker, and Bobby Whitlock just the organ or piano. The drummer, Jim Gordon, played with what the amplifiers were doing, so he was not a thrasher, so to speak. He wasn't generating pounds of perspiration to make noise. Nobody wore earphones, they simply listened to each other acoustically, playing softly enough so that they could hear each other.

Why they chose to do it this way, I don't know. When I did Cream, it was double stacks of Marshalls, a pounding drummer, and everybody playing full tilt, you wore earphones to hear yourself and to protect yourself against the din. Yet when we were recording the Derek & the Dominos album (*Layla and Other Assorted Love Songs*), if someone walked in with squeaky shoes it would spoil the take. The studio was a relatively small room for those days: about 25 feet wide and 35 feet deep, with an 18-foot ceiling. The serenity made the miking easy: We weren't building gobos and isolating people and putting them in booths — they watched and listened to one another as they played.

Incidentally, Criteria Studio B was the same room in which we had recorded Aretha Franklin, Wilson Pickett, and the Rascals. Whenever anything was done in Miami, we were always locked into Studio B.

During the 1970s, coming out of Derek & the Dominos, there were five or six more Eric Clapton albums, plus we did Lulu, Dusty Springfield, Herbie Mann, Eddie Money, Lynyrd Skynyrd, and Rod Stewart. Skynyrd and Stewart spilled into the '80s. There were a couple more Eric Clapton albums, I got the Allman Brothers back together again, and the Lynyrd Skynyrd band together for their tenth anniversary and reunion. I'm currently producing a singer named Merritt Morgan. She is signed to EMI. I only do two, or at most three, albums a year nowadays.

I have been overseeing a lot of reissues for CD and these projects are very time-consuming. I got involved in the reissues of the Clapton stuff on Polygram, where they did not just take the old master tapes and remaster them, but actually got the 16-track tapes and remixed them. And I did the same thing with the Allman Brothers with regard to the Fillmore albums, just last year.

Unfortunately, it is not always a happy experience. I don't hesitate to say that I wish the people at MCA had shown more respect for the artist when they reissued the Lynyrd Skynyrd material because, without consulting me, they had the audacity to double and triple the lead vocals with effects and so forth. If Ronnie Van Zant were alive today and somebody suggested that to him, that person's head would have been met with a bottle of Jack Daniels. If you're going to preserve something in the interest of tradition and posterity, you don't change the colors.

Then again, preservation can only go so far. Every now and then I kid with Leiber & Stoller and say, "Who the hell would have thought when we were making these records back then that they would become Muzak?" You don't even have to go back that far. I recently ran into Dickie Betts and said, "Hey Dickie, I just heard 'Melissa' on an elevator!"

The Birth of the New York Sound

The history of the prolific and unique New York City recording scene

By "Professor" Phil Ramone

Originally appeared in October 1995

In the early 1960s, the New York recording scene was undergoing a major transformation. People like Les Paul had set the pace for ways to make records sound good through overdubbing. The singer/songwriter syndrome hadn't quite caught on. And independent studios like A&R Recording were opening up and recording major records by major artists.

Many of these changes were being driven by the young artists who were coming up (i.e., Dylan, The Band, Donny Hathaway, Simon & Garfunkel, Dionne Warwick), as well as by some of the established producers like Jerry Leiber and Mike Stoller, Ellie Greenwich, and Jeff Barry, all of whom had particular musicians that they liked to work with. This amazing group of musicians made up what was developing into the New York City "recording clan," which should be credited with developing the New York sound of the '60s and '70s.

New York Minute

Certainly Memphis, Nashville, and Philadelphia had their own identities and, believe it or not, so did New York. There were jokes about New York musicians always being in a rush. Studios were expected to have house drums and house amps; there was no such thing as cartage. You'd see the same players running around town doing three sessions a day because we were pretty locked into a three-hour schedule with maybe a half-hour overtime.

The sound was characterized by the fact that these session musicians had such a diverse background and also, in order to make a living, worked at a rather fast pace. The group included such renowned players as Osie Johnson, Panama Francis, Buddy Saltzman, Gary Chester, and others, who, in the late '60s (and early '70s), became famous for the records they made. They were a "good luck-charm" for the New York producers of the period. If someone made a record with a certain drummer, guitarist, and bass player combination, they would tend to stick with them. These musicians built a reputation for becoming part of the starmaking machine, and more people would hire them to be a part of the process.

If you listen to some of these records ("Walk On By," "There Is a Rose in Spanish Harlem") you will hear some of the most inspired session performances of all time. They are all even more amazing if you consider that everything was recorded live — there was very little room for overdubbing. The musicians' union had rules stating that you weren't allowed to overdub one instrument without paying the whole orchestra. The only way you could overdub was an act of God or if a doctor's note was given to the producer to prove that the singer's voice was shot. You couldn't reschedule a date, so you had to get permission from the union to track. I'm sure there are people who remember the days when we had to lock the doors and do the vocal late at night when no one was around. It was many years later until the union and musicians agreed that you could do a rhythm date and then a sweetener like strings or horns.

Independents Day

We were also witnessing the transition from the record-company-owned studio to the independent studio at that time. The scene was dominated by the house facilities at Columbia, RCA, and Decca. A Columbia artist or RCA artist was technically not allowed to record in any other facility but their own. Certainly Columbia and RCA had great sounds — RCA in Nashville and L.A. was extremely well known. Columbia had the Seventh Avenue and 30th Street studio, which was legendary. The independent studios survived on independent singles work and, gradually, several of the studios (Bell, Regent, and A&R) developed a reputation due to the hits they were starting to record.

The engineers at these facilities were also changing the way they were making records. Tom Dowd, Bill Schwartau, and Al Schmitt were pioneers in the relationship between studio and musician. We all had to understand the style of music and what producers were expecting us to do. A client would bring in a record and say, "Listen to this," and we were expected to figure it out immediately.

I found the only way that I could have any success was to adopt the musician's point of view. We didn't have sophisticated headphones or cue systems at the time. I realized early on that my only strength, besides using my hearing, was to make the most out of the equipment. The respect and rapport I felt for the musicians made us overcome unnatural balances that occurred on many sessions. A successful engineer really had to know how to place their mics to get the right sounds. And then you had to deal with your nerves when there was some guy saying, "We've got four more minutes and we need another take." Many people have forgotten how the clock played such an important part in the way people judged you as an engineer — as well as how those recordings actually sounded.

Just as the music business has changed, so has the New York scene. Part of this is because New York has lost its various rhythm sections. We still have great players, but there isn't that same hanging out and running from one studio to another; every date seems to feature a different set of players and, as a result, the musicians aren't benefiting from the intimacy that only constant musical interaction develops. There was even a period of about five years where the rhythm sections consisted of a drum machine and a bass player, with maybe a guitar solo overdub.

All My Life's a Circle

However, everything we do is cyclical, so there is no reason to believe that there won't be an onslaught of records in the coming years done with different kinds of live rhythm sections. One of my sons recently said to me, "Hey, did you ever think about making a rock 'n' roll record where everybody is in the studio together?" and I told him, "Yeah, it's here again." In today's scene, there is a big surge toward good rock 'n' roll — which always sounds great when it is recorded live. There are also some really talented musicians out there who are working together regularly and coming back into the arena. The advantage they have is that these musicians can look back 30 years and learn, whereas the pioneers who moved from jazz to bebop to the beginnings of rock 'n' roll were the pacesetters. They had to go out and figure it out by themselves without having a starting point.

I feel this difference in today's technology as well. Even though many engineers don't have the same experience of recording everything live, they have a chance to listen to the way it has been successfully done and learn from past recordings. I think that the joy I experienced learning and growing through those decades only makes it more exciting in 1995. It is the music that drives the recording business, not just radio or MTV. When an artist walks into the office of an A&R person and plays a great tape, that's when that company actually comes to life, and this will always be the case. This is also how producers, engineers, and commercial music studios all survive. We are all dedicated to the process of capturing the magic of the performance on tape.

A Madness to His Method

Enter the strange world of project studio pioneer and audio innovator Joe Meek

By Dennis Diken

Originally appeared in December 1995

"They" say if you want something done right, do it yourself. We've heard it all before, but it's true — and it goes double when it comes to recording. Have you ever lost the immediacy and intimacy of your home demo in some high-falutin' studio at the behest of some bigshot engineer or producer? Don't you hate when you're told, "It can't be done"?

That's what "They" told Joe Meek, but he still managed to blast off with some of the most weirdly delightful and original records ever cut, and he told "They" where to get off.

If the name rings no immediate chime, here is the tale: Joe Meek is hailed as Britain's first independent record producer, self-taught and later schooled in the arid '50s British pop-studio scene where his revolutionary ideas and recording techniques turned heads and blasted UV meters. He went on to write, engineer, and produce a slew of diverse recordings earmarked by the use of echo, reverb, compression, limiting, and distortion — and featuring an assortment of outer space, macabre, and lighthearted rock 'n' roll themes, rendered with heavenly choirs, ethereal sounds, and a strong rhythm presence.

The artists he worked with were a mixed bag of bodybuilders, actors, pop combos, pretty-boy crooners, female singers, talented instrumentalists, and screaming loons. His songs celebrated Buddy Holly, Eddie Cochran, big black coffins, life on the moon, country & western themes, bublights, and dearly departed ones. He racked up 45 Top 50 chart records in the U.K., while only two releases made noise in the U.S. — "Telstar" by the Tornados (the first single by an English group to break the U.S. Top Ten, let alone #1 on the pre-Beatles American charts) and "Have I the Right" by the Honeycombs (#5 in the U.S. in 1964). And they all were recorded in a tiny apartment/studio in London!

If he was unable to create a certain sound he heard in his head he'd simply invent and build the device to deliver it. He was a tone-deaf, dyslexic, husky workaholic who was obsessed with seances. He recorded Tom Jones's first discs and rejected both the Beatles and Bowie, yet some sanely and soberly call him a genius — the British Phil Spector some even say.

If Meek to you is a mystery, take heart: We will tell you more. No doubt "Telstar" will transport you back in time to a higher plane you may have since escaped. To hear these unusual sounds for yourself (and you should), Razor & Tie Records has done us all a large favor and released a far-reaching cross section of the meat of Meek with *It's Hard to Believe It: The Amazing World of Joe Meek,* a CD compilation noteworthy to all "sound" people. So grab a listen and read on for a glimpse into this weird world of British recording circa 1953–67.

The Making of Meek

Since age four, little Joe (born Robert George Meek on April 5, 1929 in Newent, Gloucestershire, England) was captivated by wires, scraps, castoff recorders, cameras, radios, and any tinkerable electronic junk he could drag into the garden shed. He effectively grew up teaching himself the art of recording and building and modifying the gear he needed from the inside out with a blinding dedication that led to the exclusion of other childhood interests.

He applied his building talents in imaginative and unusual ways. Birds were shooed away by loud blasts of music from speakers perched in the branches of trees in the family cherry orchards, while dumbfounded crabby neighbors were treated to instant replays of their surreptitiously recorded arguments! Through his formative years, he built crystal and TV sets, futzed about with sound effects, overdubbing, tape editing, DJ'd at dances, and recorded local talent onto acetate discs.

All of this practice led up to his service in the Royal Air Force as a radar technician. By 1953, he was ready for the big black smoke of London and the world of professional recording. The prestigious IBC Studios hired him; first for location recording of the Radio Luxembourg Shows, then as a sound balance engineer at their busy London facility during the heyday of skiffle and traditional jazz. Daily contact with the cream of British stardom (Petula Clark, Lonnie Donnegan, and Shirley Bassey among others) and a wide range of musical styles schooled him intensely in the makings of a solid pop record.

There he also manned the boards on "Petite Fleur" by Chris Barber's Jazz Band (which later became a U.S. Top Five charter in '59). He honed his production skills and delivered a previously unheard prominent "upfront" drum sound on the Humphrey Lyttleton Band's "Bad Penny Blues" in 1956.

By the mid-'50s, the U.S. pop charts were waking from the doldrums of the earlier half of the decade's lightweight pop dominance. Despite pervasive white "cover" versions of R&B hits, diverse and vital production camps (such as Sam Phillips in Memphis; Specialty in New Orleans; and Vee Jay and Chess in Chicago, to name but a few) could no longer be held down.

Concurrently, England's pop scene was a rather static affair. Most — if not all — releases suffered from a vanilla, hackneyed roomy sound that was void of any distinguishable production value. The bleedin' engineers were under orders to maintain a strict decorum of white lab coats at all sessions, and tried-and-true recording "rules" were not to be questioned.

Of course, rules are made to be broken — and Joe Meek was just the chap for the job. With a "sound vision" in his head, he tore the front skin off the bass drum, put in a blanket for muffling and definition, and stuck a mic inside. Then he'd close-mic the rest of the kit, isolate the individual instruments, chuck in the occasional sound effects (e.g., loose gravel shaken in a box approximated marching soldiers in "Lay Down Your Arms" by Anne Shelton), turn up the echo, and turn heads by actually *using* distortion. Imagine the shock — this was simply not acceptable behavior for the proper engineer and technician of the mid-'50s in Great Britain!

Joe was also a bit of a kook, and he alienated coworkers who found him increasingly difficult to deal with. In the blink of an eye he could transform from a giggly prankster into a vein-popping monster, hurling ashtrays, drumkits, or even compressors across the room at the slightest hint of constructive criticism.

As a producer, Joe used various methods of coaxing good performances out of his artists. Sometimes his gentle, charming manner worked best, while on other occasions blatant threats of violence or a starting pistol to the head worked even better. Furthermore, lacking any performing ability, Meek resorted to vocally squeaking out approximated melodies of his own compositions to his head-scratching, talented players (or, at times, gifted arrangers such as Charles Blackwell or Ivor Raymonde).

Characteristically a shy loner since childhood (and being gay in a homophobic era), he became a studio hermit, experimenting until the wee hours of the morning. He was also a tad paranoid, guarding his cloistered "secrets" and devices that he was convinced the "rotten pigs" (i.e., producers, engineers, and artists) were out to steal.

Before running his course at IBC, he wrote and cut a skiffle tune called "Sizzling Hot" with Jimmy Miller & the Barbecues (no, that's *not* Jimmy Miller, the famed producer), giving him claim to the title of Britain's first producer-engineer in 1957.

New Worlds to Conquer

Leaving IBC, he set up shop temporarily at his tiny Arundal Gardens apartment and began planning and recording a "Stereo Fantasy" extravaganza. The production was "a strange record" that would "create a picture in music of what could be up there in outer space...from the studies I have made," as stated by Joe on the record's original sleevenotes.

I Hear a New World, Pt. 1, a four-song EP — one of the world's first concept albums — was issued in a highly limited release in 1960 and promoted as a demonstration record for in-store play to sell stereo equipment (which is very interesting, considering 99 percent of Joe's work was conceived and mixed in mono).

Owing to the task at hand, Meek ran amok in order to translate the "good vibrations" heretofore heard only "out of this world." The liner notes to the reissue CD offers a listing of the do-it-yourself implements employed in the recording process: "...the sound of running water, bubbles blown through drinking straws, half-filled milk bottles being banged by spoons, the teeth of a comb drawn across the serrated edge of an ashtray, electrical circuits being shorted together, clockwork toys, the bog being flushed, steel washers rattled together, heavy breathing phased across the mics, vibrating cutlery, reversed tapes, a spot of radio interference, some quirky percussion, and the odd burst of music."

This tour de force boasted exotic titles as "Orbit Around the Moon," "Glod Waterfall," and "Disc Dance of the Globbots." The new Razor & Tie collection of Joe Meek songs offers a unique pair of extracts in "Valley of the Saroos" and "The Bublight," the latter featuring an overdriven lap steel guitar (also heard throughout the LP).

Another featured "voice" on the album is Joe's beloved clavioline. David Amels, president of Voce and a vintage keyboard collector, offers a first-hand account of this curious instrument: "The clavioline is detectable on various '60s pop classics such as 'Runaway' by Del Shannon, 'Mirage' by Tommy James & the Shondells, 'Sweet Pea' by Tommy Roe, and 'Baby You're a Rich Man' by the Beatles. It's a small, transistorized, monophonic keyboard instrument that is made in France and extremely expressive in imitating violins, oboes, and horns.

"Manual vibrato can be achieved by wiggling the keyboard sub assembly from side to side. Where Moog added voltage-controlled filters, the clavioline has fixed imitative filters. It even has a built-in 15-watt tube amp in the carrying case/stand. Tailor-made for a wiggy guy like Joe Meek."

For those of you curious about the album's sequel, *Part 2* remained in the can — aside from white-label test pressings and bootlegs — until ambitious Meek aficionados saw to the entire project's CD issue in England in 1991. The odd music was performed by a transmuted skiffle group christened the Blue Men, and featured sped up "creature voices" (*à la* Alvin & the Chipmunks), gimmicky stereo separation, and Joe's beloved trademark sound effects.

Inheriting the Earth

In addition to his engineering talents, Joe also helped design and build one of England's most enduring state-of-the-art studios. Lansdowne came to be known as "The House of Shattering Glass" in tribute to the clarity and quality of its recordings. Some former IBC clients defected to the new digs to work with Joe again as he honed his skills and produced more hits.

Bolstered by the success and royalties of his composition "Put a Ring on Her Finger" by Les Paul and Mary Ford (U.S.) and Tommy Steele (U.K.), Meek cultivated a stable of artists and became partners in Triumph Records. Pitching a good fight against the powerful British majors, he scored a Top Ten hit with "Angela Jones" by Michael Cox in May of 1960 before the tiny independent succumbed to smothering distribution problems. But the real fun was about to begin....

Major Banks, Joe's Triumph partner, bankrolled a new operation that gave Joe his own studio and complete creative control in the production of masters to be leased to the British majors (Decca, Pye, EMI). This new empire was christened RGM Sound (after Robert George Meek).

One might expect a visionary like Joe to chart his world domination in a cavernous studio with great natural room reverb and space to accommodate the array of musicians required to give life to his lofty, stomping, celestial sounds of the cosmos. But Joe knew the true merit of project recording decades before the term was coined: He built his studio in a small, three-bedroom apartment dwelling above a leather goods shop on London's busy Halloway Road. In a surprising lack of creativity, he named the studio 304 Halloway after the address.

Here's the layout of the joint: The first three floors housed a tiny waiting room, an office, a kitchenette, and a 15- x 11-foot (approx.) living room. The second floor had a small bathroom, an 11- x 11- x 10-foot control room, and a main studio room (17 feet 8 inches x 13 feet 6 inches). The third floor held the bedroom, a spare bed/storage room, and an additional junk room.

Telstar Tales

It was at 304 Halloway that Joe recorded his most well-known work — the Tornados tune "Telstar." By today's modern communications standards, the quality of the original fuzzy Telstar satellite transmissions of July 1962 is prehistoric in comparison, but the specter of the then-new technology and the spacey implications gave Joe the jolt he needed to blaze into the creation of his most legendary work. When the Tornados cut the basic track before driving to their evening gig, they had no clue as to what Joe and Geoff Goddard (his writing partner) would deliver on the final product of "Telstar." When unleashed, this astounding production presented a total sound picture unheard of before or since.

A book could be written about this disc alone, but confining this masterpiece to the printed word would be like "dancing about architecture," as Jake Riviera once said. But how about the guitar breaks? Jeff Lynne has said, "I've always dreamed about getting as good a sound as that...That is the ultimate sound of an echoey guitar. It's like heaven to me, that bit." For the record, Alan Caddy of the Tornados played a Gibson ES 335 TD Blond through a small Vox AC 15 on the session.

The sound effects at the top and end of the cut are purportedly a backward taped toilet flushing combined with electronically treated vocal sounds. Serious upgrading of RGM's audio arsenal was hindered by the plagiarism suit brought against Joe by a French film composer that tied up the would-be royalties accrued from the six million worldwide sales — not to mention countless covers.

The Technical Meek

Some of Joe's techniques in the studio are legendary. His powers of isolation in a tiny room were said to be unfathomable. And if a bass drum sound wasn't cutting it in the track, he might just stomp out the beat on an exposed floor board, kick a bit in the bathtub, or instruct the drummer to play on an empty packing case (check "Just Like Eddie" by Heinz for a possible example). The 4/4 rhythm of the chorus on "Have I the Right" by The Honeycombs is the actual sound of the group lined up in the indoor stairwell clomping in tune for an overdub. Meek swears that a visitor at the session from the Dave Clark

5's organization stole this idea and used it for their smash "Bits and Pieces." Both records ended up big hits, though this is one instance where Joe's rampant paranoia may have been proven correct.

Talkback monitors and cue lights were eschewed in hopes of creating a more intimate recording environment. Instead, Joe'd hollar, "Ready!" around the control room door to the players in the main studio room or to wherever the horns, strings, or choirs might be stationed — in the stairwell, the downstairs living room, or maybe in the bathroom!

Joe's early *modus operandi* consisted of vigorous bouncing on the EMI TR 50 and 51 mono recorders (familiar to Joe from his location recording days) and a Lyrec stereo twin track (presumably a TR16). Ultimately, the bouncing track would wind up on one of the two tracks on the Lyrec with the vocals added to the other. Then both tracks were mixed down to mono.

Ken Brown writes in *Thunderbolt* (the magazine of the Joe Meek Appreciation Society) on the EMI TR 50 and 51: "These single-motor juniors in the EMI range were primarily designed to be portable for location use. Correctly set up, they made a fine recording. Many '50s hits were mastered on these machines, but they were very fiddly, needing constant tweaking to keep them on spec. Mechanically, they weren't up to the Lyrec, and the 8-inch spool capacity was only good for 20 minutes or so, running standard-play tape at 15 ips.

"The TR 50 was only a 2-head machine, robbing Joe of his beloved doubling, tape delay, and tape echo when recording on it. For this, we know, he hooked a Vortexion recorder in. The TR 51 was a 3-head machine, mechanically similar to the 50. It is safe to say that the 50-series machines would have set the limit on both noise build and wow and flutter during his overdubs."

Mixers were either self-fashioned or small Vortexions 4-15 and 3-15M. This was a brand of choice by the BBC and other British studios and labs. Ken Brown continues: "Joe would have presumably been combining [the mixers'] outputs, perhaps in a simple resistive network, in order to attain the number of microphone or other inputs needed for the session at hand.

"The Vortexion units offered high quality, low noise, and distortion. The 3-channel version had a peak program meter (PPM), which is a bit like a VU, but faster and responds better to transients. Cleverly, the makers allowed the units to be interconnected, giving seven mic inputs, all metered, mixing down to one input." Not far removed from Abbey Road's eight inputs and Decca's 12.

Brown claims that Joe could connect a 4-channel Vortexion to a self-made 3-channel unit to "give him 11 basic inputs, but he could easily have stretched the hook-up to include a few line-level feeds straight to the mixer outputs to mix in off-tape echoes or other high-level sources. Using several mixers like this sounds primitive now, but it would have offered Joe flexibility. Taking separate feeds from mixers before combining outputs would have enabled him to add effects selectively to mics or groups of mics, and he could send or return his effects to some groups while omitting others. Mixers today feature comprehensive facilities for routing signals like this, but in the early '60s very few manufacturers of large recording mixers existed. In the majority of studios, the mixer was built by the technical staff to their own requirements — usually very different requirements to Joe's!"

Eventually, Joe upgraded to the EMI BTR/2, a popular and standard-setting recorder in Britain. For a technical look, we once again turn to Ken Brown, who calls the bulky machine "technically luxurious. Overkill in every respect. In this pre-quartz-locked, servo-control era, tape drive meant huge precision motors driving an enormous but beautifully engineered tape deck. Mechanical engineering at its very best, complemented by 'conservative' circuitry, heavily underrated for stability and reliability. The steel cabinet (specially made for EMI by Morris Motors) housed the tape deck in the top, and amplifiers, power units, and oscillators behind two doors below. It had three heads, 11-inch reels, and two speeds (15/30 ips) if it was the high-speed model.

"Despite its size, the BTR was totally silent in operation, controls operated with a cushioned, sensual 'cl-o-o-mp' with air-damped tape retractors, and three reservoirs on the tape deck that had to be topped up with oil for the lubrication system!"

Mastering Meek

As dense and hot as the Meek singles sounded, it's possible that CD reissues of his work give a more realistic rendering of what he had intended for the end product. John O'Kill discusses the mastering process in *Thunderbolt*:

"Although we all loved and enjoyed our vinyl records in the '60s, the truth is it was often a monumental struggle to get the disc 'cut' to equal the master tape when the tape was finally transferred to disc. I suspect that much of the distortion for which Joe was so often accused was not there in his tapes, but occurred because of the inability of cutter heads of the day to handle his 'over-the-top' productions and carve them for all time onto a revolving disc of cellulose acetate.

"The '60s setup [for mastering was] a Scully lathe fitted with a dubious Westex cutter head, driven by a Leak TL 10 10-watt amplifier, cutting into a disc of cellulose acetate, which would still undergo endless generations of electroplating until the final stamper was mounted in the record-pressing machine. CDs cut from original tapes or good copies reveal like never before how brilliant some of Joe's recordings were."

Tell that to the Decca engineers of '62, who, upon monitoring the master tape of "Telstar," were "horrified at its unheard of levels of limiting and compression." Or to the dim bulb in the sales department who thought the record was scratched at the beginning!

—Dennis Diken

He soon ran this in conjunction with the Ampex 300 IC (console) recorder. According to Brown, compared to the BTR, this less cumbersome unit "was slightly more modern, featured better heads, and had a really warm 'American' sound to it. With a few changes, the original 'three-ton' deck would still be around for a couple of decades through the 300, 350, 351, and 440 series machines progressing from mono up to 8-track. Joe's Ampex/BTR combination, both running full-track and hopefully at 15/30 ips, would have boosted his overdubbing capacity tremendously.

"Instead of hopping from the questionable TR 50 to a mere ½-track on the Lyrec and back again, he now had two full-blown, high-speed, full-trackers do the job. They were both 3-head machines, offering splendid off-tape effects, and he would save noise by not having to go down to ½-track on every Lyrec bounce, and reduce wow and flutter by avoiding several degradations on the TR 50. He could now bounce a completely finished rhythm track onto the Lyrec once only, leaving the other track free for vocal or lead instrument as he wished.

"This new freedom could also be turned around for other effects. He could, for instance, record a split mix live onto both tracks of the Lyrec, equalize, echo, and compress each separately, then bounce them onto mono onto the BTR or Ampex, then back to one Lyrec track with something new added...and all this via his ultraflexible 'free access' mixing network, including effects inserted wherever. The permutations were endless. Technically, it meant the maximum utilization of the minimum components, which, in engineering terms, means efficiency."

Special Effects

Joe cut with his levels as hot as possible and utilized distortion when it fit his needs. He saturated the tape with as much signal as it could withstand. Brown assures us that Joe monitored full tilt, as well: "Quad preamps feeding quad 11 power amps driving 15-inch Tannoy dual-concentric 'Reds' in Lockwood cabinets. Definitely not a setup for anyone of a nervous disposition!"

Joe probably moved up to 4-track sometime in the '60s as evidenced by some later Honeycombs recordings that were issued in stereo. Ah, but Meek's masterworks shine for their monophonic majesty and unique quality that only his bouncing and individual source compression could conjure.

Some cuts ooze an inherent essence not unlike many 4-track bounced home demos we've all had experience with. Certain individually dubbed sounds fall into an eerie, surreal, almost out-of-place setting. Where Joe was concerned, some of these moments may have been intentionally placed, the fuzz guitar lick following the verse lines on "I Take It That We're Through" by the Riot Squad being one example.

Brown also notes that in March of '63, Joe "added two Altec compressors, a 436A and a 436B, to his arsenal, together with a new tone control unit, and a 220/110-volt step-down transformer to power them all." Later, in September of that year, he brought in a Fairchild Dynalizer 673, limiters 660 and 661, and a compact compressor 663.

Joe's mic selection included some Neumann condensers, Telefunkens, and the Webtrex Ribbon, a piece not found in many British studios but no doubt appealing to Meek, as it was seen in some photos from Buddy Holly vocal sessions. (Meek was a rabid Buddy Holly fan.) He also employed the ribbon Reslo RBT, used for the bass drum and occasional group vocals.

John O'Kill's article, "The Technical Joe Meek, Pt. 2" (also published in *Thunderbolt*), states that these types of mics "pick up equally from the front and rear, not the sides. Obviously, vibrating the ribbon by singing into the front will give an electrical output 180 degrees out-of-phase to that obtained by singing into the back. With a soloist, this is of no significance, but quite a lot of phase cancellation occurs when you have both front and back simultaneously. The effect can be very useful — a bit like 'free' compression, helping to contain complicated backings, and providing a curious sort of solo boost should the front or rear party pause while their colleagues opposite continue."

Play a Joe Meek-produced record and you will hear echo and/or reverb. A passage mixed dry was generally placed as such for effect as opposed to the other way around. A striking example is the wet lead-guitar line juxtaposed against the compressed in-your-face track on "Swingin' Low" by the Outlaws. Or the prominent drum against the silvery verb-laden music and vocals of Mike Berry's "Tribute to Buddy Holly."

On some occasions, Joe might cut vocals at Abbey Road, Decca, or Pye to use their echo chambers. Nevertheless, the delay sounds he achieved at 304 Holloway are simply astonishing. Geoff Goddard has made references to "a combination of tape delay echo (Vortexion) and *something up in the attic*." One could only guess that Joe had a concealed echo chamber up there.

Among his most precious and shielded inventions were the true secrets of his success. Two echo units — one with a bolt with a spring from a garden gate, the other with a broken fan beater's springs — inside a metal box taped shut hermetically. This knowledge was unraveled when brave IBC studio assistant Adrian Kerridge meticulously untaped the sacred container one night in Joe's absence. Surely there would have been hell to pay had its creator popped in during the proceedings.

Going Downhill

So, yes, the RGM domain was primitive by standards of today's overblown multitrack madness, as well as of some of his contemporaries — though not as crude as pundits previously presented. Maybe the lack of cosmetic couching and photos of a battery of tangled wires and reels with tape strewn about helped perpetuate this idea.

Joe truly believed in life on the moon and other planets (check "It's Hard to Believe It" by Glenda Collins), and immersed himself in all things otherworldly. Seances not only encouraged song ideas, but eerily predicted accurate chart positions and the demise of Buddy Holly, Joe's principal guiding light. The ouija said the singer would "rave on" out of this world on February 3, 1958. In fact, Holly's plane did crash on February 3 — *1959*! After his death, Joe relied on advice from his fallen idol from the beyond.

As the swinging '60s swung on, Joe was not able to jumpstart the inert hitbound momentum originally created by "Telstar" and "Have I the Right," though the quality of his work never diminished. With a hurting cash flow, the problems befalling the undercapitalized independent writer/engineer/designer/producer became insurmountable. Toss in his blinding paranoia, barbituates, insomnia, haunting "spirit voices," the never-ending "Telstar" case, other nagging lawsuits from artists, harassing "gangster types," a demoralizing bust for "persistently importuning for an immoral purpose," and the looming possibility of eviction from 304 Holloway. On top of all this, Joe, along with other known "gay offenders," was to be investigated as a suspect in the murder of a teenage boy whose body was found dismembered and placed in several suitcases along the countryside!

On the morning of February 3, 1967, Joe Meek took a shotgun, killed his landlady, and proceeded to blow his own brains out as she tumbled down the stairs. It was the eighth anniversary of the death of Buddy Holly.

The Meek Legacy

They say you can't keep a good man down, so wherever Joe Meek currently resides he must be having a bit of a laugh. Never a hero in his own day, he'd delight to know that well over a dozen CD compilations of his productions have been issued in the U.K. and a British Joe Meek Appreciation Society [U.S. office: 171 Lakeshore Ct., Richmond, CA 94804] is thriving.

But what would he do when he discovered that some of his priceless conundrums have been debunked? Ted Fletcher, former session singer for Joe and one of the anointed with whom Meek actually shared technical data, has recently developed and marketed the JOEMEEK compressor.

Where would we all be today had the world been a Meekless place? Joe opened doors for the British recording world and waxed sounds that did not exist on record before — anywhere. Sonically ahead of his time, he was every inch the visionary and conditioned our collective ears for what was to come and made it OK for future generations to do their wacky things — until the credit for that original vision was obliterated by arguable lesser "trailblazers."

Why isn't Joe Meek a household name? The sounds and conception of his discs were virtually *inconceivable* for their time. Suppressed and dismissed with a wave of jealousy and disregard by his peers, perhaps?

The comparisons to Spector abound. Both men are certainly giants in audio, but did Phil ever design and build his own equipment? Some may go on about Meek's schlockier tendencies (ditto for Spector), but he radiated them with such *style.* Just listen to the stuff on *It's Hard to Believe It*.... This guy had a true innocent rock & roll heart, and kicked everybody's ass into orbit (and then some).

...And he did it his way.

The L.A. Gold (Record) Rush

A quarter century of studio excellence from La La Land

By Chris Stone

Originally appeared in November 1996

During the late '60s, the Westward movement of the pop recording studio scene would soon transform the entire audio industry. Prior to that time, the mecca was New York City, while studios in L.A. and other cities primarily catered to the regional talent. Having launched Record Plant in NYC, 1968 (12 tracks), we saw the writing on the wall and were fortunate to play a part in the L.A. expansion with the opening of Record Plant L.A. in 1969 (16 tracks). As a result of this geographic re-centering to L.A., the nexus of *hits! hits!* became, in Stevie Wonder's words, "La La Land."

The Studios

In the late '60s, the main recording studios in L.A. included, among others, Wally Heider, RCA, CBS, United Western (Sinatra and Bing Crosby were investors), Sunset Sound, TTG, DCP (Don Costa Productions with his nephew, young Guy Costa, of later Motown fame), Gold Star, and Radio Recorders (where Record Plant is today), as well as the major film studio scoring stages and the early television "single mic and a 2-inch speaker" audio stages. Scoring for film, big band, and jazz was big in L.A., and had been a magnet for professional studio musicians relocating here from New York City. A handful of studios ruled the Big Apple, with prices escalating in an upward spiral.

In 1969, we opened the West Coast version of The Record Plant, proudly declaring on our party invitation that we were "L.A.'s First Hunchy Punchy Recording Studio." We wanted to shake things up and, well, we rocked the boat. Our well-documented approach was seen as revolutionary, but was actually quite simple: modern acoustics by Tom Hidley, the best equipment available, and studios that looked like living rooms because superstar engineer and partner Gary Kellgren knew it should be that way. This prompted many artists to say, "Hey man, I'd like to live here!" Best of all, it was 20–25 percent less expensive to record in L.A. than in New York City.

What followed was a cry of "Go West, Young Musician" — and they did, providing the artists, producers, and engineers to feed the new studio scene. Buddy Brundo, owner of Conway Recording Studios, remembers: "Studio musicians moved here to do film dates because the work was constant and the pay was good. Pop music producers then had a pool of pros to call upon, which attracted them and their artists here."

Village Recorders, MGM, Elektra, ABC, Liberty (which later became Arch Angel, owned by Neil Diamond), Larrabee, Conway, Motown (formerly Poppy), Sound Labs, Hollywood Sound, and Record One, among others, opened their doors and prospered. Hollywood had become the new mecca for making records, and was soon to be the largest professional audio market in the world, with close to 300 recording studios in the greater L.A. area by the mid-'80s.

Producers & Engineers

Along with the new studios came the new record producers (they had formerly been A&R guys who did mostly administration, but George Martin and the Beatles changed all that). Record producers became more like film directors, and, with more creative recording techniques, we saw the emergence of the superstar engineers. Engineers had previously been on staff in the large studios, and were assigned and shared the recording duties of the major music artists. It was expected that CBS artists would only work at CBS studios, and the same went for RCA, Capitol, and the rest of the major labels.

That all changed when the major artist's manager sat in front of the A&R executive assigned to his guy/girl, complaining: "My artist would feel inhibited creatively if he can't work at such-and-such studio with so-and-so, the only audio engineer who understands this music." We saw the birth of the independent engineer who could call the shots, a creative force that, in many cases, evolved into the engineer/producer who made the decisions of where the artist would be most comfortable for the recording. Prominent producers had their favorite engineers, artists had their engineers, and the lawyers decided which superstars would be in control in the recording of the record. The record labels quickly found themselves in the position (only with their highest-selling artists) of trying to control the excesses instead of controlling the creative output of the recording process. The carte blanche budgets were a godsend to us who were gambling heavily on the new technology.

Some of the more talented producers in L.A. at that time were: Bill Szymczyk (Clown Prince), Al Kooper (Mr. Cool), John Boylan (Quiet Force), Quincy Jones (Best Vibes), Glyn Johns (Icy Brit), Tom Dowd (Mr. Wonderful), Bones Howe (Mr. Understated), Snuff Garret (The Rascal), Phil Spector (Out of this World), Brian Wilson (Out There at the Center), Tom Allom (Heavy Metal British Dude), Tom Werman (MBA Hard Rockman), Ron Nevison (Cloak and Swagger), Phil Ramone (Lovable Genius), Stewart Levine (Mr. Expense Account), Nick Venet (Room Full of Gold), Malcolm Cecil and partner Bob Margouleff (The Odd Couple), Richard Perry (Studio 55), Bob Ezrin (Cooper and Floyd), Brooks Arthur (Opportunity Knocks), Ed Freeman (American Pieman), Bill Halverson (CS&N), Armin Steiner (Avant Guard), Lee Herschberg (Sweetheart of the Studio), Al Schmitt (Everlasting Hits), George Massenburg (State of the Art), and Paul Rothchild (Elektra Man).

A short list of top engineers (many of whom later became producers) included: Gary Kellgren (my partner in Record Plant), Eddie Kramer (British Invader), Andy Johns (Brit That Roared), Val Garay (Record One), Bill Schnee (Still Cookin'), Bob Gaudio (The Fifth Season), Howie Schwartz (Heider's 1969 tape operator), Guy Costa (Mr. Motown L.A.), Bruce Botnick (The Doorsman), Buddy Brundo (Italian Stallion), Roger Nichols (Steely Man), Bruce Swedien (Q's Sidekick), and Allen Sides (Ocean Way).

The Artists

Artists who quickly picked up on the L.A. scene of the late '60s and stayed to party included Jimi Hendrix, the Rolling Stones, the Doors, the Doobie Brothers, BS&T, the Motown roster, Simon & Garfunkel, Neil Diamond, Judas Priest, the Eagles, Don McLean, Stevie Wonder, Steely Dan, Linda Rondstadt, Boston, John Denver, Santana, Buddy Miles, and Jackson Browne. Obviously, L.A. was the place to go to make your record — that's where your friends were, and the parties never stopped at our studios.

The Technology

Along with the producers, engineers, and artists came the charging advances in recording technology, fueled by big budgets and artist demand. Bill Putnam was here at United Western with Jerry Barnes and formed UREI to design and manufacture better outboard gear, such as the 1176 (which sold for $650 new and is now worth up to $3,000 in mint condition). JBL came on strong, as did 3M and Ampex with their multitrack tape machines.

Producer Bill Szymczyk (Joe Walsh, Eagles, B.B. King) says it well: "It was really those damn Beatles and the whole London scene. Those guys were always ahead, whether it was George Martin doing something different with 4-track, tape doubling techniques, phasing, wrapping masking tape around the capstan motor, whatever. We could not keep up. What really did it for me was hearing stereo drums for the first time on *Sgt. Pepper*. That was the start of needing more tracks to do everything in better stereo. Now, the drums alone may take 12–16 tracks. When MIDI arrived, it just added to the need for more tracks, which allowed us to simply make more flexible, complex music. Technical development was definitely driven by a greater number of tracks on the tape machines."

This development, of course, required the console makers of the day (including Quad 8, API, Spectrasonics, Neve, and, later, SSL) to design larger consoles to accommodate the greater number of tape machine tracks available. The rule of thumb was to have enough channels for the number of tracks on the tape machine, plus at least eight more for effects. As a studio owner, if you bought a new console every three years you had to order a frame with a minimum of 8–16 modules of expansion space or you were obsolete by the time you got it installed. John Stronach sums it up: "The Beach Boys developed the L.A. Sound. Innovative technology gave us the capability (more tracks = more freedom of expression) and flexibility to allow the music to be driven by the artist and expressed by the recording studio audio engineer — if he had the right toys."

The same is true today, but now the sophistication of synchronizers — initiated by Gerry Block's Timeline Lynx modules — allows us to cascade machines for as many tracks as we need for any project, incorporating less expensive tape machines like the TASCAM DA-88 and the Alesis ADAT. More important, the synchronization concept allowed the audio and video machines to "talk to each other," providing a quantum leap for the audio and visual arts to crossbreed and flourish. Again, L.A. led the scene because it was also the largest film and television production market in the world.

Digital

It all started at the AES show in L.A. in 1978, when Mitsubishi and Sony introduced their first 2-track digital machines. Mitsubishi had 2-track reel-to-reel and Sony had the 1600 (Beta cartridge), which later became the 1610 and then the 1630. In February 1979, the first 3M 32-track and 4-track digital machines were installed at Record Plant L.A., with Stephen Stills recording for a crowd of naysayers. It blew everybody's mind and the industry never looked back.

The CD was introduced to the press and our industry by SPARS at United Western studios in L.A. in 1982. Guy Costa from Motown, Jerry Barnes from United Western, and others demonstrated to everyone present that the laser beam had provided a worthy replacement for the stylus of the record player. That same year Sony introduced the 3324 multitrack digital tape machine. In 1983, Dr. Tom Stockham (Soundstream) opened a hard-disk digital editing service on the Paramount Pictures lot in Hollywood with a large roomful of massive Honeywell computers. That same year brought us the Mitsubishi 32-track, followed by the Otari. In 1986, Record Plant L.A. once again led the pack with the first Sony 48-track digital recorders, still the standard in the major recording studios of today.

Acoustics

Last, but certainly not least, are L.A. contributions to acoustic technology. Tom Hidley was among the first to explore and develop the new acoustic design, isolation, and monitors capable of acceptably presenting the high sound pressure levels generated by hard rock, which had not been required by acoustic music. At TTG (Two Terrible Guys — Hidley and Ami Hadani) studios in Hollywood in 1966–68, their efforts attracted the Monkees, Eric Burden, and Jimi Hendrix, among others, who were in awe of the power and clarity when they heard their own music at incredible levels. Word spread to New York about the "new L. A. sound." I knew this would be a tremendous marketing tool and hired Hidley away from TTG to design the new Record Plant studios. Today, Tom Hidley has built over 500 studios around the world and is currently working on a $100 million Infrasonic facility in Marrakech, Morocco.

The Project Studio

Incredible advances in recording and L.A. studio notoriety led to an overabundance in the early '90s of musicians and groups who wanted to record on this marvelous equipment but could not afford to pay the high prices the leading studios had to charge. This led companies such as Alesis with their 8-track ADAT machine and other companies with major facilities in the L.A. area, such as Roland and Yamaha, to develop more inexpensive studio gear, allowing the project studio to compete and thrive.

It had to happen, but this new revolution caught the big guys by surprise. L.A.'s major studios called the alarm with HARP (Hollywood Association of Recording Professionals) and rallied against these "illegal home studios." Once tempers had quieted, the "mothership" big studio guys found that they could work with the "satellite" project guys to everyone's benefit and a reasonable level of harmony was attained through compromise.

Today, the galloping progress of technology, both for newly developed cutting-edge gear that only the motherships can afford, and lower-priced versions without the bells and whistles designed for the project studios, has provided a standard of quality recording at a low price no one could have predicted. Once again, L.A. played a major role in the transformation of the modern recording industry through its innovative musicians, producers, audio engineers, studios, and the manufacturers who serve them. After all these years, it's still great to work in La La Land, where the music never stops!

Chris Stone is co-founder of Record Plant, founder of the World Studio Group, past president of SPARS, and considered by many to be a patriarch of the modern recording industry.

SECTION II

PERSONAL STYLE

EQ was always about personal style. While the "Techniques" section of this book focuses on specific tips regarding a certain piece of gear or track, this section lets the author speak more generally about the way he records — how he captures the sound, mixes the sound, and, in some cases, masters.

Many of the subjects here are known for the particular sound, and reveal here the secrets other engineers have been trying to reproduce for years.

Tear Down the Walls

Getting rid of walls, building great relationships, and creating great recordings

By Bruce Swedien

Originally appeared in June 1991

I hate walls when I'm recording, either real or imagined. I don't like barriers or roadblocks of any kind. Anything that gets between me and the music. Between you and the feeling. It's a passion for openness and togetherness that has been a driving force in my career since I began recording music as a professional in my hometown of Minneapolis back in the 1950s.

I am fortunate enough to be in the process of expressing this facet of my character in physical form these days. I am building a very personal music studio at my ranch — and it's like no studio you've ever seen before. The main room in my new studio has no walls. There's nothing between what you would call the "control room" and the performers' area of the studio. Whoever's singing vocals can sing them right behind me, or beside me, or right in my ear, if that's what we wish.

I guess it boils down to the fact that I am bored with the standard clinical approach to music recording. Everyone being assigned to little "boxes" and the resultant feeling of us being separated during the performance of the music.

My love for togetherness is an attitude that influences all aspects of my work. It has been at the root of my long-term musical relationships and friendships with geniuses like Quincy Jones and Michael Jackson.

When you work hand-in-hand with someone on a creative musical project, you can't allow any obstacles to arise in your communication. You have to develop a working rapport that lets you accomplish your tasks in a way that allows for musical expression of both parties involved — in a way that perfectly translates the musical concepts onto the recording medium, so that the rest of the world can appreciate them, play them over and over again, and make them a part of their lives. Tearing down walls in your working relationships lets you get to the heart of the matter — the music — without any barriers getting in the way.

The Classic Touch

Working closely with the artist is something that always came naturally to me, but I have to give a lot of credit to the conductor of the Chicago Symphony Orchestra, Fritz Reiner, for bringing it out. I met Dr. Reiner in 1957 in Chicago. I had just come from Minneapolis, where I had been recording chamber music and choirs for local record companies and musical organizations. I came to the big city to work for RCA Victor, and I ended up recording a couple of albums with the Chicago Symphony Orchestra, with Fritz Reiner conducting.

Dr. Reiner was not only a gifted conductor, he also dearly loved the recording process. I think I could say that he seemed to really enjoy making records. We would work together, hours into the night, editing the orchestra recordings bar by bar, and sometimes note by note. It was, in a way, an early model of the kind of relationship I've tried to build with all the artists I've worked with over the years. It's one thing to love the music, it's another to have the kind of intellectual curiosity and passion for quality that it takes to delve continually into the minute decisions of the recording process.

There's one thing I've never been able to forget about those formative years of working with Dr. Reiner. He immediately made me a part of his innovative, new incentive program — "one mistake and you're through." It worked; I paid attention. Every young engineer should be as lucky as I was.

Starting off with a strong background in classical music has certainly made a difference for me. An orchestral balance is an orchestral balance no matter whether you're recording acoustic or synthesized music. And learning to record classical music takes an incredible ear for detail. It has to be right; there's no middle ground.

In recording music — no matter what you're recording — there's only one criterion that transcends all other considerations, and that is quality. That's what appeals to me the most about working with Michael Jackson. All Michael cares about is quality in the music we do together. Quality of melody, quality of performance...in fact, incomparable popular music is our goal.

Classical music is also a tie between me and Quincy Jones. Of course, the projects we worked on weren't classical. One of the first projects Quincy and I did together was an album with Dinah Washington on Mercury Records. We also did projects together on Roulette Records with Sarah Vaughn. Quincy later moved to Paris and became a star pupil of Nadia Boulanger, who taught Stravinsky. Our mutual love of the classics is a big tie between me and Quincy; I think it's a love that's evidenced in *Back on the Block*.

Besides, it was also classical music that got me into recording in the first place. Both my parents were classical musicians, and they poured on the piano lessons. It was soon apparent to me (and my piano teachers!) that due to a severe lack of keyboard ability, I should do something else for a living. Recording was a natural fit.

The Musical Revolution

And recording I did. I was incredibly lucky to have had the privilege of working with artists like Count Basie, Woody Herman and Duke Ellington, Stan Kenton, Jack Teagarden — and, of course, Quincy Jones, who I met very early in my career. It was this incredible diversity of experience that has served me well to this day.

Right now, I'm working on a book that goes over all this history in detail. After all, I've seen the inside of the control room through the musical revolution. This book is going to be about my experience and the people I've worked and dealt with before, during and after that revolution. [Editor's Note: Bruce's book has finally seen the light of day — he had a booth at the October 2003 AES Convention to promote it. It is called *Make Mine Music,* and is currently only available in Norway, where it was published. Visit www.mia.no for more details.]

What do I mean by musical revolution? Well, in the early days, what we tried to create was a concert-like image of the music. But in the late 1950s and early '60s, we began to think that reality in recording was not necessary, or even desirable. That's when I really started getting excited about recording.

In my opinion, one record changed pop music forever: Les Paul and Mary Ford, 1951, "How High the Moon." Only one instrument plays all the parts. There wasn't a shred of reality in it — and it was wonderful. The attempt to present it in a concert-like atmosphere was totally absent, and people dug it. Music making has never been the same since.

Miking Michael

Bruce Swedien talks about studio techniques for M.J.

The first thing that dictates my mic choice — with Michael Jackson or any other artist — is the music. For a love song, such as "She's Out of My Life," I'd use something very warm, like a Telefunken U-47 tube. For a somewhat harsher sound, like what you hear in "Workin' Day and Night," I'd put a Shure SM7 dynamic to work. For a lot of Michael's background tracks, especially for vocal block harmonies, I will even use one of my RCA 44-BX's.

I don't usually use a room mic. I prefer to move Michael around. When I do the background, I'll have him close to the mic, and then I'll have him step back. This forces me to raise the volume level of the mic, and it captures more of the early reflected sounds in relation to the direct sound, plus this technique gives a good mixture of the reflections off the floor.

I use a very visual approach, not only in miking, but in all aspects of production. This probably stems from the fact that when I hear sounds, I see color. That's the way I EQ Michael. The high frequencies appear to me as silver in color, and the lows are dark colors, brown and black. When we were at the Grammys in New York this year, Bette Midler had on this absolutely bewitching purple velvet gown. When I saw her on stage, all I could think of was the bass sound in "Man in the Mirror." Hmm....

I also like to experiment a lot; that's another reason for having my home studio. I love tubes, for example. No, I don't mean vacuum tubes. I mean paper shipping tubes. Pipes. That kind of thing. There's a line in "Billy Jean" where Michael's alter ego speaks to his consciousness. I had him say this line into the mic through a mailing tube. It gave it a real sonic personality. You can hear it if you listen.

WESTVIKING RECORDERS

[Editor's Note: This article describes Bruce's California home studio. He later relocated to Connecticut, where he built another home studio.]

For 35 years, I've been dreaming of building the perfect recording studio. Finally, I'm getting the chance to make the dream come true.

I have a ranch outside of Los Angeles. We have horses, chickens, geese, ducks, dogs, and cats. I've torn out the tennis court and put a chapel-like studio where it used to be. The studio — which I'm calling Westviking Recorders (in homage to my Scandinavian heritage) — represents a total departure from clinical studio design.

As I said, I've always hated being separated from the musicians, looking through the glass from a separate control room. So the structure contains one main room: 35 feet long x 21 feet wide with a 15-foot ceiling. It's large enough to produce a 30 Hz full wave, so it's going to be just about the sweetest sounding room you've ever heard. For recording rhythm tracks and the like, there's a large garage — fully equipped and linked back to the main room by video.

I designed the studio acoustically with double wall construction and no two parallel surfaces. The east wall is canted and the ceiling is coffered, so standing waves are kept to an absolute minimum.

The desk is a gorgeous Neve 8032 modified by my pal Stewart Taylor in Canada. It's a 32-bus board capable of running two 32-tracks or any combination smaller than that. I'm a real fan of Rupert Neve's earlier efforts — especially this particular one. I love the sonic quality of pure class-A electronics.

My dear friend Allen Sides, of Oceanway Studios, is doing all my speakers. The monitors themselves are on a perfect 10-foot, 8-inch triangle to the sweet spot, built into special soffits constructed for acoustic isolation from the rest of the building.

I've also built this room for scoring films. There's every format in there from 8 mm to 1-inch video, and I can link any audio format to picture. We'll use a 12 x 9-foot Cinemascope screen for projection.

Of course, we've got enough outboard gear in there to blow your mind. Some of the highlights are Neve limiters, Yamaha Rev5's, Rev7's, SPX-1000 and SPX-90, the Eventide 949, UREI 1176 limiters, dbx 165a's, a Dynatronic CX-5, an EMT-250, and two echoplates custom-built by Jim Cunningham in Chicago.

Tracks can be laid down on my 16-track 2-inch MCI. I have a Mitsubishi X-850 digital master machine with Apogee filters. I also have a Mitsubishi X-86HS complemented by several other analog and digital tape machines.

I have 105 microphones; it takes 15 Anvil cases to hold them. I still have the first mics I bought after high school: old Telefunken tube U-47's. I still use them in every one of my projects. I've also got M49's and M50's, along with three Telefunken ELAM 251's. But you'll also find units like the AKG 414, 451, and 452 in there, along with a ton of Neumann U 64's, KM 56's, and M 84's. There are ribbon mics too — RCA 44-BXS's, 77-DX's, and BK-5's for percussion. And how could I forget my B&K's and Milabs? I love them.

Gear aside, the point is that this is my dream studio. I'm going to be co-producing a couple of songs with Sergio Mendes for Elektra, and co-producing with Rene Moore (of Rene and Angela) — all at Westviking Ranch. I can't wait to get started.

It all comes back to what I was saying before about walls. You don't need them. Trying to re-create a concert on tape is like being a rat running through a maze — you start with a very constricted endpoint in mind and go through endless shenanigans to get there. It doesn't exactly inspire artistry or spontaneity. To me, it's not even very satisfying.

When I work with Michael Jackson, or any other pop act for that matter, the images I create are in my imagination, not in reality. Together, we create an all-new set of rules, a construct of axioms that are all our own and no one else's. That's beautiful, when you stop and think about it. Every album you hear — not just the ones I produce, obviously — is an entirely different reality. It wasn't built to conform to anyone's preconceived notions of good and bad. Thanks, Les and Mary.

Passion of the Groove

Freedom, of course, has its limits. Unfortunately, the lack of structure in pop music seems to have created a least common denominator toward which too many poorly engineered projects gravitate. A lot of what I hear nowadays in pop music sounds a lot alike; I hear far too much "knobbing around" in the control room — throwing on limiters and gated reverbs with little thought about how it affects the emotional statement.

A lack of adequate technique destroys the passion of the music. Obviously, modern studio technology — effects and the like — has opened up a tremendous new palette to musical artists. But it's important to keep them under control. My personal rule of thumb is that anything I try to do has to be involved with the passion of the groove. Any effect, any trick, has to augment the musical statement. How do you make those determinations? Gut reaction. I always trust my instincts. There's really no other way.

Another example: digital recording. On Michael's upcoming album [1992's *Dangerous*], there are two songs I mixed to analog. And not analog ½-inch, mind you. Quarter-inch. Why? Because the songs sound better on ¼-inch analog tape. Now, I'm not saying that digital is bad. What it does well, it does so dramatically well that there isn't even anything you can say. But there are times when analog just sounds better. Again, you can't let technology lead you; you have to lead technology.

If I could give any piece of advice to people getting into the business it would be this: Get some education. Engineering is a lot more than deciding which "cool effect" to throw on. Having a solid background in music and in technical matters — like electrical engineering, for example — gives you an incredibly solid ground floor from which to make constructive decisions in the studio.

As in all arts, you've got to know what the limits are in order to push things to the limit. You've got to know *why* people built walls in the first place before you can tear them down.

Producing Primer

What it takes to become a producer in today's music industry

By Robert Margouleff

Originally appeared in August 1991

The duties of a producer are both numerous and varied, which is why sometimes the initial intentions of the producer wind up lost somewhere between the studio and the record stores.

Becoming a producer is more difficult than it may seem at first glance. Before learning what a producer does, you have to know what a producer is. What follows is my personal definition of a producer and some tips for being an effective one.

There are basically three important things that producers do:

(A) They get the artist to perform to the limits of his or her potential.

(B) They achieve A on schedule.

(C) They achieve A on budget.

B and C are for the most part self-explanatory, though not necessarily easy, but it is the ability to bring out the best in an artist that truly determines the producer's quality. To achieve this goal, there are a number of things that a would-be producer must keep in mind.

• If the artist does not own his or her own studio, or does not have one that he enjoys working in the most, it is then the producer's mission to find a studio that best serves that artist and the artist's budget.

• You may have noticed that I used the term "artist's budget." Contrary to popular belief, it is the artist's money you are spending, not the record company's. The record company gives the artist an advance and it is the producer's responsibility to spend that money wisely.

• An important characteristic of the recording industry to remember is that everything is a team effort. I'm talking about more than just the producer and artist team, although that is certainly important, but a recording team also includes the record company, the distributors, and all the other people involved in making a record happen. Keep in mind that you will always have to rely on the skills of other professionals, and it is necessary to establish a solid rapport with them.

• Produce what you know. Don't try to tackle styles of music that you are unaccustomed to. I have produced rhythm and blues, rock & roll, and rap music, but each of these genres has a solid base in rhythm and blues. I would never attempt to produce a piece that was far removed from any style that I had previously worked with, like country or classical music.

• Everybody has an ego, but the studio only has enough room for one — the artist's. An artist exposes himself when he enters the studio and it is always his name that's on the line. An artist is very vulnerable at this time, so it's up to the producer to make sure the artist feels safe and is open to the performance.

• There are many different takes of each individual piece, but each number should be treated as though it were being performed live; each take should happen. When I recorded "Rock in Rio" for MTV, we did 27 bands in 9 days. There was no opportunity for a second take. We had to make it happen each time an act performed. All recording should be treated that way.

• As a producer, you should know what it is that you want to do with the particular artist. If it is an artist whose work you are unfamiliar with or who you have never worked with before, you should meet with him or her and discuss mutual interests and mutual heroes so you can decipher what it is he's looking for musically, and help him find it.

• Last, an important word for anyone interested in becoming a producer is "experience." You should come from somewhere — have some background in the recording industry, whether in songwriting, performing, or, if you are like me, engineering. It is good to work with people of different backgrounds so you can negate each other's biases. For example, a songwriter-turned-producer may favor the song more than the artist while an engineer may have a tendency to concentrate more on the technical end of recording.

My advice to anyone interested in becoming a producer: Get some experience in a studio and serve the artist. Good luck and lots of success.

Robert Margouleff is a record producer as well as a Grammy Award winning engineer and is responsible for five platinum and eight gold albums. He was the First VP of the L.A. chapter of the National Academy of Recording Arts and Sciences (NARAS).

On the Move

By Jeff Lynne

Originally appeared in October/November 1991

I was always led to believe that you had to record in a proper studio and that you had to have all this state-of-the-art equipment. This was true especially toward the end of ELO, during the mid-'80s, when I became deeply involved in high technology. I started using all these machines and all these tracks and all this digital stuff and then I suddenly thought, "I hate this now. I don't even enjoy making records anymore. I think I'll go back to the old way, the way I used to do it in the first place."

This meant analog, lots of acoustic instruments, odd little rooms to record in, and a lot less than 48 tracks.

Actually this was when it first dawned on me that you could create a great recording outside of a proper recording studio. George Harrison asked me to help out with his album *Cloud Nine*. I went to George's house and his home studio to make it and it was such a great experience. His home studio didn't have any kind of modern stuff. At least it wasn't pandering to any kind of new gadget. It was just an old — a really old — desk, a great one, a 24-track tape recorder, and that was all. There were a couple of outboard things, but not much to be impressed with. Just some great musicians, great sounds, and a great recording environment.

We made this analog record and it was a big success. And I realized, "Wow! You really don't need all that stuff." From then on I've gone on to do a few successful records using the same principles, just analog and 24-track recording. And I really enjoy myself now. I mean, I can just do it, and it's done. You don't have to hire 43 technicians just to tell you what's gone wrong with the equipment. But you do need a good engineer, and for me that's Richard Dodd, whom I first worked with when recording *Cloud Nine*.

Back On *Cloud Nine*

After seeing the kind of studio George set up at home, I set up one of my own, in my 15th century English house. It's a real analog environment. In fact, it's where I did my first solo record, *Armchair Theatre*, for Reprise/Warner Bros. I literally did almost do it from my armchair. I put in a desk, a Raindirk, which is not a famous one, but the guy who builds them makes them all by hand. It's really warm on the bass end. A lot of desks, I think, are just too hard. The Raindirk also has a nice EQ on it, which you don't have to use much anyway. For recording, I always use an Otari 24-track, which is very robust and it seems to always work for me. It doesn't go bang in the night. I got to a point where I was sick of linking up two machines. The one sound I got to hate more than any other was that "rrrhhmm, woooooow!" as the two 24-tracks got into sync. And I decided, "If I can't get it all on 24 tracks, when the Beatles used to get it on four...."

Of course, I do sometimes think, "Ah, shit! If I only had another six tracks I could really have some fun on this." But I've been trying to discipline myself. In the past I tended to go, "Well, it needs piano." So I'd have eight pianos. Of course, I retain my options. It's still an inventive process. I may still want eight pianos on it. There aren't any rules. But the way I work now has evolved through trying all these various systems and working things out. Now I'm thinking, "Simplicity is the best thing after all." The fewer gadgets and boxes and shit in the way, the better. To tell the truth, I like a microphone and a tape recorder best of all.

Bang (&O) Out of Life

That's how I got into producing in the first place. It was 1968 and I was with an English band called the Idle Race. We went in to make an album and there were just these two engineers producing on a part-time basis (Gerald and Eddie, who worked in Advision) in addition to their regular jobs. It took us a long period of time to make that record. Every Sunday for a month of Sundays. I was only a young lad then, but I knew I had what it took to produce.

At home I had a Bang & Olufsen tape recorder that did sound-on-sound, so you could start with a rhythm guitar, adding the piano by bouncing from the left to the right as you went along. Then you would add another instrument by bouncing from right to left and put the harmonies on, etc. I could get up to 20 tracks on it doing it this way. It sounded like shit; it was mostly hiss at the end of the day. But you could hear all these parts going at once, and I was fascinated by it, and it taught me how to produce. I realized that the first thing I had put on tape sort of disappeared, so I always had to put it back on again. The original rhythm guitar would be gone entirely, having gone down with each generation. So I'd put it back on and then that would sound like shit. So I'd wind up doing everything over again — on the same bit of tape, which you could practically see through by the time you were finished.

When the Idle Race was asked to do another album, I said, "Well, I'll produce it. I know how to do that." In any event, I did it. And got away with it. Nobody said, "Well, it should have had a proper producer." The second Idle Race record was my first official producer credit. That B&O was really small, too, about a foot wide. But I kept it in this great big box, with a couple of lights on it so it looked really impressive.

My next career move was joining The Move in 1970, after which we formed ELO. Producing ELO, even though we were using only 16-track back then, I used to go into the studio every day and go, "I can't believe my luck! Nobody's gonna kick us out. It's really a proper studio and I can actually do it!" It was just an amazing thing for me. I was overwhelmed, really.

Petty's Wide Open Opinions

Tom Petty produces a few comments about working with Jeff Lynne on his solo work (Full Moon Fever), with the Traveling Wilburys, and with the Heartbreakers (on the recent Into the Great Wide Open).

Jeff Lynne brings so much enthusiasm to making a record! I've never seen anyone who enjoys being in a studio that much. It's almost like he just plugs into his lifeline when he's in there. And that sort of energy rubs off on everybody else.

As a producer I think Jeff has just come into his prime, even with all he's done. He's just hitting his stride. He's usually the one who comes up with the couple of chords that make all the difference when we're recording. He's such a brilliant, brilliant arranger. He can just hear something and put it together so nice for you. I've learned a lot from him, too.

On both *Full Moon Fever* and then on *Into the Great Wide Open* we've worked very naturally together. And we never dreamed we would. But we're pretty good friends, and we like so much of the same records. And we just like sitting around playing acoustic guitar together.

Later on, I began working in the following way: I'd record the 30- to 40-piece orchestra, the choir of 20 or 30, do all the backing, lay it down first, have everything finished — but no tune and no words. That's when I'd go home and write the entire song in one go. In fact, nobody ever knew what it was going to be until I tagged it on at the very last. Frankly, I didn't know what it was either — sometimes. I had a rough idea, of course, but I operated on the theory that all that great backing would inspire me to come up with a really great tune and lyric. That's living on the edge, I suppose. I don't do it like that anymore.

When I tell people like Tom Petty now that that's what I used to do, he's totally amazed. "How'd you do it?" he'd say. Because producing Tom is a whole different procedure. When I write something with him I'll say, "We've got it" just playing it on guitar, with no fancy stuff. In fact, we're pretty much confident from there that it's going to work on record. If the melody and words stand up on guitar, then it's a proper tune. Tom'll call me up in the middle of the night and say, "Oh! I've got that verse now!" And he has got it. He really works tremendously hard.

For Tom's latest album, *Into the Great Wide Open* [MCA], we recorded in Studio C at Rumbo Recorders. It's as close to recording at home as you can get in a commercial facility. It's this tiny little studio, with an Otari 24-track and this tiny little Trident desk. We even used the kitchen there to record the drums.

I like commercial studios, and many do a great job of making you feel comfortable and at home. But that's just it — they're trying to re-create the home studio experience. Unfortunately, they can't re-create that surprise when you turn the corner in your house and go, "What a nice airy cupboard sound." These days, I don't miss anything from the studio when I'm recording at home. In fact, I think the home studio gives you more scope because you've got places like the cupboard to put mics where'd you'd never have them in most studios. At home you get different, funny-shaped rooms where you say, "Wow!" There's just an endless supply of different ambience.

Room to Work In

Of course, you can change homes as much as you change studios. I'm planning to move to France, and I'll be moving my English home studio with me. It's very modular, you see, just cables and plugs. I can pull all the plugs and take it anywhere, really.

I haven't picked out the house in France yet. But when I go looking I'll walk in, clap my hands a few times, and say, "Yeah, that's it." Or, "No, that sounds horrible." It's funny, but the same size room can sound rotten or great, and I don't know why. But I'm not worried. More or less wherever I go, I find someplace where it sounds good. Then, once I'm settled in, I find the places in the house with the most interesting sounds. Like, "Oh, this would make for a really good snare drum." I really enjoy working in real rooms that haven't been acoustically treated or anything. You get a much more friendly sound. That type of environment also helps build great musical relationships.

Nothing I've ever experienced, though, was as great as working with Roy Orbison. It had long been an ambition of mine — just to meet him. Then, becoming his friend and cowriter, was an extra special thing. He'd come into the studio to sing and just blow you away. His voice was enormous. It had such a lovely clear top, but this incredible deep bottom as well. As a producer, you had to work hard to contain it. Roll a lot of bass off. He was just so deep.

More recently, I did four tracks with Ringo for his new record and that was great, too. He wrote two and I wrote one and we did an old Elvis one. His drumming is so fabulous — you can't mistake it.

Wilbury Twists and Turns

George Harrison and I started thinking about starting a group when we were doing *Cloud Nine* in 1987. And we thought, who should we have? I'd go, "Ooo! How about Roy Orbison?" And he'd go, "How about Bob Dylan?" We both liked Tom as well, so we thought let's have Tom. And it just worked out like that and the Traveling Wilburys were born. It was to be the opposite of a super group, which none of us wanted at all. We wanted it to be a bit of fun — and it was.

I think rock 'n' roll's got to be slightly rough. When I got involved in digital about six years ago, I thought, "Oh, I guess that's the way it's supposed to sound." Very slick, very polished, very posh. But I didn't really know then because I hadn't really gone through the digital recording experience as yet. It was another one of those things where you have to have this and you have to have that. And every week somebody goes, "Ah! You haven't got one of those?"

Don't get me wrong, though. I love electronics. And I especially love electric guitar. But my favorite keyboard is still an analog Oberheim. It's really old and when you play soft it really sounds great, and when you play it loud it really sounds great. There are a few digital keyboards I like, but I just prefer the analog. Acoustics have a certain feel. Especially when I work with Tom and George. We seem to feel good on acoustic instruments.

One of these days, though, I know I'm going to have to try doing it digital again. I'm sure it's better now than when I did it in the past. But, as yet, I haven't heard any as good as what I want, as good as the analog sound. But I will eventually try a project using digital on 48-track digital. I want to do it, and then I can tell you the truth about the technology when I'm finished. And if one of those friendly digital tape machine manufacturers would like to lend me one for a project, I would be more than glad to try it!

I'm all for progress, you know. But only if it makes things better. If not, I don't see any point in changing. And it's got to be a lot better. Today, most people I know and work with prefer analog. And personally, I like distortion — what can I say.

Technology is not on the top of my mind these days. I'm actually going to France to take some time and make my second solo album. It's all still pretty much a mystery to me, but I've got a few ideas. I really want to get a fresh start — in a foreign environment — and really write some new songs.

I've done so much with other people this year that it's going to be a weird thing to sit down and do it on my own again. I wonder what the French word for "armchair" is?

The Basement Tapes

The former Cars leader is currently in a home stretch, tuning up a producing career from his basement studio

By Ric Ocasek

Originally appeared in December 1991

I love to produce. Songwriting is more important, and it's what I get the most satisfaction from, but producing is close behind. It's also something I'll probably rely on doing more of in the future. I have made a point of producing at least one record a year, mostly things that are not really pop. I'm more interested in artists whose artistic value is greater than their commercial value. Bad Brains and Alan Vega, both of whom I've produced recently, fit that bill.

The music market and music technology are changing. There's more opportunity for artistic exploration among the independent labels than ever before. More than anything, I want to maintain the freedom to do what I want to do musically. I don't want to get into having to live up to a past success. I do get pressure to bring the Cars back, but mostly from the fans, not from the record company. Warner Bros. lets me do the records I want to make. In fact, freedom was my main consideration in switching to Warner Bros. from Geffen. I know that generally these days the labels try to interfere more, simply because the music industry, both records and radio, has become so much more of a business.

Independents' Day

One factor helping the independent labels is that there are more and more alternative radio stations surfacing on the dial, and not just college stations. Another big reason for this progress is the new recording technology. It makes it possible for everybody with an original musical idea to compete in the music market. For instance, I wouldn't be surprised if in about five years you'll be able to get digital 8-track recorders like the analog 8-track TASCAMs now, and at the same price but with absolutely no noise and all the advantages of MIDI built-in.

In my own home studio in New York I have a 24-track TASCAM recorder and a CMX Soundtracs mixing console. There's also a lot of outboard equipment. Most of it is left over from the Cars' Synchro Sound studio up in Boston, which itself had been an early version of a project studio. The Cars had sort of a garage sale, but I kept some digital reverbs, sweep equalizers, compressors, and some vintage things — most of which I barely ever use now. But then, I don't think very much is essential. I have more than enough equipment considering that it's a basement and I'm not trying to get a room sound, or even an ambient sound.

For me, most of what I need are a guitar processor, which could be either a DigiTech or a Roland, and which I put the guitar through direct, and two or three keyboards, which I also run direct. In fact, the final mix of *Fireball Zone*, my latest solo album, has on it about a half dozen tracks transferred over from the original demos done on my basement studio 24-track. (Drums and bass were put on later in the commercial studio, but the musicians were just playing to the tracks I brought from my house.)

My usual procedure is fairly independent-label compatible; that is, it's not overproduced. I first write the songs on a mono cassette recorder, so that I'm not stifled by any extraneous logical considerations, arrangements, and things. I then go to 4-track (a four-year-old TASCAM) or onto one of a couple of old 8-tracks I own, an Otari and a TASCAM. (In Boston it was always 8-track reel-to-reel. I always liked those machines. I used them a lot on my first solo record, *Beatitude*. I took the 8-track tapes and just transferred them over to 24-track to make the disc.) The performance is often very good on these tapes. Even when it's just a 4-track I'll transfer it to 24-track because I don't see the point in just duplicating the same performance, unless it needs to be completely rearranged. I'm also not a purist in the sense that a musician has to do every part. I don't care how the music gets on the tape, with a person or a machine; I only care about the song.

Cars Audio

Whether I'm producing, myself or others, I'm always well prepared when I go in to record. I usually have at least a 4-track tape of what I'm going to do. And if I go in with things on 24-track I almost always opt to keep them in the final mix. It's not your sound but what you play, I think, that really makes the difference. That's also why I think the independent labels will genuinely be able to compete, as long as they come up with the good ideas and interesting music. I thought that was Greg Hawkes's genius with the Cars. His sounds were toy-like, but he had a fabulous idea of what made a hook.

That said, I always try to do something new or different each time I produce. My favorite albums are usually not strict pop arrangements. The first Velvet Underground record is number one on my all-time Top Ten. Those arrangements are just banged out; they're just lyrics on top of noise. There's even a little free-spirit, anti-mainstream folksinger sensibility left in me, from when I was in the folk trio Milkwood and before. The Cars' "Since You're Gone" is really a folk, finger-pickin' song, only played through a distorted guitar.

MIDI Life Crisis

I must admit I'm not all that interested in the music part of the new computer technology. Frankly, I don't do MIDI. I'd rather play it by hand. It's a technological language that I can't be bothered with learning. To me, that's the engineer's job. Let him put the timecode on. If I do it, it's only going to take away from concentrating on the song.

The odd thing is that photography is another lifelong love of mine and I have a Macintosh with a lot of graphics programs. But I don't have a single computer music program. And I don't have any computers in my basement studio. As a songwriter, I just can't see making music with a mouse. Or with a typewriter. I can't relate to it and never want to be able to. In that sense I am a purist.

My aversion to computerized music is even stranger when you consider that my father was a NASA systems analyst and I grew up with high-tech. Back in high school in Baltimore my best friend was an electronics nut. He loved ham radio and that got me interested in it. I got a first-class radio license when I was 16. I had to go to Washington, D.C., to take the test, building a transmitter from scratch and all that. When transistors were hot, I knew all the electronics.

By the time I got to college, though, I had settled on music and just forgot about the electronics, and even did photography only sporadically. I got into acoustic guitar because I couldn't afford an electric one. Then, 10 to 15 years later when it came time to get into the recording studio with the Cars, the technology part didn't scare me off. The process of recording was already simple to me.

Demo Derby

I played in 15 bands before the Cars. I never wanted to be part of a band that wouldn't play just my songs. Maybe that was selfish, but I didn't want to have to deal with covers. It was a shock that the Cars ever became pop stars. My goal had always been to be a big underground star, somebody shunned by the masses and loved by the few. We played in bars and most of the groups lasted three months to a year. Even the Cars was a combination of three earlier bands of mine.

Then again, the story of the Cars really began in a recording studio. There was a studio just outside the city that I was helping to build and getting free studio time in return as part of the deal. During the day I'd be there pounding up plasterboard and wiring things, and then at night I'd be recording for free, making Cars demos. Then a disc jockey at BCN named Maxanne who had been following us in the Boston clubs asked me to send some of our demos to the station. BCN started playing them and one became the most requested song on their playlist. That attracted the record companies and our underground days were over in a hurry. We made the first Cars album in London in 12 days and it only picked up speed from there.

That's why I'm still enthusiastic about making records with new groups for independent labels; it gives me a little of the old thrill. I've always wanted to keep the integrity part, and I think I've managed to do that. I've never done songs with five people to get a hit and I've never done commercials with my music, though there's been plenty of opportunity.

One of the great things about my basement studio is that it allows me to still make the record if the money isn't there to go into a commercial studio. I wouldn't bring everybody into the basement, though. I worked there with Alan Vega, whom I know real well, so that worked out. Mostly the basement setup is for my own writing, or if I want to get indulgent and finish some tracks by myself. I like to get the real creative stuff done down there. I don't want to walk into the commercial studio and wait for inspiration to hit.

In the next few years, though, I expect I'll be doing some very different things. From the new songs I already have written and from the way I'm thinking of going, it'll be a real left-hand turn for me. It's a turn no longer being signaled from inside the Cars, but I've still got my freedom of direction.

L.A.'s Top Scorer

Stanley Clarke stripes gold in films and with his new label at his Los Angeles three-car recording studio

By Stanley Clarke

Originally appeared in February/March 1992

When I see a picture moving, it's natural for me to come up with some music to accompany it. Without music, pictures seem emotionally dead. Even if it's already emotional, I can make it more so. Or, if I want, I can change the mood entirely. I can make a scene of someone walking through a grocery store, behind the spaghetti, scarier than hell. That's probably why I get such a rush from film scoring that nothing else can match. If I want to, I can even turn that spaghetti into some crazy menacing alien — just with sound.

I remember one of my first jobs, an episode I did for *Tales From the Crypt* on television. When the finished film came in to my studio and I ran it, there was nothing scary about it at all. I thought to myself, "These guys have got to be joking. They think this is scary?" But then when I put on that initial low drone, it came to life. Film scoring is like creating life, which is kind of scary in itself. It's also a great feeling of power. Regardless of what the director has done, you have the power to redirect it for the better, or for the worse. Music is more than just the final touch to a movie. You can make or break it.

Scoring *Boyz N the Hood* was probably the best project of my career. In addition to my natural love of film scoring, I had a lot of personal interest in the subject matter. There was, and is, an important message in it, one I wanted to make sure was conveyed properly to the audience. I especially didn't want it to appear, or sound, stereotypical. With all those car chases and gun blasts it very easily could have gone that way.

I needed to draw out the real emotions, the really powerful emotions, that were in the script.

Basically, the film has two main musical styles — funky modern street music and what I call "almost orchestral" music. It was the juxtaposition of these two very different sounds that created the special, dramatic, and intense feeling on the soundtrack. It made people go, "Wow! What is it?" It created a real nice vibe, one that came through even to me when I went to a theater to see it. That sound made the movie a whole lot deeper.

I do virtually all of my basic film scoring in my project studio. When I moved out to L.A. a few years ago, I bought a house with a large three-car garage in back, which was destined to become my studio. During those days I was still pretty much just a bass player. My equipment consisted of numbers of basses and numbers of bass amps. Not much more. Now when I look at my studio, it's wild to see how far I've come in so short a time.

Like many people in this business, I started out with a basic TASCAM system for demos — a 12-channel mixing board and an 8-track tape recorder. It was great for demos, but, being a perfectionist, I started to want more. And more. I ended up filling up that garage quickly with an Otari MTR-90 and a TAC Scorpion board (I'm thinking about upgrading to a Mozart) and tons and tons of outboard gear. Just racks of that kind of stuff. So much I can't even keep track of it. There's no use listing it all here. If you want to know what I've got, just go to your pro audio dealer and see what he's got. I've got the same. I especially like the Aphex gear, especially their Dominator. The Drawmer gates are great, too. I have quite a few noise gates so that our recordings come out very clean. And those new Lexicon reverb units are as good as anything I've ever heard.

The film scoring work was what made me really organize my studio. I realized that the room could no longer be run and set up as loose as it had been. I had to make it as precise an instrument as possible. I had to master it like I had mastered my bass. Suddenly, everything had to work together. It also all needed to be locked to picture, so I installed TV monitors and synchronizers.

Basically, I use the garage for writing the score and, because of this, I ran into another problem: I like to write alone. I needed an engineer, but I didn't want one hanging around all the time. So the studio then had to be redesigned, or, rather, custom-designed, so that stupid me could work the thing.

As for how I work, I pretty much follow the same routine, at least on film-scoring jobs. I get a tape that's striped with SMPTE. I have everything synchronized and locked up and the master ¾-inch tape essentially runs the show. I just start writing and "print" to Performer on my Mac. (I also use Cue.) All the MIDI stuff, everything, starts there. For the live stuff, I make notes and record that later. After a couple of days I bring in the engineer to start laying stuff down and to start transferring my sequences over to tape. If we need to, we're ready to go to a commercial facility to add orchestration or to mix.

Boyz N the Hood had a very large string section. I started by playing the basic string parts into the computer, just as a demo, so I could hear what the stuff sounded like, and to serve as a guide for when I would write it down later on paper for the orchestra. (I use a gigantic sound stage where John Williams does his stuff.) Still, all the basic ideas and all the preproduction happened at home.

I know now that building the home studio was one of the best moves of my life. I encourage every musician to have one, absolutely. When I first came to Los Angeles, if I just wanted to change a bass line or overdub an electric bass, just tune-up stuff, I'd have to get in my car, book a studio, pay an incredible amount of money, and have the tapes sent ahead of me. You're looking at a grand (at least) right there. Whereas with the project studio, especially if you're lucky enough to have 24 tracks or just the basic guts of a commercial studio, you can go in there any hour or the day or night. My studio has saved me tons and tons of money and time.

Of course, putting it all together over the last five years has been an education in itself. I feel like I've gone through med school. When I step back and look at all I've done, all the detail work, all the manuals I've read, I'm amazed at what I've learned. Just trying to figure all this stuff out is a full-time job. The upside, though, is that I now feel more professional as a musician. I know I could leave L.A. for any other major music center, like New York or London or Paris or Tokyo, and I'd be able to walk into a studio and deal with what's there to have to deal with. And that's a nice feeling. It's a vital part of the creative process that today's musician has to understand.

All that hard work has also prepared me for being a record company exec — my most recent career move. I'd wanted to start my own record company since I was 30, but, back then, when I told people this dream they just said, "Yeah, yeah, Stanley. Sure." This time, though, they came to me.

One day my wife told me the execs at CBS were coming over to the house. My first thought was, "Well, they're finally going to let me go — but they're being polite about it." I've been with CBS forever, so some of these guys I've known since they were in the mailroom. When they came over, though, they said, "Stanley, how'd you like to have your own label?"

It was my son who came up with the name Slamm Dunk. (I've been a big basketball fan and player all my life, so it was a natural.) The label's first releases will be sometime this year. Right now (November '91) I'm still getting people inked. I expect, though, that I'll release three to four artists a year. And I'm not going to produce them all. I'm going to be like a real record company exec. I wasn't, in other words, looking for more producing to do. Frankly, it's not my favorite activity. But I did want the opportunity to give a chance to some instrumentalists, who will be the focus of the label.

I owe my own career to a small label. In fact, I owe it to one guy, Nat Weiss, who got me started as a soloist. He came into a club in New York one night and said, "Hey, man, you have charisma or something." And I said, "Yeah, great. Tell me more." Then he asked me if I wanted to make my own record, which at that time was not usual for a bass player. I really had the bass player attitude then, too — to sit back and wait for the guitar player to call you. I made the record and it did very well for a first LP, and everything else just continued from that.

So now I've progressed to a point where I sit around waiting for producers to call me. After playing bass live, though, film scoring is my favorite thing to do. In fact, I've really got to watch out that it doesn't take over the rest of my life and career. It's such a rush to see those pictures come to life. It's definitely an addictive experience and I'm just going to have to be careful.

Nashville Here They Come

The "Capitol" of country is now the boomtown for all pop music

By Jimmy Bowen

Originally appeared in April 1992

I'm already on public record with my prediction that by the year 2000 Nashville will be the music capital of the whole country — not just of country music. Every day more and more young people are moving to Nashville, even transplanting from New York and Los Angeles, because Nashville's such a vibrant, reinforcing music environment. In Nashville you can walk down the street on the way to the store and run into a dozen people in the music industry. You can cut a record or get a deal in no time here because there are a ton of studios, publishers, and record companies so close together. It's a tightly knit musical community, and that's very nourishing to the creative process. It's also still a small town overall, about a half million people, most of whom are vitally interested in making music and in the music business. Nashville, in other words, is to music what L.A. is to film. Musicians, writers, or engineers, especially those with young families, can come here and live relatively cheaply compared to New York or L.A. Early in my career, I spent four years or so working in New York and then 16 in Los Angeles in their respective music industries, and by the end of my time in L.A. I was afraid for my family's safety.

In Nashville, I'm either at home or in the studio and I'm 12 minutes from everywhere. In L.A. it took me an hour just to get home, and by then I was ready to kill someone after battling the traffic. What's more, Nashville is already as good as anyplace else to record and is only getting better. We've had all the finest equipment since the mid-'80s and the overall professionalism can only improve as more and more of the talented young people gravitate here.

I'm not just talking about country music, either. Right now, Nashville is not only the capital of country and Christian music, but is soon to be the center of niche music. It will be quite a while before heavy metal will ever find a home in Nashville, but eventually, all kinds of music will be recorded here. If I were a young musician songwriter, engineer, or singer, I'd move to Nashville.

Engineering a Career in Nashville

Of course, getting in on the ground floor of engineering and producing is difficult any time, any place, but if I were a young man looking to break into the industry now, Nashville would be the place. I'd go around and knock on every door until I got a chance to start my

Taking Liberties

Jimmy Bowen has come a long way from his '50s teen-idol days in Texas (with such hits as "Party Doll" and "I'm Stickin' With You"). He has been a main force in music production and the music business ever since, but he has had a particular impact on country music since his arrival in Nashville in 1976. (He had almost single-handedly dragged Nashville production into the vanguard of the digital age.) He started off producing acts like Mel Tillis, Roy Head, and Red Steagall, and by 1978 had become vice president and general manager of MCA's Nashville operation. Later that same year he took the same titles at Elektra/Asylum's Nashville office (signing people like Crystal Gayle, Conway Twitty, Hank Williams, Jr., and the Bellamy Brothers). In 1983, Elektra merged with Warner Bros. and Bowen took over that business. A year later, he was on the move again, as president of MCA Records/Nashville. Its record sales tripled and, in 1987, Bowen produced 23 Top 20 singles (11 #1's) and six Top Five albums. Still not content, in 1988 he started his own independent label, Universal Records. Then in 1989 he was appointed president of Capitol Nashville, which he metamorphosed into Liberty. By the time you read this, he'll probably be the Governor of Tennessee.

—Greg Collins

way up the ladder. Engineering and producing is still essentially an apprenticeship process, so if you have to start by custodial engineering and producing a shine on the floors of the studio, then do it.

Then, finally, you'll get that first chance to sit down and work at the board and everybody will see if you've got what it takes, or not. It's very much a trial by fire, but that's how it works. There are, however, a couple of colleges in Nashville that offer courses in music engineering. From what I've seen of them, they're giving out useful information. We've had a few students in as trainees and have just taken on a couple of graduates in our hirings. That's an opportunity that didn't exist when I was starting. It's not easy to break in, but it's not impossible.

As a major record company president, I also think the new project studios are great. I only wish that when I was young we'd had them. When I started, at college, we recorded straight to disc. We had a band, and at night we would go in and use the college studio for a few hours. I have no idea what the equipment was, but the biggest problem of engineering back then was keeping somebody from tossing a cigarette into the trash bin with all the tape cuttings. When this happened, all we'd produce was smoke.

Anything you learn about working with music, about getting it down properly on tape, can only help you later on. There's still a vast difference, of course, between producing music on a home setup, regardless of how elaborate, and working in a major studio. I think, though, that it's the difference between flying a Lear jet and a 747...many of the basic principles are the same, but there's a lot more hardware to know and handle in the jumbo jet.

Nashville Then and Now

When I came here to Nashville about 14 years ago, my first thought was that somebody must have had a big sale on shag carpeting. It was all over the place — on the floors, on the walls. The sound would just shoot into that shag and never come out again. There wasn't a sound loud enough to last more than half a second in any one of those rooms. They usually had the drums in a small closet-like room to keep them out of the acoustic guitar tracks. The budgets were so low that artists had to record three or four songs every three hours.

When I got here and wanted to spend a day or two cutting each song, they thought I was crazy. One of the first acts I produced was Mel Tillis, who speaks with a bit of a stutter to begin with. When he saw the bill for the studio time for the record, he couldn't talk at all. I'd spend a couple of hours getting a drum sound and they'd give me strange looks.

Of course, they didn't really have drums then...or at least none you could hear. They used brushes most of the time, but I knew that a generation grows up with certain sounds and the last couple had grown up with a strong beat. They'd never start taking country seriously until it gave them that sound, and until it caught up with L.A. and New York music production. The whole town was about ten years behind the times in the late '70s. Through nobody's fault, the music publishers had become the producers, and usually if a publisher can hear the lyrics, he's satisfied with the production.

About six years ago, we finally got the SSL boards and Mitsubishi 32-track recorders, and that's the way we've been recording ever since. We rent the JVC 2-track recorders from Glenn Meadows at Masterfonics and, so far, nothing has beat out their sound.

Something I do love from the old analog days are the great tube mics, especially the Neumann U 87 and U 47's. For me, there's no need to prefer analog over digital equipment. I get the best sound I can for the particular situation, knowing it will be captured forever by the digital tape. I like to re-create the mood of a live performance when possible, and sometimes use a mixture of analog and digital equipment to do that. I really love the new equipment. Some people are afraid to try new technology, but I'm always looking for something new.

One of the areas I still enjoy very much is mastering, which I do at Masterfonics with Glenn Meadows, the owner of the facility. Although I still enjoy live engineering and mixing, my schedule is so busy that I use ten different engineers to work on our product.

And Liberty for All...

Thursday, January 23, 1992 was the first official day of Liberty Records. I really just changed the name (from Capitol Nashville), though. We were already a separate label, but because of the name everybody got confused. It was very disconcerting to my people, for instance, to open *Billboard* and see we had the #1 record in the country and it was listed as a Capitol release. Everybody just kept slashing off the "Nashville" part of "Capitol Nashville," because we weren't familiar to them as a separate company. So now it's Liberty, and at last I'm "at" Liberty. Coming up with that name was a pretty simple process. I asked the parent company what names they already owned and when I saw they owned Liberty, which had been an old company run by a good friend of mine, I grabbed it. What's more, every time you open a newspaper these days, some country is gaining its liberty, and so it seemed a perfect concept for these times, and for Nashville.

Mix It Raw

Capturing the sound of Nirvana meant re-evaluating the strengths and weaknesses of today's technology

By Butch Vig

Originally appeared in April 1992

The first time I heard "Teen Spirit," the first single from Nirvana's #1 debut album *Nevermind*, I knew it was an incredible song. And that's saying a lot, considering I was hearing a completely distorted demo recorded in a basement, on a boom-box through a cheap PA.

I couldn't even hear the vocals on that version, but when we went into rehearsal with it I could hear everything. It was incredibly intense and loud. The first couple of times they played the song I was up and jumping around the room.

The entire recording of *Nevermind* was a tremendous experience. It was both Nirvana's and my first time recording with a major label, although I had worked with them on some demos for Sub-Pop, an independent label. The band was concerned about "selling out" and losing their intensity and raw energy. It was my job to capture them live and reproduce their energy and passion as best I could.

We never expected this kind of reaction to the record, though, I mean, achieving a #1 album on the same chart as new releases from Michael Jackson, Guns 'N roses, and U2 — it's still hard for me to believe.

I think one of the reasons that people have responded so well to this record is that it sounds honest and real. It doesn't have a real high-processed sound where everything is perfect and glossy. You have all these high-tech productions all over the radio, and here's this band that's passionate and real and you can hear that they gave everything on each and every track.

Despite the sound, this wasn't some basement recording. In fact, we recorded at Sound City, which is an older studio in Van Nuys, CA, using this great old Neve board that gets in the way as little as possible when letting the sound through. I think that board had a lot to do with capturing the live sound. I also didn't use much signal processing when we were recording. No tape on the drums either — I just tried to get the drums to sound as good as

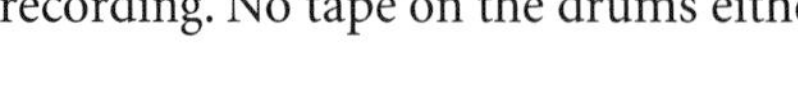

they could in Sound City's big room. I was going for the hottest sound I could get from microphone to preamp to tape.

The mics I usually use are Sennheiser 421's and Shure 57's and Neumann U 87's, but we also use some great old tube mics, like Neumann U 47's, U 48's, and U 67's. I like the fatness and warm sound that tubes produce. I used EQ only when it was absolutely necessary. If something needed more bottom or top, I'd EQ it, but I usually don't like to do a whole lot of processing. I try to make it sound as good as the original source.

Nirvana's Down-to-Earth Method

Working with the musicians was what really made it happen. In order to keep the band's intensity, I tried not to bore them. Most of the time I was engineering, they weren't even in the studio. I didn't want them to sit around bored, waiting for me while I was trying to get a certain drum sound, or burned out on a song because they kept hearing it again and again.

Even when we were recording we wouldn't stay on one song for too long. Kurt Cobain, lead vocalist, guitarist, and songwriter, told me he was very impatient. That meant that whatever was being played, whether a warm up or whatever, was always being recorded. If we didn't get something right away, we'd just move on to something else and go back for it later. I think that's why the band always sounds fresh — they kept their spontaneity while recording.

Nirvana for the Masses

Kurt is an amazing songwriter. He has this knack for wonderful pop sensibilities, even though it's amidst all this heavy metal noise and chaos. He writes these really strong melodies with lyrics that are intriguing — filled with rage and mystery. You may not always understand what he's thinking, but it draws you into the songs just the same.

There's a whole audience of young people who haven't heard stuff like this before. Sure, they've heard heavy metal and punk before, but here it is with this commercial-wide appeal to it. And besides, this is how music began and should be — people playing their instruments.

It's refreshing to hear something that honest on the radio and see it achieve mass popularity. I'm sure we'll have more processed bands appearing on the charts, but at least Nirvana has made people turn their heads a little — especially people in the industry.

It's tough to say what Nirvana will do next. What happens next depends on Kurt. They might do a rawer album, or maybe something acoustic. Perhaps a real slick pop record. Kurt's a good enough songwriter to pull all those off.

Whatever they do, they're going to do it with energy and spontaneity — and, of course, volume.

Knowing the Score

Scoring for film or rock 'n' roll doesn't require compromising your musical integrity

By Michael Kamen

Originally appeared in June 1992

Mano Hadjidakis [sic] once said to me, "You mustn't write at the keyboard because you become a prisoner of your technique." You can also become a prisoner of the technology. This is especially true with film scoring, where it's best to learn the mechanics when you get the gig. There's no need to preoccupy yourself with all the functions of a piece of equipment or the politics of meeting producers and directors, because when you finally do get an assignment, you might have stopped concentrating on something far more important — making beautiful music.

As is the case with most film composers, I actually backed into writing film music. I specifically set out to compose for ballets, but there wasn't much of a call for it. (I was damn lucky to be able to do a few.) My background has always involved writing or playing orchestral and chamber music, and I have refused to let go of my personal style — whether it's for films or rock & roll.

Never Surrender

Perhaps the most difficult aspect of film scoring is having to surrender some personal style to a film score's needs. You can't write Western music if you're working on a space movie, right? (Or can you?) Merely because a piece of music is intended for film does not mean that it should be shoved into the background and not have an identity of its own. Film music has a more noble notion than simply filling a void. Internal or self references can be injected into a music score's theme, giving a composition a consistent feel throughout a film and causing the audience to easily acquaint the music with either a feeling in the movie or the entire movie itself. Such themes can be most easily identified by little pieces of recognizable melody. And when you have a melody to rely on, scoring becomes an arranger's function. All you have to do from that point on is ask yourself, "What version of the melody can I play now?"

For example, the score I wrote for *Robin Hood: Prince of Thieves* had a boldly obvious melody. The hook in the theme song "Everything I Do" became the theme for the movie, and the melody itself actually became a "character" cropping up throughout the film. And that is the best function a film score can perform. The other functions are basically cosmetic, designed to help get around tough bits of filmmaking such as when a scene isn't scary enough or when a scene is frightfully too long. However, a film composer is not a miracle worker. Film music can help a good movie, but it can't save a bad one.

The rest of the scoring process is really just a series of cinematic problems that require musical solutions. Any scene can have as many as a dozen musical solutions, and everyone's approach to a similar scene is different. My approach is to take a reactive position, as if I were watching the scene as a member of the audience or as if I were an actor trying to relay the feelings of the scene to the audience. You want the viewer to feel a specific emotion. Fear, love, hate, exhaustion — whatever the emotion, you need to get it across musically.

Of course, there are some basic things all film scorers must do. For example, a motion picture always exists within a time frame and a location. Establishing the crucial elements of time and place musically is the second most important goal of film scoring. The most important goal is getting the score done on time. And that's where the right pieces of equipment — properly used — turn out to be critical.

Equipment of Note

When I first heard that there was an instrument that provided notation, I immediately went and bought one. The original Kurzweil 250 had an intelligent design that represented a more solid investment pound-for-pound than any other single piece of music technology. And though its notation system wasn't quite there, in my opinion, there was still a lot to offer. Considering it was and still is an instant 12-track MIDI sequencer, the 250 is endlessly fascinating because I can play a reasonable facsimile of an idea into it and then come up with something that sticks. It has become part and parcel of why I've been able to score seven or eight films a year.

My project studio in my London home is where I work most of the time, and, while it has just an average run of equipment, it's functional and easy to work in. I use a Macintosh computer with Performer to access files from the Kurzweil, and also to edit sequences. There have been numerous times when I've pasted an assortment of ideas together using Performer, and have come up with wonderful-sounding cues. I also have an Akai A-DAM digital recorder and an old Seck mixer that I run to the Akai. I use a pair of Yamaha NS-10 monitors (because they won't blow up). My video equipment is all multi-standard since I work on movies made in the U.S. and the U.K. I also use an old Sony monitor and a U-Matic tape machine. A Sanyo LCD video projector is the most recent addition. Not exactly your major high-tech environment, but it gets the job done.

Bach Off

The other side of my studio is devoted to state-of-the-art 16th-century technology: pencils, paper, rulers, and brains. Listening to Bach, I sometimes wonder if his brain worked so much better than ours simply because he kept so many of his ideas in his mind. He certainly worked a lot faster than most of us, his music is painfully better than anything else written

Bach & Roll

Michael Kamen has always felt that combining classical music with elements of rock & roll was a viable means of composing beautiful music. Music that would be right for the modern era. Music that has taken him a long way.

After dropping out of Juilliard to play oboe with a rock band in the mid-'60s, Kamen wrote ballet music and moved on to work in such diverse arenas as musical director for David Bowie's "Diamond Dogs" tour, scoring feature films, working with Pink Floyd, and directing a 100-piece East German choir. In the process, he has also worked with David Sanborn, Eric Clapton, the Eurythmics, George Harrison, Queen, Kate Bush, Queensryche, and Tim Curry. He wrote the score of *Robin Hood, Prince of Thieves* and the film's hit song ("Everything I Do) I Do It for You," with lyrics by Bryan Adams and R.J. Lange, which is presently the second-largest-selling single record of all time, having gone triple platinum. The song also won him *Billboard*'s Song of the Year and was nominated for the Golden Globe Awards' Best Score and Best Song. The song was also nominated for an Academy Award, where Adams and Kamen played it live for the Oscars' audience.

Kamen's gifts find him performing many roles, including musical director, producer, and arranger, as well as composer and scorer. His other feature film credits include *Shining Through, Die Hard I* and *II, Lethal Weapon I* and *II, The Krays, License to Kill,* and others. Scores for England's Channel 4 and the BBC, Steven Spielberg's *Amazing Stories, Christina's World* (an Andrew Wyeth documentary), and the ABC series *Animals, Animals, Animals* are among his TV credits.

How does he get so many gigs, and in such varied musical fields and styles? Kamen feels that all forms of music have something for everyone. "I speak the language of music, which I feel is the language of human emotion," he says.

That belief has certainly worked quite well.

today, and he did it all with a quill and a piece of paper.

But then again, Bach was a musician and all musicians are, to some extent, tweak freaks who love to play with the latest gadgets. You never know when that one piece of equipment that will make a colossal difference may come along. Some time ago, I thought that piece was the NED Synclavier, but now I feel as though a few layers of Synclavier can sound like a giant theater organ. I just don't like its harsh tonalities. But when its sounds are kept simple it can cover a fairly wide emotional range. Nevertheless, I still feel a more immediate relationship to the Kurzweil than to the Synclavier.

When composing, I prefer to use as few electronic devices as possible. I almost never write to timecode, and I've become accustomed to working without a click track. In fact, I hate to use a click track when creating an emotional soundtrack, although sometimes it's unavoidable. The time frame for *Robin Hood* was nearly impossible (about three and a half weeks), so I had to use a click track just to be able to get more than two hours of music done in time. Scoring *Shining Through* on the other hand, I had almost six months to write and virtually none of that was done to a click.

No Small Halls

Of course, sooner or later I have to leave home to record. When I'm working with an orchestra, I prefer to use the biggest hall available. In a small studio you're forced to listen to an amplified sound effect that compromises the music, which doesn't allow it to sound the way you imagined it. Likewise, electrical interference is kept to a minimum. Miking depends on what we want to hear and it's basically done through trial and error.

Once it's all down on tape, the mixdown is where I turn into a techno-freak, practically pulling all the faders myself. But I try to remain focused on the musical goals I originally set at home rather than on all the electronics in front of me.

Carefully used, electronic equipment may be a saving grace. But don't let electronics lure you away from your musical goals. The concept of music is inside your heart and not inside your equipment.

Swinging Lessons

Teddy Riley takes the birthright of New Jack Swing and heads toward "The Future"

By Teddy Riley

Originally appeared in August 1992

When people ask me to give them a definition of the New Jack style, I tell them to look at the musicians who are currently swinging it. Johnny Kemp. Keith Sweat. Jodeci. And now, Michael Jackson. Every time an artist incorporates my style into his or her music, it adds a different element to the mix, changing the people's perception of New Jack Swing once again. Already, the New Jack movement has felt the influence of a wide variety of musical genres, ranging from dance to R&B to funk to pop. However, no matter what styles come together to create my vibe, there's one factor that will always remain constant: The roots of this new music lie in the sights and sounds of the town in which I was born, Harlem, New York — otherwise known as New Jack City.

Basically, anyone who was born in Harlem is going to have some sort of rap or gospel background. That's why at the heart of New Jack Swing there lies a strong commitment to the sounds of street music and the rhythms of gospel. I love to blend big, rich sounds with dirty sounds in order to give my music a natural, yet hard-edged feel. Plus, I only record in analog so that none of the warmth is lost during the swing. If I didn't go analog, I wouldn't receive the same fat texture that keeps the bass drums boomin' and the snare drums slappin'.

Instead of using stock drum sounds, I prefer to sample live acoustic drums and then loop them into a natural beat. I don't sequence the drums in a quantized fashion because it's not natural — it doesn't produce any grooves. The drums must have an authentic feel to them if they're going to have a positive impact on the listener. I also like to go for the natural sound when I'm recording vocals, lead and background. Some of the best examples of my work, like "Remember the Time" from Michael Jackson's *Dangerous,* were recorded naturally, with minimum use of effects. A lot of people will record their vocals with a barrage of delays and echoes, but I prefer to use the microphone plain, so that the voice sounds clear.

Regarding Michael

When we recorded Michael Jackson's voice we didn't EQ very much. There wasn't any use in overloading him with too many effects when his voice sounds so much better dry. The real challenge was to create an effect that brings Michael right to the front of the speaker, in stereo. Even though he's the closest thing to a legend that we have living today, there's a very intimate side to Michael — a side that I wanted to bring out and into the listener's room. Besides, I think that the lead and background vocals sound best when they're smack-dab in your face.

Larrabee's Future Enterprise

When Teddy Riley decided he wanted his dream studio, he chose the sky as the limit.

When the King of Swing, Teddy Riley, was selected to write and produce new material for the "King of Pop" (guess who), it came as no surprise that Larrabee Studios, Universal City, CA, won the coveted coup of housing the dynamic duo during the recording of *Dangerous*, the latest album offered by a very New-Jack Michael Jackson. While many producers and musicians alike consider Larrabee to be one of the best studios this side of the Atlantic (Prince and Paula Abdul are on the A-list), Riley refers to the recording facility as *the* studio for maximum comfort and high-quality sound. As a matter of fact, the young producer's experience at Larrabee was so positive that when it came time for him to build his own music studio, The Future, he turned to the premier recording powerhouse for advice and inspiration. What began as words of wisdom from the horse's mouth, however, quickly escalated into a full-scale construction project, with Larrabee turning their words into action, and eventually heralding the enormous task of building Riley's high-tech dream studio.

"Teddy was very specific about what he wanted in a recording studio," says Larrabee's owner, Kevin Mills. "His first priority was building a facility that would be capable of handling any challenge, problem, or piece of equipment — pronto. The quest for maximum efficiency was the key here." One way Mills went about building Riley's super-studio was to wire everything up so that all of The Future's major racks could be plugged in with just one connector. Thanks to some Larrabee handiwork, long snakes with large connectors were designed so that Riley's MIDI gear could be plugged right into the back of outboard racks and spontaneously show up under the patchbay without any hassles.

Other Riley objectives included creating an environment that strongly resembled that of Larrabee's elaborate recording haven. Everything from the acoustics design to the lighting system was built with the Larrabee mindset in tow. Even their custom George Augsberger speaker system was incorporated into the framework of The Future, enabling the modern-day maestro to pump up the bass to thunderous levels without worrying about speaker blow-out. Other pieces of equipment that came readily approved by Mills's production staff included Pultec Equalizers, AMS reverbs and delays, Lexicon 480Ls, UREI 1176 compressors, Neumann U 47 and U 87 microphones, and a Studer 827 multitrack. Not to be outdone by Larrabee's mind-blowing arsenal of audio consoles (they have four SSLs), Riley himself purchased a 60-input SSL with plans to one day install a 100-input board. "I want to create the most technologically advanced studio around," says the man who recorded Michael Jackson.

At only 25, it looks as if Teddy Riley is more than halfway there.

Life Of Riley

In the parking lot of The Future studio complex there sits a row of black and red Porsches, one of which bears the license plate NEWJAK1. There's only one person who can lay claim to this title, and that's Teddy Riley, the 25-year old wunderkind who has been revered as the founder of New Jack Swing, a smart mix of brash, jacked-up street sounds and fresh gospel rhythms that is currently ruling the radio airwaves.

Riley has been revered as top dog ever since he delivered double-whammy productions of "I Want Her" by Keith Sweat (1987) and "Just Got Paid" by Johnny Kemp (1988). His own band, Guy, also hit mega-platinum status, further laying down the groundwork for his billing as a major player in the music biz. It wasn't long before Riley's New Jack hybrid of snappy drums and hardcore horns caught fire, opening the door to a variety of artists seeking his vibrant new sound. Bobby Brown, Stevie Wonder, Kool Moe Dee, Boy George, and Heavy D. are just a few of the majors that Riley has worked with since his induction as the newest whiz-kid on the block. But it wasn't until his friend, comedian Eddie Murphy, introduced him to pop-phenom Michael Jackson, that Riley entered the realm reserved for only a chosen few.

In true New Jack style, Riley stood up to public scrutiny and created a unique compilation of Jackson songs (heavy on strings and dry on vocals) while still presenting him as the king of cutting-edge pop. More recently, Riley has finished working on Bobby Brown's latest album, hoping to recapture the glory heaped upon him after producing the super-star's hit album, *Don't Be Cruel.*

—Jon Varman

Most of the vocal tracks that were taken from Michael Jackson, and Bobby Brown for that matter, were completed on the first or second try. I like to keep it that way because if you're going to make a mistake in the studio, you're going to make that mistake on stage. And when it comes to recording, we like to remain as true to the original sound as possible. If you can't come into the studio and sing a song the way it's supposed to be sung, then you don't need to be working with me. Jackson tunes such as "Remember the Time" and "In the Closet" were done in only two takes. But a song like "Jam," which requires a strong attitude (and an even stronger voice, which Michael nearly lost) was completed on the second or third take. If the singer feels the music, and you've got the melody recorded beforehand, you're going to get the vocals down cold.

Along with the recording of a Michael Jackson album comes the fun job of incorporating sound effects into the songs. On *Bad,* there were a lot of unique sounds recorded with high-tech finesse, including the live beat of Michael's heart. For *Dangerous* I went out and got live car sounds that can be heard on "She Drives Me Wild." For the song "In the Closet," I drove home some door-slams and created some videogame-like effects that appear throughout the melody. I've been sampling and recording effects for some time now, even during my days with Guy, when I used Performer software to sample bomb sounds and loop beats.

Back to the Future

Even though technology has greatly expanded our recording horizons, I find myself going back to the old style that existed in the '70s, when real instruments were the norm and live recording was *it.* Equipment such as the Minimoog and the old Juno 106 are coming back, while rap vocals are being recorded right in front of the console, closed in by gobos, rather than windows. As far as sound inventions go, however, I'll use whatever stock material I can find and put it through the technological ringer to come up with something new and exciting. I don't spend too much time analyzing the techniques of my heroes — Stevie Wonder, Prince, Quincy Jones — because I'm always looking for a different way of doing things. For example, if you give somebody a Vocoder or a Vocalizer, he might come up with some great stock sounds, but if I get my hands on it, we'll put it through any given piece of equipment and create some sounds that you've never heard before.

We have a whole slew of sound-altering techniques that I like to keep relatively secret because I want to be able to use them for the next three years without anybody capitalizing on them. There are just too many people in this industry who treat music like a competition, and that makes it hard for me to pass down a bit of information without someone going out and saying that he discovered it. That's just the downside of the industry, and it comes with the territory.

The upside is my studio, The Future, which I've settled down in Virginia Beach. I like the fact that I can work here in quiet, away from the hype of the big cities, and do what it is I have to do without any interruptions. I never leave this place, unless I absolutely have to, and even then I won't go unless I've completed the basic essentials. I'm not looking to be a gigantic star or the big guy on campus. I just want the freedom to make music that people can appreciate, and it's here in Virginia Beach, among the relative calm, where I can best achieve my primary goals.

Word to the wise: Studios are not built overnight. I realized that after I was told I would have my studio completed in three months and it ended up taking a year. Now that I have it, I'm ready to take it all the way. My plans are to have the biggest studio with the biggest sound. I don't think any other studio besides Larrabee, and a handful of others, can get the bottom that The Future gets. I used to go into studios and complain about their speakers because they used to bust off of my music. Now, when I go into my own studio, I couldn't bust them if I tried.

Teddy's CADillac Ranch

Riley's SSL room may be the main attraction at The Future, but as business continues to grow, more and more New Jack Swingers are being drawn into the CAD room — a compact yet versatile studio that features Tannoy and Yamaha NS-10 monitors, Macintosh and Atari computers, and, of course, the CAD E-frame mixing console.

Franklyn Grant, a Future engineer/producer, says "The Future's CAD room is primarily used as a writing room for producers and artists alike. It features crisp, clear sound and provides inhabitants with an explosive experience.

"When we first heard this machine," says Grant, "it really hit us. Teddy and I really love the frequency response of the CAD. And the fat bass on this board is incredible!" The E-frame works in conjunction with a Mega Mix computer system, enabling the operator to utilize quick muting, gain increase, and voltage control features in a completely visual environment.

Currently, The Future is laying down basic tracks and vocals for Wrecks N' Effects and Big Ty & the Hoods in the CAD room. "We're looking for that hardcore, New Jack sound," says Grant, who in addition to working for Teddy Riley has also engineered and produced albums for Father MC and the Fat Boys, respectively. "And in this room, we can do more than simply achieve our goals."

The Future is made up of two studios, an SSL room and a smaller CAD room, both of which I use exclusively. A MIDI room has also been set up to house computers, sequencers, and keyboards. We're currently in the process of building a new room that is going to feature every technical and vintage element known to man. Like Larrabee, I want my studio to have the capacity to create any sound and manage any production technique. My dream would be to have a little bit of everything — Neve, CAD, Focusrite, UREI — not a console of each brand, but a whole soundboard made up of the best of the best. Right now we're trying to get an 80–100 channel SSL board in here so that we can go all out.

Take It to the Charts

Working on the Michael Jackson album was an all-around great experience. Not only did I get the chance to bring the New Jack sound to Michael's music, but I also received the opportunity to work with Bruce Swedien, one of the masters of modern recording. Most recently, we worked on a remix of the new single "Jam," with some help from my co-engineer, Jean Marie Horvat, whom I like to call "Little Swedien." Currently, I'm finishing up the funk flavor for Bobby Brown's new album. I think that as Bobby Brown creeps up to the level Michael Jackson is at, Michael will move up to the Sammy Davis Jr. level of stardom, where legends are made.

It's funny, because a lot of the guys I used to go to for help are now coming to me for advice on building their own studio. I guess, when I really think about it, I've learned a lot over the last few years.

Opening New Doors

The Doors guitarist Robby Krieger takes us into his project studio

By Robby Krieger

Originally appeared in November 1992

Yeah, it was a halcyon time in the '60s and, sure, I experienced my share. After all, I was in a band with Jim Morrison. But all the legend aside, we were a hard-working group that sought to express ourselves artistically, and many feel that we succeeded. For the past few years I've been concentrating on my playing, recording albums in various music genres, and I've built my own workplace where I can record my ideas the way I hear them. I recently released a new album.

At home, my project studio contains a Fostex B-16D ½-inch 16-track running at 30 ips, a Ramsa WR-1820 24x4x2 board, Alesis Quadraverb, Yamaha Rev5 and Rev7, Eventide Harmonizer, Roland D110, Roland U220, Roland GR50 guitar synthesizer, and Hybrid Arts digital workstation. I do a lot of live stuff to DAT and we use the workstation to edit and tweak those tracks. I also sync it up to my sequencer, which allows me to run live digital guitar tracks along with the sequencer and enables me to edit them. Usually I drive the system with the GR50. Roland recently came out with software that allows you to load in with your sequencer and it kind of makes all of your Roland equipment compatible. It's called the Roland User's Kit.

I also lock up the workstation to the 16-track, stripe SMPTE on track 16 of the Fostex, and lock it up to the digital master. Normally, you would have to hook your sequencer up to a 16-track, and the end result wouldn't be in the digital domain. I have a pretty cool patchbay that links all of this stuff together with TT plugs. My speakers are Westlake Audio, with the addition of a homemade subwoofer, and I mix on the little Yamaha NS-10's. I built this studio myself and it evolved by just sort of doing it piecemeal as I went along.

Riders on the Storm

If there was a '60s act that lit a fire under the seats of the music-buying public, it was The Doors. Perhaps no other American rock phenomenon has had the historical impact and importance of this band. Oliver Stone's film *The Doors,* and its success with the general public 20 years after, helps bear witness to this fact.

When "Light My Fire" hit the charts in the summer of 1967, it shot to the Top Ten on Billboard's pop chart almost immediately. But The Doors didn't hit overnight. In fact, they were playing the tunes that fill the first album throughout the L.A. area for about two years before the record was made. And this intimate knowledge of the music, combined with the relatively primitive recording technology of the time, made for an album that was recorded almost entirely in one or two takes. It was recorded on an Ampex 350 4-track workhorse through an old tube-powered console that had rotary gain controls. Only the vocals were overdubbed. (Later albums would be recorded on Scully 8-track recorders, first with the one-inch format in 1967. The last few albums were 16-track that were recorded on Ampex MM-1000's.) Incidentally, "Touch Me" from the *Soft Parade* album (1969) was the first stereo 45-rpm record ever released.

There are, arguably, several factors that may be responsible for the Doors' continued acceptance and their historic significance. The quality of the music is certainly one factor. Keyboardist Ray Manzarek and guitarist Robby Krieger had classical and jazz backgrounds, respectively, and brought to The Doors' sound a melodic complexity that few other rock bands have been able to outdo. Some may say that romantic images of the times and The Doors' connection to them are among the reasons for The Doors' afterlife.

Whatever the reasons, there is one factor that is difficult to dispute: the quality of their recordings. These records stand out today almost as strongly as they did when the technology utilized to make them was state-of-the-art. More proof that it's not always the equipment at your disposal, but how you use it that can make the difference.

—David Jacobs

In-Doors or Out?

The technology that lets you have all this at your fingertips in a relatively small space is truly amazing and, with digital, the sounds of today are really clean. But the fact is that some of the big old clunky machines we used in the past still seem to sound pretty good — mainly because they used wide tape. Of course, 2-inch tape is still in common use for 24-track analog, but now 1-inch 24-track is becoming popular. Like my ½-inch 16-track, this kind of machine is great because it's economical and space efficient, but — let's face it — you don't have a lot of room on the tape for the tracks, and you do get some bleed-over.

For projects that are to be released, I generally prefer to use outside professional studios for certain things. In the past I've used Cherokee and Devonshire, which are both really good studios. But this time, I'm trying to do as much of the album at home as I can, and so far I haven't needed to go outside. The only thing I might have to use a big studio for will be live drums, vocals, or maybe some guitars. When it comes to digital versus analog, I don't have a personal preference. Some of my jazz friends, horn players in particular, say they don't like the way they sound on digital, but I can't tell the difference.

Strange Days

When The Doors first recorded, it was at Sunset Sound in L.A., which still exists today and remains one of the great studios. Of course, in those days, project studios were uncommon and the technology that produces the gear such as that in my project room didn't exist. After Sunset we switched over to a place called TT&G. Still later, Elektra Records built their own studio, and we used that. The final album, *L.A. Woman,* was recorded in our rehearsal hall on a 16-track machine we had brought in.

Multitracking, which we take for granted today, was in its infancy and we had to do a lot all at once. The first album, *The Doors,* was 4-track, the second, *Strange Days,* was 8, the third, *Waiting for the Sun,* was 8, the fourth, *Soft Parade,* was 16, and *Morrison Hotel* and *L.A. Woman* were 16 — we never did get to 24-track.

On the first album we didn't do overdubbing because there was only one extra track. But we did do second passes of vocals. With the second album, we started doing a lot of experimenting. That was when *Sgt. Pepper* came out and everybody thought they had to put a million things down. If you listen to the second album, there are some backwards piano parts and some other weird stuff.

At that time the tape machines were the big old Ampexes and Scullys. You didn't have the variety or the miniaturization that makes the project studio possible today. The first album was done on one of those old tube boards with the big black round knobs. At the time, Sunset Sound had the best echo chamber in the United States and I think that accounts, in part, for the great sound they were able to achieve.

Bruce Botnick was pretty much our exclusive engineer. A guy named John Haney also did a few things for us, and Fritz Richmond was sort of assistant to Paul Rothchild [founder and president of Elektra at that time]. Bruce currently owns Digital Dynamics in L.A., which was one of the first digital studios.

Prior to The Doors I had limited recording experience. My experience included sessions at Gold Star, the "wall of sound" studio, which was one of the few independent studios in L.A. at the time. This was back in the early '60s. In those days the record companies like Capitol had their own studios for the most part, so independents were uncommon.

In the Beginning There Was The End

I'd say the most interesting recording session I did with The Doors was "The End." That was at Sunset Sound and Jim was on acid that night and was raving. It took us all night to get "The End" down on tape. Actually, we did two takes and edited them together to form one.

It was during this session that I witnessed one of the most amazing techniques I have ever seen. It was called a "window edit." We needed to cut track 2 from take 1 and insert it into its corresponding place in take 2. In other words, take 2 was the better take except for a problem with an instrument (I don't recall which) on track 2, which was fine on the first take. So it involved cutting past track 1 on take 2, moving ahead on track 2 to the given point, cutting out that track from that point to another given point, and inserting in its place the piece of tape containing the good track from the other take. Confusing, isn't it?

The splice was about eight feet long and a quarter of an inch deep into the one-inch tape. Bruce Botnick had to make the two pieces of tape fit together like a jigsaw puzzle. He did it, and luckily the tempos matched almost perfectly.

When the session was over we were all getting ready to leave and, unbeknownst to us, Jim sneaked back in the studio, grabbed a fire extinguisher, and destroyed the grand piano, the harpsichord — practically the whole studio. Paul Rothchild had to drag Jim out of there before he got arrested. Someone's insurance covered the damages — it wasn't our insurance, for sure, because we didn't have any.

I think that *The Doors,* even though it was 4-track and recorded through an antiquated board, sounds as good as the other albums and its sound stands up to this day. One of the reasons for this is the fact that we did only have four tracks and we had to get our stuff down initially, which I think in some ways is better than the way it's so often done today, piecemeal — one part at a time. We had the songs down cold because we had been playing them around L.A. for about two years, so we only needed, for the most part, to do one or two takes per tune.

Thinking back, a lot of the elements just seemed to go together better in those days. But then again, I wouldn't want to give up the creative freedom my project studio and workstation afford me — and all the new doors they can open!

The Madonna Diaries

Erotica's coproducer brings us into the inner sanctum of Madonna's labor of lust

By Shep Pettibone

Originally appeared in December 1992

I remember when Madonna and I first started working together on *Erotica.* We were listening in my home studio to one of the first songs and I turned to her and said, "It's great, but it's no 'Vogue.'" She told me that not every song could be "Vogue" — not every cut could emerge as the top-selling record of all time. She was right, but I pressed my case anyway: "I guess I'm always trying to out-top myself," I told her, "The next thing should be bigger than the last." Madonna just turned and looked me straight in the eye. It had been a long time since I'd been star-struck by her, but she was glowing differently now. "Shep," she began, "no matter how fierce something is, you can't ever do the same thing twice." She sat down to record the final vocals on "Erotica" and looked out onto the terrace and into the New York City night.

"Ever," she repeated.

July – August 1991

I wanted to start writing again. The last project I had worked on with Madonna was *The Immaculate Collection* but that was just a month and a half of working with that QSound stuff. I knew I could do something great after "Vogue" and "Rescue Me," so I just started putting tracks together with my assistant, Tony Shimkin. I wanted to have a few songs for Madonna to listen to when I went out to Chicago, where she was filming *A League of Their Own.* I had no idea that she was planning to do an album at that time, but then again, neither did she.

I arrived in Chicago on July 8 and gave Madonna a cassette. I told her to give it a listen and tell me what she thought. She said she'd listen to it in the car, in the trailer, wherever she could. A few days later, I heard back from her. Madonna liked all the songs — three out of three. I decided to work on a few more.

Usually, when I sit down to write, it isn't as if I have a specific person in mind for any one song. By the time I get to a certain place in the music, it begins to mold itself an identity and I think, "Hey, this person would like that." At the time, Cathy Dennis, Taylor Dayne, or Madonna were the primary inspirations for a variety of songs.

October – November 1991

Madonna returned to New York and we began to work on demos in my apartment. It's cool working at home. It's convenient, cozy, and there's no studio time ticking by. Plus, if you wake up in the middle of the night and you have an idea, you just go upstairs, turn on the equipment, and go. Our schedule was kind of sporadic in the beginning. I'd work with her for a week and then she'd go off to work with Steve Meisel on her book (*Sex*) for two weeks. Occasionally, Madonna would meet with Andre Betts, her coproducer on "Justify My Love." While she was away, I would spend time coming up with other tracks or work on Cathy Dennis and Taylor Dayne material. At this point, I wasn't working on any remixes — just writing.

"Deeper and Deeper," "Erotica," "Rain," "Bad Girl," and "Thief of Hearts" made up the first batch of songs we worked on together. I did the music and she wrote the words. Sometimes I'd give her some ideas lyrically and she'd go, "Oh, that's good," or, "That sucks." I remember when I gave her some ideas lyrically for "Vogue" and she said, very curtly, "That's what I do." Essentially, her songs are her stories. They're the things she wants to say.

I did everything upstairs in my home studio: keyboards, bass lines, and vocals. Depending on the mood I was in, I chose from an Oberheim OB8, Korg M3, or a Roland D-50. On the sampling side, the Akai S1000 was our prime workhorse. We used it to sample snake charms for "Words" and Kool & the Gang horns for "Erotica."

When it came time to record demos, we laid down a track of SMPTE on the last track of my 8-track TASCAM 388 Studio 8 reel-to-reel, which has dbx. Usually we'd put the track down on tracks 1 and 2 in a stereo mix, and then bring Madonna's vocals in on 3 through 7 — a lead, a double lead, the harmonies, and the background parts. Ninety-eight percent of the time, the vocals recorded in my apartment were the keeper vocals, the ones you hear on the album.

It took two or three days to write a song from beginning to end. Still, sometimes even after they were done we'd want to change the flow of the song and ask the song a few questions: Where should the chorus hit? Should it be a double chorus? Sometimes Madonna would call me in the middle of the night and say, "Shep, I think the chorus should go like this," or, "I hate this verse, fix the bass line." "Deeper and Deeper" was one of those songs she always had a problem with. The middle of the song wasn't working. We tried different bridges and changes, but nothing worked. In the end, Madonna wanted the middle of the song to have a flamenco guitar strumming big-time. I didn't like the idea of taking a Philly house song and putting "La Isla Bonita" in the middle of it. But that's what she wanted, so that's what she got.

Shep Pettibone – Mix Maestro

If remixing was the music industry's latest monster, then Shep Pettibone was its Dr. Frankenstein. After tailoring his craft as a part-time DJ and record-store owner, Pettibone plunged headfirst into the remix craze in the 1980s by re-creating hard-hitting versions of songs for a variety of dance queens, including Loleatta Holloway, Gloria Gaynor, and Alisha. Suddenly, Pettibone found himself in the eye of the pop hurricane, where New Wave acts such as Pet Shop Boys, Thompson Twins, New Order, and Erasure were spinning out an enormous web of dance songs ripe for the remix. Not surprisingly, clubs immediately took to this new form of dance music, but radio still handled the genre with kid gloves. Essentially, they needed an excuse to play New Wave. Pettibone gave it to them.

By inventing powerful dance versions of "Chains of Love" (Erasure), "Something About You" (Level 42), and "West End Girls" (Pet Shop Boys), Pettibone transformed the way radio listeners heard music. It seemed as if anything, no matter how staid or played, could be given an enormous backbeat and transformed into a dance hit. As a result, remixes began to influence the way songs were marketed, and, more important, how they were created.

By the time the 1980s came to a close, Janet Jackson, Paula Abdul, MC Hammer, Lionel Richie, Prince, and Cyndi Lauper had entrusted their work to Pettibone. In the meantime, an icon-in-waiting by the name of Madonna approached him to remix her song "Get Into the Groove," thus initiating a relationship that would span several hit records, including "True Blue," "Where's the Party," and "Causing a Commotion."

"By the time I worked on 'Like a Prayer' and 'Express Yourself,'" says Pettibone, "it looked as if Madonna liked the remixed versions better than the ones that were on the album. That was great, but producing was still at the top of my wishlist."

Pettibone got his wish when he was asked to write and produce a B-side single for Madonna's *I'm Breathless* album. That B-side eventually became "Vogue," which, in turn, became the largest-selling single of 1990. Pettibone had arrived on the production scene, in a big way.

With a bonafide smash under his belt, Pettibone went back to work for today's hottest entertainers, while juggling a client list of post-modern disco divas that included Cathy Dennis, Taylor Dayne, Mariah Carey, and, of course, Madonna. Of all his compatriots, however, it was Madonna who most encouraged Pettibone to continue writing, spurring on what would eventually evolve into Madonna's tour de force, *Erotica.* With a ground swell of multimedia publicity, the album entered Billboard's Top 200 at #2 in its first week.

—*Jon Varman*

December 1991

"I hate them." That's what she said to me when we listened to the first bunch of songs we'd recorded. I thought it sounded great because some of the songs had a New York house sound and some of them had an L.A. vibe. "If I had wanted the album to sound like that, I'd have worked with Patrick Leonard in L.A.," she told me. I got the point pretty fast.

Madonna wanted *Erotica* to have a raw edge to it, as if it were recorded in an alley at 123rd Street in Harlem. She didn't want some light, glossy production to permeate her sound. I got back into my usual style of mixing, which is pretty bass-oriented, analog, hit-you-over-the-head kind of stuff. When you're recording songs for Madonna, the attitude is: Either make a song work, or it's not going to be on the album. That's that.

Typically, Madonna would get over to my place by one in the afternoon and we'd work until eight or nine at night. Improvising vocals took one or two passes and by the time the third pass came around, she'd get on the mic and say "Let's go." Madonna has an incredible mind; she locks the melody into her head and memorizes the words immediately. She doesn't even have to read the words off the paper when she's singing.

The only problems were during sequencing, when we had to do something on the Mac that would take some time. Two minutes into it, Madonna would ask us: "What are you guys doing that's taking so long!" — and this was just after the first few minutes. We'd tell her to go downstairs and make some popcorn or phone calls so that we could put the song together and she'd do that for about five minutes before screaming: "Come on, guys, I'm getting bored!" I had to keep things moving as fast as possible because it's one of my jobs to keep Madonna from losing interest in what she's doing.

As far as the music went, it was getting a little melancholy by that point. It definitely wasn't up-and-happy music. Maybe I inspired songs like "In This Life" and "Bad Girl" because they were written in a minor key. But Madonna's stories were getting a lot more serious and intense and she was definitely driving the creative direction of the songs into deeply personal territory.

January – February 1992

I spent Christmas on vacation in Jamaica and when I got back on January 2, I was like "Oh man, I am not ready for this." There were a lot of intense songs to work on for Madonna, but all I had was this reggae-ish vibe going around in my head. Jamaica had really had an impact on me. I put the vibe down on tape and played it for Madonna, who immediately took to it. Once she got all the lyrics down, the song became "Why's It So Hard?"

After it was done we thought: "How about if we get a male Jamaican rapper in here to do some stuff on the record?" We found this guy, Jamaiki, who runs a Jamaican record store uptown. He was this big guy with a real deep-ass voice. When we were trying to explain the song to him, he just looked at us and said, "Do you have any rum, man?" By the time Jamaiki was laying down the tracks in my studio, he was dancing around, swigging rum and spilling it everywhere. We ended up not using the track because it sounded too rough for the song, but it was a very fun day — completely different.

By this point, people had begun to realize that Madonna was recording in my penthouse. All day her fans would wait outside, even though it was freezing, just to catch a glimpse of her or take a picture. One particular day, when I walked her down to her car, the lobby was filled with building residents getting the mail, hanging out at the front desk, sitting on benches. It was weird because usually the place is empty. After I walked her outside and ran across the street to get the day's newspaper, I came back to find nobody there. People were coming downstairs to the lobby just to get a look at her, even if it was out of the corners of their eyes.

March 1992

Now I knew we were doing an album. We had 15 songs demoed and she liked them all. The last song we did was for the movie *A League of Their Own*. Madonna just started singing a melody over and over again into the Shure SM57 microphone while the Mac with Vision was playing strings, organ, piano, and a basic rim-shot loop. It sounded really timeless, very nostalgic. I spent all night filling in the verses and the song became "This Used to Be My Playground."

The day after "Playground" was finished, Madonna went to Oregon to work on her next film, *Body of Evidence*, with Willem Defoe. This gave me some time to wrap up work on some songs with Cathy Dennis and Taylor Dayne at Soundworks Studios in New York. The workload had grown quite intense since the beginning of the year and it showed no signs of letting up. Thanks to my manager, Jane Brinton, we were able to coordinate all the ongoing projects without a hitch.

May 1992

I met Madonna at Oceanway Studios in Los Angeles to complete the orchestra parts for "This Used to Be My Playground." We had to record a string arrangement — something I was excited about but had never done before. Madonna chose Jeremy Lubbock to do the arrangements because he had done such a good job with her *I'm Breathless* material and came highly recommended. Everything went fine until the point when the orchestra played their parts; we didn't like what we heard. Madonna and I had to change the whole arrangement, right there in the studio, with a full orchestra sitting there getting paid for taking up space — around $15,000 for three hours, $3,000 for every half hour over that. And of course, Lubbock was talking to two people who didn't know a *C* from a *B* natural. The pressure was on.

I can only sing the notes I hear at the moment, so that's what I did. Madonna and I stood there over my little Mac, singing the notes, and Lubbock would go, "Oh, that's a *G*. Oh, that's a *B*" and that's how it got done. We completed the session in two hours and 58 minutes — two minutes away from another three grand.

The last day of recording fell on Memorial Day. Madonna wanted to do the lead vocals again, insisting that it would sound better. It did. I finished off some edits before going over to a party Madonna was throwing in her Hollywood mansion.

June – July 1992

The schedule for recording at Soundworks in New York went something like this:

- June 8 — "Erotica"
- June 9 — "Words"; "Why's It So Hard"
- June 10 — "Why's It So Hard"; "Thief of Hearts"
- June 11 — "Thief of Hearts"; "Goodbye to Innocence"
- June 15 — 8-track dumps w/no timecode
- June 16 — "Deeper and Deeper"

And so on and so on...

We transferred everything we had on the TASCAM 8-track onto 24-track. I decided to produce the tracks at 15 ips with Dolby SR because it has this warm bottom in the bass and I wanted to capture that for *Erotica*. Plus, I was listening to some of my old remixes, which were recorded at 15 ips, and was amazed at how much more you could feel the music. Compact discs seem to move you one step away from the music, while records put you right in the mix. So I figured that if I overemphasized that LP feeling, it would rub off on the CD, which is the primary format manufactured for American audiences today. Strangely enough, our country can't get any LPs of *Erotica,* while the rest of the world can.

On July 7, we did the mixing for "Erotic," the ode to S&M that Madonna wanted to include in her book, *Sex.* She felt it should sound the same as "Erotica" (the song on the album), with just a bass line, her voice, and some sensuous Middle Eastern sounds. But by then I had seen the book and had come up with an interesting idea. "You have all these great stories in the book," I told her "Why don't you use them in the song?" I knew that Madonna was developing a 1930s dominatrix-look for *Erotica,* but I didn't realize how far she was willing to go until I saw *Sex.* It contained stories authored by her mysteriously dark alter ego, Dita.

Madonna took the book and walked out of the room and didn't come back until about half an hour later. Suddenly she was on the mic, speaking in this very dry voice. "My name is Dita," she said, "and I'll be your mistress tonight." I knew that the original "Erotica" would never be the same again, and it wasn't. The chorus and bridge were changed entirely and the whole psyche of the song became sexier, more to the point. It seemed as if Dita brought out the beast in her, actually serving as a vehicle for the dangerous territory she was traveling. Actually, it was the name Madonna used when she'd stay in hotels around the world. Not anymore.

When July 10 came, I felt my 30-something years hit me full-force. It was the day of reckoning — my birthday, and yet I was stuck in the studio with Madonna, Tony Shimkin, and an animal-balloon-twisting clown to celebrate it with. It was fun for about five minutes, until Madonna said, "Shep, you gotta get back to work."

August 15, 1992 — Mo's Birthday

One of the tracks, "Goodbye to Innocence," just wasn't working. There was something about the song that didn't grab Madonna, so we had to fix it. I worked overnight in my studio and came back to Soundworks with a brand new bass line that seemed to do the trick.

Miking Madonna

When miking a singing superstar, do you pull out all the stops? Or do you just stick to the basics, record in your apartment studio, and employ the help of a beat-up old mic?

If you chose option two, then you're striking the same studio pose as Shep Pettibone and Madonna. Simply put, Madonna would sit in the middle of Pettibone's cozy apartment studio and sing into an old Shure SM57, while two Yamaha NS-10 nearfield monitors blasted out the goods over Manhattan's Third Avenue.

"Madonna didn't use headphones," says Pettibone. "We had these monitors pumping out the music, which definitely makes for more leakage. But who knew we'd be using the demo vocals in the final mix." When it came down to isolating vocals for remixed vocal dubs, Pettibone used Drawmer gates to eliminate drumbeats and sounds that would otherwise show up on a track because of leakage.

When smooth melodies were called for, a Yamaha SPX900 or Roland DEP-5 came into play, while spoken parts were recorded dry. For one track, "Bye Bye Baby," Madonna and Pettibone searched for an old 1940s feel, which would make the vocals sound as if they were coming out of an antique radio. They found their sound with a Pultec HLF filter.

Although the *Erotica* production team would eventually go high-tech behind Soundworks' 48-channel SSL board, the mindset was still mostly one of low-tech standards. One example came during the overdub sessions for "Bad Girl," when Madonna came up with some new lyrics for the song. "We had to record new vocals for the second verse," explains Pettibone, "and they had an SM57 handy. The only problem was that it was a brand new microphone and we had recorded the original vocals with the old SM57 back at my apartment. We knew the song wouldn't sound cohesive, and it didn't." Pettibone ran back to his studio and returned to Soundworks with the tried-and-true mic. "Sometimes," he adds, "older is better."

—Jon Varman

Madonna put on headphones and got ready to lay down the vocals for "Goodbye to Innocence." But instead of singing the original words, which were written last year, Madonna started toying with the lyrics, singing the words to the lounge-lizard act staple, "Fever." At first we thought: "This is cool," and it was. It sounded so good that we decided to take it one step further and actually cover the tune. Too bad no one knew the words. What we needed was a copy of "Fever" if we were going to record it that day. So, Madonna got on the phone with Seymour Stein at Sire Records, and, within an hour, we had the lyric sheets, the Peggy Lee version, and the original version of the song in our hands. I was really impressed by how quickly we got it all. That was the last track on *Erotica* and we finished mixing it just in time to celebrate another birthday — Madonna's.

That night, she had a birthday party on a boat circling Manhattan. Picture about 50 people dancing on a boat with disco blasting out of the portholes and you get the idea. In between dancing and celebrating, I spent the time reflecting on the album. I was confident that it was a great compilation of songs, but I was wondering how people would react to it. It was definitely a different album for her in that it was a dance/pop album, instead of a guitar-laden pop album designed just for Top 40. That was a conscious decision on her part because it seemed that the more pop she went, the fewer of her albums people were buying. This time, she's giving the people what they want.

September – October 1992

After three and a half months of working in the same studio and hearing the same songs day after day, it was a relief to have the album finished. Everything went smoothly except the last two songs, "Why's It So Hard" and "Words," both of which we had to recall for changes. On September 12, I walked out of Soundworks with the completed master of *Erotica* in my hands.

A month later, I went to the *Sex* party. The *Erotica* blitz was about to hit in music, video, and book form and a variety of stars were coming out for the party. Madonna herself surveyed the scene during the midnight hour. I walked over to meet her in the DJ booth.

There was all this wild stuff going around us: people tattooing one another, couples simulating sex — it was crazy. And when I went to talk to Madonna, who was in the middle of it all, our conversations turned to music. For all the multimedia extravaganzas that were braying for her attention, it was still the music that mattered and it was the record that we fawned over. I realized that no matter how far I've come, I still feel the same way that I always did.

And then she put the handcuffs on me. NOT!

Dynamic Duo

Jimmy Jam explains how he and Terry Lewis work as a production pair

By Jimmy Jam

Originally appeared in February 1993

Terry and I have a saying that helps us come up with a solution to any problem, whether it be musical or technical: We have no slack. It means that if one of us is experiencing a creative block for some reason, the other one picks up the slack. If, for instance, there are four or five projects going on at the same time — a Johnny Gill vocal in one studio, a Sounds Of Blackness track in another, and so on— we'll split the duty. Terry tends to be the one doing most of the vocal work, while I gravitate toward tracking and mixing. In fact, Terry calls me "Trackmaster," and I call him "Vocalmaster." It's a tribute to our friendship that we've been able to collaborate so successfully and for so long.

Terry and I originally met in junior high school. He was a very gifted athlete, but he liked to play bass as a hobby. As a matter of fact, it was Terry who interested me in playing keyboards, even though my initial love was the drums. It was while I was taking a beginning piano class that I came in contact with another person who, in addition to Terry, would have a great effect on my life. While the teacher was showing everyone how to play "Mary Had a Little Lamb," I would be jamming and writing songs with this other kid. It wasn't until a few years later that I would audition for my ex-jam/classmate, who was forming a band under his own name, Prince.

Go for the Gold

I didn't make it into Prince's band, but I gave it my best shot. (Matt Fink got the job.) I play well enough to write songs, but if I had to make it as a pure musician, forget it.

I learned early on that there are different approaches to songwriting depending on the artist you're writing for. For example, we write very melodic songs for Janet Jackson and Ralph Tresvant, because that's where their true strengths lie. The power of Johnny Gill's voice alone can bring a melody to whole new levels. Melody is very important to a good song because you want to have something that people can hum or sing along to, even if they don't know the words.

Soundwise, I think our music has a lot of different vibes. For each artist, we change what we do because Janet Jackson isn't going to sound like Cherelle and Cherelle isn't going to sound like Karyn White. For instance, some of the drum sounds and synth vibes created for Janet would sound great on songs by other artists, but we can't use them because we would end up getting caught in one mode.

Overall, we record in a very old-fashioned way. We just turn on the tape and go for the gold. That's how you make those wonderful mistakes that give your song the unique touch you're looking for. It's like when you do a demo of a song and you know it's not the real thing and some unexpected things get in that you initially don't like. But, when it comes down to recording the song for real, you usually end up trying to duplicate those things — those wonderful mistakes. That's why it's always important to save the original tracks, or the scratch vocals. Nine times out of ten, the scratch vocals are better than the real thing because the artist doesn't have the pressure — that "this is it!" rolling around in his or her mind. We used to give the vocalist a tape and say, "Here's how it goes. Learn it and come back tomorrow." We never do that anymore. You can catch gold (or platinum, as the case may be) while an artist is in the process of learning a song and playing around with addictive new melodies.

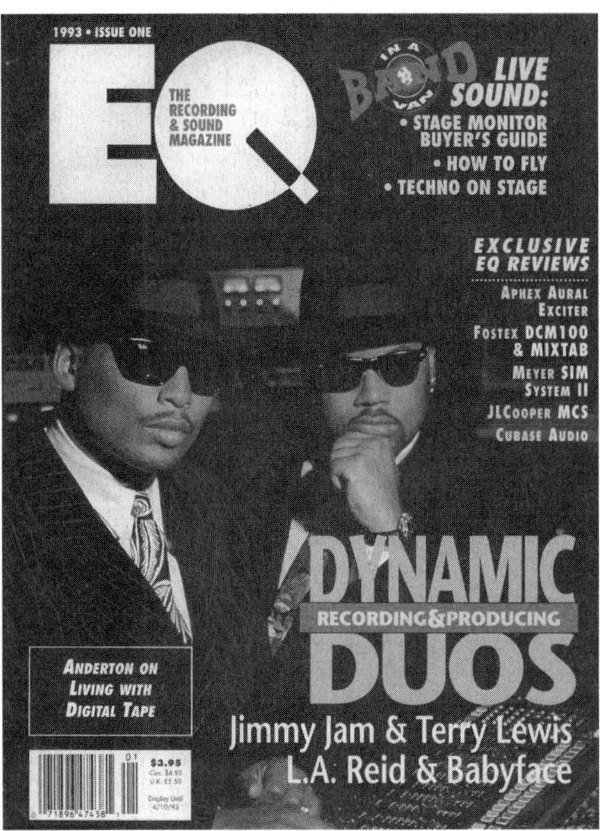

Janet's Last Jam

Strangely enough, one of the biggest singles off Janet Jackson's last album, *Rhythm Nation,* was a song that went straight to wax with a scratch vocal. "Escapade" was a very upbeat, festive melody that craved for a certain feeling. I laid down four minutes of bass, keys, and drums on tape, and then Janet came in to sing the guide vocals. We had every intention of going back into the studio and cutting the vocals for real, but we never did. Subsequently, when we sent the work tape to Shep Pettibone to be remixed, he asked us where the individual tracks were and we told him that what he had was the record. Basically, the demo version of "Escapade" was what was released to the public, except that it was demo'd on a 24-track. There are a lot of tracks that Janet has done that way, simply because we like to keep them as skeletal as possible and then fill in the other tracks around her vocals. "When I Think of You" was also released in its original, raw version.

Janet's voice is especially unique since it actually adds rhythm to the track. After we have a track done, she'll sing on it and make it funkier than it was before. It's a combination of her breath, her style, and the way she pronounces certain words. Plus, she sings in beats, which makes it much easier for us to work. As far as EQ'ing goes, we put Janet on tape flat and let our engineer, Steve Hodge, choose the right mix to go with the flow. On the song "Nasty" (*Control,* 1987), we used a lot of high-pass filter while on "Rhythm Nation" we overloaded the tape so that the effect would sound very frantic, very urgent.

For Janet's duet with Luther Vandross, "The Best Things in Life Are Free" (*Mo' Money* Soundtrack), we tried to separate the vocals rather than blending the two. Janet's voice has more of an edge to it with some light high-pass, while Luther's voice is just Luther. He seems to glide above the track, kind of playing around with the melody. I think that "Best Things in Life..." shows that Janet can't necessarily sing like Luther, but Luther can't necessarily sing like Janet.

In a creative music business, you've got to be where you can create good music. That's why we chose the town we grew up in, Minneapolis, as the home for our studio, Flyte Tyme. We settled in this city ten years ago, and stayed here when we opened our new state-of-the-art headquarters in 1989. It's great in Minneapolis because you don't live under a microscope the way you do in L.A., where everything is so music-oriented. Plus, all our friends and family live here, and that enables us to maintain a well-rounded lifestyle.

There are four studios here at Flyte Tyme, each with its own Harrison console. Both Studio A and D have a Series-10 while the other rooms hold Raven and MR-4 boards. We record some of our biggest acts (from our label, Perspective) in Studio A, including Sounds Of Blackness, a 40-person gospel group that I'm very proud of. That room is really great for string sessions, which I prefer over sampled string sounds. Studio B is our personal studio, located directly across from our office. That is the place where Terry and I can be found during the midnight hours, letting the creative process run wild. Our funkiest stuff comes out of Studio C ("The Funk Room"), which has its own Synclavier setup. A couple of producers around here, Lance and Prof T., really like that room because it has two JBL monitors that were left over from the original Flyte Tyme, and they are just too big for the tiny studio. When you go in there all you hear is this loud, crazy bass.

Since we're not a commercial operation we don't have to compete with the other studios over having the latest "whatever" just because it's new. For most of our artists we'll pull out vintage equipment, such as an OB8 for Johnny Gill or an old EMAX for Janet. Out of ten new products, there'll probably be only one or two that will really stick around. The Akai MPC-60 has become the drum machine of choice, but a lot of times we prefer to program basic beats into an old Linn LM-1 just for simplicity. It's quick, easy, and you don't have to spend time assigning outputs. I tend not to get too involved with a lot of drum programming because, even after the beat is down, we'll go back and add live cymbals and toms.

Some of my favorite samples are the really dirty ones we did on "Rhythm Nation" and "Alright," which featured loops from Sly & the Family Stone and James Brown, respectively. We also used the Ensoniq Mirage for sampling trashcans and factory sounds (which actually originated from the old Linn machine), while the EMAX system supplied us with everything from gun shots to white noise like that you hear on a TV. As far as keyboards are concerned, I'm a preset guy at heart. The SY77 by Yamaha is not very pretty, but it's great for bass and Wurlitzer piano sounds, and recently we started playing with Ensoniq's SQ2. Basically, I'll roll with any keyboard that has a good bunch of presets, but I don't like to spend all my time creating new sounds because there's some guy sitting at Yamaha or wherever, getting paid to come up with good ones. If that's what he does for a living and he can't create an incredible preset, why do I need it?

Finally, when it comes to miking vocalists, the AKG tube is big on our list. We like it because it's very forgiving with all types of singers, loud or soft. Janet likes to sing with her mouth literally on the mic and her headphones at full blast, yet the tube mic never breaks up. We also use AKG's 414 mic. As a matter of fact, when we recorded Luther he insisted on using one. That's one of those mics that will never say die. But in the end, we set up two or three mics to see which one sounded best, and 90 percent of the time it was the AKG tube that would have us smiling.

Mo' Movies

Before *Mo' Money,* we had never done a complete soundtrack, just a few songs that appeared in movies like *Krush Groove* and *Ghostbusters II*. So when Damon Wayans asked us to write and produce the soundtrack for *Mo' Money,* we jumped at the opportunity. I've always been a big movie fanatic.

Terry and I would like to continue doing soundtracks, but it's a very time-consuming process. I really like Ennio Morricone (*Bugsy,* 1991) and guys like that, but Quincy Jones (*Color Purple,* 1986) is the real cat. And he goes way beyond movie scoring — he's the godfather of producers. We're not even in the same ballpark, or the same city in the same ballpark, that he's in. Quincy was one of the people instrumental in getting the general consumer to know who the producer is.

After *Thriller,* everyone wanted to know: "What exactly does a producer do?" The producer's not just a guy who simply sits in the studio and spends all the money. The producer can be a writer, an engineer — a self-contained entity. And Quincy's the man who proved that to the world.

As far as the future of music goes, I see kids moving away from the sampled beat and going back to live sound. Now that a lot of musicians are hooked on samples by bands like Arrested Development and Black Sheep, they're saying, "Instead of learning how to sample this, I'm gonna learn how to play it." Technology is here, and we're obviously going to use it in new and inventive ways, but I hope that it doesn't affect too drastically the way people write and produce songs. There's something about playing together, in a band or in a duo, that just can't be replicated with the crutch of too much technology.

Tag Team

How L.A. Reid and Babyface, another dynamic duo, work it out

By L.A. Reid

Originally appeared in February 1993

One of the biggest advantages of having a producing/songwriting partner is that you always have someone to bounce ideas off. Working by yourself can sometimes get a little stale, so it's better to have a collaborator around to help keep up the inspiration level. There are always ideas out there that you may not have thought of, and that your partner has humming around inside his head. Plus, you don't have to second guess yourself when working with someone whom you trust. As my partner, Babyface, says: "By working as part of a team, one always has the benefit of a second opinion."

I first met Babyface in Indianapolis, Indiana, sometime around 1980. We were playing in rival bands at the time, which ended a year later when we hooked up and started to write songs together. We formed a group called the Deal, with me on drums and keys, and Babyface singing lead vocals. It was obvious from the outset that we were able to trust each other's musical instincts wholeheartedly. Instead of making choices separately, we began to make choices as one.

Today, we continue to make hard choices together, whether they involve our music, the business, or our recording facility, Studio LaCoco. The primary goal these days is to establish LaFace Records as a major label within the next few years and to then move into film and television. After the success of the *Boomerang* motion picture soundtrack, we now have time to work with a variety of diverse and talented artists who may someday appear on future records or soundtracks. By working out of our studio's home base in Atlanta, we're able to maximize our privacy while still keeping one hand in the creative process.

L.A.'s Women

The label has had a head start thanks to TLC, an all-girl trio that has taken off in a big way. My wife, singer Pebbles, played a major role in helping "Ooooooohhh...On the TLC Tip" go platinum, considering she's the one who discovered the act. Actually, there are a lot of groups that Pebbles discovered that have come to LaFace for future development.

After she introduced the girls to me and Babyface, we knew right then and there that TLC was going to be a hip act with a strong connection to America's youth culture. We wrote songs for them that essentially jibed with their attitude that they "can have any man they want — and that's actual and factual!" The song that inspired those lyrics, "Baby, Baby, Baby," was recorded in our studio with a musical mindset that lay somewhere between hard and soft sounds. The melodies went down smooth and mellow, while the drumbeats remained relatively hard.

While we were recording Boyz II Men's "End of the Road" at Studio 4 in Philly, Babyface turned to me and said, "What we have here is a very good song." But when it was originally being written, I don't think we even tried to ask if it was going to be a big hit or not. [*Editor's note: "End of the Road" has become the longest-running #1 pop single in rock history.*] Our responsibility as producers and writers is to create quality music, not to worry about how big a song's going to be or what star is going to sing it. Most of the time, songs don't go to who you think they're going to go to, anyway. As a matter of fact, there have been times when we wrote something for a woman and it ended up going to a man, and vice versa.

We only had six hours to record all the vocals on "End of the Road," which is not a lot of time. Each guy sang on his own track and then the group sang together live while an MPC-60 drum machine and a Forat F-16 sampler kept the backbeat. There wasn't really any set way for recording the song. It's just an old-time R&B tune that sticks to the basics and never lets up on the harmony.

Whitney & Bobby

Working with Whitney Houston on "I'm Your Baby Tonight" was an incredible experience. She cuts songs so fast, your head is spinning by the time she's done. Some people have given her a bad rap by painting her in a pop picture, but that's not the real Whitney. She's a very real artist, and she has the soul to prove it.

Bobby Brown is a different type of artist entirely. One day, he can come in and not feel it at all, while on others, he'll simply blow you away. I came in contact with Bobby just as he was maturing out of his key role in New Edition. By that point we had already made a few dents in the pop charts with songs like "Rock Steady" (the Whispers, '87) and "Girlfriend" (Pebbles, '87), but we had no idea of just how big we'd hit with Bobby Brown at the mic.

Now it's five years later, and a lot of time has passed since Bobby put out his last album, *Don't Be Cruel.* This time around, Bobby's sound is a lot thicker than it was back in the late '80s. The song "Humpin' Around," for instance, with its operatic voices and hard-hitting drums, is a lot different from songs like "Every Little Step" and "Don't Be Cruel." It's not that we're using different equipment, because everything we have is still the same — old Yamaha REV-5's, Eventide 3000's, Focusrite EQs, etc. I guess we've just been influenced by some of the younger producers who are making waves around us.

We tried not to EQ Bobby too much, because our main goal when working with an entertainer is to capture a person's essence and build the music around that. Babyface and I prefer to EQ the music so that it fits the voice, rather than EQ the voice to fit the music. If we had a miking philosophy, it would probably be: Don't mess with the natural sound of a singer's voice. We have several mics that have been customized for great sound, including an AKG tube, a Neumann U 47, and a real old U 87.

Look Ma! No Computers

Essentially, LaCoco is a vintage studio with everything harking back to the old school of sound. Whether it's vintage microphones we're dealing with or a brand new guitar, it is an analog operation all the way. We don't sample beats or use loops, and computers are only necessary when a song's lyrics have to be written down and stored.

The reason we're not that into the high tech is because we try to concentrate on great lyrics and awesome grooves. If we spent all our time paying attention to technical tricks, then we'd never get around to the melody, which is the most important aspect of a song. After all, the melody is what we all pick up on when we're listening to a song. And isn't that what loving music is all about — being a good listener?

Not the Same Old Song & Dance, Part 1

Aerosmith's lead guitarist lets the music do the talking in his project studio

By Joe Perry

Originally appeared in March 1993

I've had something to record with at home ever since 1975. However, I didn't start building a serious project studio until about five years ago. And, although it's not a part of my Massachusetts home, it is close enough by that I can get to it whenever I want to.

One of my favorite things in the studio is a rack of Neve 1066 and 1073 EQs that I send everything through. I also have a bunch of effects, including Eventide's H3000SE and Roland's SDE-3000, that I go right to tape with. That way if I want to record another mix, I won't have to repatch everything. I also own a Lexicon LXP-5, which I used for a wild effect at the beginning of a song called "Fever" off of our new album, *Get a Grip*.

With *Get a Grip,* we were talking about going out of town to this place called Longview Studios. It's an old farmhouse with a bunch of 24-track rooms that we have used before for writing and recording. You go up there and play and sleep. It's all pretty cool, but I didn't like the prospect of spending the entire summer up there. I wanted to stay close to home.

Steven (Tyler) and I had already been writing at my project studio, the Boneyard, and I had just purchased a Macintosh LCII with Performer software, so I suggested that we keep working there. As it turned out, the band really enjoyed the close and personal experience.

In the Beginning

"Fever" was the first song that we developed for *Get a Grip.* Steven and I were just doing some demo stuff in the Boneyard about two years ago, and that's where that song and the new album began.

We write songs in various ways. Usually I'll have a few pieces of music that we start playing around with — with lots of guitars on it, as you may have guessed. And we'll sit there and start pulling stuff up and seeing what works. That's the way it's always been — for over 20 years.

Sometimes the demos are better than expected. For example, the last song on the second side of the new album, called "Boogie Man," is a little piece that we had done at a different rehearsal studio and that was taken right off the DAT machine. We always have a DAT machine running, just in case. This way, if we hear something we like, we can go back to it. "Boogie Man" had a guitar riff that we just hadn't planned on. Steve sat down and played the slap bass on the keyboards and I played guitar, and after about 45 minutes it gelled into something really decent. What you hear on the album is the last two minutes of that jam right off the DAT. We played it once two years ago and that was that. If we had taken it one more step, I would have written a melody for it, but it sounded so good that we decided to leave it alone.

We do a similar thing when we're recording with the whole band. Aerosmith always records live in the studio — everybody playing at once, with Steven doing a basic vocal. Then we sit back, take a listen to it, and then add to it and fix whatever's wrong. In fact, on some of the songs we recorded I did the lead first and then went back to record the rhythm track. This is how we get the best energy.

We used to do 30 takes, and then take the best performance of each track — the best first chorus, the best third chorus, the best lead, etc. Now we get it all in one whole take. These days, it's pretty rare that we actually cut up a song. We usually get it on the third or fourth take — one of the benefits of being in a band that spans more than two decades. The Boneyard helped, too. Most of the demos we recorded there for *Get a Grip* were really templates. And in some cases, when we couldn't play out the original feeling that was captured on the demo, we would lift them right off the tape. If I got an effect one night that I couldn't reproduce, the demo made a great backup. (I have to get in the habit of writing stuff down — some nights I would bring up 24 tracks and I don't even keep track sheets!)

Drawing the Line

Aerosmith contributes to the producing of its albums, and, of course, we benefit from the input of a talented producer. Every producer has a different style and every band has a different relationship with their producer. Basically, the way we work with Bruce Fairbairn, who did *Permanent Vacation, Pump,* and *Get a Grip,* is that we will have our songs at a point where we all like them. Then

Bruce will come in and listen for the rough spots. As part of the band, you get in the middle of the music, and you need someone with some distance from it. He comes in and listens with fresh ears and works with us to make it the best it can possibly be. If we had one part that we all thought was really smoking, and had something like two months away from it, maybe we would come back to it and see that it needed more. Unfortunately, we never have that luxury, so we get the next best thing: Bruce.

Personally, I think being a producer is such a harrowing experience that I'm glad I don't have to do it to make a living. "Producer" is like a catch-all title. It's a very important position, but I don't want to get any closer to producing Aerosmith than I am right now. Everybody in the band has strong feelings about it, too. I don't think it's wise for us to get to the point where we don't have someone to act as a mediator.

I can relate to the problems that producers face. When I was with the Joe Perry Project, I was in charge of everything — and that taught me the value of working in a band like Aerosmith. I had a good time doing it, but I won't do that kind of solo work again. Maybe someday I'll put out a bunch of outtakes from the studio, but right now I just don't have the time. Besides, there's no need to put out anything that I can't release with Aerosmith.

Done With Analog

Like *Pump* and all our other albums, *Get a Grip* was recorded analog. The reason why is simple: We prefer it. So far I haven't heard digital sound as good, at least when recording. I even hate the way a DAT sounds until it's gone to tape. With analog, there's a certain warmth that just can't be created with digital. And we tried. With *Pump,* we put everything through the AMS AudioFile. Listening to the record now, I think it sounds kind of harsh. This time around we didn't do any of that — we sync'd right to ½-inch tape.

All of your in-studio problems don't have to be solved digitally, either. Just a few weeks ago we were getting ready to mix a song we had recently finished recording, "You Gotta Love It." Steve and I thought we had overdubbed all the parts. We hadn't played it back and we had put it away because it originally wasn't intended for this album. So the day before we were supposed to be done mixing, we put the song up and there was nothing on it. None of the keyboard parts, none of the strings, none of the background vocals. Nothing. We figured it would take days to re-create it.

Enter our hero: engineer Brendan O'Brien. He came in and played us the demo so we could hear what it sounded like. He suggested we get a couple of keyboards and start screwing around, but we called all over and couldn't get hold of any. We were starting to pull our hair out! So we ended up flying the keyboards off the demo. Steve figured he could place the vocals in about two hours, but Brendan suggested flying them, too, and it sounded good to us.

But we weren't on easy street yet. We placed the demo side-by-side with the new tape and the tracks were slightly out of time. The SMPTE wouldn't lock up. Brendan flew it in and every four or six seconds he had to stop the tape, fly it in, and slap one reel with his hand because it was moving too fast. I hadn't seen that done in 15 years. It worked great, and took him 45 minutes tops.

On the Road Again

With the new album just released, we'll be going out on tour to support it. Right now I'm not sure exactly how we're going to do it — every time we go out we do something different.

One thing I know will be different: Whenever I have any effects like reverb or echo, I would rather have it go into the board than through pedals. I prefer to have it go straight to my amp and then have whatever effect I want put on at the monitors. This time around I know I'll have a system like that set up.

What I'll probably do is set up a console backstage just for my guitar effects. That way, the signal can go right to that console, where we can add the effect and adjust the EQ. I figure the chain will go: guitar, amplifier, microphone, my backstage console, and, finally, the house mixer.

Perry-spective

The reason that Aerosmith has stayed so strong for so long is that everybody's got an equal say. Everybody's got their strengths (Brad, for example, goes really wild with the videos). If anybody is given too much free rein, then they'll get carried away with it. I think back over the years to some of the decisions that have been made on stuff I really loved, and it causes a lot of sleepless nights. But I know it makes a better album, and therefore a better band.

Well, I gotta go now. With this album just finished and a new record deal, I'm going to be busy for a long time.

Permanent vacation my ass.

Back in the Saddle

For the third album in a row, producer Bruce Fairbairn helps take Aerosmith where they want to go

By Bruce Fairbairn

Originally appeared in March 1993

There is never a dull minute with Aerosmith. In the studio they're always very willing and open to challenges. In fact, they almost demand to be challenged. Steven in particular is always working away at a song — throwing new ideas, parts, and arrangements at it.

Personally, I feel very comfortable throwing an idea out to the band. Sometimes we'll even laugh about it, but they'll always try it — no matter how crazy the idea sounds.

Usually, differing opinions or point of views are very difficult for everybody when you're recording. To Aerosmith's credit, however, this is not a major obstacle. With all the members of Aerosmith, once they've put their point out, and argued passionately for it, if it doesn't go their way, they'll accept that and try to make the most out of the decision. This makes it a great atmosphere to work in, even during the explosive times.

This quality also makes working with the band exhausting — but extremely rewarding. Steven, especially, has so many ideas and moves so quickly through them that you have to be right there with him or you'll miss some gem that'll never be there again. It's very intense, but, again, it's tremendously rewarding.

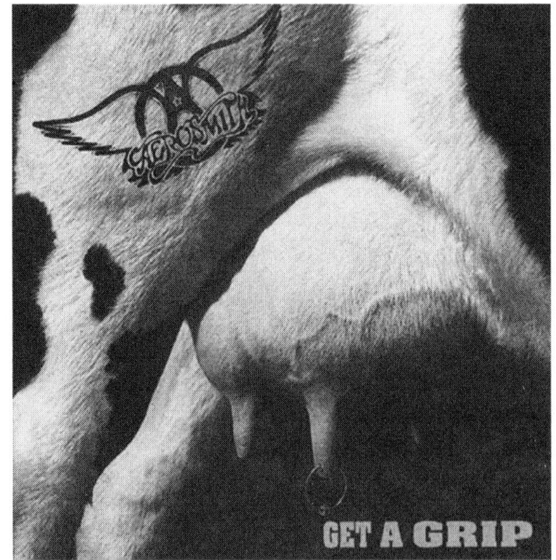

Every band is different in the studio. Aerosmith is definitely different from AC/DC, and AC/DC is different from the Scorpions, the group I'm working with now. If, as a producer, you plug whatever band you're working with into your system, you end up taking away their individual creativity and style. When I work with a band or an artist, we do things a certain way to a point, but then everything changes depending on who you are and what your style is.

Take Joe Perry, for example. Joe is one of the most creative and spontaneous guitar players I have ever worked with. There are plenty of guitar players who are good technically and who can execute well, but Joe plays on his feet. You can ask him to play a solo five times and each time it will be different but just as great. He's also always trying to open up new sounds. For example, on this album he must have used 50 vintage amplifiers. We dragged them into the studio, dusted them off, and fired them up. There were some great sounds that came out there — like the old Parc we split with an aged Epiphone Combo amp. It looks totally bizarre when you see it, but it sounds amazing when you get it right. I have to thank Joe for opening my eyes to the weird world of old guitar gear.

I didn't get the chance to work at Joe's project studio, but I feel that I know it well because I've heard so much music come out of it. Here's how we used it: First, I would come down to Boston and work with the band for a week or so, rehearsing. I would then identify some areas that needed work and Steven and Joe would head back to Joe's studio to work on them and come up with new song ideas. Then they'd send it out to me in Canada and I'd come down and we'd rehearse again.

Their efforts at Joe's studio certainly paid off. In fact, some of the stuff from his studio ended up on the album in one form or another. The uniqueness of an idea combined with a sound that happened at a particular place in time was such that we couldn't hope to recreate it. There's great potential in his place. Now, if we could only get him to fill out track sheets....

In addition to Aerosmith's last three albums, Bruce Fairbairn has produced many of rock 'n' roll's heavy hitters, including Bon Jovi, Poison, David Bowie, Blue Oyster Cult, and Gorky Park.

Not the Same Old Song & Dance, Part 2

Aerosmith's frontman takes us inside his writer's studio and shows us the toys in his attic

By Steven Tyler

Originally appeared in March 1993

My writer's studio is a floating room over a barn that I use as a two-car garage. The room is about 40 square feet and is surrounded by a two-inch space that separates it from the rest of the barn, including the floor. The room is lifted off the floor by rubber stoppers at about 40 points. Why a floating room? The best way to get an entirely soundproofed situation is to put air between you and the rest of the world. There are things like water and lead that work, too, but that's a little ridiculous when air will do the job.

The idea came from one of our past albums. We used a floating room in the recording of *Draw the Line,* which was recorded at an old nunnery called the Cenacle. There was no place to put the console, so we built a floating room and I liked the way it worked. Now I can crank it up to 120 dB before anybody'll hear me. If I want to have someone over to write and play with, we have someplace to go and crank it out until three, four, or five in the morning and no one will complain. You all know how that shit goes — you pick it up and you don't stop for dinner.

I'm not looking to build a big studio. Joe's is close by enough that it's not really necessary for me to have one, too. Besides, I'm really not into the tech-head thing yet — I have enough trouble remembering my own lyrics, and to start worrying about where the bus sends go is something I don't need right now. My short-term goal was to write for this album and have a place with a drum set, a couple of Korgs, and a toaster oven — a place where I wouldn't have any obstacles in my way. And that's what I did. I'm sure I'll get some small board when it gets real easy, but for now, if I get some idea that requires more than I've got, I'll work it up properly in Joe's studio.

My writer's studio is a fun place to work and I love it. I've been having this gentleman come in, named Marshall Ross, and he's carved this huge eagle for me there. It's got a 30-foot wingspan and a huge head that lights up. You can see it through the woods — it's the eighth wonder of the world.

We took a quantum leap from the old days to now. I used to spend a lot of time getting high and looking for outside things to make my insides right, but nowadays, instead of the infamous Aerosmith lost weekends, I'll go find a friend to write with. I'd rather leave my studio with a cassette in my pocket and a couple of songs from my heart then have a lost weekend with someone whose name I can't even remember. Coincidentally, it's like the best of both worlds because you get sounds on tape in a project studio that you wouldn't normally get in a larger studio unless you were high.

Work This Way

For the new album, *Get a Grip,* we went to A&M Studios and put down an album's worth of songs. When we stepped back and looked at the big picture, we weren't sure if this was what we wanted to follow *Pump.* The whole band wished we could go back into Joe's studio (the Boneyard) for another month or two and keep writing because we were on a roll. The question was not whether the songs were any good, but rather: Did we have the time to make them better? We decided to make the time. David Frangioni (who I like to call Gyro Gearloose because he could rewire a Walkman to record 4-track) had everything up and running at Joe's place, so we came back home and went to work.

The atmosphere in a project studio is absolutely better than the one in a large commercial studio. I want to have fun doing what I'm doing, or one day I'm just going to say "forget this." In the Boneyard, even if we get nothing onto tape, I know I'll still have a great time. And nothing is lost. Whenever I sit in a room with Joe and let the tape run, we get at least 10 to 15 solid seeds. For every song that was a hit over the years, I could get a tape from my vault downstairs and let you hear where it came from. We always have the DAT machine rolling, acting like a drip net catching the ideas.

I think Joe's room is perfect. It's small, about 25 x 9 feet, with a 12-foot ceiling. Joe's always looking for new stuff to put in it, too. He was talking to Shelly Yakus at A&M about EQs and decided on Neve, and Gyro's given him a lot of advice. I don't really have anything to do with picking out the equipment that goes into the Boneyard.

Let the Music Do the Talking

The secret to success for any band or songwriting team is communication. The relationship between Joe and me has always been about communication. Sometimes I have a hard time talking to him one-on-one, but I know I can always communicate with him musically. Music is such a strong language that when I lay down a drum beat, I'm saying something more than words can ever say. You can really let the music do the talking if you have an instrument in hand. I can answer him with anything he "says." That's the secret to teamwork between two people or five or whatever.

I think it's more difficult to work with a producer. Everybody likes to come in and rework your stuff to validate their punch cards and say that they were part of something. It's like a bunch of people telling you what the sugar cone beneath a big ball of vanilla ice cream tastes like and, oddly enough, it would taste different to you from what everybody else described. Everybody has their own interpretation of things and you've got to decide whether you take a hard-nosed stand and say, "No way man, this is me and this is the way it stays," or take chances. That's why we let people into our camp all the time. With each album, it gets harder and harder to listen to other people, but every album gets better and better, so a producer is definitely necessary.

Personally, I love producing. If I had the time, I would love to produce another band or my own album. Someday I'll put on the brakes and do it. When I do an Aerosmith album only a piece of me is shown. Being part of a band, you have to try everything. There are four other fingers in the pie and it's not the Steven Show. There's a part of me that wants to do all the stuff I love. Someday I'll do it. I don't know exactly what it'll be; it depends on which side of the bed I wake up on that day.

Getting Vocal

When I record my vocal tracks, I don't like to go in and just throw them down. I like to do them at my own pace, which is pretty quick anyway. I prefer to have six or seven tracks and keep singing the same song with different voices and in different ways.

I like after-hours vocals. It's what I did on *Get a Grip* and it's what I did on *Pump.* I go in there after the band leaves — so it's just me and an engineer. That's when I can have the most fun. No one's listening and there's no pressure. After hours is when I can get closest to a song and its real meaning. The emotions that come out of me then are always in sync with the song.

When we head out on the road, as we'll be doing shortly to support the new album, I fall into this little place I call my road voice. With it, I can't hit the high notes I can hit now, but I hit another kind — a raspy, bluesier high. I used to have a tiny switch on my mic that I could hit with my ring finger and it would switch me between straight signal and DDL, but now I don't do any of that. The thing I'm looking forward to on this tour is trying out some in-ear monitors.

Sweet Aggression

We had a problem with *Pump* in that it was too bright, which is one of the problems when transferring analog material to digital. Digital hurts. Digital burns. Rock 'n' roll has a certain warmth that gets lost in digital recording.

Sometimes in our analog mixes, we're coming off the board on tape and we're mixing my screams and Joe's lead guitar, which are both high register, and we've got them where we want them — really loud. You transfer that to digital and it bites your ear off. So you roll some of it off in mastering and it loses something.

In the old days we went through so much outboard gear, and some of it sounded real good. When I listen to something like *Toys in the Attic,* I can hear things that I never heard before. In that sense, digital is a wonderful medium, but I haven't been able to master it myself, nor do I know anybody who can go from analog to digital and make it sound really good — especially for us, because we like to record and master really hot. Case in point: *Get a Grip* is 4 dB up from *Pump.* This is our most aggressive-sounding album to date. It's gonna make ears bleed.

Catch a Wave

Now that the album's out, I'm going to go surfing — or at least it feels that way. I've got my surfboard, which is the album, I've got a wave, which is the tour, and now I've got to ride this mother into the shore. If you're going to bother standing up on the board, you might as well take it as far as it'll go.

It's rough sometimes, but I still love what I do. There are times when my ears burn from exasperation and I get so frustrated, but it all pays off when I listen to the album at the end.

Somewhere along the line I get this dream that I can make something work and I go at it with a vengeance. And I've always been the sort who, if you tell me I can't, will. It's that rebellious nature that I've had since I was a kid. It's what got me into so much trouble. Now I'm here to do it again with the new album: to go where no band has gone before.

The Ramones: Separated at Birth?

The Pope of Pop is interviewed exclusively for EQ *by the Prince of Punk*

Originally appeared in June 1993

J*OEY: This has been a long time coming, hasn't it?*

PHIL: Yeah. Everybody always asks me if we're related. Usually I tell them that our ancestors came over on the boat together and got separated at Ellis Island. That usually satisfies them. I've discovered that interviewers get ticked off when I tell them we're not related — I guess they think I'm pulling their leg.

JOEY: I thought it was cool when you thanked us in your Grammy acceptance speech.

PHIL: I remember that — I got a telegram from you the next day thanking me.

JOEY: Actually we took the name because we heard Paul McCartney used the name Paul Ramone when he traveled.

PHIL: When I worked with Paul on *Ram,* he told me a story about when he first started out he took the name Ramon, very close to our name, huh? He said he felt it was a very showbiz name, but finally decided on McCartney. He did write a song called "Ram On," however, which is a little ditty that appears on the album.

JOEY: Tell me about the making of Ram. *That's an album that I really enjoyed listening to. It was kind of experimental.*

PHIL: Ram was an adventure. Paul got involved with a lot of American musicians, which I think is responsible for a lot of the charm of that particular album. He has a very masterful way of working with the people around him — he's very genuine about his music and tries to keep things as raw and as simple as possible. When we started working on *Ram,* Paul was definitely on his way to making a new statement.

JOEY: Recently, when we were on tour in Spain, we were watching Wings Over America. *He performed "Uncle Albert," and I sucked it up and really enjoyed it. I like the fact that it has a lot of character, is fun, and has a real feel to it.*

PHIL: That was part of his style. I think that was where *Sgt. Pepper's* had broken the mold for record people: It had complete character from a style point of view, and there were no rules. Paul will tell you how the first album was made in a day, but as the years went by they were finally able to make music more the way they wanted to make it. So when the Beatles split up, this was a chance for him, although he was going to be compared with John no matter what he did, in terms of who was the more aggressive lyricist, and so on. People always accuse Paul of being too sweet and cutesy-pie, which is not at all the case. Those are not his roots. He just has this weird attitude that he sometimes pulls, he's like a vaudeville performer in that way. He's a throwback to some other part of the decade or early part of this century in some cases. He's not a recent soul. In fact, I think that both he and John are from a different planet!

JOEY: There are certain people that seem a bit extraterrestrial. Take Jimi Hendrix, for example. He's most definitely not your average next door neighbor. With Hendrix, the guitar is an extension of his being. It's not as though he has a guitar, it's more like an extra limb. Every time I hear a Hendrix track I'm blown away. It's all emotion and feeling and almost as though he's saying, "This is me. I am my guitar."

PHIL: You also have to realize that he was a very good showman. He could hold an audience captive for hours. The amazing thing is that when you listen to his recordings today, you still get the feeling that you are there with him, even though they're not that well recorded.

JOEY: That's another thing. I feel that to a certain degree modern-day technology has ruined — and in some cases even killed — the feeling and raw emotion in music.

PHIL: Well, it has probably forced some people to become more anal about the way they work, and, from my point of view, less interesting in terms of where the drama is in the band. When it takes a whole day to reach a certain point, that's not playing. Playing is about what comes naturally and what you feel at a certain point in time. When you have a piece of equipment that can change the rhythm pattern simply by pressing a button, you've changed the attitude of the player. When you're young, you play with a certain aggression, and even if you only know two chords, you play them with a certain amount of feeling. That's what the basis of rock 'n' roll bands is really about, and, as you well know, it's also the biggest thrill. It would be interesting to see whether Living Colour is an extension of what Hendrix would have been today because of the style and the aggression of the guitar and the way the rhythm comes off. The Ramones certainly don't pamper the music business either, though.

JOEY: We're all rock 'n' roll fans. The Ramones like being exciting and raw, and everybody in the band has his own distinctive style. How do you feel about the old approach to making records, in comparison with the new?

PHIL: The new approach, believe it or not, is not that far removed from the old. The only difference is that techno freaks tend to put a screen in front of themselves when they start to play, removing themselves from the atmosphere instead of playing into the character of the music. If you are going to stabilize and establish yourself as an artist, you are going to have to play with other people. In the past four or five years, bands have not been playing in isolated rooms, and that's why the Seattle scene, for example, started to happen. There's only so much time that you can remain alone — even singers and songwriters know that.

Currently, there's a major push toward capturing the feeling of the '60s and '70s. I don't like to say it's a repeat of those years, because it's always new and fresh, but it has that same approach and earthiness to it, the sound that people want to hear when they go to see a band.

Using a sequencer is great because you can get certain effects, but if it becomes part of the band, then you've lost the essence of why people make music. But I'm not against the style; I just think it's a question of how you produce. You need to convince the people you're working with that what you're after is immediacy. They have to believe in themselves and you have to make them trust you to tell them that something is great. The key to production is to stay in the background; a good director knows when and how to get the artist to react and emote, because the chemistry of a band will only work when everybody is in the mood.

A good example is Paul Simon. Paul is a real perfectionist, but he does recognize the feeling and emotion that comes from a street musician. That passion is what recording is about. When we were in Brazil, we came across 20 or 30 drummers playing on a street corner. We pulled out the small 8-track we had with us, and the whole thing just came together emotionally. It certainly wasn't planned, and I personally think that because of what goes on in the music business, a lot of the best instinct records are missing.

I'm not blaming the engineers — I think they're very unaware of how important it is for the band to come into the studio and not have to wait around. If the band feels like playing in the first five minutes, there's your record. Time is wasted when the band has to wait for gates or lights to be put up. I plan my spontaneity so that no one knows that it's ready. You're not supposed to know it's ready, because you really turn on a different light.

But you can make great records today — it's just a matter of beating up the old rules. When I'm in the studio, I say to the artists, "Look, if you were going on the air in 30 minutes to do a live rock 'n' roll broadcast, you would make it." If they don't believe that, then they won't get anywhere in the business. Today it's retarded in terms of the amount of time it takes to make a record. Dylan is a perfect example: He would make a record in one night because he had already written the tunes. Just like you, I imagine — you probably have the five or six tracks that you know you are going to do already prepared, and the best thing to do is not record them one at a time. What Dylan does is record them one after the other, no sequence, no rules. You put two rolls of tape in the machines and run one alternately with the other.

JOEY: We're really impatient and we just want to do it. With our last album, we got nine basic tracks down in one night. I remember how things were back in 1977. I wrote "Sheena" and played it for Seymour [Stein, Sire Records company head] who flipped out and said, "We've got to record this song." So that same night we went to Sundragon, recorded the song overnight, and put it out the very next day.

PHIL: That's what I like.

JOEY: Yeah, it's cool because there's a kind of a romance about the old days in the business and the ways things worked back then. It wasn't an industry the way it is now. You wrote your song and knocked it out immediately. It was both an exciting and emotional time. Seymour is a kid at heart and he has that real spirit a lot of record company heads don't have. A lot of them aren't even into music.

PHIL: What you are referring to are the guys that used to come to recording sessions. They made the decisions and when they ran back to the office with a cassette and a dub, they'd say, "Listen to this!" I remember a time when we would have songs at all the radio stations by the next morning, if not by the end of the same night we had been at the studio. Getting this stuff on the air was the most important thing of all. That lack of immediacy is what I really miss in the business today, because I love the feeling of making a record on a Tuesday and knowing that by Thursday it'll be out. And when you have written a song, there's something about not having to wait a year for its release.

JOEY: I can't wait either. When I write a song, I'm excited about it and I want to put it down immediately. I don't want to have to wait a year or until the next album is due. I'd love to be able to record it while it's fresh and while I'm excited about it, because the spirit of it will come through. I was really excited when I wrote "Sedated," but then I had to wait a year before I was able to record it. By that time, I wasn't even sure if it was a good song anymore.

Today it's exciting because of all the new labels that are coming up and all the grass-roots stuff that is happening, but when you're in a situation with a large record company, all the execs have to approve everything. They don't have to know what a good song is (most of them don't). To them it's all dollars and cents, so it's really frustrating.

PHIL: I totally understand that. I wish committee approval were not needed, because the audience is not that way. But I hear and understand their side of it, because their investment is so big.

JOEY: Nowadays I realize that when you are investing hundreds of thousands of dollars, it's not just a case of, "Yeah, it's a good song." It's all very political, and this Arbitron crap really undermines people. People know what they like and what they want. Listening to the radio in the '60s was a real educational experience; you got turned on to everything. I used to listen to the WMCA Good Guys and Murray the K and I got into the Beatles, the Stones, the Who and the Kinks. Nowadays, I can't listen to the radio. The only radio I enjoy and am truly inspired by in this day and age is Vin Scelsa's program on K-Rock (WXRK) on Sunday nights. There's no other show like his in the entire world. It's totally eclectic and a total learning experience.

PHIL: Music is educational. It's a foundation that makes you want to pick up an instrument and be creative.

JOEY: Kids today are not adventurous, at least not in America. I was amazed when I went to England for the first time in 1976. Kids there knew everything. They had all of the Gene Vincent and Little Richard singles and were totally knowledgeable about music. They literally knew everything about everything. Kids in America don't know anything about anything. Everything today is visual, like MTV for example. But what we need is a really good cable show, something that uses archival footage.

PHIL: You could do that. If you're 10 or 12 years old, you're about to enter your adolescence and are about to discover music. And you'll find music about yourself, music that becomes personal to you, but I feel that you need to know where it came from. We are still watching footage from World War II and Vietnam, and people don't seem to tire of it. I think that the music world could stand to see something similar, with radio being its first sponsor, creating their own channel. Using Larry King's show as an example, you don't have to physically watch it. You can turn around or walk around the room because if the character on screen is interesting, the TV basically becomes radio with a picture. The imagination takes over, so it doesn't matter if it is blasting — "the viewer" is not glued to the screen. New York radio used to be that way. Do you remember when FM first went on the air, particularly WPLJ? We used to do a live show out of the studio I worked in.

JOEY: WABC FM?

PHIL: Yes, exactly.

JOEY: I remember Elton John in particular.

PHIL: We had Elton John, the Allman Brothers, Roberta Flack — so many people I can't remember exactly who. But it wasn't commercial. It was about playing for as long as you wanted, with no rehearsal, while 75 to 100 people sat around listening and drinking wine.

JOEY: I think that we really should do something on the TV so that kids will watch and so we can open and expand their minds.

PHIL: It's a good idea. As a kid growing up, the radio was my salvation. I would take it to the back room to get some privacy from the family. I'd even put it under my pillow and sleep with it. But that generation has gone because people now tend to have three TV sets per household. Currently, people are talking about the pending arrival of hundreds of new cable stations as technology improves. So we should definitely give them something to go on.

I have a ten-year-old who flips through the radio dials as quickly as he does the TV remote, so his music education is strictly up to him. Even though I'm the parent, I don't influence him. Sure, he hears some of the music I listen to, but I have to give him freedom of choice. I feel it's important for him to know where it all comes from.

There's definitely not a problem with crossover between the generations. For example, if you go to a Crosby, Stills & Nash or Beach Boys concert, it's frightening because the audiences are twice as young as you would expect them to be, while these old guys are up on stage doing the same act they did 20 years ago.

JOEY: We're currently in our third generation of fans and I think that with the Ramones the beauty of it is that we get fans into metal, into alternative, into rock 'n' roll, and into punk. The whole spectrum. And the fans are from all age groups. We get mothers and fathers coming to see us with their kids. I think that that's what is so great about music today. There used to be barriers where you were either into rock or soul or jazz, but now the charts are one big mix of every music type. It's open for everyone to listen and enjoy.

PHIL: I'm happier that there are no barriers, although I think that the music business has no choice because they tend to have to categorize you in the record store. There they say, "That's rock 'n' roll, that's folk, and that's jazz." If they didn't, it would be totally whacked.

JOEY: Phil, it's been great meeting you, but I think we're out of time.

PHIL: Same here. Guess I'll see you at the next family reunion.

JOEY: Right.

At Home With U2 — Daniel's Song

Getting the right sounds in all the wrong places. All the world is U2's project studio

By Daniel Lanois

Originally appeared in December 1993

I've always been more of a musician than a technician, which makes it rather ironic that I have become known for producing the likes of U2, Bob Dylan, and Peter Gabriel. I've always followed the musical route; it's just that I've gotten more fame as a studio guy over the years — although, with the release of my second album, *For the Beauty of Wynona* and winning a Grammy for U2's *Achtung Baby,* both routes remain very important to me.

I suppose I was always interested in the technical side — I built my first project studio with my brother Bob when I was 16 years old. It was in my mother's basement and it was made up of a homemade console and two Revox machines. We would record as much as we could in one pass on the first two tracks, and then run that back through the console. After that, we would overdub once and record it to the second Revox. Essentially, the second print would be the overdubs plus the mix. Surprisingly, the quality was excellent. There was not a lot of tape noise or hiss, considering the setup.

One of the reasons that I think I became pretty good technically was that I took a lot of chances with interfacing. I would always try to integrate unorthodox gear together. For example, I would use a guitar amplifier as a processing device by remiking and then setting up a chain of effects and processing gear. I would then use that as part of a feedback loop.

Most of the time in studios, a track will be sent to an effects box and a return will be brought back to that console and that will be the end of the chain. But I would always choose to send it to yet another processing device that would then go to another processing device and then to another — and then at that point the link in the chain would be regenerated back to the first link, creating a very musical regeneration and producing a very organic result. Much like the way a musical instrument amplifier has a personality because of the frequency response limitation. The limitations of this regeneration, or the emphasis of a certain frequency, would allow the sound to develop its own personality.

Castle Rock

One of the most unusual places I have ever recorded in was Slane Castle, where U2's *Unforgettable Fire* was recorded. It was the band's idea to move out of the studio and to go out

on location. Fortunately, this idea was not foreign to me — I had been doing this kind of recording in Canada where I experimented with different locations, including a big old library in town that had been closed for years. I feel that I can record anywhere as long as there is a good musical setup and, technically, there will be no complications. I'm less fussy than I used to be.

We set up three different rooms for U2 to work in at the castle: the ballroom, the library, and the workshop. The ballroom had a long reverberant decay time, therefore it could only be used for slower tempo songs. That's where the song "The Unforgettable Fire" was recorded. The library, on the other hand, had a very dense sound without much decay at all, making it easier to play in because the sound wasn't splashing all over the place. That was the room where the harder tracks were recorded; and, as such, it was the most active band room. The workshop was just another name for the control room.

Because much of the recording was done in the library, we set it up like we always do for U2 — stage setup complete with floor wedges. U2 always records live with a PA. The drummer, Larry Mullen, always has a stack of PA equipment right behind his kit. It has become part of his drum sound — it gives a lot more bottom to his kick drum. We try and keep the band as close to Larry as we can, because when they are close like that they play more in sync.

Most of the unusual sounds were created in the workshop. That's where the harmonies were worked out and where the solos were done. It was an interactive room and, anticipating that, I kept live mics, a guitar amp, and miked percussion at the ready.

Whenever I work with U2, whether in Slane Castle or the rented house just outside of Dublin where *Achtung Baby* was recorded, I try to become a temporary member of the band. I usually like to plug in a guitar or play a piece of percussion. It gets me involved in the arrangements and increases the adrenaline.

U2 is really about performance. We generally try to get something on tape as a foundation and then add a lot of detail to that. Many studio compositions come about from jam sessions based upon a riff that they had prepared. That tiny riff provides the inspiration to come up with other chords, in a different type of arrangement. What we wind up with is very different from what was originally planned.

My Way

The way I produce myself is not really all that different from how I would produce, say, Peter Gabriel or U2 — the tracks are recorded in much the same process. The part that gets difficult is recording the vocals and picking which tracks you put on the record.

Regardless of the artist, whether it be myself, Peter, or U2, I generally use the same miking techniques. For example, my favorite piano is a Steinway. When I mic a Steinway piano, I use a single microphone, usually an RCA 77 ribbon mic. I find that I get the most pure, clear sound with it. I like to place it center, slightly favoring the hammer hitting point. When you hear it back on radio, it sounds big and clear.

With guitars, the room has a whole lot to do with the sound. In my experience, the best sounding guitar rooms are rectangular-shaped with tall peaked ceilings and a solid wood floor. My favorite mic, usually placed favoring one speaker, is a dynamic mic, like a Shure SM58 or a Beyer 88. I also like to put up a room mic, which can be a nice tube mic like a Neumann U 47.

I prefer to make the decision on the spot about blending. If there is too much competition in the room between instruments, I'll use the close mic. The strangest thing about this is, even though you are tight-miking, the room that the amp is in still has a huge effect on the tight mic sound. I believe that the amplifier responds to the room and the two become one.

These are the miking techniques that I used on all guitars sounds on my new record. For example, the solo in "Messenger" was recorded that way in a very pure sound — no processing. I used a '58 Fender Strat for that. An example of the room playing a big part of the sound would be Edge's sound. For *Achtung Baby,* we put him in this tall, rectangular room when he played his lead. Actually, in the house we recorded in, there was an isolation corridor between the drum room and the main studio. It was maybe 6 feet wide, 14 feet tall, and 14 feet deep. That's an extreme example of the tall rectangular room, but we found that we always got the best guitar sounds in that shaped room.

I also use a Korg SDE3000 as my preamplifier before I hit the box. It has a controllable output level that lets me hit the amplifier harder. I will always use that — even in bypass. With the Korg as a link in the chain, I find that it makes for a more musical result.

Brian's Song

Brian Eno, who shares the Producer Grammy with me for *Achtung Baby,* has been a very big musical influence on me. When I first started with Brian, I was engineering for him, but he quickly made use of my talent.

When working together, we have a simple agreement — I agree with everything he says and he agrees with everything I say. With the differences out of the way, you can concentrate on what is more important — getting the machine rolling — and once that's done, nature will decide the course. In my experience, where you are five hours after you started is not where you thought you'd be.

In closing, I would just like to add that I was very happy to get the Grammy. Not just because of the recognition from peers, although that's certainly appreciated, but also because I have been working with Brian for more than ten years, and it's a nice thing to share.

The Zooropa Story

Recording U2 in the studio, at the Factory, and on the cutting edge

By Flood

Originally appeared in 1993

When it came time to record *Zooropa* with U2, there was no conscious decision made saying we were going to create a new sound. But there was a decision that we didn't necessarily want to make *Achtung Baby II.* That was a very furrowed-brow type of record with a very intense, very heavy outlook. This time around, U2 wanted to enjoy themselves and have a good laugh. If *Achtung Baby* was U2's *Sgt Pepper,* then *Zooropa* was their *Magical Mystery Tour,* an eclectic and experimental mix of sounds and ideas.

We had to finish the songs in a very short time. Sometimes U2 would have to record early in the day, fly off to play their next date, and then come back at around two in the morning to listen to the mix. Plus, the vision of *Zooropa* was beginning to expand. One second we were recording an EP; the next, an album; the next, a B-side. There was some pressure involved because U2 is a high-profile band, and it was more than just a challenge of finishing it in time. It had to be good as well.

Zooropa was recorded in Dublin at a studio called Windmill Lane. We also worked out of The Factory, a rehearsal complex that features a quasi-control room with a Soundcraft board and an Otari MTR-90 recording machine. When recording, we would use a Fostex synchro-DAT, so that rather than slaving, we could do ten guitar takes or ten vocal takes onto the synchro-DAT and then compile them onto one track.

For actual sound, we would generally use 15 ips, because you don't use as much tape if you're doing hour-long improvisations. You can fit it all on one reel. Plus, the sound is much better at 15, not truer, just more musical. But, if you use 15 ips, you've got to be a lot more on the case with your drop-ins and edits.

Techno Talk

Recording the album was a mutual exploration in different areas. Having come from working with people like Depeche Mode and Nine Inch Nails, who are based more in a technological style of music, it was very challenging to have cross-fertilization with people like U2. It's stimulating because you can say: "Here is a drum loop, what do you want to do with it?" and U2 will probably respond in a way that's entirely different from what you would normally expect.

Initially, U2 was coming from the conventional band point of view, which says, "Here we are — drums, bass, guitar, and singer." This was different from a band like Depeche Mode. But both bands were similar in that they wanted to explore areas that the other had already explored. For instance, U2 wanted to push new venues and ask questions like, "Can we sequence that?" while Depeche Mode wanted to play with real guitars and drums on *Songs of Faith and Devotion.*

When working in the studio, one of my favorite pieces of gear is the Eventide H3000, because it's probably the most versatile effects unit there is. It's creative with delays, harmonizers, and weird distorted sounds, and anyone with any imagination can go completely mad with it. If you want straightforward delay or straightforward pitches, you got it. But if you want some sort of totally bizarre pitch-shifting reverse, then you could just as easily do it.

The hookline in the chorus of "Daddy's Gonna Pay for Your Crashed Car," for example, is half made-up of the H3000. When used in tandem with the Zoom 9010, a very effective guitar multieffects processor, you're allowed a great amount of flexibility. There are seven effects in a chain and you can have them in any order. You're not restricted by any predetermined order.

In Pieces

The title track, "Zooropa," is actually in two halves. The first half was created from scratch in Dublin, but the second half was taken from a soundcheck the band did in New Zealand or Australia about two years ago. The engineer and Edge sat down and took out the best elements of the jam using SoundTools to construct an arrangement. Both parts were then edited to get a stereo mix. To create a dovetail to the whole piece, Brian Eno laid down a track of a squishy, mad-synth sound that connected both halves of the song. Edge laid down some guitars, and then he used an EMS Synthi A, which looks like something you'd see in a '50s sci-fi movie. I tend to collect and use those types of things — vintage pieces of equipment.

In addition to "Zooropa," some of my favorite songs on the album are "Crashed Car," "First Time," and "Numb." "Numb" was originally something leftover from the *Achtung Baby* sessions, so we were just trying out a few ideas on that to see if we could take it one step further. Edge started working out the basic rhythm for the vocals. He took it, worked the lyrical idea out, completed the song, and it came out sounding great. Edge comes from a sturdy musical background, but his knowledge of technical aspects is great as well.

Lemon Heads

The song "Lemon" started off as a disco tune until Brian Eno got through with it, gating guitars and adding backing vocals, making it a very bizarre folk song. Bono sang in falsetto on "Lemon" using a Shure SM58. We spent one evening going through "Lemon" countless times, changing things here and there, but the first take we had was the best. Rerecording a song over and over doesn't always pay off.

Personally, I'm a firm believer in the first impression when it comes to recording artists. That's why I'll sometimes mix and record guitarists by going straight into the board. The guitar's always going to sound different if it's going into a board instead of an amplifier, and it's stimulating to the player to play in a way that breaks the song. It captures the element of spontaneity.

For example, let's say you have a great part, and you want it to be on your record. You can put it through an amp and go through all the business of doing so and find the sound you want, but by the time you do that you can have easily lost the spark of the moment. I tend to weigh things up like this when recording — what gains priority: sound tinkering, the original idea, or the song itself? First impressions mean a lot for any artist.

Essentially, I believe that modern technology is an instrument in the music. I am an advocate for technology as long as it's something that's used rather than something that somebody is used by. It's very easy to become a slave to technology and do something over and over again. Even though you have the ability to try a lot of options with a computer, that doesn't mean that it will be done any better or quicker. It is important that you make sure you use technology to your advantage and don't ever let yourself become used by it.

That Was Then...This Is Now

The Master of Modern Jazz on the technological timeline

By Herbie Hancock

Originally appeared in February 1994

A few years after I left Miles Davis, I put together my first project studio, Garage Sale Sound. This was sometime in the early '70s and the studio was nothing fancy: just a minimal mixing board and some crude pieces of equipment that I set up in my garage. It was important for me to have a space nearby so that if I got an idea (and they can be gotten at the weirdest times) I wouldn't have to rush off to another location; I could lay down tracks right there in my garage.

In the early years, I was using the facility solely to put ideas down on tape. Had I not set up my own home studio, a lot of valuable ideas would have gotten lost. Soon I added a mixing console, the Soundcraft 2400, which gave me the ability to mix my musical ideas and complete preproduction for albums such as *Thrust, Treasure Chest,* and the soundtrack for *Death Wish.*

I bought my first digital keyboard in the late '70s — the E-mu Model 4060. It served as a master controller for my analog synthesizers, meaning I could trigger the notes of external synthesizers directly from the 4060. I don't recall there being, at that time, any other keyboards that enabled you to perform this function.

E-mu had incorporated a built-in sequencer in the 4060, which I fully loaded with RAM memory. Like most built-in sequencers, it was designed to record and play back short ideas, but I wanted to use it in the same way that we use external sequencers today. This was the pre-MIDI age, but I didn't want to record just short ideas; I wanted to record whole songs.

The sequencer was accessed from a telephone keypad mounted on the unit. So when recording, I divided a song into sections and used the keypad to store those sections in different locations. The instrument, however, wasn't designed for seamless sequential playback of those stored areas, so we attempted to come up with a solution to this problem.

My technical engineer, Bryan Bell, worked closely with E-mu engineers Scott Wedge and Dave Rossum to modify the keyboard for seamless playback. Subsequently, this led to our developing a digital patchbay accessory for the 4060 keyboard. It cost me thousands of dollars to manufacture, but I strongly felt that the end would justify the means. Then MIDI came into the picture, and made the device we had just finished building obsolete.

Another device that was born of necessity was our "master clock." Bryan Bell wanted to utilize the Linn drum machine as a master device, using the 4060 keyboard as a slave. The dilemma lay in every manufacturer saying that the keyboard had to be the master; there was no universal timing source. So we hired John Vieira to build a 4-channel clock-dividing network with tape sync capability, while Roger Linn provided us with some tape-chip syncs that he was using. Bryan Bell, meanwhile, made a two-rackspace box that interfaced with our SMPTE reader and the old tape sync that the Linn drum machine used. These efforts resulted in a device that could drive any sequencer; we could now have four different devices following our homemade master clock.

After we had this device set up, Dan Garfield visited our studio to show us his own synchronizing device, Dr. Click. To his surprise, we had already invented our own version of this product. But while his device had two channels of clock dividing, we had a 4-channel unit that also read SMPTE. With our master clock, we could use mixers and sequencers to chase tape, a function that nobody else was able to do in 1981. Dan Garfield actually went on to do very well with Dr. Click. For us, however, creating new technology was never a matter of marketing, but of necessity.

Many years ago, I dreamed of being able to control all the synthesizers in my studio from one source, and then save all the information to a computer. Today my dreams have come true. We're using four Apple Macintoshes and two IBM PCs in the studio for music applications.

I consider myself a Macintosh person at heart. In fact, my first computer, which I bought in 1979, was an Apple II Plus with 48k of RAM. Bryan Bell created a multipage software program for the Mac called Cosmic Keyboards, and it provided pages for lyrics, record information, written music, and a sequencer. He began writing and learning BASIC at the same time, but the program was amazingly sophisticated for its time.

Even though I have two IBMs (which came with the Euphonix and the Waveframe), Macintosh is the foundation for the studio. A Mac IIfx contains all my sequencers — Opcode's Studio Vision, Steinberg's Cubase Audio, Passport's MasterTracks Pro, and Mark of the Unicorn's Digital Performer. I usually use StudioVision, but having these various other sequencers allows me to accommodate the different tastes and preferences of others who work on my projects.

Our most recent acquisition is the Euphonix CSII mixing console. The primary reason for purchasing it was to enable me to do final mixes in my studio, and I needed an automated mixing console because we are working with so many tracks. Moreover, this console has all the features I need to work on my music — Snapshot Recall, MixView screens, and, of course, Dynamic Mix Automation. Automation was a necessity because some of the songs we recorded contain up to 62 tracks. Without automation, it would have become almost impossible to mix a song with that many tracks in it.

Before acquiring the Euphonix CSII, I compared it with my previous mixing console, a Neve 8068. I did a comparison test by trying to A/B the EQ of the 8068 (the 8068 is famous for its EQ) against that of the Euphonix. The EQ of the Euphonix compared favorably with that of the 8068. Plus, the CSII has the features of a larger board despite its compact size.

These days, I'm using the Korg T-1 as a controller. Other models I have include Proteus's 1, 2, and 3, a Korg Wavestation, a Korg O1RW, a Kurzweil 2000 rack model, the Roland JD990 (with an incredible orchestral expansion board option that we added), a Waveframe, and a Synclavier. The Synclavier sounds fine, but its architecture makes it a bit slow, so I tend to use the Waveframe more.

Digidesign's SampleCell is great for sampling. The Sound Designer II board allows us to have four tracks of hard-disk recording. Among our signal processing devices, Ensoniq's new DP/4 enables us to have signal processing going from one unit to four different devices independently.

Even to this day, after a new device comes out its features will inspire me to conceive of uses that go way beyond the original vision of the manufacturer. I try to incorporate my vision into the product by customizing and modifying it for my needs. I can see other possibilities for a product, possibilities that the manufacturer may not have even considered when the product was originally introduced. Essentially, I'm a closet techie in a musician's body.

On the Road Again (and Again)

The world's premier punk band has seen and done it all — and they're not done yet

By Joey Ramone

Originally appeared April 1994

On February 9, 1994, in Tokyo, Japan, the Ramones played their 2,000th show. To celebrate this event, as well as the band's 20th anniversary and the success of their most recent release, *Acid Eaters*, *EQ* correspondent Joey Ramone discussed with his soundman of some 15 years, John Markovich, life on the road with the Ramones.

Joey Ramone: So how did you hook up with us?

John Markovich: Originally I owned my own sound company and I was doing shows in the Ohio area. I think we happened to meet up at one time without knowing each other. I used to do a lot of work with Kenny Slater of Blue Sky Records, who took care of Rick Derringer and Johnny Winters, and he asked to do a favor for a friend of his named Danny Fields. At the time I took the job I really didn't know who it was till I got to New York and met everybody, although we did do a Ramones show a few months before that…

Was that at the Tomorrow Theater?

Yeah, in Youngstown. The way that came about was Kenny Slater said I have a friend who needs a soundman for a group that's going to be opening for Iggy Pop. When that tour ended you guys went on to record the live album [*1978's highly acclaimed* It's Alive, *so far unreleased in America, which was recorded at London's Rainbow Theater, New Year's Eve*] and when you were done, that's when I started full-time with you.

So how do you get the raw club sound that our fans expect when playing the large, European gigs?

Basically, it's just volume and knowing the Ramones' sound from playing clubs. Sometimes it's hard to get the right sound. I think the smaller the PA, the more "rocky" we can make it sound, because there's a fine line between a big room that is very rolly and has a lot of overtones as opposed to clubs, which you can tighten up to make it sound carpeted. Clubs have a much rawer and richer sound.

Which do you prefer?

I prefer the smaller venues. I like a small theater with nice sound, that's got a high ceiling and places that are partially carpeted. I don't like it when it's too dead. I like it sort of between a ringing place and a dead room.

On touring, it's never boring. We're on the road about 150 days a year.

We went up to 2 something — 250. It was like the neverending world tour. We came back from Europe and went on tour in the States, then back overseas again. That was all in 1982/1983.

I remember. It became an in-house joke with us. On the laminates it read "The Non-Stop World Tour." With all the extensive touring, is there anything you do for hearing protection?

For the last 15 years or so, there's only been a limited number of times where I know that I've hurt my ears because the room was too loud. Even if you turned it down it would have been too loud — that kind of room. Most of the time from the distance where I'm from, I get pretty much covered up. I know we're reaching levels of around 124 dB near the stage, but coming back to me, I'm at about 114 dB near the board.

Yeah, it's loud on stage. We tried those in-ear monitors recently, and I didn't like them. I think the ear monitors are good if you're playing softer music. The people who seem to wear it the most often are in a very open situation like Bono or Rod Stewart. Actually, for a while there I'd hone in on these people because sometimes my situation drives me crazy. I have a lot of trouble hearing the monitors because the band won't turn down — it's like a competition. It's a rough situation. When I would sing with the ear thing it would cancel me out. I love it loud, but I want to be able to hear myself too.

I've been in situations where people use these monitors. They're on a stage that's not too confining. They're all over the stage. If you were on a big stage and walked away from your monitor, it would affect your levels. With in-ear monitors, you can walk wherever you want to and have the same level all the time. For us, because we're more stationary, we need the power to throw it back at them. It's a lot of watts, about 2,000.

Let's talk gear. What do you use on us?

We run into the same equipment everywhere when we travel all over the world. I try to stick to things we can find everywhere. I prefer the Yamaha PM3000 console, Drawmer gates and limiters, and dbx limiters. Speaker-wise, I prefer the EAW cabinets, but that's a thing where you can't find it everywhere, so you get into a lot of different types of cabinets. For effects, I use the Eventide 3000 for your vocals and the Roland XTE2000 and SPX900 on the guitars. It's kind of a simple setup. There's not a lot of gear there. We don't really overdo it.

Does stage diving affect the equipment?

We do have problems. Most of the time we have people that like to climb the PA and jump into the crowd. Most of the problems we have is that people start pulling the monitors over in front of you and they screw up the wires.

We hit some pretty high volumes. How do you protect the gear from blowing?

That's hard to say.

I've seen it blow a few times.

I just go on my instincts. I can tell by the meters on the console and there are limiters and all kinds of compression on the crossovers for each section. We're using a three-way crossover that has protection for each section of the sound system. Currently we're using a Yamaha digital crossover. Other than that, I would say that after 15 years I know how far I can take it.

Remember that time in Texas when the speakers caught fire?

The strange thing about that was it was the top cabinet. It was one of the very few times that we stacked the cabinets three high and the very top speaker was on fire. That was because the speaker had a loose terminal or something.

That was pretty wild. Speaking of wild, what was the craziest experience you've had working a Ramones show?

I would think that one of the craziest experiences was around 1982 when we were doing shows in Italy, in the big sports arenas. We were in Genoa and there was a riot going on between the fascists and communists or whatever the parties were, and you guys were on stage surrounded by Italian Green Berets and I'm out in the audience standing by the console out there in the wind by myself.

I felt we were like this cocktail band playing with this full-scale riot taking the forefront.

I remember them shutting down the show for a slight bit of time between the U.K. Subs and us, and I remember "God Save the Queen" by the Sex Pistols.

That was the show where it was three balconies high and somebody threw a giant stone down on Mark. Pretty insane.

That was the same tour, but in Milan.

Right. Now that was an exciting show.

To me, Milan was the most exciting show I had ever done with the Ramones. Totally, insanely packed with people. They were breaking down the doors and throwing down rocks. We had more crazy experiences during those shows in Italy. Remember the time when the lighting tower fell into the crowd?

That was crazy. Tell that story.

You were playing onstage and I can't remember what song it was, but we were cruising along. It was an outside venue, a bicycle track called the Belodrome. It was a huge place. It was another place that they broke the doors down. There were about 25,000 people there, and we were doing the show when the lighting tower was pulled into the crowd and I see people's heads change in color because they didn't know the light tower had fallen and we're still doing the show. The next thing they do is turn the power off and five ambulances drove through the crowd to the stage.

I remember we made the front pages of several newspapers with the ambulances and all.

The European tour we did was very exciting.

I remember it being very scary with the Red Brigade, German shepherds, and the Uzis.

That was the security at that time. We were doing outdoor shows. In the middle of the town square. We had two semis. Back then we were using old Martin stuff.

What was that show we did with Mike Oldfield?

That was in Barcelona. That was a very big outdoor thing. There was enough PA for a

1,000 people to hear and there was another PA behind me that I had no idea what it did. It was one of those shows that you couldn't do too much about. It was one of those shows where you showed up, played, and left.

What's your least favorite venue?

My least favorite would be the place in Asbury Park — that old ballroom on the boardwalk. The toilet of the world. I would say my favorite venue, however, is the old Ritz in New York City.

That place was great.

I always enjoyed doing a show there. It always had a nice sound.

Remember that time we were playing in Japan and there was that big earthquake?

That was in Tokyo. At first I though the people were shaking, then the speakers were moving and everybody was just grabbing onto everything. That was exciting.

It was weird. We went into the dressing room and there was giant cracks in the wall.

We were on the 9th floor.

That was weird, too. It was a department store, wasn't it?

It was a department store all through the whole building except for that room on the 9th floor. It was like a small amphitheater. That was a good one. I guess that was back in 1980.

How many years has it been now?

Since 1978. We've spent a lot of time doing a lot of things together. It's become like a family thing.

I'll say. You ready to do it again?

Ready whenever you are.

Can't We All Get Along?

Now it can be told: Project studios and commercial facilities can coexist

By Buddy Brundo

Originally appeared June 1994

This is a constantly changing world. Project studios won't go away; they're only growing in number and importance. And, likewise, there will remain a healthy and important role for commercial studios for many years to come. How are these two industry segments going to work together in the future? As far as I'm concerned, we just need to work out a few details.

Every commercial studio will appreciate the growing problem. We are all getting a lot of project studio tapes with incomplete information on the tape boxes and on the track sheets. And we spend a great deal of time trying to figure out what really went on during the sessions. Sometimes it is as simple as telling us which tracks are safeties and which are masters or which are unusable scratch material. Or letting us know what preamps or microphones were used on the vocals.

Sure, project studios are growing. But so are their needs for professional studio services. Project studio people are coming in here to have ground buzzes removed, or they are looking to replace a drum machine with a real drummer, or they are after a string date, or they need to overdub new vocals. They don't live in a vacuum and neither do we. As I've said before, we're here to help the music.

There are some things we can't help, however. We can't help a project studio operator who just doesn't know when to let go of a project. I'm hearing this more and more from record companies — that project studios can also lead to creative excess. If you don't have a time limit to doing a music project you can simply go on and on and on. It's like overcooking a sauce. Overcooking the music can take the edge off of it.

The Story Behind the Story

The mid-'90s was the peak growth period for project studios, and the commercial studios were feeling it. The tensions were particularly high in Los Angeles, where project studios were being closed for violating residential/business zoning regulations. Popular thought was that the commercial studios were "ratting out" the project studios to the authorities.

Buddy Brundo, owner of one of the larger commercial studios in L.A., wrote this article for *EQ* in the hopes of finding a place for both types of studios to co-exist. Many of his predictions came true.

Another problem is that a project studio is usually just one person — alone in a room. How can one person ever compete musically with a group of musicians in a comfortable, creative environment? Isn't this taking the one-man band to an extreme? It's like the film that was written, directed, produced, and starred in by the same person; the collaborative effort, the interaction between creative individuals, is what usually results in the most meaningful music and the project studio, with all its space limitations and isolation, often can't provide this type of space. Of course, creative people should have their own creative studios; they should be able to get up in the morning and have their tape decks and consoles in their den and have the ability to put on tape whatever's in their mind. But that creative space is only one part of the creative process. Music is not meant to be private. Importance of musical interaction will grow in the years ahead, especially if we continue hearing more and more acoustic music on records.

It seems like acoustic music is "in" again. Sometimes project rooms have trouble making good acoustic records. I'm hearing a lot of acoustic tapes come into the studio from project rooms that are equipped with an [Alesis] ADAT and a pair of [Yamaha] NS-10's. The musicians are simply blown away by what they hear at home. But when they play the tapes in our perfectly tuned rooms, they end up wanting to replace everything. There are always exceptions (there are some fine recording spaces at home), but sometimes a project room may have a sound that is not very musical; and if you get bad room reverb over a vocal it is very hard to fix regardless of where you go and what you do. Recording style and recording space have a much greater effect on the quality of a recording than the actual mics or equipment themselves.

There's another thing to consider — lifestyle. Everyone's heard the story about this local musician who was running a project studio in his house that kept getting bigger and bigger. He had a few cartage guys walk into the house one day, just as his wife was walking naked out of the bathroom. The guy didn't give up his project studio, but he did end up getting divorced. There is no privacy. Musicians work all hours of the night. People come and go. Rental equipment is in and out. There are numerous technical breakdowns that occur. It's impossible to live your life in a recording studio — and I should know.

What's more, project studio owners who get bitten by the techno bug start trying to figure out ways to finance their equipment habits and to justify the 100-input SSL and twin Sony 48-tracks. That's when they start looking for outside business — and that's when they start crossing the line between a project studio and a commercial studio.

We're well into the '90s. Project studios are here to stay. Brilliant, cost-effective technology is upon us. Project studio operators are learning the basics of recording. And they are hungry for technical information.

Commercial studios have that type of information and we know how to communicate it so that musicians and producers clearly understand what we mean. We've had experience and plenty of it. This is probably the most important role we will be playing in the changing recording scene. We will be the mothership where projects are finished. We will continue to serve an elite clientele of producers and musicians. And, for the rest of the project studio world, commercial studios will be the primary source of expertise. Better information and more open communication between all levels of recording studios will ensure that the music keeps getting better and better. That's what it's all about.

Buddy Brundo is owner of Conway Recording, a commercial studio in Los Angeles, CA.

Home Sweet Platinum Home

Queensrÿche's drummer tells the story behind making the Platinum-selling album Promised Land *— with 11 ADATs in a log cabin on an island*

By Scott Rockenfield

Originally appeared in March 1995

In many ways, Queensrÿche has always been somewhat of a do-it-yourself band. Our first recording back in 1982 was a four-song EP; we spent our own money, had a mother and father management team at the time, and set up our own record label called 206 Records. We did all the selling and marketing ourselves. A couple connections with distributors got us into the stores, and we received a great two-page review in an English magazine and some domestic press. We got lucky and the EP sold 15,000 copies in a week, so once we had that type of interest, record companies started pursuing us — the vibe was different back then, and companies were signing people more readily. Believe it or not, we still hadn't played a single show at that point.

Fast forward to 1994, and a lot has changed. The cost of gear is getting so low, and the quality so good, that we didn't see the need to spend the money to go into a corporate studio to do the follow up to *Empire*. We also wanted the freedom of working in a more relaxed environment; besides, when you work at home, you own the gear so you're not spending two grand a day on somebody else.

This was the first time we'd taken this approach, and like most bands we figured we'd do the demo work at home, then go to a commercial studio to cut the "real" tracks and do the mix. But we underestimated just what technology can really do. When you listen to the *Promised Land* CD [which was certified platinum during the writing of this article—Ed.], most of what you're hearing is really a home recording. We ended up keeping what we recorded at home because the spontaneity and relaxation comes through into the actual performances. When you're not thinking you're doing a "keeper" part, or worrying about watching the clock, you often get a better feel.

The whole project started when we got off the road from the *Empire* tour and took a year off. We were all writing and coming up with ideas, so we decided to buy the same type of tape recorder to allow all the band members to exchange musical ideas easily. We ended up getting 11 Alesis ADATs, and, generally, we've been very satisfied with them. Even though the technology is really new, Alesis deserves credit for soliciting feedback from ADAT owners and constantly improving its machines. For example, we just updated all our ADATs to System 4 software, and the whole feel is a lot better and faster.

We did all the preliminary work at home on our ADATs, sometimes individually, and sometimes collaborating with other band members. For example, I wrote "Disconnected" with a drum machine and some keyboards at my place; I gave it to Geoff (Tate), and he liked it so much he wrote the lyrics. The song was basically finished when it went to the guys in the band, who redid the keyboard parts with guitars and real bass. Other songs we worked out together. The final recording was a combination of many different approaches.

Isolationists

After a while we had a lot of tapes and music in semifinished form, and we decided to continue the mode of feeling we were working at home by going to a 5,000-square-foot log cabin on 20 acres of land in the San Juan Islands, west of Seattle. We bought a bunch of Mackie consoles — we have eight among us — set up a studio in the log cabin, and lived there, basically spending five months compiling all the ADAT tapes that we had done, along with some additional sampling and recording. We finished virtually all of the actual recording process at the cabin.

Dealing with all those ADATs got to be somewhat time-consuming after a while, so we transferred all the tracks over to a Sony 48-track digital to keep all the audio in one place. Most of the time we transferred tracks digitally through the Alesis AI-1 (an AES/EBU digital interface/sample rate converter), but because transferring 48 tracks two at a time took a while, sometimes we transferred multiple tracks through the analog outs. It didn't make any real difference in the sound, anyway.

When it came time to mix, we went into [Seattle studio] Bad Animals because the tracks were complete and James ("Jimbo") Barton, our coproducer, knows an SSL like the back of his hand. It may not be the best-sounding console, but we wanted to have the freedom of using the SSL recall options. Besides, we'd been in the cabin for five months, and were ready to get out of there! We also did some work at Triad studios, which, like Bad Animals, is local and convenient to all of us. A few people have asked about "The Dungeon," another studio credited on the CD; that's actually my parents' basement, where we've rehearsed every record we've done together.

However, we still did a lot of mixing at the cabin while tracking, and because we like Mackie mixers we decided on a configuration of a 32 x 8 and two 24 x 8 consoles hooked into a custom-made patchbay made by Tom Hall of Triad. We used the 32 x 8 and one 24 x 8 for tracking, while the other 24 x 8 was used mostly for playback. We pretty much used what the Mackies had to offer; for example, most of the drums went into the stock preamps

Anatomy of a Tune

"9:28 a.m." is almost like classic electronic music: sound effects, manipulated vocal samples, and no beat. Since Scott wrote the song, *EQ* asked him to elaborate on how it came about.

"Part of the reason is that I'm into doing film music, *à la* Tangerine Dream or Vangelis, and I had an intro to a film I was working on for a director. Everyone in the band liked the basic piece, so we worked on it and I did the whole thing in my apartment. For the sound sources, I went to Triad for the tweaked piano sounds and various other beds. Most of the sound sources were my voice; I plugged in the mic and daisy-chained about 18 million effects. I find effects to be extremely inspirational. Also, we have a CD library of sounds. Finally, a lot of the sounds are sound bites from my laserdisc collection, but they've been so altered that no one could recognize them, so clearance wasn't a problem.

"'Disconnected' also has a film-style intro that we added on. A lot of the natural sounds you hear on 'Disconnected' were recorded with a DAT and microphone outside the cabin in the morning. Compared to a CD library, there's nothing like the real sound you record yourself."

and that was all we needed. But we also used outboard gear, like guitar preamps, along with gates and compressors.

We reconfigured the Mackies depending on what we were doing. Although the second 24-input mixer was supposedly for playback, as more and more inputs became necessary we stole them from the playback mixer. We also had a separate ADAT station with three Mackie 1604's set up so that some of us could be working with ADAT while others were working on the main part of the album, and there was also a separate computer station with an Atari and Macintosh sync'd together for doing sequencing and some weird sound effects (you can hear these on tunes like "Disconnected" and "9:28 a.m.").

For sampled sounds, some were recorded directly into the computer and for others we used conventional samplers. The main sampler was an Akai S1000; however, Chris DeGarmo has a Digidesign Session 8 that was also used.

Although we didn't do any MIDI-controlled signal processing, currently I'm working on a film score with Eventide H3000's; they're great for MIDI control, especially because you can spin the knob to create effects and the sequencer will record the changes and play them back.

Under Advisement

I would advise anyone working at home not to become too isolated, because the gear can let you do that if you're not careful. We've tried to use the technology not to distance ourselves in our own studios, but to increase the level of interaction and spontaneity. And luckily, the relationship we have with Jimbo is great. It's too easy to turn inward, so having someone with an objective viewpoint to bounce ideas off of is invaluable. We started working with him in 1988 on *Operation: Mindcrime* as an engineer, and by the time we did *Empire,* he was becoming more of a producer. Toward the end of *Promised Land,* we realized his input involved a lot more than twisting knobs, and he helped push us in different directions, so we felt a coproduction credit was well-deserved. He certainly came up with things I never would have thought of.

As to the future, we're not completely through with this project yet because we're working on a companion CD-ROM. We had a videographer, Mark DeGarmo, and a small crew at the cabin; every day we filmed whatever we were doing — eating dinner, making the record, etc. The CD-ROM starts when we bought the ADATs and ends when we left the cabin. This project is very different from what else is out there; most of it takes place at the log cabin, but we animated a lot of it to give a more virtual look — a *Cool World* type of thing. You can walk about the cabin, explore, and talk to us; but there are also some game elements. For example, if you click on something like a shelf, you might find me taking you into an alternate world where a disaster is about to occur that you have to prevent, otherwise it will cause a chain reaction into some of the other characters' worlds. Currently the CD-ROM is for Mac and PC, but eventually we want to do versions for Sega and other CD-ROM platforms. We're also thinking of doing a movie soon — not a documentary, but a real movie.

Hopefully the success of our "home recording" will be inspirational for other people who prefer to work at home. Of course, there are lots of musicians who work out of their homes, and would like to have the same thing happen to them that happened to us. But just having the gear isn't enough, and sometimes even having good music isn't enough. We're fortunate that we have a combination of five guys who have been together for a long time doing what we love. We don't try to emulate the flavor of the month, which is (probably ironically) a reason why we've been successful. We don't try to be successful; we do what we want to do and hope that it's successful.

When we did our first record 14 years ago, we decided to make it just the way we wanted because we were going to have to live with it for a long time. We've done that with every recording since. We're fortunate that our fans don't put us in a box — they don't tell us what we have to be. I don't know what we're going to do next time around, but I'm sure we'll go off in some other, new direction. That's what keeps things interesting and fresh for us as a band, and for our listeners as well.

My Life in Recording

From the big band era, to the psychedelic '60s, to today's contemporary sounds, I've seen it all (and lived to tell)

By Al Schmitt

Originally appeared in May 1995

I've been in recording studios since I was seven years old. I had an uncle who owned one of the first independent recording studios in New York City, and as a child I used to go over there all the time. He'd have me sit and clean patch cords while they were recording. Guys like Art Tatum would come by and teach me little boogie-woogie licks on the piano. So as a kid I got to hang out with a lot of musicians — which was great. In those days the engineer would record with one mic and would move the musicians around to get a balance. This was even before tape machines. The musicians would have to take their shoes off because you could hear their feet stomping on the studio floor. I was always wide-eyed and awed by it all — I never thought I could get involved with it. The equipment was so delicate that I thought you had to be a Swiss watchmaker to deal with it.

The First Run

When I got out of the service, my uncle called me and told me that he had a friend who owned a recording studio and was looking for someone to break in as an assistant. At this point I had no technical experience in audio — only what I had seen as a child. I wasn't sure that this was what I wanted to do for a living, but my dad and I talked it over and we decided I'd give it a try. If I didn't like it I could always go back to college and do something else. So I went to the studio, Apex Recording Studios on 57th Street in Manhattan, and took a job as a runner. I'd make coffee, clean up — all that kind of stuff. The head engineer there was Tommy Dowd. Tommy had started there about nine or ten months before I did. My hours were from nine to six, but I remember on the first day they were doing a date and I stayed until midnight. Every day I'd stay there from 9 a.m. to midnight. I got myself a notepad and I drew diagrams of the setups — which microphones were used, how the engineers set up and placed things, how they laid out things on the board, and so forth. Watching Tommy was an incredible experience and he taught me a lot about recording.

After about six weeks I was upgraded and allowed to do what they called "demo records." On Saturdays (and sometimes Sundays) people would come in and demo their songs. Usually it was just piano and voice. We would do it directly to disc and they would have the disc when we were done. There were a couple of cutting lathes and turntables in the control room. We also had a wire recorder and a tape machine called a Brush Sound Mirror — this was just before we got our Ampex 300.

Three months into my career I was working on a Saturday and we had a bunch of demos booked. I did two or three of those and then at two o'clock was something marked "Demo/Mercer Records." At around 1:30 these guys started coming in — musicians with horns and all this stuff, and I was starting to freak. There was no one there at the studio. So I said to these guys, "Well there is a mistake here — I am not qualified to do this." I tried to get Tommy and my boss on the phone, but it was Saturday so I couldn't reach anyone. To make a long story short, it was a big band and it was Duke Ellington's band. So I went to my book, looked at the setup diagrams, and I set everybody up. This date was for Mercer Records, but Duke Ellington was signed to Columbia at the time, so he was not allowed to play piano on the session (Billy Strahorn played piano). Duke sat next to me and I kept apologizing and saying, "I've never done anything like this before. I'm not qualified. I'm in way over my head." Duke kept patting me on the leg saying, "Don't worry son, we're going to get through this." We did two sides and it came out OK. It certainly wasn't the best record I ever cut, but it came out all right. That was my first record. I got thrown in, and if I had time to think about it I might have had a coronary. But it came on me quickly like that and I didn't have a chance to run away and hide. I had to do it and I did it. I think I was 19 years old at the time.

We did a lot of work at Apex for a guy by the name of Bobby Shad, who had a label called Sittin' In. And the idea was that it was sitting in with James Brown or Lightning Hopkins or whoever. He did a lot of what were known as "race records" in those days — R&B records. Bobby liked me, so one day I was the only guy available and I wound up doing a session for him. Then he started using me all the time. Bobby produced for Mercury and later on he had another label called Mainstream.

Hitting the Atlantic

Tommy (Dowd) and I did a lot of dates for Atlantic Records, which, at the time, consisted of Ahmet Ertegun and Herb Abrahmson. They were kind of a fledgling label. I remember coming in and doing two records with the Clovers; "Don't You Know I Love You So" and "Skylark." We did them in about 45 minutes and it was a big hit record for Atlantic. It was probably my first hit record. I would hang around when Tommy was doing dates because he was cutting a lot of the big artists and making a lot of hits like "If I Knew You Were

Coming I'd Have Baked a Cake" by Eileen Barton for National Records. We also did a lot of jazz and bebop records, which was great because that was what I grew up on. All of a sudden I was working with all my idols like Dizzy Gillespie and Charlie Parker. It was really amazing. They were recording for Atlantic, Prestige, and Sittin' In, so I started building a relationship with these people.

About two years into my career, Apex folded up and I started working for a place called Nola Recording. This lasted about a year until I got a call from someone at a studio called Fulton Recording Studios. Tommy Dowd was working there as well as at Atlantic in their studio. I went for an interview and I got the job. So I worked over there with an engineer by the name of Bob Dougherty who was another major influence on my career. He did all the big MGM dates. We had a pretty large studio, so we were doing a lot of orchestra dates and I learned how to record French horns, woodwinds, and the instruments of the orchestra. Bob and Tommy did most of those dates, and then I started getting into it. I also did a lot of jazz things there like the Modern Jazz Quartet and Chris Conner. In the meantime I was also doing dates with Gerry Mulligan/Chet Baker and Bobby Brookmeyer/Jim Hall for Dick Bock at World Pacific Jazz. My reputation was building, and I was keeping busy.

We were all on staff salaries in those days, working three or four sessions a day. I was doing Tito Puente, Tito Rodriguez, Machito, and a lot of stuff for Tico Records. I was recording all kinds of music and it was just a fabulous experience because I was not set in a mold. I learned how to do everything from a marching band to religious music. I was totally in love with what I did. Every day when I was on the subway going to that studio I was thanking God. I couldn't believe they were paying me to do all this fun stuff! It was nerve-racking at times and a lot of work, but just the fact that I was working everyday with people that were my idols was a major thrill.

Al Schmitt in the '90s

While Al Schmitt is certainly well known for the projects he has done in the past, the man is definitely not letting up. When *EQ* spoke to Al in early April of this year, he had just finished mixing an album with Marilyn Scott. In the past year he engineered albums for David Sanborn, Dr. John (says Schmitt, "It was Dr. John with a big band and it reminded me, of the early recordings I made for Ray Charles"), and Quincy Jones. His up-and-coming projects include producing the next Diane Schuur and Natalie Cole albums, as well as a special project that is still in the discussion stages.

EQ asked Al if he thinks he will slow down and here is what he had to say: "I'll keep working until somebody says to me, 'Hey it's time to go home.' I'm having way too much fun and I love doing it. I'm an addict and it's not only making the records, but it's also that all my friends are in the business. I love being with my friends, and musicians are my favorite people. When the phone doesn't ring anymore, that is when I'll stop doing music. When nobody calls me, that's when I'll stop."

—Steve La Cerra

Go West Young Man

After being at Fulton for a while, Dick Bock called me from California and said, "Al, I got you a job in a studio out here that is the best studio in California: Radio Recorders." I worked at Radio Recorders doing all kinds of hits. Bones Howe and I did the Henry Mancini *Peter Gunn* album, and I did a bunch of records for Connie Francis and Jesse Belvin. RCA did not have their own studio so they did a lot of work at Radio Recorders. I worked a lot with Dave Pell and Thorne Nogar. Thorne was the guy that was doing all the Elvis Presley records and I learned a lot from him. He was great and also a big influence. Bones and I were young guys, people liked us, and we were getting great sounds. We had a lot of fun.

Then, in 1960, RCA decided to open up their own studio in California, and since I was doing almost all the dates for Mancini and other RCA artists, I was the first engineer they hired. RCA was on the corner of Sunset and Vine — it used to be the NBC Building. We took over two studios and made them into recording studios. They were probably two of the best studios I have ever worked in. All the great Mancini stuff was done there, including *Hatari, More Music From Peter Gunn,* and *Mr. Lucky*. I had done some work in the smaller room with Elvis on *GI Blues* when he got out of the service. At this time we were starting to record in stereo as well as mono. I was also doing albums with Ray Charles and Betty Carter. Around 1962, I did *Hatari* and that was when I won my first Grammy. (I have won six more Grammy awards since then.)

Burning the Midnight Oil

At that time, I was so busy I couldn't do any more work. I was the main guy at RCA and I was working from nine in the morning until midnight, six days a week. People I didn't even know were calling, saying they wanted to book the studio, but they had to have me. There was one guy that I didn't know from Adam and he insisted the only way he would book the studio was if I could do the dates. I wanted to get a little time off and let some of the other guys do some work. But he insisted and insisted so finally I said I would do it. Dave Hassinger (my assistant in those days) and I got a hearing aid and I put the hearing aid on. This guy came walking in and started talking to me and I made believe I couldn't hear him. Then finally I turned and hit the volume on the hearing aid. In those days they were big, cumbersome things. So I said, "OK, now it's working," and this guy turned snow white. I thought he was going to run out of the room and I finally had to take the thing off and tell him we were only kidding. I wound up doing the session.

I think it was a blessing to the engineers that were recording back then to record everything at once. Whatever you put up is what the record sounded like. When we were doing mono and 2-tracks you learned to balance things quickly. We would do four songs in three hours. You had to learn the arrangements and had to be able to follow charts. You had to be musical. You had to know when the vocalist was going to get loud so you could hand-limit and tuck it back. You also had to learn how to keep everything on meter so things weren't pinning all over the place. I get some tapes that I'm asked to mix nowadays and when I put them up I can't believe the levels. We had to get it right the first time and without distortion. Most of the time we'd get a run-through. Usually on the first run-through I would stand next to the conductor in the studio and listen. Then on the next run I'd go into the control room and get my balance, and by the third time through we were off and running making takes. You had to be on top of it.

A Big Production

I got to a point where I was working my tail off at RCA, and then I got an offer from Bill Putnam who owned Universal Studio (not the film studio) for a lot more money. I wanted to get into producing because a lot of the producers I was working with would come into the studio and use me and while I was making the records they would be on the phone. They were doing nothing and getting the credit for producing all these records and the engineers were doing all the work. It wasn't always the case — there were a lot of great producers — but in many cases it was true. I decided that's was where the money was, so I told Steve Shoals (my boss at RCA) that I had an offer for another job and would leave unless I got promoted to the production staff at RCA. So I got promoted to the production staff — and took a big cut in pay! But I started making records and made a bunch of hits right off the bat. I was doing Jefferson Airplane, Eddie Fischer, Sam Cooke, and the Limelighters. I had a roster of eight or ten artists and most of those artists had three albums plus four or five singles a year, so I was jammed.

While I was a staff producer at RCA I was not allowed to touch the board. The union was so strong that for about five years of my career I did not do any engineering at all. What bothered me (and I had some really good engineers working with me at the time) was that by the time I told them what I wanted, I could have reached over and done it myself. I used to get turned in all the time because the union guys would come in and see me reaching over and doing something. I was always being brought up on the carpet for meddling and getting in the way.

At one point I called my boss in New York and I told him it was too crazy. I was doing Eddie Fisher in the afternoon from 2 p.m. to 5 p.m. and Jefferson Airplane from 8 p.m. until 4 or 5 a.m. I'd go home to sleep awhile and then I'd get up and come in to do paperwork and all this other stuff. I finally said I can't do it and I quit. RCA told Jefferson Airplane to find another producer but there was no other producer at RCA that they wanted to work with. RCA said, "Fine you can use an outside producer," so the band called me. I made more money producing that album than I had in the prior three years before. So I thought I had made the right step.

That was my start as an independent producer, and I was really nervous about getting enough work because I had a family to take care of. Jackson Browne and I became good friends so I produced *Late for the Sky* with him. It was very successful and I kept busy. Tommy LiPuma was a partner at Blue Thumb, and he asked me to mix an album he was working on. I said, "Gee, Tommy I haven't sat at a board in five years. I don't think I can do that." So we made an agreement that if it wasn't working he'd let me know or I'd let him know and we'd just stop. It was Dave Mason's *Alone Together* and it came out fabulous. While I was mixing it I realized that this was why I was in the business in the first place. This

Schmitt Talks Hardware

I was always aware of the progression to better recording equipment. Around the time I graduated to producing they started bringing in the old Neve boards, and they sounded great. Most of the boards I worked on were either custom-made or Neve boards with good preamps. I listen to some of the records I made 30 years ago and they sound as good or better than some of the things I'm doing today. It's careful mic selection and good tape machines. Sometimes I will do what Bruce Swedien does — record the rhythm section on analog tape and then bounce it over to digital for the overdubs. In general I prefer analog tape. If it's something that's got a lot of dynamic range I might use analog tape with Dolby SR. When I mix down I use ½-inch 3M 996 tape, +5 at 30 ips.

When I was working at RCA in the '60s I had everything I wanted. If there was a new mic out and I said I wanted to try it, I had four of them the next day. They were just fabulous and I was always one of these guys that wanted to try the new stuff that was coming out. I think that what really changed recording was when we started getting into multitrack. I remember when we got to 8-track — we were all standing around going, "What are we going to do with all these tracks?" Then when it came to 16-track we were all thinking ,"Oh this is ridiculous. Who is ever going to use 16 tracks? What would you use them for?" Now I'll go ahead and lock up two 48-track machines!

Some of that old equipment we still use today, like the Fairchild limiters and the tube microphones. I still use AKG C-12's and Telefunkens all the time. I use mostly tube microphones on my dates. The thing about the old tube mics is that you had to pair them up. When I was at RCA I had all these mics and I knew which mics sounded alike and which ones sounded different. I'd have maybe five tube Neumann U 47's, and two would sound a little brighter than another pair and those would be different from the fifth one. I had them all numbered and knew which ones worked well on which instruments. I used a lot of Neumann M 49's and M 50's in those days. I knew which ones to use to achieve equalization. My equalization came from my technique of where to put the mics and which ones to use. EQ had to be patched in, and when I started we had one equalizer. You had to equalize everything — you couldn't EQ individual microphones. So if I put up a mic and it wasn't bright enough, I would change it for a brighter microphone. That is how I changed my EQ.

was my love so I started doing more and more engineering. The money wasn't as good as producing, but it was my first love.

I wound up working with Tommy again on George Benson's *Breezin*, and that was my second Grammy. Then I mixed a few things on the *Aja* album with Steely Dan and won my third Grammy. My fourth Grammy came when I worked with Roger Nichols on Steely Dan's "FM" from *Gaucho*. My fifth Grammy came when I did all the tracks on *Toto IV*. That was such a great record and we knew it was special from the first moment — those kids were such great players. I won my sixth Grammy when I did the *Unforgettable* record with Natalie Cole and David Foster.

The Stand Outs

There are two artists that I worked with who particularly stand out as being really special. The first was Sam Cooke, who was brilliant. He knew exactly what he wanted to do in the studio. It was like fishing in a barrel. We had so much fun together in the studio. We laughed and hung out and he was a friend as well as a brilliant talent. He sang like a bird. He had it all.

The other was Henry Mancini, who was a brilliant composer and always a gentleman. He had a great sense of humor and he always was appreciative of us. I remember sessions where the date was supposed to end at 11 p.m. and it was three minutes to 11. We already had the take, and Henry knew it but he would say, "No, no we need one more." In those days if the session went one minute past the hour, all the musicians would get paid an extra half-hour overtime. So he would make it go until 11:02 or 11:03 and it was his way of saying, "Thanks guys." He was such a terrific, classy guy and he was fun to work with. You laughed, got quality stuff done, and got paid for it!

Busy, Busy, Busy...

I have never been busier in all my life then I am right now. I can work as much as I want. Last year I worked about 46 weeks and the year before was similar. I've had very little time off. If I get two or three days off between projects, I take off with my wife and just go somewhere to try to rest. It seems like one thing after another. Now I have a manager because I simply don't have time to make the deals. I still get the calls, but I turn them over to him and he makes the deals. I don't have to worry about working for a certain fee. But on the other end of it I'm one of these people who believes you have to give back, and if somebody is broke or it's somebody I like, I'll go in and help them out. I think that we need more of that in this business — especially for the people who are struggling. And I get people who call and say I'd love to have you but I can't afford you, so I try to work something out. I'm not rich, but I'm happy God put me in this position. I love what I do, I do it every day, and they pay me for it. You can't beat that.

I still produce, but when I do I try not to engineer unless I am doing something with a group as a coproducer. I may mix the project myself, but I'll have an engineer do the recording. If I try to produce and engineer at the same time, the engineering distracts me from producing. I am so particular about the sounds and I concentrate on that aspect so much that I might start to forget about the music in terms of pitch and arrangements. During the mix, the music is down and I'm not distracted, so I can do that by myself.

Some people call me just to mix their records and I like that. That is kind of like putting the pieces of the puzzle together. I mix quickly — in most cases I'll mix two songs in a day. I really like to use GML automation on a Neve console or Flying Faders. I don't work on SSL boards because I'm not crazy about the sound. I do a lot of stuff at Schnee Recording with a custom board and I have my own gear as well. I have some of the Mastering Lab preamps from Doug Sax and Mastering Lab speakers that I take wherever I work. I also have some

Talking Mic Technique

Probably the most important thing you can do when recording an orchestra is to stand in the studio next to the conductor during a run through. With a good conductor, you'll be able to hear what the arrangement is all about. I usually have the orchestra set up in the symphonic arrangement — first and second violins on the left, woodwinds and violas toward the center, French horns to the right of center, and low strings (celli and basses) on the right. You have to use high-quality mics. I like to put up a pair of Neumann M 50 (tube condenser, cardioid pattern) mics 15 or 20 feet over the conductor's head, spaced four or five feet apart. These mics get recorded to separate tracks and most of the sound will come from this stereo room feed. Most of the time the orchestra is recorded all at once, but once in a while we might overdub the brass or the strings to get a little less leakage. But that leakage makes the orchestra sound big, so a lot of times you want it in there.

In addition to the stereo feed, I spot-mic the different sections of the orchestra — but not too close. I'll put a couple of Neumann tube U 47's on the basses, tube U 67's (set to omni pattern) or KM 84's on the celli, and U 67's on the trumpets and trombones. Sometimes I might use some old RCA 10001's on the trombones. Alan Sides has a great collection of hard-to-find mics that he lets me use, and if it wasn't for him my recordings might not sound as good!

I don't like to get too close to these instruments or I'll lose the leakage, and that's what makes it sound natural. Also, if you get too close to the strings you get too much of the bow sound, so I like to keep the mics at least four or five feet away from the strings. Sometimes I will put a gobo behind the French horns to get more reflected sound and then use the Neumann M 49's to mic them. For percussion, I'll use an AKG 452 or one of the Schoeps or B&K mics because these mics are a little faster. The spot mics are all recorded onto separate tracks, but the stereo feed makes up most of the sound. I use the spot mics to accent certain instruments or maybe fill a hole in the sound from the room mics.

The secret to getting a good orchestra sound is using the best mics. My EQ comes from my mic selection, not EQ on the board, so if I need a different tone, I'll change the mic.

—Al Schmitt

tube limiters and a TC Electronic M5000 that I carry everywhere — I love that piece of equipment.

Keeping the Fire Burning

At one point in my career in the '60s, I got involved in the drug scene when the acid groups were popular. There was a lot of grass and cocaine going around and, like a lot of other people, I got caught up in that. And that's when the burn out started to happen. I'm not so sure it was work. It was a lot of the drugs, staying up late, and not getting enough sleep. Once I woke up to the reality of what was happening and stopped doing it, my life became simpler, work became easier and more pleasurable, and I don't have that problem anymore. The only time I get burnt is if I go from project to project to project. I get a little tired and want some time off. But I can usually work it out to not schedule something for four or five days so my wife and I can just go away to an island somewhere and relax. A little R & R has to be built into the schedule. I have a lot of energy and I'm a workaholic, so sometimes it can get to be too much, especially if you are doing things that you are not too happy with. But for the most part I can be picky about my projects and I get a lot of respect from the artists. So it's at a high quality level and there is already a good foundation. They respect me and I respect them.

When I work with Tommy LiPuma and even Dave Foster I do what I want in the studio. I set up the way I want, I record the way I want, and they don't bother me. If it wasn't right they would say something. These are top producers who hire me because I do what I do. They don't have to worry about it and that leaves them free to worry about the things they have to. If they are in there worrying about the creative end and then all of a sudden have to worry about why it doesn't sound right, it's more than enough burden on them and they wouldn't call me.

Getting the Call Back

I think the reason I get so many calls is that I'm easy to deal with in the studio. I don't have a major ego, I'm always willing to try something, and I listen. I get a lot of respect from the artists, and that works out well. When somebody hires me to engineer they not only get an engineer, they get somebody that can produce records and will throw out a good idea once in a while.

My best advice for young engineers is that, if you believe in something, really stick with it. If you have a passion for what you do, hang in there and stick with it. Don't let outside influences tell you to forget it. If you really believe in it, it will happen. And have good work ethics — be honest and put in a good day's work. Give your best all the time — it works for me.

Patience Makes Perfect

Some of my tested techniques for getting what both you and the artist want on tape

By Kevin Killen

Originally appeared in August 1995

While working as an assistant engineer at Windmill Lane early in my career, I was exposed to a lot of different engineers and producers. As an assistant engineer, you really had to learn to hear what the instrument was doing and choose the right microphone. Most of our sessions were with live musicians, and that really helped my microphone technique. You'd get to know what the engineer wanted and set the session up for him. It's difficult to be a good assistant because you have to be polite, diplomatic, and unobtrusive, but if you were really good at what you did, you helped the session run smoothly.

This early experience helped me make the transition to engineer (and later to producer), and I have found that diplomacy skills are as important as engineering skills in making a great record. How do you tell somebody that the performance they thought was stellar was actually terrible? How do you put that in a way that won't make them feel bad? And at the same time, how do you still encourage them? You never want to be negative toward an artist's performance, but a certain amount of candor is always important. You ultimately have to gain their respect, and there is always a way of doing that which they will appreciate and respect you for. They'll know in the future that you are not just saying things to appease them. From such honesty, trust is built.

The most important thing in the studio — besides technical ability — is to have patience. You have to wait for great performances to happen and be ready to capture them.

So What

The project that has probably had the most impact on my career was Peter Gabriel's *So*. That record was a struggle to finish and required a lot of patience because we encountered many technical difficulties and synchronizing problems. The project was originally started as a 48-track situation with two analog 24-track machines. Peter had a synchronizer installed in his studio the day before the band came down and apparently there were a couple of wires that were misconnected. One tape machine was running slightly slower than the other, so when the tapes were copied from one machine to another, that slight pitch variation was also transferred across. Therefore, the tapes would not lock together. In 1985 there weren't a lot of samplers around, so we had to fly parts off to ½-inch tape and then fly them back onto the master.

At the time, AMS had just come out with a 14-second sampler, and the gentleman who owned AMS at that time (a friend of Peter's) was kind enough to lend us one for the duration of the record. We would sample sections off, pitch shift them, and then fly them back. There were some great performances that had been recorded and it required a lot of discipline to sit there for hours on end and fly them back. I vowed from that moment on that I would never use synchronizers again, and I have pretty much been able to avoid using them. Occasionally, if I want to stack a particular part, I might make a quick slave or wild a piece of music over to another piece of tape, sample it, and fly the parts back in. Synchronization is seductive in that you can have more tracks, but I think that it ends up costing you time in the long run because you don't make decisions regarding parts or performances.

Elvis Costello Live

More than ever before, artists are approaching me about doing their records "live." To them, a live record probably means getting all the necessary dynamic shifts that they would do if they were performing in a public space. Unfortunately, the mic is very unforgiving when recording; it really can showcase both the good and bad things about someone's performance. Sometimes you simply have to approach making a live record in a different fashion from walking into a room, setting up the guitar, bass, and drums, plugging in, and running tape.

My image of a "live" record is to cull together the musicians and essentially allow a day per song to work through the arrangements. Then try to be patient enough to wait for a great performance or two or three takes that you can edit between. If there are some timing anomalies, but they are musical and you accept them, then you augment the track. But you work on it pretty quickly, and the way I have been approaching it recently is that I record the track so that it sounds pretty much like I want it to sound. Then you do the overdubs to that song almost immediately, and the next time you come back to the song it sounds almost like a finished record. You don't put it away for three weeks, then come back to it and say, "What was I going to do with this song?" You might have forgotten what your initial idea was.

If you decide you have made a mistake with it and must re-record it, that's only a day out of the schedule. You haven't spent three months trying to make it pop or groove a little better by adding one more thing. This way it's a little bit more painful for the musicians because you are pushing them through the day, but when they walk into the control room they are hearing a very good representation of what the song is about.

Elvis Costello's *Kojak Variety* was very much a live record. Elvis had said that he always wanted to do a record like this. We took musicians from England and the West Coast and went to Eddy Grant's Blue Wave Studios in Barbados. We would listen to the version that Elvis liked from the original artist, decide what our approach was going to be, and pretty much capture everything on one take. The band would play, we'd get a take that we liked, and then we would overdub immediately. In a two-week period, we recorded 16 or 17 songs. On the last day of recording, I did about 14 rough mixes. I took a real simple approach — I think I had one reverb and a tape-slap going. That was it.

Elvis had a bout of laryngitis while in Barbados, so we went to London to retouch some vocals and add some guitar that Elvis wanted to do. That essentially ended up being the record. In fact, a lot of those rough mixes ended up being the final mixes for the record.

There was a period of about two years between that day and the day we sat down to mix. We thought that remixing would really add something extra, but Elvis had fallen in love with the rough mixes so it was hard for him to hear anything else. We swapped out a couple of mixes, but the majority of the record was the raw mixes. I had roughly half an hour to do each mix and I'd just throw them up and maybe do a couple of moves. There was no automation involved.

The Direct Approach

For the past four or five years I have really been avoiding signal flow through the console when recording. I have a rack of Neve 1064A mic preamps that are housed in a flight case. I put them out in the room, amplify the signal close to the source, and send it directly into the tape machine at line level. Sometimes this is not practical for every instrument, but it really makes a difference in the way things sound if you get the main instruments down like that. I also find that you tend to EQ a lot less to make up for deficiencies that you might otherwise not hear.

I now carry a pair of Proac speakers and a Cello amplifier with my own cables. I started doing this in the last year and a half for both tracking and mixing and it has been an interesting educational experience. Since I have started using the speakers consistently, I have noticed that when I take the tapes for mastering (I master exclusively with Bob Ludwig) we are using less EQ in the mastering suite. It's more of level changes and an odd bit of compression. I am hearing more fidelity when I am in the control room so I tend to do less in mastering. Sometimes I'll have additional speakers set up like Yamaha NS-10M's or some other bookshelf speakers that the artist is comfortable with so we can toggle back and forth between the two. When you pop around from studio to studio, you realize the inconsistencies in the way speakers can sound even when they are the same speakers.

Engineer as Producer

I was always making the transition between engineer and producer. There were people (especially in Dublin) who gave me the opportunity to produce some things even though they were small local recordings. I did a reasonably good enough job to get a second opportunity and it mushroomed from there.

I don't feel that I am doing anything differently in the studio now than I have in the past. But I do have to deal with the label, the business affairs people, the studio, and the A&R administration. That is a whole other side of production that soaks up time. It is your responsibility to deliver the record on or close to budget. You are the point person for the label, and if things aren't going well they can talk to you or fire you. You always hear about producers getting fired from projects, but you rarely hear about artists getting fired for not living up to what the label thought their potential was. That's when they get dropped, but sometimes it takes four or five records for the label to realize that maybe an artist is not so great.

Occasionally I'll get hired as an engineer if it's another producer who wants to hire me, but I find the role of producer/engineer much more interesting. I like to be involved from the outset and, after doing that for 16 years, I feel that I can contribute something to the recording process. I think it's disrespectful to anybody who works in a studio, down to the assistant engineer, to expect them to sit there and not have an opinion. Given the right approach, a debate in a control room or a studio space can be healthy to getting a particular take. Every opinion is valid — even if it may not be the opinion you want to hear at that particular moment in time.

In my own sessions, I like an assistant who is capable of engineering. I'll let him run the tape machine or even do some engineering. And I respect his opinion because it is another set of ears, maybe equally as musical as mine.

Producing a record is like getting married to an artist for three or four months and then getting a divorce. You hope that the divorce is amicable. After being with artists 12–14 hours a day you learn all their wonderful and idiosyncratic qualities. You go through this really intense relationship and when the record is finished it suddenly stops. Then you go back to square one and start the process over again. Sometimes it is very difficult to let go of the project you just finished and start the next record, so I usually end up taking time off after a record to recuperate. It's a very emotional experience. You want people to love it, but it takes about six months before you can sit down and be truly objective. Once you have finished it you think it is the best work you have ever done. It's the closest I'll ever physically come to having a child.

Kevin Killen has worked as engineer, remixer, and producer for recording artists such as Peter Gabriel, U2, Tori Amos, Kate Bush, Roy Orbison, and Elvis Costello.

Homestyle Sound

Home project studios are the way to go for performers, songwriters, and parents (or all of the above) — like me

By Bruce Hornsby

Originally appeared in September 1995

I have just gotten back from attending a party. Not a big, fancy record company party, but an end-of-school-year pizza party for my 3½-year-old twin boys, Keith and Russell. This is one of the main reasons why I built a project studio in my home. I never wanted to be an absentee father and miss out on spending time with my family. And my family is the main of four key ingredients that make up my life's activities — the other three being touring, writing, and recording music.

The studio is approximately 30 feet away from my house, and I love that. Another reason I built the studio is for creative freedom. I never liked the pressure of watching the clock in commercial studios. It's restricting, and I feel that they are not the best creative environments. Recording in your own studio, your own element, brings on a whole new feeling of relaxation, and it works great for me. I've become much more prolific since I've built the studio three years ago. After having a studio, I can't imagine ever going back.

The Hair Club for Men

That's the unofficial name of my studio. Mainly because all of the key people involved with it are not so well endowed up there, if you know what I mean. There's the mastermind who designed the facility, Ross Alexander (who also designed John Mellencamp's project studio in Indiana), my brother, Bobby Hornsby, who built the place, and my engineer, Wayne Pooley. Even my drummer, John Molo, is losing it upstairs, and I myself am not that far off either.

I wanted this studio to keep me grounded, and it has. In the planning stages, we knew that we

For the Record

Wayne Pooley, Bruce Hornsby's engineer, tells how Hornsby's album, Hot House, *was recorded.*

Bruce likes to have a performance-oriented feel to his sessions. When we tracked his latest album here at The Hair Club for Men, the entire band was recorded live for the most part. If you can stop and try to envision this — there were seven parts being played at once. The keyboardist's Leslie cabinet was in the bathroom, the bass amp was in the amp closet (a.k.a., the equipment room), and the two horn players were in the garage. Back in the main studio were the drums, the bassist, and the keyboardist and his rig, while Bruce's two pianos were in the piano room. It was totally maxed out.

When recording in a less than optimal recording environment, such as the bathroom, you can offset it with a nice blend between a DI and cabinet. This is the setup we used for most of the basic tracks that featured the band.

We had an interesting arrangement for the recording of this album. Rehearsal and recording occurred simultaneously. They'd be listening to their headphone mixes that were derived from a separate part of the console. This allowed me to listen to a soloed hi-hat for ten minutes straight without disturbing the band's cue mix. Our Neve is a 40-input console. We set up channels 25–40 to record and used additional API mic preamps to augment the Neve mic preamps. These channels went unprocessed, and were recorded straight to machine "A," one of our two Sony 3324 24-track digital tape machines. The tape returns from machine "A" were routed to the line inputs 1–24. Channels 1–24 were recorded on machine "B," and were processed with compression, EQ, and all that fun stuff.

By using this method of sync'ing the "dry tape machine" with the "processed tape machine," two purposes are achieved. For one, it gave the musicians a taste of a "finished product" because, although they were fed from the unprocessed 25–40 channels, they heard the full 40-channel output — effects and all. Second, it protected us from being limited later during mixdown because we had those dry signals to work with. So even though there were wet and dry signals simultaneously happening, they always remained as separate entities.

Just this past spring, we acquired Digidesign's Pro Tools III software, and we're using it for premastering applications. For the last album, using the Pro Tools III, we took all of our mixes and mastered them to 2-track. This allowed us to bring a preassembled DAT complete with edits and spacing to the mastering house as opposed to bringing in a whole bunch of unorganized mixes. (A good way to save some bucks!)

A fairly extensive MIDI routing system is maintained throughout Bruce's studio. We are using an Opcode Studio 5 to pump out MIDI to all the various parts of the studio, and it makes it easy for us to, for example, start and stop drum machines and record MIDI data from synthesizers. Also, Bruce's piano is outfitted with a MIDI controller called the Gulbransen KS-20. Using this and Opcode's Studio Vision, I'm able to record microphones and MIDI data from the piano simultaneously.

wanted certain things and Ross did a good job of giving us what we needed. One particular thing that I requested was a good-sized keyboard isolation room because I knew that I was going to spend a lot of time in there to practice and record. We also wanted a window looking outside of the control room. Here on our land we've got some nice woods and just outside the control room is a creek. It's much different from the dark and confined conditions commonly found in commercial studios.

We're not just cutting demos here either; this is a fully functional studio. In fact, we cut my new album, *Hot House* [RCA Records], here. The console that we're using is an old Neve 8068 that we bought from Unique Recording Studios out in New York. I'm sure that board has seen many interesting recording sessions. We retrofitted the console with the Neve Flying Faders. For now we have fader and mute automation, but still have to document the EQ the old-fashioned way. But it's been great nonetheless. We can leave our mix up on the board for days, hit the road, do a gig, then come back, and get a good perspective on the mix. You could never do that in a studio that wasn't your own.

Instrumental Setup

The piano is my instrument, and it plays a big role in all of my recordings. In planning the studio's design, I knew that I'd want to have a separate live room dedicated to my Baldwin and Steinway pianos (the Baldwin is a MIDI piano), particularly for situations when I play live with the band — which is quite often. John Molo, my drummer, plays real strong — in fact, he plays loud as hell and I can't be in the same room as him or all you'll hear are drums on the piano tracks. In any case, we usually use some great old Neumann U 67's to record my piano. I've used some AKG 414's and C12's, but we've had the best luck with the Neumanns. I am interested in the Barcus Berry piano pickup as a means to mic my piano for live gigs, and it's an avenue that we will explore in the future.

Being the lead singer and the piano player of my band brings on a whole other variable to recording. How to record vocals and piano simultaneously is the key question, and I do it both ways. During a session, my vocals usually serve as guides. It's common practice for me to kind of talk the band through a song and primarily focus on my playing. When I've got the instrument tracks down, I'll cut the vocals and overdub them in on the mix. I don't follow the standard format of going into an iso booth to record my vocals. I record my vocals right there in the control room all alone, sitting at the board. I put on my headphones, turn the control room speakers down, and that's my isolation. I punch myself in and out as desired, and I've gotten pretty good at it. I've tried all different kinds of vocal mics, and I have found the best success with a Sanken CU41 mic.

For situations that require a different means of isolation, we've got a total of three live rooms: a big room, a small room, and a piano room. Actually we have an "unauthorized" other live room — my garage. The band and I were just experimenting one day and found that the garage had a really bright, strong sound to it. The horn players were just dying to record out there. So there's my other "live" room. It's adjacent to the studio, and we've recorded some horn tracks there that have made it to the record. Being that it is situated so close to the control room, there was no need for any kind of special tie lines; we run the cables just like most guys do. The sound in the garage has that "live" ambience to it — the horns sound great coming from there.

I Write, Therefore I Am

When I write my songs, I don't use any kind of sequencing software. Even though we do use Digidesign's Pro Tools III in the studio for certain applications, songwriting is not one of them. Sometimes I write the lyrics first and then put the music to them. Other times I write the music first and then the lyrics. If you listen to my albums, it's obvious to me when I've done one or the other. For example, the music on a track will be noticeably more complex if I wrote the lyrics second. If I've written lyrics first, then the music will be simpler.

I've also been known to sing and play piano into a boom box. In fact, I do that a lot when I practice. When I'm ready to present material to the band, I'll lay down a drum machine track, overdub my piano, and then a scratch vocal. This will all be recorded on the Sony 24-track. The use of a drum machine plugged into a small amp puts me into a groove that I might not necessarily get from playing solo piano, and further assists my songwriting process. Other times I could be driving in my car and find myself in the process of creating a song. And I always carry a notebook with me on the road because you never know when a lyrical idea can pop into your head. Because there are so many different ways to write songs, it helps the songs have stylistic variety.

True Lou

Lou Reed achieves his dream of having a recording sound exactly the way he played it

By Bob Ludwig

Originally appeared in April 1996

I have known Lou Reed since I consulted in mastering his *Metal Machine Music* album in 4-channel discrete quadraphonic. Lou has always been very interested in faithfully capturing his true sound on record, including experiments in binaural recording. Like most artists, he has found this to be a very difficult thing to truly do.

Since then, I have worked with Lou on three other albums: *New York City, Magic and Loss,* and his latest release, *Set the Twilight Reeling.* With *New York City* and *Magic and Loss,* Lou was still not satisfied in that he felt that the sounds he heard in the studio were still not being captured on tape. With *Set the Twilight Reeling,* Lou finally captured what he wanted. The record finally met 100 percent of his vision. This article is about how he captured that vision.

This interview took place at Lou's New York City apartment shortly after completing the mastering of the record up at my place in Portland, Maine. Steve Rosenthal, the engineer on Lou's record, joined us.

The Recording Process

Bob: Let's talk about the record. I was going to ask you about the sequence because I remember what trouble you had doing it.

Lou: I told everybody involved in the recording to make out a sequence, which we did, and they were really pretty close. That is really interesting. And I would just sit here with the CDs we made up and make different versions of it and listen to the end of one song going into the beginning of the next. And some songs would be *destroyed* by being in the wrong place. And then other ones, like "Hang On to Your Emotions" going into "Sex With Your Parents," seemed destined.

Bob: It's as though there's some omnipotent thing looking down on this sequence!

Lou: We cut "Sex With Your Parents" on July 4th, which I don't think we knew. We were ensconced up here in the studio I made in my apartment, so who knew what day it was. We've got these little trees on the balcony outside the room, and there was this incredible storm. I had gone downstairs to get something, and when I came back upstairs, Steve and Struan Oglanby [production coordinator and programmer] are outside and the trees are taking off — they're flying! This is during the session! And Steve and Struan are hanging onto this one tree! It's one of the funniest things I've seen in my life. To be up here and see these storms going on and all this equipment — it's incredible. [*Lou shows me some the gear involved in making the record and the list of guitars used on each track.*]

We found this direct box from Avalon for the bass, the DI-U5. It costs $600, but they could charge $10,000 and it would be a bargain. We found an SVT setting where you would swear you were listening to an SVT. We would mic a little Hartke bass amp with an old solid-state Neumann, I forget what the number of it is, and there would be your bass. And then Fernando Saunders [bass player] could monitor it through the ATCs. Everything went through the ATC SCA-50's, God bless them.

Bob: Do you own all these mics?

Lou: Yeah. We were renting the bass mic, but then I put an order in and they found me one, but I rented it during half the session. All the guitar mics, all the vocal mics — that's all me. The only thing we rented as far as other mics goes was the Schoeps Stereo Sphere. The rest is from Roof Recording Services' small but extensive collection.

I think one of the big secrets was the Manley microphone that was always used as the vocal mic, but you could use it for anything. The leakage into it always sounded great. It wasn't like, "Oh, the leakage is horrible." On my vocal track you can hear the electric drums Tony "Thunder" Smith [drummer] is playing, and you can hear him hitting the pads. The guitar is also raging through the vocal.

Bob: How did you have the guitars lined up?

Lou: We had anywhere from two to seven guitar mics set up. That's why we didn't have a lot of instruments, but we made a lot of tracks. That's also why we had to mix in a place that had automation with moving faders. There were so many tracks used to make up this sound. Between the drums and the guitars we were at 24 tracks, and we hadn't even done anything yet! That was the kind of attention we were paying to the guitars. Any one of those microphones would get a great guitar sound on its own, but it's the combination that gets that sound on tape like what I heard live. I said I was never going to release another record unless it sounded like what I heard when I made it.

When we moved down to the Magic Shop [also in Manhattan], we brought in all the big rigs that we couldn't use in my project studio. At my place, there was not one square inch you could move. Fernando was playing opposite me; we were playing staring at each other.

It was a tight space. We had it all baffled off with eight bath mats. They were like little houses for the amps.

[*Steve Rosenthal, engineer and owner of the Magic Shop, arrives.*]

Bob: Steve, had you used those Coles mics before?

Steve: I'd used ribbon mics for horns before, but never for guitars.

Bob: How do these Coles compare to, say, an RCA ribbon mic?

Steve: They're more accurate, they color the sound less, and they can take a higher sound pressure level. In the old days, they used to be used as drum overhead mics. That's originally where I saw them; they were in that Beatles recording session book. There's one sitting on top of Ringo's drum kit. So they can take high sound pressure levels.

Lou: This is one of the world's foremost Beatles fans, by the way.

Steve: Drummer Tony "Thunder" Smith was sitting on a special platform Lou had built for him.

Lou: It was made of plywood, but it was filled with this stuff from Ultrasonic up in Maine. What we had noticed, and tried to continue at the Magic Shop, was that we had the ability to get the exact guitar sound I always wanted by using that acoustic sound stuff with Seisel carpet on top of that for absorption (it's Seisel because wool would give you static shock). So we did the same thing at the Magic Shop.

My studio was a nightmare live room because if you snapped your fingers, the sound would go on for eight seconds. At the Magic Shop, we measured out a portion of the studio, covered it with the same soundproofing treatment we used at home, and put a Seisel carpet over it. So the amps are sitting on this stuff, and you're not getting that hard bounce-off. Do you still use that at the studio?

Steve: Yeah, it's still sitting on the drum platform.

Lou: We had tried a couple of things. At home, we are always listening through speakers aimed directly at us. But when we tried to do this at the Magic Shop, it didn't work because the room was so live, and not meant for listening to music like that. The control room, however, was a different story. I went into the control room with a pair of Aerial speakers, which were set up in the back of the room. There is a sweet spot on the couch, and that's where I had my guitar controls, which were linked out into the studio. I was sitting in between those big Aerials there — and added a set of ATCs at the front! We mixed through six systems. Starting with the little mono speaker built into the Neve, to the ATCs, to the Colberts, to my Cambridge portable system, and to my custom-made Richard Rose Tannoys.

Steve: The headphones! Tell him about the cool headphones system!

Lou: Oh yeah, we had eight pairs of Grado Prestiges, some Sennheiser headphones, and my Sony 999's. Everybody fell in love with the little Grado headphones. They are such fun.

Steve: Not really expensive, but very accurate.

Bob: How was the band set up?

Steve: The drums were back on a platform, and Lou was kinda mobile — it depended on how close he wanted to be to his amp. Or how close, in effect, I could have him be to his amp. Sometimes, when we had these big hairy sounds, we had to get the Manley away from the guitar amps. Everything was in a pretty confined area.

Bob: The Manley has switchable patterns?

Steve: Yes, and Lou has a custom-made Manley.

Lou: They shaped the bottom end for me. Made it work with my voice better. I called David Manley up and said the mic does this and this and this, but for me it does that and that. He said, "I know just what you mean, I can do it in ten minutes" — and he did! And it came back and it's this amazing microphone. The beauty of that mic is that all the other things going through it sound good.

Steve: It was almost like having a room mic in a way, because it's so accurate. And it was picking up everything that was going on up here. If we had a mic that was coloring what was going on [the off-axis sounds], we wouldn't have gotten the tones that we got. This mic is so dead-on accurate that it really reproduces the tones that you give it. It's a big part of why the record sounds the way it does.

Steve: The way the drums were set up was really fascinating. It was done with the Roland electronic drum set hooked up to an Akai S-3000 sampler. Struan and I spent a couple of days in the Magic Shop sampling drums, including some favorite kits that we like, some really old snares, old kick drums from the late '20s, and a giant parade kick drum. How many sets of drums would you say we had there?

Lou: They brought in four or five bass drums and about four snares. But Steve let us use his drum room so that we could get this great live sound on the drums, and we just went through all kits that we like. He has *his* favorite, I had *my* favorite, and then we'd bring the samples here. You didn't have to put an effect on them because they were done in a live room in the first place. It was like a classic sound right off the bat. We had a bunch of them!

Steve: Struan would do the programming, and he could combine sounds. Lou might say, "I like this kick drum sound; it's really fat, but I wish it had a little more attack." Struan could slip another kick sample in there and get it to where Lou liked it, and all of a sudden we had a unique kick-drum sound. They were both live kick drums, but we were able to manipulate it through the sampler in a way we could have never done in a live situation where the cymbals were clashing and everyone was banging and slamming. There was a lot of control, which was really important.

We were thinking in the beginning of putting a live hi-hat in here and having some of the drums live. We brought one up one day, hit it once, and everybody went "No!" It would have been impossible. Tony Smith came up and saved our collective lives because he knew how to play this stuff. A regular drummer cannot just sit down and play it — it's not gonna happen.

Lou: I figured out I spent about two-and-a-half years preparing for this in the sense of gearing up, which included A/B'ing equipment and calling people up. I called people I trust, obviously including you, Bob, and I'd ask what is your mic of choice, what's your "this" of choice, and we would go out and give it a listen. People were very helpful. Guys would actually lend us their favorite thing to check it out.

Steve: I came on board about a year before we started recording, when I started coming up to Lou's place. We would have a great time, too. We would sit here with really high quality pieces of equipment and just go, "Do you like that? How about this? What sounds good? What doesn't sound good?" We did that for microphones, we did that for equalizers, we did that for compressors — we just went through the whole recording chain.

Lou: We would do blindfold tests for each other. And, almost without exception, we would pick out the same thing. Some of the answers were a little shocking; a lot of times the answer wasn't what you'd think it would be, which was the beauty of the blindfold test. For example, Steve knew a guy who had an original EMT gold foil. One day we had it lugged up here…

Steve: It weighs 400 pounds…

Bob: Thank God it wasn't the steel plate!

Lou: And he compared it to the Sony "Gold Foil" program on the R7. Blindfold test again, and guess what? The Sony was way better! The schmootz wasn't there.

Steve: I was very surprised. We are not really digital reverb fans by any stretch, so we were excited about having this EMT plate here. But as soon as we closed our eyes and listened, it was a revelation. What Sony has done was take all of the good features of the Gold Foil and they got rid of all that junk that we'd have to spend two hours in the studio trying to filter out. The poor guy had to take his box back — he thought he had a two-month rental!

Lou: It's like that Avalon bass direct box, which has a little button with a high-end filter on it…

Steve: You know when you take the DI (Direct Insert) into the studio there is this high-frequency junk that sits on the top of the bass sound, and usually when you try to get rid of it you get rid of some of the bass tone, the high harmonics. Wynton at Avalon is really an amazing character. He was a musician and thinks about his equipment in a musical way. He put a low-pass filter into the DI that basically removes the high-frequency junk and it does not change the harmonics of the bass.

Lou: Steve went crazy when he heard it. He said, "My God, whoever built this really knows his stuff."

Steve: That's such a nightmare, DIs and stuff. Lou had found this great Hartke Systems bass amp that we used an awful lot on the album.

Lou: $349. It's got a little contour button that, according to Hartke, is the Motown [bass instrument] EQ.

Bob: Uh huh [laughs sarcastically, knowing something of what actually did go into making the Motown bass sound].

Lou: So the button was always in [*everyone laughs*], and then Fernando would shape it after that. And then we found our SVT setting with the Avalon. There's a whole bunch of other settings, too. You just do it with a click.

Steve: They were all very useful. Lou's got EQ, a tone control, and a boost. We used an awful lot of Avalon equipment on the record.

Lou: Steve thought so much of the Hartke bass amp that he got one for the studio.

Steve: Yeah, I bought one for the Magic Shop, too. I've got a B-15, but I didn't have any modern amp that I though was really great, but as soon as I heard this thing I thought, "I want one of these." People have been using it at the studio. You don't have to play at loud levels to get a really punchy tone. Sometimes with bass amps you have to put the thing up to 150 to get some sort of tone out of it.

So the bass was a combination of the Hartke Systems and the Avalon DI through Neve preamps. Lou had gotten a rack of 3-band Neve preamps that we used on the album per our A/B testing. And one of them was used for the bass.

Bob: When you were doing this A/B testing, there are a zillion permutations one can go through. Did you get into changing cables and interconnects and stuff like that?

Lou: No, we stuck to what was here.

Steve: We used regular standard cabling.

Lou: We had already gone through the Kimber Cable and Monster Cable trips, but that stuff was for guitars. All we discovered, for whatever it's worth, was that we introduced tones that you wouldn't *want* to hear. You did get more, but it was something you'd want to take out if it was there. The Kimber and Monster cables were only hooked up to the monitors.

I am using special cords for my guitars. The cable from my guitar and all of the amps was specially made for me by Pete Cornish in London. I've got no idea what's going on, but one end of the cable *has* to be connected to the amp, and the other end *has* to be attached to the guitar.

I've got a bunch of varying lengths that Pete has made for me, and all I know is it really sounds great. I've tried other guys' cables where they say they're doing something, and they sound midrangey and weird and thin. You know they say they get more, but the only thing they do that I notice is I lose bottom. Then I had these special guitars made by John Bolan with the design by Ned Steinberger — that was my last move. And these special Telecasters by Rick Kelly that all have 100-year-old necks.

Joe Bardon, who built the pickups in there, said, "If this was stock-car racing, having a 100-year-old neck is like having nitro in back of you — it's not even fair to anybody else!" I mean, there's old Telecasters, but this is from Stradivarius's time!

Bob: What is it about the age of the wood that makes it sound special?

Lou: It's the seasoning…I don't know. "Seasoning" doesn't really say anything. I don't know what it is, but you can certainly hear the difference.

Bob: Just as an aside, is Lou's studio hum-prone?

Steve: Actually it's very [RF] quiet in here.

Lou: As long as I don't put on any of the lights that had dimmers.

Steve: You couldn't have dimmers, which is a regular studio rule — so in that sense the rule followed the rule.

Bob: There's not a transmitting tower near here?

Steve: There was no RF, but we had birds flying into the window.

Lou: We had birds crashing — attracted by the sound! But we've been playing up here since I've been living here, and I knew there wasn't any of *that* kind of hum. But when we were getting ready to record, Steve was gracious enough to help me set it up and he brought in his assistant Joe Worda. Worda brought in a guy to wire all of this stuff and we were all looking for hum.

Bob: Let's talk about guitars…

Steve: There was an incredible guitar forest here. There were so many guitars to choose from it was just amazing. And each one of the guitars really does a special thing. If there was a particular color that was needed, you'd just pick one up and there it was.

Lou: When I figured that out, it solved one of the greatest problems I've had in the studio: Even from hour to hour you can't necessarily depend on going back to an amplifier with the same exact guitar, the same settings, the same everything. You do the same thing you did before, only now it doesn't sound good. *Everything's the same, nothing's changed!* But you go back and you can't get that sound back. So we suddenly realized we had a lot of choices we could play with.

Steve: It's really true because you can't repeat this stuff — I don't care what anybody says. We would try a couple of times and then it would be totally different. There were forces beyond our control, so we would just go on....

Lou: We had a lot of fun because we were trying to avoid EQ'ing. I knew if we got the right sounds matching we would not have to worry about EQ'ing. We could just place things and they ought to be able to sit right, which is essentially what we did — we spent time placing things.

Bob: This record's got so much space in it. That's the thing that's so impressive to me; it's a rock record with space. I mean, I think the 100-year-old guitar necks come across on the album!

Steve: Yes, it's not filled up with a bunch of overdubs.

Bob: Was the original version of "Egg Cream" the first thing you recorded?

Lou: Yes.

Bob: So it was almost like a demo for the record.

Lou: That *was* the demo for the record. It was what we could really do. And from that song we saw that if you can get some really good people in here then this thing's a real go.

Bob: I'll never forget when you called me up and said, "I captured on tape the way my guitar sounds for the first time!"

Lou: Yeah, it can be done.

Steve: One thing about recording it up here was that you could record it and then immediately play it back through the ATCs.

Lou: Instant feedback!

Steve: So you didn't have to walk into the control room. It wasn't as if Lou and I were separated; we were a half a foot from each other. It was like instant communication because we'd play it live, then play it through the ATC, and he would go, "There's something missing…" and then we would figure it out.

Lou: Steve didn't have to get up out of the control room and walk in. We're sitting right there practically cheek to jowl!

Steve: Yes, and that's a very different thing to do. That's one of the things about recording up here in Lou's studio that was very different, which I think facilitated getting those kind of tones. Usually the artist and the engineer hear two different things. The artist is in the room hearing his guitar amplifier and all the body around it and the room tone, and the engineer is listening to a set of speakers. So, in a sense, they're not even hearing the same thing. But in this particular case we actually heard the same thing. So we could make sure that what was on tape was what we were hearing next to us.

Bob: Steve, how has it been for you since these sessions back at your studio?

Steve: I've been using the Cambridge a lot. I bring the Cambridge Soundworks in when I do mixes and stuff.

Lou on Lyrics

Bob Ludwig: Were these songs written over a long period of time? Did you start writing them right after you completed Magic and Loss?

Lou Reed: These songs all came in one shot pretty much after I had the production elements under control and I could just concentrate on writing and not have anything else interfere with it. They came fairly quickly over a period of two to three weeks.

Do you remember which was the first song of the group that you wrote?

That's easy: It was "Egg Cream." It was written for a movie called *The Face,* and I really fell in love with the song. Because I was in "writing" mode, if anyone wanted a song for a film I'd say, "Yeah, but I have to be able to use the song on an album." This happened with the TV show *Friends.* I did a song called "You'll Know When You Were Loved," which I didn't keep on the album. It seemed like this album was going to be a collection of songs from various projects, and I didn't want that.

I know that "Hooky Wooky" came early. I think I was in Europe at the time, I was doing this TV show called *The White Room,* and for some odd reason I found myself apropos of absolutely nothing suddenly saying, "Let's do the hooky wooky!" I *love* to hooky wooky! I hear these things in my head now and then, and this went on to such a degree that I said I've got to write a song. So I came back and wrote this song and it took this odd turn during the lyric. Hard left! That was one of the earlier ones. "Finish Line" was one of the last ones.

Did the press say anything to you about "Sex With Your Parents"?

They say things that I don't know what they mean like, "Are you worried that you'll get in trouble?" Like this is an Eastern Bloc nation.

As though Robert Dole was going to send his hit men after you!

They ask, "Is the label giving you a problem?" I said no, nothing like that. And I say, "Don't you think it's really funny?" Then they seem relieved that *I* say it's funny. I don't for a second expect to change anybody's mind about anything; I'm just making a joke because I hate those people. So it is getting noticed.

Lou: The Cambridge Soundworks system is by Henry Kloss up in Boston. It comes in a little suitcase. Inside the suitcase is the amplifier, two bookshelf speakers, and cables. The suitcase is a subwoofer. We brought one right into the studio, and it's amazing to go back and forth between the speakers because I found them to relate perfectly with the ATCs.

Things were essentially geared off my Tannoys, and the Tannoys went well with the ATCs. The Tannoys have also gone well with the Colberts. So there's this line through all the speakers. I've been listening and listening to everything that people recommend to me and in the end the Colberts related to the Tannoys, the Tannoys related fine to the ATCs, the ATCs related fine to the Cambridges, the Cambridges related fine to the Aerials — if you heard something on one, it wasn't a mystery on another.

Bob: So there are no [Yamaha] NS-10's on this record?

Steve: No NS-10's! I have a pair of Genelecs at the Magic Shop, and when we were

"Finish Line" was written in the studio 'cause it had been something else, and the something else it was did not make it. I loved this little basic track we had, but I couldn't dislodge the old song. It was very difficult to rewrite, and then Laurie Anderson kind of jump-started me. She said, "Remember you've got this lyric in your computer?" And I said, "Í do?" I went in there and started rewriting that, and lo and behold it gained a life force as strong as the other one and was able to dislodge it because it was better. The only thing that remained of the original track was Fernando's bass. In fact, when Roy Bittan overdubbed his piano part it was to the other song! He's never heard the song the way it actually is!

I hear about these serendipitous things happening when artists write songs, and it amazes me. It's beyond my understanding.

It's almost like taking dictation. I don't know what to make of it at all. I can't even image how that gets done, and then you do another one! It makes me think that you're able to get in touch with another section of your mind that is really very much in touch with your soul on a level that's different from everyday experience. Sometimes there'll be words there that I don't know or a spelling that I think is wrong and I'll go check and the spelling is not wrong, and the word is not wrong. It's just a word that I'm not really acquainted with! I don't know what to make of that!

In "Set the Twilight Reeling," the word "borne" is spelled with an "e" at the end. I'm doing this proofreading later and I thought, "I don't make mistakes like that." So I went to the dictionary and looked up borne with an "e." Borne with and "e" means "to carry." The other born, of course, means to give birth. I kept looking for who put the "e" there. Some part of my brain no doubt remembers this fact from some English class. I wouldn't normally use that word in normal conversation; it's really a word for writing. It's not even archaic.

Without getting new-agey, I don't think when you look at a beautiful painting it does the same thing that music does. A record actually physically moves you. Today, in rehearsal, we hit this power chord together, and you could feel your solar plexus go, "oh, man!" The bass kicks in and you go, "Whoa!" And then when you put *words* to that and get your head involved — that's really great.

overdubbing and mixing we sometimes used the Genelecs, but we bailed on them pretty quickly. Lou got the Aerials brought in from his office and we got another pair of ATCs to put in on top of the console, so there are no NS-10's on this record.

Bob: So you must have done some EQ'ing when you were mixing or recording at the Magic Shop?

Steve: I have to tell you that basically what was EQ'd was the kick drum and the bass (which was EQ'd a little bit on the Neve preamps). Just +1 at 10k on his vocal on the Neve preamp. There is a little bit of EQ through the Sontec on the kick drum, but that's basically all.

Bob: So you didn't record through the Mackie at all?

Steve: No, the Mackie was what I would call our monitoring console. We had Avalon preamps and Lou has eight Hardy preamps. So between the Hardys, the Avalons, and the Neve, that was what we used to record everything to the multitrack.

While nothing was actually recorded through the Mackie, I have to say this about it: One day during our A/B tests, we had all four of the preamps (the Avalon, the Neve, the Hardy, and the Mackie), and we ran a bunch of blindfold tests. And the Mackie was always the worst, but I have to say that it wasn't the worst in some cases by that much. We were impressed, especially considering that you get 32 of them [preamps] for basically the cost of one Avalon preamp.

Bob: What was the maximum number of tracks you ended up using when you were mixing?

Lou: Fifty-six.

Bob: So you owned seven TASCAM DA-88's and you needed to still rent another?

Lou: Yes.

Bob: Just one thing about the vocal: I know that there's almost no sibilance problem on this album. Is that just the Manley mic?

Steve: I think there's a combination of elements. We are using the Manley mic, the 3-band Neve mic pre, and an LA-2A tube compressor. And I think the tube compressor has a tendency to do nice things to the top end. I also think the combination of those elements gave us a really nice, bright, accurate vocal sound. But we didn't do any de-essing when we mixed; there was no de-essing done.

Bob: Yes, there wasn't a problem with it. Usually, on past recordings — even with that fantastic Sony vocal mic — there would be some sibilance stuff.

Lou: Yeah, there was that problem.

Steve: Talk about A/B'ing. We spent about a week and a half trying to get the perfect vocal sound. I mean we tried every combination of elements we could get right now. And what we ended up with is the classic sound of the old Neve and the LA-2A. It's the most accurate thing we could get to what it sounds like to have Lou sitting in the room singing. All the other combos would be coloring it, some would bring sibilance, some would make it thinner, some would make it fatter, but this actually sounds like Lou!

Bob: What a concept!

Steve: What a concept to have the artist actually sound the way he sounds! But that brings up another point of things exceptional about this record: I think it is so great and I felt it was really important that Lou plays while he sings at the same time. You see the size of this room, you would say that was impossible: How could he sing live in this room with everybody playing at the same time? But it happened.

Bob: What mic pattern did you end up using, super-cardioid?

Steve: No, straight cardioid.

Lou: It was mic positioning....

Steve: When it was the clean stuff, he could literally be sitting next to his amplifier, which is very liberating I'm sure. Again, when you are performing in the studio there is a sense of disconnection — you're in the isolation booth with your headphones on, your guitar amplifier's 50 feet away, and there's all that dislocation. But I mean here is Lou and here is Lou's guitar amplifier three feet away from him.

Lou: Plus, you were with the guys! You're all in it together and you're performing and you want it to happen and everybody's rocking. The music is pounding right up your back, but up to a controllable level.

It was, in a sense, a dream come true. It was the optimal situation: hearing it just the way you want it, the amount that you want it, playing with the people that you want, in a completely controlled but really cool situation.

For me the goal was: "How can I hear it the way I really like to hear it and not be so disassociated from it?" I've always felt like I'm just a ghost, a little bit removed and not really there. And you're always trying to conquer that. If you didn't have to conquer that you could just play. A recording should be something that captures the spirit, not a construct at the board. This is what we heard, this is what we want you to hear. It is what we heard.

Steve: The bass amp would be going while Lou was singing, and sometimes you would hear these really cool percussion parts on the record...

Lou: ...and they are on the vocal mic!

Steve: It's the vocal mic's ambiance.

Lou: It's Fernando or it's Tony. The sound of the pick is heard through the entire record — a perfect added percussion track right off the bat. And that's something I've been doing since an album I made called *Coney Island Baby* where I used to mic the electric guitar — a mic in front of the guitar to just pick up the picking. We didn't have to do that because the Manley picked it up anyway. It's so amazing how things sound when you put them together. On "Finish Line," you'd swear there's a Jew's harp at the beginning.

Steve: We were looking for it, but it wasn't on the tape.

Lou: It got to the point where we went out and got a Jew's harp. I thought since we hear it maybe we can define it better by actually playing it, but none of us could play it and we were saying, "Who do you know that plays Jew's harp?" Then we said, "Oh forget it."

Bob: You could look at your 802 book.

Lou: We finally figured out which instrument it was — it was the high end of the bass,

I think *in* with the electric guitars. When they blended together, a fourth sound came out that separated. There's like this fourth force! Well it's there, leave it alone. We got a guy playing the Jew's harp in there...great!

Bob: How much guitar layering was there on the album? Every guitar sound on the album is you?

Lou: Yes.

Steve: Not a lot of layering, though. The thing was, we did a lot of stereo guitar recording. I recorded a lot of the amps in stereo. So they sound bigger and they're very real sounding.

Lou: "Egg Cream" sounds like it's more than one guitar, but it's just one guitar and seven mics! People have said to me, who is playing the other two guitars? It's just one...

Bob: ...in real time!

Lou: Yeah! The most layering occurs at the very end of the album — that's four guitars at the end of "Twilight." That's the most.

Steve: When Lou wanted to play through his big giant cabinets — he has a really great Soldano and a Cornish cabinet — those guitars were done at the Magic Shop, 'cause he obviously would have been evicted! There were at somewhere around 150 dB.

Victor Victorious

How I broke my new band in my project studio

By Alex Lifeson

Originally appeared in May 1996

Alex Lifeson is lead guitarist for the famed power trio Rush. He recently went on the other side of the board and did his first producing gig for his new band, Victor. The recording was done at Lifeson's project studio, and here he discusses how it was done.

We finished the last Rush tour in May of '94 and Geddy [Lee, bassist and lead singer] and his wife had a baby girl a week later. He really wanted to spend a year off the road with her. And Neil [Peart, drummer], as always, had a number of things on his agenda, so our break stretched out to 18 months. I just couldn't see myself sitting around for a year-and-a-half not doing anything, so Victor was born.

I'd always talked about doing a solo record, so it was really the opportunity for me to put my money where my mouth was. I dove in head first with no real plans for what I wanted. I knew I would need about a year to do everything I needed to accomplish, so I set some goals for myself and I just worked it out day-by-day.

Studio Scene

I have a studio, Lerxst Sound, here at home, so it was only natural to do all the recording here. My studio is outfitted with a Mackie 32-channel 3208 console, four ADATs, and Acoustic Research AR18's and DynAudio monitors. Everything is powered by Bryston power amps. I have an assortment of microphones, including Sennheiser 421's, and Neumann U 87's and KM 84's. For guitar, I use the 421's and Shure SM57's. I picked up a Shure SM7 for vocals, which is really a great vocal mic because you can get right on it and it sounds clear and warm.

I also have a pretty big assortment of compressors including a Trident Audio, a couple of UREI 1176's, and a Brooks Siren. For effects, I'm using a couple of T.C. Electronic 2290's, the TC 1210 spatial expander, a 15-year-old Lexicon 224, a Lexicon PCM 70 for additional reverb, and Neve 1073 EQ strips, which I like to use primarily for guitar.

I also have a Digidesign Pro Tools 16-channel digital system with Emagic Logic Audio that I'm running off of a Macintosh Power PC 7100 with two 1 GB drives. I prefer to record in more traditional ways rather than doing it on the computer, but it's a real benefit to do the writing and arranging on the hard-disk system. I'd sit down and I'd fool around with a guitar idea, establish it, and then I'd lay down a basic drum pattern that I could play to for tempo more than anything. I'd thrown down a couple of tracks of guitar, a track of guide bass, then I'd do any sequenced stuff — keyboards or any additional drum sounds that I wanted to do as the song developed — and then all my cut-and-paste editing would be done on the computer. Once that was established, I would transfer all the guide tracks over to ADAT and run the BRC on the ADATs through SMPTE with the sequencing program so that I could fly in any additional things I'd do afterwards with keyboards. From there, I would rerecord all the other instruments.

Things With Strings

For my guitar sound, I used a 50- and 100-watt Marshall JCM 800, and one of the 6300 Anniversary series that I use with Rush live. I also used a DigiTech GSP 2101 Studio tube preamp that I ran direct through a Palmer PDI05 speaker simulator.

The Palmer's really great; it's warm and it has got a couple of variables that you can dial in. The 2101 was probably the most valuable piece of equipment I had for recording guitar. With any kind of guitar sounds I got through the amps, the 2101 seemed to knit them all together, warmed them up, and made them more focused in terms of sound. With this new Rush record we're working on, I'm using the 2101 on just about every song for that same reason — it just seems to glue everything together into the perfect mono track.

I miked the guitars in the room, but I ended up building a little enclosure for them. Because the room is basically a square, there's lots of standing waves and the reverberation is really weird. I put up all kinds of pieces of carpeting and anything I could find to deaden the room a little bit, and it was close miked so I wasn't really relying on the room to add any character to the sound. However, I could still hear the room when I had it set up, so I built an enclosure for the cabinets out of foam padding, carpeting, and pieces of Styrofoam to deaden the reflection. I ran the mics through the Neve strips to warm up the sound just a bit. The Mackie is a great console — it's very clean, very clear, and very quiet, but the EQ on it for something like guitars is just a little tough to handle. It tends to be a little bit brittle and a little hard-edged, and the Neves just help to warm that up.

Quite often, I had the two Marshalls going as well as the 2101, and I'd just find balances and maybe make slight EQ changes. I tend to not EQ too much. I'd rather move the mics around until I got the sound I wanted and then make small EQ changes from there. I find that it's a little more controllable. From there I would fiddle around with the mix of all those components.

I would lay down a rhythm track with a Les Paul [guitar] and then I would double that. Then I'd lay down two tracks of Fender Telecaster, again, just to give the impression of one big guitar sound. I find that with the Tele/Les Paul combination I get all the clarity, top end, and edge from the Tele, and the Les Paul adds that nice round bottom. Not everything was like that, but generally that's my rule, to build up the guitar presence that way.

All the acoustic tracks were direct. I had a Fishman stick-on transducer pickup that I used on the mandola, as well as on all the other acoustic instruments. Plus, I have a couple of Ovations that I either ran direct into the console or through the 2101 on a clean sound and fiddled around with it a bit. This technique started out as being convenient at the writing stage: I could just pick up the acoustic, stick the pickup on, plug it in, and get an idea of how the acoustic part would work. However, I found that with a little bit of time spent on shaping the sound, I could get the kind of character that I wanted out of the acoustic. I could hear the pick against the strings a little more than I would have by doing it traditionally, plus it was slightly more aggressive and more present doing it that way.

The Producer's Life(son)

Producing the Victor album was a liberating and clarifying experience. Becoming so focused on the material and the mental image of the finished work, I felt a great sense of control. In Rush, we've always worked with a coproducer and made decisions among the four of us. Being completely in charge was both exciting and refreshing. I would very much enjoy working with other artists as a producer. The most important lesson I've learned after working with the producers Rush has used over the years is to be sensitive to how the musicians hear and feel their music, and not interfere with this basic energy and vision. A good producer will enhance all these characteristics and retain that special quality that makes the artist unique. It is, after all, their music, and the producer's job is to make sure they hear it in the best way possible.

—*Alex Lifeson*

Rule of Drum

I used an Electro-Voice RE-20 and the 421 on the kick drum. Again, the RE-20 had a nice bottom end to it and the 421 has got that "smack in the mids" that worked out quite well within the limitations of the room. I used couple of AKG C414's as overheads, and a KM84 on the hi-hats. I miked the top and the bottom of the snare with 57's, and 421's were used on the toms. I split the 421's so I would have one 421 on the two top toms and two separate 421's on the two floor toms.

As for the bass, I used a Gallien-Krueger single 15-inch front-loaded cabinet with an SVT head (both on direct), miked with a 421. In retrospect, I think I lost a little of the deep bottom end on the bass sound. Perhaps if I used different mics I could have gotten some of that back. I think I was going for a sound that was a little more "middly" and sat in the track a little more clearly rather than filling that bottom.

In the Mix

When I started the mixing process, I bumped everything over from the ADAT onto 2-inch analog. I hit the tape pretty hard because I thought I might be able to get a little bit of warmth out of it. When it was all said and done — on Ampex 499 tape with Dolby SR — I didn't really find that much difference between what I had on the ADATs and what I ended up with on analog tape. It's much more convenient to work on Studer multitrack machines. The transports on the ADAT are slow, and going back and forth is a bit of a headache. So that was really the main reason for doing that transfer.

When I went to McClear Pathe to mix, I did the first few mixes through Apogee filters, and maybe I was hitting the Apogees a little too hard, but I found that it softened the sound and made it kind of "spongey." So I ended up going back and redoing those mixes, and then I started taking mixes out because I wasn't happy with the bottom end, so I went back in once again. I remixed the record a total of three times. I intended to spend about two and a half weeks mixing. I figured that gave me a little bit more than a day per track. I ended up spending a month, and I worked six days a week from 11 a.m. to 3 a.m.

I tried to be very careful with the guitar mixing. If I were to remix the record, I think I would try to find a bit more of a balance between the rhythms that I mixed up front and the leads that I sort of buried. I didn't want the solos to feel like, "Here's the solo — it's in your face." I wanted the sonic impression of it to be tied more deeply into the song and with what's happening with the rhythm track and more knitted with everything that's going on. I don't know if that always works, and maybe I was a little bit oversensitive in downplaying that aspect. Certainly on a song like "Mr. X," I think the main lead guitar line is a little too low in the mix, but you learn from these things. At the same time, when I listen to that song, I find myself leaning forward, and there's this sense of being wrapped around the music when I do that. So, perhaps I did create an impression.

I'd certainly like to do another project like this. Whether it's a Victor project, I won't know until the time comes. I want to keep an open slate and just start on it on the first day and not think about it that much. I'd love to do some soundtrack work and I'd love to do some production. But, since the new Rush record is winding down to an end, and touring always follows, it's going to be quite a while. Maybe. Sleep tight, Victor.

With a Little Help From My Friends

A combination of many studios and talents help me finish my record the way I wanted to

By Jason Miles

Originally appeared in February 1992

I grew up listening to some really amazing music: Miles Davis, Wes Montgomery, Hendrix, the Butterfield Blues Band, etc. And it's my quest to keep that quality of music alive. That was my main concern when I was offered a deal to make my most recent record, *Mr. X* (now available on Lightyear Records). I've worked on some pretty big-budget projects and I know the value of being able to do a record in a great commercial studio. Making *Mr. X* was a great challenge because I had to figure out a way to keep the quality very high with a budget that was very modest for making the kind of record I needed to make. I realized that mixdown is probably the most important part of a project, so I planned to record as much as I could at home and then mix in a room that would really tell the truth.

I used ADATs on my first record, and after I saw the XTs at the AES show, I decided to get a couple. We're in a time where there is so much gear available, it's ridiculous, and it's up to your creativity as to how to use it. I am a big proponent of sample CDs — you can have the greatest band in the world playing with you if you work it out right. I had all these resources like *Steve Gadd Drum Scores* (which I helped produce), *Psychic Horns, Marcus Miller: Bass Legend, Bashiri Johnson's Supreme Beats*, and *Raphael Padilla's Percussion Slam*. These have loops and grooves on them and it was like, "Wow — look at all these people I can get playing on my records without even leaving my house!"

I ran my loops and percussion on my Akai MPC3000 and Emulator IV, which has 100 MB in it. Although these are both samplers, the MPC3000 is also a beautiful sequencer/drum machine. I can get a grip on my tracks by knowing everything is right in those two machines. I also have an Apple PowerBook with Opcode Vision, but I ended up really just using the MPC because the feel was right.

I recorded all of the instruments and keyboard parts down on the XTs — but you just can't throw it down on tape. It's got to be on tape *right* — especially when you do it at home.

You don't want somebody listening to your tracks at mixdown and finding that they're all buzzing and humming. My studio is properly grounded to keep everything quiet. I have a massive synth system here — three racks of synths, a workstation, master keyboard, Ensoniq TS-12, and about 20 keyboards. I have a Soundcraft Spirit 32 x 8, a couple of Ensoniq DP4's, some dbx 160x's, and a Yamaha SPX90.

One of the most important things — and this is no joke — is that you have to spend money on a mic and a mic pre. There's none of this, "I'm recording my stuff with a $150 microphone." I bought a Microtech Gefell UM 70 (which is a wonderful mic) and John Hardy mic pres. Whenever I've had people here at my studio and recorded them into the mic and pres, it sounded great. I had musicians like Victor Bailey, Lisa Fischer, D-Train, Bill Washer, and Dean Brown come in and their tracks came out great because of the microphone. I monitored through Tannoy NFM 10's and Yamaha NS-10M's. I like listening and recording with the Tannoys and actually putting it all together on the Yamahas.

I definitely took the time to clean up the tracks as much as I could along the way. Most of the time it was right after I had recorded an artist because I didn't want to waste time while they were recording. Basically, I would solo it out track by track after the artist left while it was fresh in my head — rather than going back and looking for it later. It's part of your daily chore. Before mixdown I went over the tapes for every song, made sure that I had all the parts I needed, and got any remaining noises out. I don't believe in fixing it in the mix. I think that whenever you say that, trouble is looming.

Most people say, "Jason, when I get your tracks, I put them up and they are ready to go." They are not worrying about how to fix this or that. And if I'm going to use great people like Frank Filipetti and Doug Oberkircher to mix the record, I don't want to waste their time or my money having them fix tracks. That's baloney. I learned from watching engineers come in during the beginning of the day, clean up the tracks, and erase little bits that don't belong. I also learned that when the tape is not recording, don't have the recorder in RECORD, because then there is more noise on tape. So I always make sure that when I'm not recording, I'm always out of RECORD.

The Real Thing

There were five songs from *Mr. X* that needed real drums, so I bounced them to 2-inch and worked off that. I would bring the tapes around with me to get musicians like Steve Ferrone, Chris Parker, Herbie Mann, Jay Beckenstein, and Michael Brecker to play, because I could go to where they were. I also had friends like Ivan Lins in Brazil who I wanted to work with. Ivan wrote some tunes for Miles Davis that Miles never recorded and I had a tape of them. I picked out two that I really loved the most and I did those. I knew Ivan wanted to sing on one of them, so I put all the backing tracks on ADAT and sent him an ADAT slave tape. He went into his studio in Brazil, did his vocal, and sent me back the ADAT tape.

I have another friend named Sussan Deyhim who is one very special person with an amazing voice. I wanted to work with her as well, so I sent an ADAT to her in London and told her, "Write anything you want on top of this, because I'll pick out what I want, sample it, and make it work." She did that and sent it back to me, and we put together this tune called "Prophecy." Once I got material back on tape from people, I had to hone through it and put together performances. With Ivan, I had to figure out what tracks I liked the best and comp them in the Emulator. I did all the comps at home by myself and took my time without worrying about the clock.

But not everybody got just tapes from me. It was February and the New York winter really sucked, so my wife and I figured that we had enough frequent flyer miles to get out to L.A. and stay with some friends while we worked on the record. We needed a live room to record drums (which I couldn't do at home) and there were people I wanted to play on the record that couldn't get out to New York. So I took my ADAT tapes with me and found a modest studio in L.A. called Skip Saylor Recording that had ADAT XTs and a 2-inch machine. I'd send out tapes for people to listen to ahead of time and then they'd come in to record their parts. I was working with musicians like Marcus Miller (who had done many records with me in the past), Janis Siegel, Ricardo Silviera, and Buzzy Feiten.

After months of working, I had all the tracks in order and it was time to mix. I sent rough mixes to two or three people that I trust to get some feedback. I called Frank Filipetti (one of my really good friends) who I think is one of the most brilliant engineers ever in the history of music. Frank mixed *People* for me (my previous record), and his ears are worth their weight in gold. He mixed six tunes, one of which ("Cara's Theme") was originally from *People*. I asked Doug to mix the next six songs.

I believe in using any studio because they are going to have great compressors, reverbs, automation, and a great room that you can mic (for natural ambience or reverb). You shouldn't be doing it at your house. I decided to mix all of the tunes at BearTracks in Suffern, NY, and we mixed 11 tunes in seven days. This is a lot of music to mix in a short time — partly because of the not "fixing it in the mix" thing. The bottom line is that I took my Emulator IV, my two ADATs, MPC3000, EIIIx, and also an Ensoniq ASR-10 into the studio and basically plugged my studio into their studio.

For some of the tunes that ran off of 2-inch, I had to slave the BRC to tape — which is a scary thing to do, but it worked really well. Some of the tracks were run virtual. We used a DB Electronics A-to-D before the DAT machine, and that really made the mixes sound great. When I ran my ADATs without 2-inch, we would mult the SMPTE output from the BRC so that the automation and MIDI tracks would chase the BRC.

Finally it came to the mastering. Greg Calbi at Masterdisk mastered it for me and the mastering engineer is the final component in the chain. People are mastering on Pro Tools and that's cool, but you have to be a guy that knows how to master a record. When you get into a place like Masterdisk and you finally listen on such a high-resolution system, it's a way different story. Nobody has that kind of playback system in their home or even most studios. So I thought, "Here's my chance to listen to my record through $20,000 speakers." Hopefully there aren't any surprises (there weren't) because when it's over, it's over! Greg did a great mastering job and at this point, I can't ask for anything more. I've definitely hit a stride with this record and I am happy with the results.

Jason Miles is a producer and composer who in the last few years has worked with artists such as Peabo Bryson, Sounds Of Blackness, Vanessa Williams, Suzy Bogguss, Chaka Khan, and Ann Wilson. As a keyboardist and synth programmer, he has worked on projects with artists such as Miles Davis, Marcus Miller, Luther Vandross, and David Sanborn. Miles was also nominated for an Emmy Award for the theme song from "Children of the World."

Sloppy Seconds

Some suggestions for up-and-coming engineers

By Phil Ramone

Originally appeared in August 1998

Does "sloppy seconds" refer to picking up the scraps and eating lunch after the Big Famous Engineer has eaten? Or could it really mean "How do I possibly read these track sheets? I'm sure you were never taught to write a general track sheet for live dates...."

When confronted with such a situation, Engineer #2 often says, "I didn't do the original date." A phone call to the original studio (to get more information) is answered with, "#2 is off today." So we sit and watch the meters for signs of life...It appears OK to use those seemingly empty tracks for another instrument, so let's go ahead. But surprise! Remember those two vocal endings that were recorded on what was to be the empty horn tracks? Whoops. Uh-oh. The artist is gone for the day and was certain the vocal ending was great. And now the New Big Famous Engineer spurts words not found in any dictionary.

Is this scenario happening too often? A few years of servitude in the "minor leagues" of internships just might be necessary for Engineer #2 to break in by helping established engineers and producers. Twenty or 25 years ago, there was no such thing as a recording school, so we played in the minor leagues before we could get into the majors. You were trained in a big studio like a Power Station or an A&R, and worked from the tape room all the way up to engineer. By the time you got to be on a date with a Frank Fillipetti or an Al Schmitt, you were pretty well trained. If you didn't accept the training, then you wouldn't get the opportunity to work on those kind of sessions.

Great Expectations

Unfortunately, there are a lot of people who expect to sit in the chair of the first engineer without first being an apprentice and really knowing what's going on. Instead of thinking about how important it is to do a good take sheet, he doesn't pay much attention to that kind of stuff, so things get sloppy. Some people attend a recording school, but that doesn't necessarily open a magic door. I'm not knocking recording schools, because most are responsible, but the desire to learn isn't always there in the students. I have spoken to some students who say, "We have this old crappy console." I ask, "But does it sound OK?" "Yes, but you know, it's not automated." Understand that you have to pilot that thing and position microphones in the right place. Your degree does not mean that an internship is not needed.

No Sheet

We no longer make records by ourselves in one studio — we share material all over the world. As a producer, I'm liable to pick up DA-88 tapes that have been recorded by an engineer in one studio, overdubbed with another engineer in a second studio, and then rough-mixed in a third studio with yet another engineer. I get tapes without proper track sheets or take sheets, and sometimes the timecode doesn't work. Studios and #1 engineers need to unite so that responsibility can be shared. We ask a lot of assistants. We need to explain our needs, and the importance of DATs and cassettes. In this day and age, it may be wise to learn digital editing and tuning.

Pilot to Copilot

Many years ago — before automation — the #2 was the copilot; a second hand on the faders was helpful. Tape machines were also the responsibility of the #2, and I recall a session where #2 erased a phrase. I realized he was only looking at numbers on the tape time readout, so when the tach slipped, we had a disaster. Learning song structure (verse, chorus, turnarounds, and bridges) is an important start since the "VU watchers" have their hands full.

Is it imperative to be better than the #1? Yes. And save his back when he gets in trouble? Surgeons rely upon assistants to do this every day. As a #2, producers closely watch your attitude, and your ego will soon be fed when you become the most in-demand #2. After being the Number One #2 for a while, you can make the step into being a #1. I got into the #1 spot because the then-#1 was late for a session — so I took over. The relationship with the artist and the producer was nervous, but I had been trained by the #1, and knew what to do.

Chain of Command

It's a good idea for a #2 to remember who booked the room and put together the recording team. It's artist first, producer next, #1, and then #2. When the engineer is tired and the producer wants to stay late, you have a brief opportunity to temporarily move up a notch and take a chance at engineering. What's that? You have a date with the "most adorable" in town? Choose one. You choose to be of help? You'll have to apologize to the adorable one. It's your chance to do things like comp the vocal, or do some vocal fly-ins, tune the vocal — be successful! By the way, it's not cool to be reading the manual.

#2's Rights

As a hard-working #2, you may ask yourself if you're being violated or if this is the best part of "school." Things you are required to learn include open heart and brain surgery, basic psychotherapy, and knowing where to find good food (you also need to learn how to work 20-hour days on three hours of sleep). If you're a complete #2, the phone is also your gig — fielding calls like an all-star shortstop. Responsibility? You bet. Dues? You bet. Will you become famous? That's up to your ambition and your ability to listen for what's needed. As Quincy Jones says, "Check your ego at the door."

Did all the #1's do the same crap you are asked to do? Yes. If you don't like the music you're recording, stay cool. Not everything you do will be your favorite. Does your opinion count? First check the room temperature and then respond when asked. People respect a #2 that shows interest even if Lithuanian folk songs seem boring to everyone else. Being unprepared or blaming the studio because they were late in getting your room back does *not* belong on the #1's or producer's table. Keep interior problems inside the company, and *never badmouth the studio.*

Truth or Consequences

Lying about your qualifications is certainly not an answer. I remember a session I did about ten years ago with a #2 that was highly recommended and had worked with some very famous engineers. He walked into my session about five minutes before it was supposed to start. I said to him, "Don't you think it's a little pushy not being here an hour before the session?" As he started to put up the microphones on a set of drums, I realized that he was searching his memory to remember how somebody famous had wired the drums in a past session. So I said, "Hey man, I'd be happy to help you." It was obvious that he was more used to direct patching. OK, but it's also important to know acoustic recording. What was missing from the #2 was a willingness to learn the basics.

The Commandments

If you have to be away from work for two days out of the project, be kind to your sub. He'd like to succeed and never have to hear about how stupid he was when you continue working on the project (or vice-versa). For both of you, that means keeping accurate session notes. Know thy patchbay.

Think about this: When you write down a patch, can it be easily figured out after you're gone? Note the mic on a vocal session so you can match the sound when it comes time to do some fixing. If it's vintage, also note the serial number, because they do sound different (the same can be said for vintage processors). In addition to writing down the patch flow, mark the settings of the devices, either by saving a program into memory or using a picture of the front panel (photocopy from the manual) to indicate knob positions. Study how comps are made. Sometimes you should comp using the board, because adjusting levels and EQ can make the roughs and final mix a joy. Reverbs help the artist feel good, but be careful about soloing a vocal in the control room. It should be done with no guests or musicians in the control room.

Probably the worst thing that could happen at a session would be missing a take. When I have a group of musicians playing together in the studio, I roll tape and never go back — I rarely rewind. It's a bad habit of mine that comes from the school of, "I can always edit that intro. It was great." Or, "I'd like to use that take even though all of the mics aren't up because there was a great feel going in the room." Some assistants will not continue to run the tape because someone, somewhere has said, "No, let's go over that take." When you have a $20,000 (or higher) payroll out there, who cares if you spent $400 on a roll of tape?

Here's where the second engineer can become extremely helpful by keeping an accurate take sheet. I used to always say, "If you're going to read a magazine in the back of the room, then obviously my date is boring." There are hours upon hours during mixing or vocal overdubs where that #2 either impresses us (or not) with how he keeps track sheets and watches the lyrics. Can he or she type a lyric? Can the assistant understand how we do comps? If they need more experience, then they should take my vocals when we leave and do their own comps. The next day they can show me how good they are.

Copilot to Pilot

It's great to have confidence in what you do, but sometimes you also have to move from copilot to pilot. Copilot is really the role that's missing in the industry, and I (as well as other engineers and producers) depend on these people. These are the people that make the dubs after the superstars go home. If I get a bad DAT or cassette as my only reference, it's not a good thing. That's why #2 is such an important job. Always be sensitive because we're all in the studio to capture the moment. When you hear a cassette of your work in a car or on a boombox and it raises the hair on *your* arm, you no longer have to fear the adjective "sloppy."

Recording for Fun & Profit

How and why I built and used my project studio to record Left of Cool

By Béla Fleck

Originally appeared in September 1998

The Problem

I used to record albums for Rounder, Warner Brothers, and others the old fashioned way, which is to say that, out of a typical recording budget, the studio and engineers would end up with the lion's share. The musicians would be rushed, and end up over budget with a finished product that we were not always proud of. The record would sell a reasonable number, but never enough for you to receive any significant royalties by the time you started the next one. Due to something evil called "crosscollateralization," any artist profit would be applied to the previous unrecouped records, and as soon as you started the new one, all costs would be applied to any previous records that were recouped. Pretty amazing, huh? So you could have a very successful career, sell up to and well over 100,000 units consistently, and still end up in the hole.

A Solution

My old friend Leo Eilts, who had been a bluegrass musician, was now also the Digidesign Pro Tools dealer in the Kansas City area. Leo told me all about the gear and it sounded like just the right thing for a live album the Flecktones were about to make. So we dove in head first, got the system, spent the studio budget on gear, and did all the edits and mixes on the computer.

The money previously spent in the studio could now go into equipment that we could keep (an asset). Future albums would be cheaper to make, allowing me to either bill for studio time or just have a lower budget. Albums would recoup sooner [even] with the same number of albums sold. I could actually show a profit on my own records!

What a concept.

Hard-Disk Recording

I had been a Neve/Flying Faders freak ever since producer friend Garth Fundis showed me what VCAs did to the sound. I could hear them on the mixes of that time. And, being a fidelity freak, I was very suspicious of the sound of hard-disk recording. As hard as I tried, however, I couldn't find anything missing except perhaps the hissing sound of tape, which

I had given up on early in the digital age. The mixing capabilities were powerful, although they took a little getting used to.

Of course, we did have some experience with hard-disk recording: We got excellent comments regarding the sound of *Live Art,* recorded live to ADATs and edited and mixed on Pro Tools. This double album also won the Grammy for Best Pop Instrumental.

The Plan

When it was time to make the next studio album, *Left of Cool,* with the Flecktones, I decided to go all the way. The *Live Art* experiment had gone well. Roger Nichols (perhaps you've heard of him?) had consulted on that project, checking on the EQ of my office/studio for accuracy, critiquing mixes, and just reassuring us that it was going to be OK. He also mastered the project. So I thought it would be really cool to have him engineer the tracking dates, which he agreed to. Roger was helpful in so many ways — basically setting up a studio from scratch in my new home. He helped hook us up with Alesis, getting prototypes of their 20-bit machines; Pro Tools, getting prototypes of Pro Tools|24; an early Apogee AD8000; and a Yamaha 02R for playback.

An extremely important part of the equation was Richard Battaglia, the Flecktones' live sound engineer, whom I have worked with for 16 years, since *New Grass Revival* days. Along with a great ability to get the most out of live performance situations, Richard works individually with band members to systematically improve their electric sounds. He built a preamp for acoustic instruments (AcH 104) that I, Sam Bush, Jerry Douglas, and many fine musicians use. Richard has become a Macintosh computer fanatic over the years, and this proved to be extremely important as we got the studio working.

Richard, the biggest Steely Dan fan on earth, also was excited about working and learning from Roger. Rich put in an incredible amount of time, handling the setup, backups, and computer in and outs. By doing so, he freed up large portions of my brain so I could be a "creative type."

Rounding out the team was Tracey Hackney who kept precise notes (with numbers) of the takes, kept a DAT reference in Record, and generally helped out.

The Musicians

Béla Fleck & the Flecktones includes Victor Lemonte Wooten all over the electric bass. On this album he also played cello and upright. His brother, Future Man, plays drums on a bizarre instrument he invented, basically triggering sounds from samplers and drum machines with his fingertips in real time. He also played acoustic percussion, including the cajon, a Latin percussion instrument that he sat on. Jeff Coffin plays all the winds. He added flute, clarinet, bass clarinet, baritone sax, and finger cymbals. I played banjo, electric synth banjo, and, occasionally, guitar or mandolin.

Setup

One of the first things Roger did was to set up a pair of Meyers HD-1 monitors. We also had a pair of Genelec's 1030A's and some Yamaha NS10M's, along with a Velodyne sub that we used sporadically to check for surprises in the low end. We inserted an Oxmoor DEQ1 digital EQ to compensate for the room, which is an "extra room" over the garage.

We ordered some monoliths of gray foam and some ASC Tube Traps. We rented a bunch of mics and mic pres and began shootouts. Roger had some BSS DI boxes that were great for Future Man's digital drum kit, which required about a dozen channels. These were routed through mic pres, something we hadn't tried before. The signals with kick or other low information seemed cut off on some pres, so we used the NightPro PreQ for these. This preamp ended up being our favorite in general, so we bought one. The Avalon was really nice for Victor's bass, although he liked the BSS DI almost as much. The Avalon 2-channel version was excellent, and we used it for banjo. On sax we used PreQ or Massenburg.

So all we were miking was banjo and sax. Banjo went in the kitchen with a couple of shotgun mics and a Sony C-800G in closer. Sax was in the dining room with an A-T 4030 and an old Neumann U 67. The walls of foam kept the sax out of the banjo mics in the next room.

Tracking

Our approach was to simply play the tune for a couple hours until we were tired of it or confident we had it. Then we would move on. We rarely listened to playbacks and we never played to a click. After a while, we did start using a click for countoffs so the tempos would match up later for edits. Sometimes we would cycle solo sections around so we could have ten or so banjo, sax, or bass solos to choose from later on, and so we could really concentrate on soloing, which is a different mind set. This way we would also end up with solos that interacted naturally with the rhythm section, which usually doesn't happen when overdubbing solos.

After playing a tune for a couple of hours, we would take some time getting the sounds and headphone mix right for the next one. For headphones, we used our Crest monitor console and bought a four-stereo-channel headphone amp from Music Row Technologies right here in Nashville.

We set up for two days, and recorded for five on the first session. A few weeks later we had a similar time allotted, of which we only used three days. We completed tracking with 21 tunes in the can.

Pro Tools|24 wasn't here in time for the first session, so we started out on the new Alesis M20 20-bit dudes and 16-bit Pro Tools as our backup. Then we would store everything from our Glyph Technologies hard drives to DLT tapes using Grey Matter's Mezzo.

On the second session we were able to use Pro Tools|24 as our master and the ADATs as our backups. Therefore, everything was at least 20-bit and much of it 24. After processing with plug-ins, it was all 24-bit info.

Alesis was kind enough to send Don Hanna with four of their babies, so we had some real good help for the first several days. At that time, these were prototypes, so there were several inevitable stressy moments where things didn't quite work. These machines had a couple of flaws that they obviously fixed immediately, but we were in session with two of the Alesis M20's going down. Suddenly Roger realized that the drums were only 16-bit anyway, so we sync'd up one of our 16-bit ADATs just for the drums, did a quick test, heard no difference, and continued onward. Roger is amazing at figuring stuff out and getting it working fast, often with brand new gear with glitches in it.

Whenever we had a couple hours' break we would get in the habit of backing up the DLTs with Mezzo. These would run all night as well.

Editing

After tracking, the band went on hiatus and Richard and I started figuring out a procedure for editing. Often this is what takes the most time — figuring out the best way to do something. Once the procedure is in place, you can really cover some ground.

I started listening to the 2-tracks of takes on airplanes and road trips. There were anywhere from seven to 21 takes on each tune. I would put together a comp chart and grade all the takes, underlining my favorite parts. As I studied the takes, it became rather obvious what the best stuff was, but I really had to get to know the material.

Then we dumped in or restored (depending on whether the masters were ADATs or DLTs) to Pro Tools and went to town. It took a day or two per edit, so I decided not to edit everything, just the stuff that seemed strongest. After the tunes were edited down, we compacted the files (a Pro Tools term for throwing away excess audio files that are no longer used in the session document), getting rid of everything we weren't likely to use. When in doubt, we made sure the additional audio could be recovered.

Sweetening

Because Future Man was going to Spain for a couple of months, I edited the tunes that he would be adding vocals to first. He did his vocals in the dining room on a C-24. We experimented a lot. I kept everything, and he left town.

Then we got into other overdubs such as synths, basses, horns and flutes, guitar, mandolin, or extra banjos. We were always adding layers, as opposed to fixing. All the basic tracks and solos came from the tracking session with no exceptions. Now we were sweetening and getting creative with what we had. Rather than bring outside people in, we did it all ourselves, which was a lot of fun.

In the past we had always taken a live approach in the studio, so this actually made the process fresh. Anybody could try anything. The only guests we did have were vocalists Dave Matthews and Amy Grant. I traded services with Dave, playing on several cuts of his DMB album, and he came and sang some for us. I think I got the better end of that deal! We had toured together, with us opening shows for Dave, and so there is a neat friendship between our groups.

Amy lives just down the road from here, so Richard suggested we ask her. She likes the sound of stacking her voice four times, so we tried that and liked it.

At every stage of the project, members of the band would drop by and OK each tune, solo, etc. If someone didn't like something, we would change it right then and there and hit "Save." This was a great benefit of the system: Anyone could contribute at any time.

Mixing

Now it was soup; mixing time had arrived. As we went along, we found reverbs, EQs, and panning we liked. We saved the plug-in stuff and kept notes on which external 'verbs were used on the sends themselves. Then we merely dialed up the right programs when we opened each tune. We used the digital 'verbs (Lexicon's PCM 80 and 90) with digital I/O, so the levels were always the same, even when we took them out on the road for shows and replaced them. We had to keep an eye on the input and output levels of the (analog) Lexicon PCM 70 and keep them the same for every song. We used the volume and pan graphs to set all the levels, automate sends, etc. I actually prefer this to faders, because you can see it and make minute changes.

Plug-ins are really cool. We used Waves and occasionally Focusrite EQs, Drawmer and Focusrite compressors, Maxxbass and TrueVerb, Waves L1 Ultramaximizer, LexiVerb, Multi-Dynamic's Tool, Antares Master Tune, DUY's DAD Valve, and the Aphex Aural Exicter.

Now it was time for Roger to come back to town and critique our mixes and solve problems. I found him to be great at clarifying things and we generally agreed on stuff. When I left the room and came back, it usually sounded better than when I left. On this project I found him to be more of an "if it ain't broke, don't fix it" type of engineer, rather than a "let's try everything and anything," which was an appropriate approach since I was doing a lot of the latter. The ability to live with something for a while, then change it once you know what's needed, is so great. Developing the mix over a period of time is also a pleasure.

I took the tapes to various places to listen and see how accurate the mixes were. In each listening setting I took notes as different things popped out. Then I went home and made minor adjustments. Garth Fundis and Justin Niebank made some good comments. Justin came over a couple of times and tried some of his ideas in terms of vocal compression and tweaks, and introduced me to the SansAmp, which we sprinkled onto a vocal and sax.

Mastering

We went into the mastering facility (Georgetown Masters with Denny Purcell) and spent a morning critically listening to the mixes. Things sounded really good, but could use some more way high up stuff. Denny found the frequencies on his board, then we went home and opened up those areas on certain reverbs and particular instruments.

We assembled a sequence one night with the whole band collaborating and turned in the record. While mastering, we were looking for stuff to do. We kept adding tiny bits of EQ and, in most cases, decided against them. There was no leveling to do. We did like the HDCD process, so we did that.

Emergency!!!

At this point we were over the length that the Warner Brothers plant would cut onto a CD (76:30), so we needed to find some edits or delete a tune. Plus, the label didn't like the sequence. We were going to lose our June release date, which coincided with some stadium gigs I was playing with the Dave Matthews Band, plus the Flecktones' Colorado tour including the Telluride Festival. It would be a real drag if the record wasn't out by then, and yet I was already out of town on tour!

Because I had Pro Tools 4.0 on my Apple PowerBook, I worked out the proposed edits and resequenced the album on a dawn flight to Nashville with Chris Palmer from Warner. I met Carlos from Georgetown Masters at my house, did all the edits to the multitracks, resequenced, and got back on a plane to Philly by 2 p.m. the same day. Carlos ran the finished master off to Sony optical, and we made our release date.

Single Edits and Remixes

With the album put to bed and Roger safely out of town, it was time to cut some of our vocal tunes down and try some creative remix ideas. We called another Nashville resident, Richard Dodd, to assist us with this project. He had considerable experience with radio as Tom Petty's engineer, and a very different approach to Pro Tools. As far as I was concerned, the singles could be quite different from the album versions and Warner Brothers was OK with that. So we dirtied stuff up, shortened, rearranged, compressed, and got loose with the stuff, eventually using the T.C. Electronic Finalizer, and sent off our singles to Warner Brothers.

Now we'll see what happens. Wish us luck.

Left of Cool *entered the Jazz Charts at #3 and remained top 5 for its first five weeks. It also entered the Billboard Top 200, the first time for Béla Fleck & the Flecktones. The single "Communication" was 3rd most added on AAA radio in its first week.*

Inside Bruce Swedien's Microphone Collection

By Steve La Cerra

Originally appeared in July 2000

Bruce Swedien is a man who loves his microphones. Not only is the size and depth of his personal collection impressive, but if you want to know how to treat and keep track of your mics, then just ask Bruce! All of his microphones are carefully packed in some of the most serious road cases I've ever seen (he recommends also putting ribbon mics into plastic and then into either their covers or cases). All cases are numbered, and Bruce has a computerized inventory indicating case number, contents, manufacturer, model number, serial number, and value of the contents. His inventory also specifies accessories that may be packed in the cases, such as power supplies and shock mounts. Seeing this system in action is a true testament to an artist and his tools.

I've seen a lot of vintage mics — but none that are so well cared for by their original owner! Here are a few of Bruce's favorites from his collection, along with his recollection of historic and important sessions they were used on and tips for getting the most out of them. Enjoy!

Bruel and Kjaer 4006

"I have a pair of these that were calibrated in Copenhagen at the factory, so they're absolutely matched. These are omnidirectional condenser mics, and I have a set of acoustic modifiers that fit over the front of the mics to change the response. Depending on which one you use, you can give the mic a boost in a certain frequency range or change the directionality of the mic slightly."

Altec 21B

"I have several of these old Altec microphones that I purchased new. They're omni condensers, which kept them from being very popular, but it's a good mic. I used it on bass a lot. I'd wrap it in foam and place it into the bridge, or I'd place it up under the fingerboard where the neck meets the body of the bass. It's a tube mic with an external power supply. A strange-looking bird. It's probably the only American-made, high-quality tube condenser microphone. The power supply looks like something from a submarine! Check out the high-pass filter: 20, 40, and 120 Hz. The mic would actually go below 20 Hz, so it was good for capturing the low end.

"You have to be real careful with these mics because you can get a shock from the case. There's somewhere around 700 volts from the B+ supply — really dangerous. If you hold it here (across the cable connector and the mic body) you can act as the conductor between the mic and the ground, which is not a good idea! You can see one of these in the movie *An Affair to Remember*."

Royer SF-12

"Royer has done a tremendous job in furthering the cause of ribbon microphones. I have three of their mics, a pair of R-121 (mono) mics and the SF-12 stereo mic, which is gorgeous. I don't know exactly how the SF-12 is different from the R-121, but it sounds a little different tonally from the mono mic. The difference is maybe more in spectrum than in color. To my ear, the stereo mic is a bit brighter. They're both velocity mics. The R-121 is bidirectional, and the stereo is two bidirectionals in an XY pattern. I use it as a coincident pair, like it's two mics. I absolutely love these mics.

"You know how I feel about ribbon mics, and I was excited when they came out with this because one of my favorite ribbon mics was the B&O (Bang and Olufsen) ribbon. I have a couple of them, but they're in terrible shape and can't be repaired. It's good to see Wes Dooley and the guys at Royer working so hard to come up with these new ribbon mics. The guys at Royer keep telling me, 'Put them in front of a guitar amp. You can't blow them up.' But I would never do that with a ribbon. That's sacrilege. I told them forget it. I am not doing that!

"I used the SF-12 to close-mic congas and timbales for the Cyrius project. With pop music, I like to get in close so that the sound is in-your-face."

Shure SM7

"At one point I had about five of these mics. This particular mic is serial number 5210, and was the first SM7 that I bought. The ones I purchased after this one don't quite sound the same. This is the one I used on *Thriller*." Bruce looks up his session notes on *Thriller* and informs us, "I used it for all the vocals on the title song, 'Pretty Young Thing,' and probably 'Billie Jean.' For 'Pretty Young Thing,' the mic was very close.

"The U 47 windscreens fit over the SM7 perfectly, so I put one of those right over this mic. The foam on the SM7 is more of a cover for the element than a windscreen. Even though it's more of a cosmetic thing, it should not ever be removed. For Michael, it worked perfectly.

"I also used it on James Ingram with great success for 'Just Once.' It sounds wonderful on James. The main thing with James was that I didn't want the slick, space-age studio sound of a condenser mic, and this worked perfectly."

Audio Engineering Associates (AEA) 44C

"This is Wes Dooley's new re-creation of the RCA 44BX. The 44C ribbon is an incredible mic for vocals. I recorded Cyrius singing a soft ballad on his new album with one of these fabulous mics. I placed the artist about ten inches away from the mic, and, of course, I used a windscreen. I wanted to get a bit of the lovely proximity effect that the 44C has in abundance. I bought these recently and found that they're wonderful mics, but, like all ribbon mics, they're very sensitive to air movement. They have to be stored in plastic — you even need to be careful when closing the lid of a case on them because the ribbon could be stretched. That'll damage the high end; the ribbon is slightly corrugated, and, if you lose some tension in it, the high end suffers."

RCA 77DX

"I purchased these 77DX's new after I had purchased the 44BX's, probably sometime around 1957 or 1958. They're a few serial numbers apart. This particular pair has a low-luster 'umber' finish to reduce light reflection in TV studios. This was an attempt by RCA to make a directional ribbon microphone — at which they failed. It's very hard to make a truly directional ribbon.

"I love these on trombones. I place them pretty close to the bell — there's no problem with air blasts unless you shove the mic into the bell."

Neumann U 47 FET

[When Bruce pulled these out, I almost fainted. His U 47 FET's are absolutely immaculate — like they just came from the factory. Someone please get me a box of tissues, because I'm gonna cry!]

"I think that the U 47 FET was an attempt by Neumann to replace the tube '47 or at least to come out with something similar in appearance and sound quality. It uses the same capsule, but it's a field-effect transistor amplifier. I purchased mine quite some time ago from Neumann (like most of my mics, I purchased these new). I love these mics, and one of my favorite applications for them is on trombone. I recently recorded a trombone player from Stockholm named Nils Landgren with these mics. As far as I'm concerned, Nils Landgren is the baddest trombone dude on the planet. I get in real close, and the U 47 FET can take the sound level without a problem."

Neumann M 149

"The project at Egram was when I fell in love with the Neumann M 149. I have a pair of M 49's that are great, but they're a little hard to keep in perfect shape. Sonically, the M 149's are close to the '49's — maybe a little brighter. The M 49 has an output transformer, but the M 149 doesn't, though the '149 is a valve [tube] mic. For historical purposes, I wanted sequential serial numbers. With the newer Neumann mics you can buy them many serial numbers apart and they'll sound exactly the same. Vintage mics are all over the place due to the PVC diaphragms. I used the M 149's all over *Le Sang des Roses* with Cyrius: strings, horns, the girl singers, and a lot of lead vocal."

RCA 44BX

"I purchased two of these new in 1956 for around $395 each — a lot of money back then! They're about ten serial numbers apart. You might remember a vocal group called the Hi-Lo's, a very popular close-harmony group that recorded for Columbia Records. I used one of these 44BX's with the four singers around the mic, two on each side. These two have been re-ribboned by Clarence Kane in New Jersey, but they haven't been restored. They're in the original, excellent condition.

"With this mic, if you get closer than three feet to the sound source, proximity effect is going to be quite conspicuous. They're not high-output mics, and if you have to go for a lot of EQ, you're going to have a noise problem. If the mic is in good condition, it won't be a problem, but you do need a sensitive mic pre with low noise, like a Neve or an Avalon.

"A lot of my old big band recordings were made using these 44's, not to mention a few recordings for Quincy Jones and the Seawind horns. When you set up this mic, don't set it perpendicular to the floor. Tilt it forward slightly so that gravity puts a little sag in the ribbon. That way, you'll get about a dB or so of free, no-noise, 10 kHz EQ."

Brauner VM1

"The best use I have found for the Brauner VM1 is as a vocal microphone. It's a three-pattern tube condenser mic with very low noise, and the construction is beautiful! On certain voices it's wonderful. It can be a bit bright, so it's best for a voice that isn't overly sibilant. It has a nice degree of proximity effect, so if the singer works the mic a bit, you can get some free low-end EQ without noise or distortion. It can work in a very intense sound field, and has an incredibly wide spectrum."

This prompted me to ask Bruce if he felt certain mics were better-suited to male or female vocalists. "I don't think it's a male/female thing. I think it's a timbre thing. I have recorded both male and female voices that have an edge or brightness that ribbon mics would work great with. But on other voices you wouldn't dare use a ribbon mic because it'd be too dark."

The Power and the Beauty

Bruce Swedien shares his thoughts on working in Cuba, the analog versus digital debate, and his project studio

By Bruce Swedien as told to Steve La Cerra

Originally appeared in July 2000

Approximately six years ago, world-class producer/engineer Bruce Swedien moved from California to a new home on the East Coast. Naturally, Bruce has a studio in his home, known as Westviking Farm. He's worked on numerous projects there, such as A Guitarra *by renowned Portuguese guitar virtuoso Antonio Chainho (Movieplay Records of Portugal, 1998),* 5000 Miles *by Nils Landgren (ACT Records, 1999), and* Les Go — Dan Gna *by the Ivory Coast-African group Les Go (Juna Records, 2000). In October of last year, Bruce mixed a new single at Westviking Farm for the rock band Survivor. His most recent projects there were mixing* Pasajes de un Sueno *for BMG artist Ana Torroja, and the as-yet-untitled release for Sony-France artist Cyrius.*

Until lately, Bruce's studio was based primarily around analog tape technology, but for these most recent projects he stepped into the digital arena with impressive results. In this article he discusses why and how he and studio accomplice Andres Levin used a mixture of technology to record and mix both the Ana Torrja and Cyrius albums.

Home Sweet Home

Here at my home studio, Westviking Farm, I've just completed a major project for Sony Music from a world-class singer and songwriter by the name of Cyrius. Cyrius's music is absolutely wonderful, and he's one of the most fantastic artists I've ever worked with. That's not easy to say because, as you may know, I've recorded some of music's most remarkable artists! The producers of the project are myself and Andres Levin. Originally from Caracas, Venezuela, Andres has produced tracks with Caetano Veloso, kd lang, Carlinhos Brown, Tina Turner, and David Byrne.

Since Andres is now based in Manhattan, we have worked together on a number of projects. Andres says he finds mixing in my studio very relaxing and soulful, with Bea, my wife, supervising the hospitality aspect of the activities. All of us involved in the work have dinner together as a family every evening; I know that this feeling of oneness has had an inspiring effect on the music.

Until a few months ago, my studio revolved almost completely around analog technology. The centerpiece of my room is a beautiful old Harrison 32C desk from 1979. It's essentially the same desk I used for Michael Jackson's *Thriller* (though that particular desk was a very early 32 Series). When I bought this desk five years ago, it was literally unused, so I consider myself very lucky to have found such a gem. First and foremost, I'm committed to using this console due to its wonderfully musical sound. Needless to say, I am very familiar with operating the console, knowing where every button lies. To me, it's important to be able to react instinctively to the music I am involved with. I don't like to interrupt the creative process to get the technical process going. If I have to pause to think out the signal path every time I want to make an adjustment to the sound of the music, by the time I have it under my fingers, the musical inspiration has more than likely vanished. In my opinion, gut reactions translated to popular music recordings make the most meaningful recordings. I always felt that pop music is an emotional experience, not an intellectual experience.

My Harrison console has been fitted with Geoff Michaels's Virtual Faders VCA automation for ease of mixing. It's an absolute joy to use — very powerful — and makes my old Harrison behave like it's almost "state-of-the art." My main recorders are a Sony/MCI JH-24 2-inch, 24-track machine as well as an Ampex ATR-102, which I purchased new quite a few years ago (we'll talk more about the ATR-102 in a little while).

Many *EQ* readers might already be familiar with my love for the sound of analog recording — it has a "beauty" that I don't always hear with digital recording. It can be elegant. To my ears, analog tape has wonderful proportion and symmetry. In all aspects of music recording, I have never been intensely interested in technical specifications. I have always been intensely interested in how the sound of the music affects my soul.

At the other end of the spectrum from my analog world is the digital world. In all fairness, I must say that what the digital recording medium does well, it does *dramatically* well. On this subject there's really no room for discussion. For instance, digital recording is very robust and consistent. Every time you play back a digital recording it sounds the same — which is not necessarily true of an analog recording. Running an analog master tape over and over again during the overdub and mixing processes can wear the tape somewhat, resulting in a loss of high frequencies and transient response. With a digital recording, this is not a concern. When digital recordings are stored to hard disk, there's an added advantage of random access to the audio — I don't even have to wait for the tape to rewind!

With the refinement of high-resolution digital recording formats, the line of distinction between analog and digital recording methods is beginning to disappear. For the two most recent projects, Andres and I put together a rather large 24-bit Digidesign Pro Tools system right here in my beautiful little studio. Andres feels that, with the 24-bit Pro Tools rig, we have the best of both worlds because we can experiment with arrangements and processing right up to and including the mixdown process — but still mix without looking at a computer screen.

Havana, Here We Come!

Cyrius's album is a combination of Cuban music with French lyrics. We had the opportunity to record all the basics and most of the overdubs at Egrem Studios in Havana, Cuba during January, March, and April 2000. The musicians we used for the project are some of Cuba's finest players, including Guillermo Rubalcaba (piano), Changuito and Don Pancho (percussion), Pancho Amado (tres), and Roberto Caracaser (arrangements), among many others. Almost 30 of Cuba's finest musicians participated in the album.

The first thing I had to do when I got there was to spend a whole day re-EQ'ing the control room, repositioning the large monitors, and testing all the lines and channels. We recorded straight to a great-sounding Studer A-80 analog 2-inch, through Egrems's Amek/Mozart mixing desk.

Egrem is the studio where all the great Cuban recordings have been made, not to mention Ry Cooder's legendary production of the *Buena Vista Social Club* in 1996. This has been the #1 recording studio in Havana since the 1940s. The room has so much sonic personality that it comes through even when close-miking. When 'Dre [Andres Levin] and I walked into the room and heard the rhythm section rehearsing, we just hit the floor — we knew immediately it was a great-sounding room. We were told that a lot of history was made in that studio since the 1940s and 1950s, and no one has touched it since. It's literally like the day it was made. The roof has a few leaks, so there are buckets sitting around the studio floor with cloth in them — so they don't go "clink" when a water drop hits them! The room doesn't look that great, but if you're into the sound of music, it'll grab your heart immediately. It is one of the best-sounding rooms I have ever recorded in, anywhere in the world.

All the basic tracks were recorded live to 2-inch tape with no click track. At that point in the project we didn't even put SMPTE on the tape! For the second trip to Havana (in March and April), we brought a 1970s Korg Rhythm machine to use as a time reference on a couple of the songs that we would later edit in Pro Tools. When we returned to New York, we transferred all the 2-inch analog tape to Pro Tools at Kampo Studios in New York. We used Kampo's SSL MT Axiom digital mixing desk for its exceptional analog-to-digital converters.

Once in the digital domain, we did final overdubs at The Fun Machine in Manhattan (Andres's place) and my Westviking Farm. For the overdub recordings in both places, we used Neve Class A 1084 EQ/preamps and Neve Class A 1066 EQ/preamps. When we finished about half the overdubbing, I started mixing. A day or so later, Andres drove up to the farm from New York, with all the new overdubs on a hard drive. We popped them into the mix and continued mixing.

We have five Digidesign 888/24 I/Os, a Mark of the Unicorn MIDI Timepiece AV, and a Digidesign Universal Slave Driver for synchronization. The SMPTE flow is very simple and straightforward: out of the computer through the SSD (SMPTE Slave Driver) straight to the Harrison. We would slide the start of each song forward so that the music would start 20 to 30 seconds in, giving the Virtual Faders automation system a bit of pre-roll before the music started.

Recently, we heard about using the Aardvark external digital clock with our Pro Tools system. So we got one and compared the sound of our music from Pro Tools with and without Aardvark. We were instantly convinced! With the Aardvark, the sound has a much improved clarity.

Andres uses a Pro Tools rig based around an Apple Power PC 9600 400 MHz computer. We used Pro Tools hardware and Andres used MOTU's Digital Performer software. All data was stored on two 18 GB, hot-swap drives, and everything was backed up later to DDS3 format.

It's incredible to think that now the whole album exists on the main drive, instead of a huge stack of 2-inch tapes. We have a special shock-mounted case for the drives because they are fragile.

The Power

A wonderful thing occurs when combining the analog and digital worlds. If we originate a recording in the analog medium and then transfer this recording to digital tape (or disk as the case may be), virtually all of the beauty and elegance of the analog recording will remain in the soundfield.

I think I could go so far as to say that at least 95 percent of the radiance of the analog sound remains in the sonics of the music when you transfer to digital. I think it's a lot like transferring a motion picture film to videotape. A huge percentage of the depth of field and symmetry you get with motion picture film remains in the images when you transfer it to videotape. Of course, once we have our tracks on digital, we can work wonders with the sound due to the incredible power of digital technology.

Some of Cyrius's vocals were recorded directly into Pro Tools, but we were very careful in our selection of the equipment used on his voice (as well as on the project in general). Digital can sound cold when used or overused as a medium of origination in music recording. We chose our gear to help avoid that as much as possible, using Neve Class A mic preamps and my own microphones (for details, see the accompanying story on Bruce's microphone collection).

I love the Neve 1066's because they have variable mid-high, and low-frequency bands. On the Neve 1066, the single high-frequency control is absolutely wonderful once you learn how to use it. For instance, as you crank on more substantial amounts of high-frequency EQ, the knee of the curve moves down the spectrum a bit, making the resultant high-frequency EQ more dramatic. Yet, if you use just a small amount of high-frequency EQ, it adds a gorgeous open, air-like character to the sound. I also have two Neve 1272's for recording synths and guitars direct. They're Class A (to me it's the ultimate signal path) with a lot of headroom, which makes them quite forgiving — so whether you hit them hard or not, they still sound marvelous. And they add a little character, a little color to the sonics of the source.

Do I Amuse You?

I'm a funny guy in that I don't like to use other people's microphones. To protect my sonic integrity, I've tried to use microphones that only I have handled — mics that haven't been beat up. I want to know what my microphones will sound like. For example, when I put my U 47 in front of a trombone player, I know what it's going to sound like. This is especially a concern with the inconsistency of most vintage microphones. I have mics in my collection that I bought new in the 1950s, and I can still use them on my projects today because I really take care of them. I have quite a few old RCA ribbon mics that are all wrapped carefully in plastic to protect them.

There are some new mics out there that are absolutely incredible, but I have a feeling that microphone technology matured about 30 years ago. The noise level of the microphone amplifiers has gone down a bit, and the newer mics are more consistent. For example, if you buy a new Neumann M 149 pair, they don't necessarily need to be close in serial numbers to sound alike.

Please Hold the Reverb

Andres and I did not use Pro Tools merely as a "multitrack tape recorder." We used it to develop and shape the arrangements of the songs during the mixing process (as well as using it to clean up tracks, comp vocals, record effects, submix, and pitch-shift certain elements). Since hard-disk editing is not only random access but non-destructive as well, it gives Andres and I a lot of creative options during the mixdown. There's discrete tracking, plus this tremendous power to create editorially. On one particular song, we needed to spice up the introduction. So Andres copied some snare hits from a drum fill during the song and used them to create a new fill for the beginning of the song. It took him about five minutes to do this. Of course, I have to say that Andres is seriously good and quick at Pro Tools. If we were using tape, we could have done the same thing, but it would have taken hours and hours just to do that one drum fill.

One of the really great uses we found for Pro Tools was as an effect "holder." Though it'd be nice to have more than one at Westviking, I have only one EMT 250 reverb. What Andres and I have done on several songs is set up the EMT 250 for a distinctive reverb on a particular track, and printed that effect in Pro Tools. Then we can re-set the EMT 250 with a different reverb for another sound source.

The Responsibility of Power

I feel there's a certain responsibility that goes along with all this digital power. In my beloved profession of music recording, I've been very fortunate to have spent my life in the recording studio with the very best musicians in the world. I've learned a great deal from them. I have found virtually all of them to be very open and giving. In fact, I think that perhaps my real role in music recording has been that of the fortunate student. Those incredible mentors taught me that my first and foremost responsibility is to the music I am involved in. Duke Ellington or Quincy Jones would kick my ass all over the place if I didn't keep the music in focus!

When Quincy and I are working on a project together, if I get sidetracked or deeply involved in a technical issue, Quincy will announce to everyone in the studio, "Hey look,

Bruce is having another AES meeting!" What I'm getting at is that, when your heart is in the right place, the kinds of editing and controlling options that we have access to today won't get in the way of creating believable music. However, if you turn the digital manipulation process into therapy, then it could become a problem. Listen to that little guy who sits on your shoulder telling you what's good or not so good. If you do that, you can't go wrong. Don't just have fun with your computer. That's not where it's at.

The Balancing Act

What's interesting to me is that the sound of the recording coming off 24-bit Pro Tools is not that much different from the analog tape. I also think that my Harrison console — with its relatively simple signal path — has such a warm and clear sound that you can run darn-near any signal into that desk and it'll sound good (whereas a lot of other desks are not so forgiving). The EQ on my lovely old Harrison is 4-band, totally parametric, with the best high-pass and low-pass filters on the planet.

The only other desks that I work with on a regular basis that have high-pass and low-pass filters of this quality are the SSL 4000, 9000, and Axiom MT. Filters of this magnitude can be very dramatic, and I rely on them a great deal. Once you learn their effectiveness, it's incredible what you can do. I always try to clean up the low end of the spectrum so that the bass and other low-end sound sources can be as clear as possible. With careful use of the high-pass filters on sound sources that have no real low end, you can work miracles.

For instance, I recently recorded and mixed a fantastic acoustic band from Stockholm. There was some secondary mic pickup in the studio — the guitar amp was miked in the same room with the drums. If you listen to the mics on the guitar amp, you will hear a bit of the kick drum. With the high-pass filters on the Harrison, I can virtually make that low-end, secondary pick-up of the kick-drum disappear, without affecting the sound of the guitar. Outside of the fundamental frequency of the note being played, there's no real low end in the guitar amp. If you have a quality high-pass filter you can safely edge the corner frequency up until you clean up the bottom end without destroying the sound of the guitar. Doing that on tracks wherever possible is dramatic — you can leave the whole bottom end of the spectrum wide open for the bass and the kick-drum, or any other low-frequency sound source. I think it was on Michael Jackson's *Thriller* that I really discovered how super-high-quality high-pass and low-pass filters can be used to the best advantage.

These filters can be equally useful on vocal tracks as well. When you hear a little room rumble that may color the sound of the voice, an effective high-pass filter can virtually make that rumble disappear. You might not hear that stuff in a mix as a specific sound, but it does take up space in the overall image of the music.

If your vocal or solo instrument is being played live at a distance from the source that's creating the problem, you'll have a delay from the source sound that'll be creating phase problems. By using these filters carefully, you can really help things out. I also use the high-pass filters for overhead mics on the drums, or in-the-room-mics in the studio, because secondary pickup and the resulting out-of-polarity problems can cause some nasty mix complications.

Am I A Nut Case, or What?

Over the years, I've learned that, in music recording, it's the often overlooked "insignificant" details that can actually be extremely important. In fact, when Quincy Jones and I discuss this very subject, "Q" has said to me, "It's *all* important!"

I think I am lucky in that I absolutely love detail in anything I am involved in — especially music recording. I'm such a nut case that I even carry my own wire to every project that I do! My heavy-duty wire case full of Monster Cable goes with me everywhere, and my beautiful little studio at home is entirely wired with Monster Cable.

Now Hear This!

The main monitoring system in my studio consists of Westlake BBSM-8's, passively bi-amped. Using the Westlake-designed Speaker Muff's, the stereo imaging of the BBSM-8's is astounding, and I consider this to be the finest music mixing/listening system in the world. You can discern minute degrees of left-right position in the stereo panorama with no effort at all! My Westlake's are powered by Electrocompaniet, mono-block, Class-A amplifiers. The BBSM-8's are very fussy about the amplifier they're powered with because they have a very low impedance in the midrange. To sound as good as they possibly can, they must be connected to an amplifier that will deliver a lot of power at very low impedance in the 1,000 to 1,800 Hz frequency range. The Electrocompaniet Mono-Block's will deliver 600 watts at 1,500 Hz with no problem at all.

For my truth-check speakers, I have a pair of older Auratones, powered by an Electrocompaniet Class-A amplifier. My little Auratones are mainly a slice-of-life observation point for my mixes.

An important part of my music-mixing situation is the acoustical treatment for my control room. I use an ATTACK Wall from Acoustic Sciences Corp, which I discovered a few years ago at my studio in L.A. when filming my video series. My old pal Arthur Noxon brought down an ATTACK Wall and set it up in my studio. I whipped out a couple of my mixes, and, as I listened, I was amazed to see mic positions in the stereo panorama that I hadn't seen in decades. I ordered an ATTACK Wall right away, and it's been a part of my studio world ever since.

The ATTACK Wall consists of a set of studio-grade Tube Traps placed as closely as possible around my mixing desk. The dead side of the Traps faces the desk and the bright side faces out into the room. The result is a virtually reflection-free listening environment as far as early reflections are concerned. Early reflections in a music-mixing situation are a detriment to stereo imaging. They blur and obscure lots of important detail that exists in the original recorded soundfield. On the other hand, late reflections are quite valuable when listening in a mixing room. If they are a little on the quiet side, very diffused, and incoherent in direction, late reflections will enhance stereo imaging and musical transparency. Sound from the speakers that escapes over the ATTACK Wall splashes back and forth between the bright side of the traps and the walls of my control room to create that wonderful diffuse backfill.

Whenever I travel (and I do travel a lot), I always carry a little aluminum foil box of DATs in my briefcase. On those DATs are tracks and mixes I've made over the years. Since I know the sound of these mixes intimately, I play them whenever I get ready to work in a new studio. Every room I work in sounds different, and these mixes help me to know what compensations I have to make in the mix. I've mentioned that I carry my mics and even my own wire around with me when I work. Now you know that I also carry my little box of DATs. I guess I'd better confess that I also ship my ASC Tube Traps around when I have the chance. I think they've been back and forth across the country about five or six times with me.

The Bitty Nitty Gritty

I record my mixes at 30 ips on my ½-inch Ampex ATR-102. I hit the ATR pretty hard, and the machine likes that; +2's, +3's are not a problem. The machine is aligned at +6 over 185 for BASF 900 tape. When mixing, I monitor the stereo mix path of the console through the ATR and then also through the converters for my DAT machine (I use Apogee converters). By monitoring my mix through the DAT machine, I get a good idea of how the digital recording medium is going to affect my mix, especially the low-level dynamics of the mix.

I don't record the DAT while I'm recording the ½-inch master. I've heard that some people run the analog machine and record the DAT off the repro head at the same time that the mix is going down. My experience is that the sound is different when you make the recording on ½-inch, rewind it, and then play it back to the DAT. To me, the sound warms up just a bit. I usually elevate the level going to the DAT by a dB or a dB-and-a-half, and I almost always use the "soft limit" function on my Apogees. I want every bit of resolution available to me on the DAT to enhance the character of my mix — especially if it's complex music (with a big orchestra, for instance) where, if you lose even a small amount of resolution, the audio quality suffers drastically.

You have to be very careful with levels on digital. If the ending is a fade out, you can crank up the volume at the end of the fade out and hear all kinds of doo-doo as the level gets lower. The only way to help that is by maximizing resolution during the mix. That's part of the reason I like ½-inch tape as an archive format. At the present time, CDs have a severe bit-limitation. So why bother with a mix medium that is any better than present-day

CD resolution? Well, that resolution is 16-bit, 44.1 kHz. If I were to finalize my mixes at that rate of resolution, all those bits that are missing in the current CD release format are forever gone. My much-loved music would be doomed to sound like that for eternity! No way! I think of analog tape as a mix medium with an infinite sampling rate. I look forward to the future — when we will have digital systems with finer resolution. When that happens, all of the fine detail of my mixes will be present on the ½-inch tape, waiting to be transferred to the new medium. To me, that's exciting!

I've always felt that music is life's only true magic! Treat it with all the respect that it deserves!

SECTION III

TECHNICAL

There are technical tips to be found in all sections of this book, but the stories in this section are devoted to a certain technical technique, be it from a specific track or from a particular piece of gear.

The best thing about these stories is that typically the writer was so excited about his experience with the project, or so jazzed about a piece of gear he just got, that he was thrilled to be able to inform our readers.

Some of the gear in the section is long gone, but the philosophy behind its use remains in effect.

So dig in and see what all the fuss was about…

The Return of the EMT

The famed EMT Plate is ready for the all-digital audio environment thanks to a new modification

By Tom Jung

Originally appeared in June 1992

You've probably heard of it. You've definitely heard it. Maybe you've even seen it out-of-the-way in a studio closet, storeroom, or maintenance shop. The historic EMT 140 echo plate was one of the most important devices in record making throughout the 1960s and '70s. But due to the impact of digital technology, plate echo was almost rendered obsolete. Now, due to an ingenious but simple modification developed by Jim Cunningham of Chicago, it's ready for a comeback.

For those of you who are too young to remember this studio classic, an echo plate is actually a large, flat, thin sheet of steel suspended from its four corners within a protective frame. A transducer (the driver element) transfers the incoming (echo send) signal to the plate, exciting it and causing it to ripple and "wave" imperceptibly to the eye. These "waves" are analogous to sound waves bouncing off the surfaces of a room. Two transducers pick up the echo signal created by the plate's movements and send it back (the echo return).

You've heard the result of this sound process thousands of times. It can be heard on just about every quality popular recording made between 1960 and 1980 — until suddenly it almost disappeared overnight, another victim of the digitization of the modern recording scene. The output of the plates was simply too low by today's standards, requiring a great deal of amp gain, and thus adding too much noise to the mix.

The old accelerometers that served as the pickups on the EMTs had to touch the plate at a very small point in order to maintain high-frequency response, and this minute point of contact resulted in the low output. Jim Cunningham's improvement consists of a new "Unimorph" pickup design that covers a large area of the plate while still maintaining sonic integrity. This larger mass provides a much stronger output simply due to its contact with enough of the surface to "feel" the waves, rather than a tiny portion of them, requiring less amp gain and improving the signal-to-noise ratio substantially. So even the modification that brings the beautiful plate sound up-to-date is analog in nature.

The modification itself was relatively easy to do. Within a couple of hours, I was able to replace the original pickup with the Unimorph design. I simply shaved off the old pickups with a razor blade and attached the new ones with the supplied cement. Then I changed two resistors in the amplifier, lowering the gain, and there it was — a 20 dB increase in signal-to-noise ratio.

The next step was to interface this newly modified gem with my Yamaha DMR8 all digital console. Of course, the signal coming from the console has to be converted from the digital domain into analog, and the analog signal from the plate needs to be converted back to digital. It may look like a lot of effort, but believe me, it's worth it.

A Little History

EMT plates were invented in Germany by Dr. Walter Kuhl of the Institute of Broadcasting Technology in Hamburg back in the 1950s. When the earliest plates were introduced to America they sounded terrible. Harvey Radio was the original importer and sold a dozen of them to Columbia Records, which couldn't get them to sound right. At the same time, Phil Ramone and Don Frey were in the process of opening A&R Recording in New York, which was destined to become one of the most famous and successful studios of all time. Harvey asked Phil and Don to see if they could figure out how to improve their sound and, in return, they could have one for A&R, while Harvey could maintain the Columbia sale. It was Phil Ramone who discovered that the EMTs had to be "tuned" by adjusting the tension of the steel plate. The rest is recording history.

Back to the Future

The record label I founded, Digital Music Products (DMP) of Stamford, CT, specializes in presenting live performances of modern jazz with audiophile sound quality. Celebrating our tenth anniversary with 50 releases currently in our catalog, we're an all-digital label and we always have been.

I am known in the industry as somewhat of a digital guru — my studio is digital, but there are still some wonderful analog things that have that warm, round sound that you just can't duplicate with digital equipment. The EMT plate had a sound that no digital device can imitate. But what about the noise level? Until recently, it simply didn't make the grade. But thanks to Cunningham's inexpensive modification, the noise level of the old plates can be reduced by around 20 dB. And I've been using an Ecoplate with the modification ever since with great results.

Cunningham, who in the late-'70s designed and manufactured the Ecoplate (an improvement on EMT's design), has come to the rescue and EMTs and Ecoplates can now do their stuff in the digital environment. His modification has reduced their inherent noise to an acceptable level for nitpickers like myself. And don't get the impression that these things were nothing but bundles of noise in the first place — they weren't. They just didn't have the noise floor of today's digital devices. In fact, some facilities still use them in their original state quite frequently. But now even my recordings can take on the plate's dense reverb sound.

Can you obtain a reverberation plate or two for your facility and still keep that digital cleanliness you depend on? Should you? The answer to the first question is yes. There are many used plates available out there. At least 4,000 were up and running in this country at one time. The answer to the second is — it depends on your needs and budget. If digital reverb systems, which can offer many types of echo sounds in one box, are suitable for the sounds you require, cool. But if you want one echo that stands out on its own like no other, check out a plate. Until Jim Cunningham's mod catches on, used EMTs are affordable, selling for as little as $1,000 on the current market. And the modification is available for under $75 simply by contacting Jim Cunningham at 708-831-5628.

May your music resound like never before!

Bringing Up Babyface

Giving a classic studio the ultimate state-of-the-art "Babyface-lift"

By David Hampton

Originally appeared in February 1995

Over the last 12 years, I have worked for many musicians, artists, and producers in the entertainment business, from technical support to studio consultant. Recently, Babyface and his wife Tracey were considering moving into a previously existing studio that was in dire need of technical, as well as cosmetic, attention. There was a need for a large production facility to house both Babyface's needs as well as Tracey's Yab Yum Entertainment activities. They needed someone who could coordinate the total renovation of the facility in keeping with their financial and creative vision and also maintain the confidentiality required when working with a high-visibility personality such as Babyface. They contacted me around April of '94 to meet with them at the facility for the purpose of discussing my involvement in this project. After viewing the studios and discussing their goals, we agreed that I would coordinate the project.

The studio was originally ABC/Dunhill back in the '70s; then it became Lion's Share, Cherokee, and finally Winsonic Technologies. It is a multiroom complex with plenty of space and excellent isolation from outside noise. Plus the control rooms (which had been designed by Lakeside Associates) sounded good. The studio also had more than a little history to it: It was one of the places where "We Are the World" was recorded. Some other artists who have recorded here in past years include Chaka Khan, Lionel Richie, Kenny Rogers, and Barbra Streisand.

Getting Started

Before we made any renovation plans, I located all the blueprints that existed and found several different versions. We discovered that once you get down to it and open up (for example) the ceiling, the final result is not always what it says on paper.

I could see that the original construction was top-quality (albeit unmaintained) and worth keeping. The people who originally built the facility were very good carpenters. The walls are all built on staggered studs and floated on neoprene rubber. Isolation between rooms is excellent. The finished materials (such as the marble and wood accents) used in the control rooms were kept because of their high-quality workmanship. The previous tenant's "renovations" included dark green carpeting, low-level lighting, and full-length mirrors throughout the entire facility. Needless to say, while working there, I fully expected Super-Fly to come pimpin' through the halls at any given moment.

Restoring a studio is a lot like producing a record — calling the right people for the session sure helps. My next step then was to assemble a technical translation team with each person being responsible for a key area. The team consisted of Nathaniel White Jr., general contractor; Ralph Lawson, chief electrician; and Mitch Robertson, senior technical engineer.

In a facility that has seen so many occupants, the term "pre-existing condition" was meaningless. The electrical system in all the studios was totally redone. Ralph and Mitch worked closely together to facilitate any potential systems-interfacing problems that might arise. The equipment was checked for phase and noise as it was installed in each studio. As you can imagine, over the years Babyface has amassed quite a trainload of equipment.

Room Roundup

There are three studios at the complex: A, B, and C. All of these rooms have good acoustical properties. The A room is primarily a live tracking room. We've set it up so that we can have a drummer and a vocalist each in their own booths and then have a piano player and a guitar player baffled and miked with major isolation. This control room will truly be our "A" room. We are installing a modified E Series SSL with G Series automation and EQs, a Sony 3348 digital multitrack, and two Studer 2-inch 24-track machines. The monitors are custom-designed using TAD components and, of course, there will be a full complement of outboard gear.

Control room B is our multipurpose room, containing a CAD console, Studer and MCI 2-inch machines, 24 tracks of Alesis ADAT (which is an important consideration since our MIDI production rooms also have the ADAT system), a custom synth rig, and a good-sounding live tracking room. Room B has everything needed with the exception of automation, which we plan on upgrading in the future.

The designs on room C have not been finalized and no work has been done as of now. We will proceed with C when time allows.

The building (which used to be an apartment building) is actually built over a swimming pool. You can go down to the basement and see that the contractors did not bother to fill in the pool. They just sank girders right through the bottom of it so there is this great live chamber sitting underneath the building. At some point we will probably activate it as a live echo chamber.

Along with the three main studios, we decided to build two MIDI rooms that are designed around the preproduction needs of the facility. Both rooms contain ADAT machines and an Alesis X-2 console. We felt that it made sense to standardize some of the gear in order to maintain consistent quality levels. Each room has the same patchbay layout and processing gear so that Yab Yum's songwriters can comfortably work in one room or in the other. Since we have three ADATs in Studio B, tracks can easily be recorded in the MIDI rooms and then brought to B to be transferred to another format. We are installing a third MIDI room with a VCR, disco mixers, turntables, and CD players to enable alternative productions to take place. People who come from a DJ background, for example, don't necessarily know much about MIDI, so we designed our rooms to help them understand what it's all about.

The Creative Edge

Tracey and the Yab Yum staff have selected writers and artists that have totally different musical ideas in which everything they're doing has their own musical stamp. A true production facility should give songwriters a chance to work on their songs, exchange ideas, and have access to equipment, as well as the guidance of creative people working in the industry.

As studio owners, Babyface and Tracey have also been able to establish an internship program in conjunction with the Long Beach City College Commercial Music Program. It provides experience to those who desire a career in the music business.

At the time of this article David Hampton was working with artist/producer Marcus Millon and producer Dave "The Cat" Ward in Los Angeles and NBA basketball great Terry Cummings in San Antonio. Some other artists that Hampton has worked with include Peabo Bryson, Whitney Houston, Eddie Murphy, Larry Graham, and Sinbad. Recently, he has been working with Herbie Hancock.

The Pope of Pop Blesses the Digital Domain

How I use the TASCAM DA-88 digital multitrack as a production tool for my latest projects

By Phil Ramone

Originally appeared in February 1995

Having been involved in the music industry for so many years, I have seen a lot of technology come and go. Some of that technology was doomed from the start (like the 8-track cartridge) and some of it was not accepted because it was ahead of its time (like quadraphonic sound). Aside from the development of multitrack recording, most of the technological changes haven't radically altered the manner in which I make records. But the proliferation of affordable digital multitrack tape machines has forever changed the way many producers (including myself) go about recording a project. For the most part, that change benefits not only the producer but the artist and record company as well.

The Lowdown on Mixdown

In an effort to solve this recurring problem, I began to treat audio mixing like film mixing — working in stereo pairs. As we proceed with the mix, the drums, keyboards, horns, strings, backing vocals, and (sometimes) lead vocals are mixed into stereo pairs and then I store the pairs. In the past I used a Sony 3324 24-track digital machine to store the pairs, but now I am using the TASCAM DA-88. The DA-88 is a good-sounding machine with a quick, reliable transport and is affordable enough to rent or own.

As John Patterson, my engineer, and I mix down, we print the instrument (or grouping of instruments, like horns) *and* the effects into stereo pairs onto the DA-88's. Since I like to spread things out, we usually use three of the TASCAM units for a total of 24 tracks, and at times we print the effects separately from the dry instrument sound. In the event that we need to do a remix, I have the song premixed in these pairs and each section of instruments has their respective effects either mixed in or stored to another pair of tracks. Making a small adjustment (like pushing the lead vocal a bit louder) is now easy. We don't have to waste time and money doing a recall and we don't have to worry about whether or not we can book a particular room in order to obtain a specific sound. In fact, if we print the return from the echo chamber at Capitol onto a separate pair of stereo tracks, I virtually have the room with me on tape, no matter where I might execute the remix.

When we are ready to remix, we come out of the DA-88's and go into Digidesign's Pro Tools where we can assemble or refine a mix that may need only small changes. Also, if I am out of town, I can send tapes back to John at our studio/headquarters in New York (The Shire) where he can reassemble or re-edit the song using Pro Tools.

We are finding that anywhere we go, the TASCAM machines are easily accessible and many studios are happy to have them around — even when there's already a digital multi-track in-house. It's a lot safer for us to print the sounds in pairs of tracks, and we don't feel that there is any loss in printing those pairs to digital tracks on the DA-88.

The Production Deal

Earlier this year, John and I worked on a record by an English act called EG (pronounced "egg"). The DA-88's were used throughout the project, but not in the manner of which you might think. The basic tracks were recorded on 2-inch analog tape (24-track) running at 15 ips with Dolby SR. We like to run analog tape at 15 ips because the low end is much more punchy, and, by using Dolby SR on the tracks, noise is not a factor at the slower speed. As the project moved into the overdub stage, we had a need to put down more keyboard parts, so we formatted a Hi8 tape the night before the session and then put it into a DA-88 machine that had a TASCAM SY-88 sync card installed. We striped SMPTE code on the tape, using both TASCAM's internal timecode track as well as an audio track for redundancy. Now we could record the various keyboards without worrying if specific tracks were changing from piano to synth or organ from song to song. We had clean real estate to work with.

At this point in the life of a project, John and I usually get into making work reels that are used to record lead vocal and solo takes that will later be "comped" (composited) down to a smaller number of tracks. Most people would normally get a second analog machine to make the work reels, but renting a second machine and a second SR rack can really bust a budget. Our solution was to get a second DA-88, also with a sync card, and use it to record a work mix of the 2-inch analog tracks and the DA-88 keyboard tracks. This work mix (which now existed on a Hi8 tape) was then transferred back to a fresh reel of 2-inch analog tape onto which we would record vocals. The DA-88 gave us the luxury of doing overdubs on 2-inch tape with Dolby SR without the added expense of renting a second 2-inch machine and a second Dolby rack. We were afforded all of the advantages of having that machine while *still* having all of the advantages of deciding whether we wanted to record a particular sound in digital or analog.

It seems to me that people have forgotten how unforgiving analog 24-track can be in the long run. The drum tracks start to deteriorate no matter what you do or what anybody tells you, and the truth is that you want to run the master tape as little as possible.

The Mechanics

I have become quite spoiled, having used Sony 3348's, 3324's, and Studer machines for so long. With these machines there is very little mechanical failure, and the 3348 may be the best musical tank known to man. It's a workhorse, but it's just not always affordable in the budget. John and I did a session where we recorded drums to the DA-88's, as well as to analog tape, to see if they could play back all of those transients — and the DA-88's sounded great. If we want to, we can even use the TASCAM IF-88AE interface to connect Apogee converters to the digital input of the DA-88. From the engineer's point of view, I appreciate the reliability and fast lock-up that the units provide. The machines have been consistent, whether we are using the ones we own, rentals, or in-house studio machines. Lock-up has not been a problem whether the DA-88's are chasing a 48-track digital machine or a 2-inch analog machine running at 15 ips.

Balancing the Budget

I recently had a meeting with a particular record company whose artist was quite creative and was very comfortable in the home environment. I explained that it's *very* reasonable for them to get the artist a Mackie board and a couple of DA-88's to use at home. My biggest recommendation, whether for a young artist or a veteran, is to be able to record their vocals at home. Bring in an engineer, sit them down wherever they are comfortable (most people have a room that is sensibly quiet), and go to work. There won't be the stress of working in an expensive room. I'm not trying to talk people out of going to big studios, but there *is* a stress factor, driving up through a gate and then showing up in the studio and saying, "OK, now be a star." It doesn't always work. An artist may get some nighttime vocal ideas, and, even if they have to self-operate the equipment, it's better than having them in a demo studio for $50 an hour. The low tape cost encourages artists to experiment, and a final performance can always be comped at a later time.

Through my years of working as a producer, I have heard many great performances recorded on home tape machines that had to be reperformed because of poor sound quality. There have been far too many bass parts that I've loved that I wish I didn't have to redo. If the artist has a quality recording machine in the house, you are on the road to incredible music because you can now edit, comp, or overdub, and before you know it you have good material — *without* the pressure of the clock.

The Final Track

The TASCAM DA-88's have proven to be reliable, durable machines that happen to be affordable and use tape that is easily accessible. Adding tracks to our productions is as easy as adding another machine (providing that the first one has the sync card) and backing up both the original tracks and our mixdowns is quite cost-effective. In our business, time is money, and by reducing the amount of money required to achieve quality recording, the DA-88 leaves more time for making music — and that is the bottom line.

Some Thoughts on Mastering, 1995

The Master Masterer himself tells how to keep up with the rapidly changing technology and techniques in mastering

By Bob Ludwig

Originally appeared in April 1995

The mastering process continues to evolve as the technology changes. There are so many different technical options available that many engineers/producers are confused about how to approach the final stage of their recording project. The mastering sessions of 1995 do not look as they used to even a short while ago. I want to share my thoughts about what new ideas are good, not so good, and what old ideas still work!

Analog or Digital?

In my opinion, the *average* recording we receive to master tends to sound better mixed to analog rather than digital. To me, if you are mixing rock music, there is often nothing better than mixing to a good ½-inch Ampex ATR 102. With a great 20-bit analog-to-digital converter (properly re-constructed to 16-bit via an Apogee UV-22, Sony SBM, or Weiss ANR redithering scheme), the best one can say about the sound is that it sounds exactly like the output of the mix console. Of course, this is a great situation! However, many producers say mixing to analog sounds *better* than the console output — it sort of "glues" the sound together. If you are Bob Clearmountain or Hugh Padgham and the sound from the console is, in fact, *exactly* what you want, then digital can certainly be the best format. I usually suggest mixing to both and hearing which sounds best for the particular music.

Make several mixes of the same song, some with the vocal up higher and lower than you think is right. Many times, after the mastering process, the vocal up (or down) may prove to be better than what sounded best premastered.

If you decide to go analog, please write down the *kind* of analog machine you used. Ampex, Studer, Otari, Sony, MCI, etc., do not sound the same. I have four different kinds of analog playback at Gateway Mastering to ensure the tape is being reproduced at its best.

If you decide to go digital, please note what *kind* of DAT machine you used. The automation of the session depends on knowing what kind of code your machine recorded which will then be interpreted by the pro DAT machine timecode reader.

20-Bit Recording

Mixing to a proper DAT machine using a good DAT tape is probably the cheapest way to make a decent recording. But hey, it's 1995, and if you are a professional and you want to record digitally, there is no reason why you should not be mixing down with a 20-bit dynamic range. What is your excuse? Sony, Wadia, Prism, Yamaha, Lexicon, and others have been making 20-bit analog-to-digital converters for years and now Apogee is finally shipping theirs. Even if you do not think you need the extra 24 dB dynamic range, at least bits 14, 15, and 16 will probably be more accurate with a good 20-bit converter. You will record the noise floor more accurately, and it has been proven that music can be heard beneath the noise floor!

How does one store 20 bits? Lots of ways: D-2 video machines and digital Betacam machines store 20-bit. Sony, of course, offers the rather expensive but elegant Sony PCM-9000 magneto-optical 24-bit recorder. One can also use a Mitsubishi X-86 machine that has been converted for 20-bit recording.

The cheapest way is to record onto a TASCAM DA-88 with the Prism MR 2024T box hooked up to it. This turns your Hi8, 16-bit 8-track machine into a 20-bit 6-track (or 24-bit 4-track if anyone ever successfully builds a 24-bit converter in the future).

The PCM-9000 has built in sequencing features. For the other formats, dump the approved mixes to a SADiE, Sonic Solutions, or other 20-bit hard disk editing system, edit it, and dump it back to the DA-88/Prism unit or archive it at 20-bit with an Exabyte tape.

Of course, one can record directly on to one of these hard disk systems, archiving to Exabyte as one goes. The future holds high-density CDs and other means of storing 20-bit information.

DATs

If you are recording 16-bit, the Sony PCM-1630 can offer computer verification that the data has been recorded without any errors. Some pro DAT machines will tell you if they detected any errors while recording, but DATs as a rule are less dependable than the PCM-1630/U-matic format. These days, DAT is by far the most commonly received digital format. At Gateway Mastering Studios, the majority of *all* masters we receive to work on are ½-inch 30 ips analog.

Record at 44.1 kHz especially if your final product is going to be a CD. If one is going to work in the digital domain, converting from 48 kHz to 44.1 for the finished CD usually hurts the sound. I recently purchased a sample frequency converter from dB Technologies and it sounds good. Most sample frequency converters do not sound so good.

What to Write

Besides writing what kind of DAT machine you used to record the tape, write down the sampling frequency, and what kind of timecode (or lack of code) is printed along with the sound. Make sure that the tape is clearly labeled. If the tape and the box were to be separated, could you identify your tape amongst a pile of 20 other tapes?

IDs on DATs. When one is making a tape to send to a mastering facility, record a balance tone at the reference level you used at the beginning of the DAT. Please, with a big cherry on top, do not give the tone an ID number! Just start your DAT master, let it go for a few seconds, and begin the tone. As no one but the mastering engineer will ever want to listen to this tone, do not index it! Have the first song be the first index. Working with a client's DAT that says track "5" when it is actually song 4 drives me nuts and makes me make mistakes.

It may seem obvious, but if you are sending your DAT to be mastered, please be sure each song is properly numbered. If the song fades up, it is nice to have the index start at the beginning of the fade-up, not where the auto-ID feature of your DAT decides to put it! Especially if two songs are crossfaded into each other, it is nice to see exactly where the new track should begin for the CD PQ code (track numbers).

Digital Workstations

Digital workstations are wonderful things. We have three Sonic Solutions systems all networked together at our place. Using one common SCSI drive, while I am recording to the drive in my room, one of my engineers can be editing my recordings in the second room and another running a double-speed CD ref. from it in the third! Amazing.

It used to be that one took for granted that a sequenced recording coming into a professional mastering room would be properly put together. With tens of thousands of sometimes inexperienced operators now owning inexpensive digital workstations, this is unfortunately no longer the case.

The most common mistakes that end up costing the client money to correct are:

- Using the workstation in a way that it does not properly clone (make exact copies — the sound is being changed from the editing process). Most good workstations can clone, but many operators don't know when to turn dithering on or off, or if they should remove DC offset filters, and so on. Not knowing the answer can harm the sound of your tapes!
- Chopping off the ends of songs because of monitoring too softly.
- Using software that does not put a slight crossfade at the beginning of each song, resulting in a click from the DC shift. All these clicks will have to be removed.
- "Normalizing" or otherwise changing the level of the music during the editing process. Normalizing makes all the maximum *peak* levels the same. In mastering, we try to make the *average* levels the same. If you are making a tape for the A&R department and want to even the levels out, go ahead, but the tape you send to the mastering house should only be edited, not level changed or "pre-EQ'd." Let the mastering house add it with good gear. Once the sound has gone through a bad digital EQ (and many of them are), that gritty, brittle sound cannot be undone!

If you own one of the systems that prints out a nice track sheet but doesn't allow you to actually synchronize your machine to the actual timecode, please note it on your sheet! We professionals are used to getting timecode sheets that actually mean what they say. It is nice to know that your timing sheet, with timings purporting to be accurate to the 80th of a frame, in fact has little to do with the real timecode your DAT is putting out! I am not saying not to send the track sheet, but simply to note that it is all relative to when you actually started the DAT machine by hand.

Final Thought

So much of my time is already wasted due to computers that crash or malfunction and tapes that drop-out and other acts of God that if it is possible to help the things we *can* control, it will be a better world for me and a cheaper world for you!

Miking In-choir-y

How to use an unusual mic setup to capture a choir

By Bruce Swedien

Originally appeared in March 1996

In the August 1995 issue of EQ, we ran a MicroPhile on Bruce Swedien's Neumann M 49 microphones. In that article, Swedien discussed a rather unorthodox mic technique that drew a large response from our readers. Following is a detailed description of how Swedien uses that technique in the recording of a choir.

Making a truly superior recording of a choir is really fairly simple once you understand a couple of things. First of all, you need a truly superior choir! Of course, I am kind of spoiled because with the projects I normally work on, I usually get to work with a choir like the Andre Crouch Choir (which I consider to be one of the best choirs in the world).

Next, I look for a studio with a very musical sound, and by this I mean a studio built by someone who is aware of the refinements of studio design. I like room proportions that are such that standing waves are minimal. Usually a nonrectangular room gives the best diffusion and the least voice coloration. The studio that I like to use for this type of choral recording is Westlake Audio's Studio D in Hollywood. This magnificent studio was designed by Glenn Phoenix of Westlake Audio. Because of its fantastic sound on voice, I often use this studio for choir recordings.

Mic Moves

My favorite mics for recording a choir are my two identical Neumann M 49's (they are consecutive serial numbers that I bought new in 1962). They are the pair that you saw in the MicroPhile a few months ago. That photo very clearly illustrates a pretty standard "X-Y" situation with these two microphones, and that is the way I have used them for recording the Andre Crouch Choir.

Inasmuch as I usually set the mics to the omni polar pattern for this technique, I have a feeling that perhaps the term "coincident pair" might be a better description for this application. By definition, when a coincident pair of microphones are used in any non-MS configuration, the two microphones are frequently identified as an "X-Y" pair. They can also be set to bidirectional and they will do essentially the same thing. [*The M 49 has three switchable pickup patterns: omni, bidirectional, or cardioid, controlled from the power supply. —Ed.*] They could be set for cardioid, but then you will have to deal with the fact that there will be a dead side to the mics. You will also need to pay a lot of attention to the front side of the mics — the coincident axis will have to be aimed at the sound source. The way I use them in a choir recording is usually in omni.

I put the choir in a circle about 30 feet in diameter around the two microphones so that the singers are about 15 feet away from the mics. I will move the choir members farther away from or closer to the mics if the balance needs help, and from that point on, the room does all the mixing. Of course, I have the choir standing (not sitting), and the mics are placed between 4 and 5 feet high, just near mouth height. Once you have the balance of the harmonies and vocal timbres set, the room really does all the work. From this point on, if you can find the red button, all you have to do is put tapes on the machine and sit back and listen.

I'm sure you have heard "Man in the Mirror" from Michael Jackson's *Bad* album or "Will You Be There" from M.J.'s *Dangerous* album. These two pieces are classic examples of my recording the Andre Crouch Choir using these two mics in an omni "X-Y" or coincident pair setup. Now, more typically, some engineers would use the mics set to cardioid for the "X-Y" technique.

What happens when you use them in cardioid is that you basically end up with a directional microphone system. The reason that I use the mics in omni for "X-Y" is that, primarily, what I am trying to achieve is to get the arrival time of the sound from the source to hit the two capsules at as close to the same moment in time as possible. This way there is little phase difference for any given frequency in the output of the two mics. As a result, you will get a dense, wide feeling of a very unified choral sound. Of course, the sonic image that you get has almost no left/right intensity.

Because of the fact that there are virtually no phase problems, this technique makes the most incredible mono for monophonic broadcast that you have ever heard in your life.

In addition, I have also always had a feeling that by using these microphones set to the omnidirectional polar pattern, there will not be any off-axis coloration. Off-axis coloration is a distortion of frequency response that gets progressively greater as the arrival angle of the sound increases. This type of distortion would be the greatest with the mics set for the cardioid polar pattern. As an additional bonus with this technique, I think that the acoustics of the room and particularly the early reflections from the sound source are heard very accurately by the mics, and thus preserved in their natural order.

In the Mix

I will then connect these two incredible mics to my Neve 1084 discrete Class A mic preamplifiers, which I consider to be the close-to-ideal audio signal path as far as microphone preamps. These mic preamps are the same as those that might have been found in a Neve console, probably in the early 1970s. I have a bunch of them that I carry with me wherever I work, and two in particular are in an elegant oak case that I take with me just for choral and vocal recording.

For these recording sessions, I will invariably go so far as to bypass all the studio microphone wiring. I run Monster Cable microphone cables from the studio under the control room door into the Neve 1084's. If I have enough time to run back and forth to set a little EQ, I will put the Neves out in the studio so that the mic-level signal path is very short. I use Monster Cable and come out of the 1084's and go to the tape machine either through the jackfield or straight in. I try to bypass the console as best as I can. Most of these newer consoles have a lot of ICs — even in the bussing stages where you think that the signal is at line level and is pretty safe from too many amps in the circuit.

Each mic is then recorded to a separate track. When I mix, the tracks will be panned hard left and hard right. When you are trying to retain an acoustical image in its entirety, you will minimize its drama if you don't pan the tracks hard left and hard right.

Trap Keeper

If that isn't enough, I always take my ASC (Acoustic Sciences Corporation) Studio Traps with me to my recording sessions. I have the traps that are 5 feet high and maybe 9 inches in diameter. The Studio Trap is adjustable for height. Each trap actually has two sides with little marks to identify them: One is reflective and the other is absorptive. In certain recording situations, I won't pay too much attention to those little marks! I wouldn't carefully organize them, aimed in one direction or face them all in one neat little row or something. I'll generally make a random Tube Trap setup and try to get the room sound as natural as I can. I usually put the Traps more toward the outside perimeter of the room and not between the sound source and the microphone.

If the room has an area that might be sonically hot or too reverberant, or if I hear a reflection or standing wave I don't like, I can use the Studio Traps to change the soundfield. They make a dramatic difference. In *this* situation I always pay attention to those marks that identify which side is reflective and which side is absorptive. You can experiment by starting out with a lot of Tube Traps and then remove them two at a time — you will hear the sound liven up incredibly. They allow you the ultimate control of the room reflections mixed in with the direct sound, almost like having movable walls.

Here's something to remember: This microphone approach doesn't allow you to do any remixing or rebalancing of the "X-Y" stereo image, so you have to go for your balance while you are recording. I have always felt that this is good mental discipline.

Although proximity effect does also apply to omni, it is not nearly as exaggerated as in cardioid, so you won't have one mic with more proximity effect than the other, emphasizing the low end a little more and thus distorting the stereo image. It takes a little bit of experimenting, but this microphone technique will very definitely hear the source as it sounds in the studio. Usually, just playing back a take for the choir will let them hear what parts need to be made louder or softer.

The omni "X-Y" or "coincident pair" microphone technique is decidedly forgiving as far as balance is concerned, so if the music you are recording is in balance in the studio, then it will go to tape in balance.

Lights! Camera! Audio!

Getting the most important part of the movie down on tape

By Frank Serafine

Originally appeared in September 1996

A lot of where I'm coming from in terms of sound design is the result of my being a composer. I really think that, if I hadn't had strong orchestral training behind me and wasn't a trained musician, I wouldn't have been so successful at the process of sound design. It's such a creative art form that it's good to have that background in order to do interesting textural sound design.

When I start work on a motion picture, I get a copy of the film on ¾-inch video from the producer. What they do is transfer the 35mm film to video tape. At the time that they transfer from film to video tape, they stripe both longitudinal SMPTE timecode on audio channel two, and VITC (Vertical Interval TimeCode) onto the address track portion of the videotape. We get what's called a window burn timecode. The window burn shows the actual timecode numbers on the screen and makes locating specific scenes of the film very easy. Production audio will be mixed and recorded to channel 1.

The reason that we stripe the tape with both types of code is that the longitudinal code can't be read in shuttle or jog mode. So most of the time we're dealing with the SMPTE from channel 1 for lock-up, except when you're in shuttle or jog mode — then VITC takes over. We begin our work by striping the reels. We start the timecode at 01 hours for reel one, 02 hours for reel two, 03 hours for reel three, and so on, so that we keep organization throughout the whole film. So when we look up on the screen and see 05, we know that we're on reel five.

The next thing we do is get the video and spot the film with the director. Spotting means sitting down and viewing every single frame of the picture in actual scrub (frame by frame), and writing down every single tiny detail. We're looking for *everything* while we're doing this — a guy in the background screaming, someone talking, someone walking, etc. — every little nuance of the film, and we make notes of all of these. I'm not just a sound designer on the films that come to my facility, I also supervise the entire sound process on many of them. So I have to look at all the problems that are in the dialogue track.

The video tape I receive is an unedited version of the film. Once everything is set up and I've gone through and logged scenes with the editors, they'll start going to work on editing the film. What I do is start looking through my library to see if I have any stored sounds for a particular scene, and how that particular frame corresponds to Foley.

Fun With Foley

I create a lot of my sound effects in the Foley process. What I'll do is create the sounds with props so that I don't have to go out and record something. I'll have the Foley artist make something that I then put into my sampler and make ten times bigger. So I'm constantly looking at ways to get sounds out of Foley. I actually cover everything needed in the film with Foley, as well as sound effects, because when I finally get to the dub stage, I'll notice that some sound effects don't sound natural, and then I'm able to bring up the Foley. Sometimes I'll even blend a little of both.

In terms of recording, we record all the sound effects and Foley flat with a Neumann KMR 81 shotgun mic; it's the microphone of choice for Foley and ADR (Automated Dialogue Replacement). We run that through a Millennia mic pre, then it goes straight to the TASCAM DA-88, so it's as pristine as you can get.

Usually really big sounds are created with effects, but all others are created in the Foley process because sounds that are created live in the Foley room sound natural. In recording the Foley and sound effects, every single sound and effect is on a separate track, and as we're laying down our effects we're also mixing and redubbing them as we go, so that when we get to the dub stage, the mixer doesn't even have to bring up anything — it's already mixed for him. He brings everything up to 0 on his console and it's all premixed.

Diken Berglund is our Foley mixer. He records the actors, the looping of the actors, and he records the Foley. When we go to mix, he mixes on the dub stage. This creates a situation where everything he's recorded, he knows...and then he mixes it, too. It's really a good system.

Special Effects

While the Foley is being created, simultaneously we're slugging in sound effects from the library and we're consulting with the Foley artist. For years I've gone through not only my own library to find the sounds I wanted, but until my library was developed, I'd go through everybody else's libraries as well. Over the years I've collected literally thousands of sounds, which we've recently just taken the best of and released to the general public in a specialized series called *Platinum Sounds* (which is now available through L-Squared Communications in Santa Monica). For the most part, though, I'd find a lot of the sounds from most of the older libraries were not of the quality that I desired. Some of the performances of these old sound effects are just so unbelievable — like in an old Frankenstein movie for instance — that you'd never be able to create again. So what I've done on some of these older libraries is run them through EQ or Pro Tools, NoNoise, or DINR to extract sounds out of the library and delete some of the noise problems occurring in them. We also use DINR when we master a new sound into the library.

I also create many sound effects with electronic musical instruments, such as the Yamaha VL-1 interfaced to a WX11 Wind Controller, the new Korg Trinity, and Kurzweil 24X. I love utilizing the physical modeling technology of the VL-1 combined with the SansAmp rock 'n' roll distortion technology. I've been able to create some new and unusual sounds from this combination that I've yet to hear in the marketplace.

In recording my own personal sound effects, one of my favorite microphones is the Shure SM81. I go on a scout for sounds with a really good mic and a portable DAT recorder like a Sony or a Technics (I have a variety of them), and I might come back with 50 sounds. I then take the sounds back to the studio, we log every single sound effect into the computer and listen to it, and then begin sampling the good sounds into the E-mu Emulator IV. Once the samples are in E-IV, it's really incredible what we can do with them — they actually become like Silly Putty. It's totally elastic reality. Also, we now work with the Avid AudioVision system, which is really a great editing tool. Over the years I have found that many of the digital audio workstations available tend to be very rigid in that you couldn't do things like cluster a bunch of sound effects together, or manipulate the pitch or EQ. You'd have to go in and actually harmonize the sounds down if you wanted it that way, which was always such a chore for me and why I never chose to go with all the "traditional" hard-disk workstations — because they weren't really that developed yet. So we use AudioVision in conjunction with the E-IV. We have a lot of E-IV's in my facility because they're workstations that can be used in different rooms for different functions.

Station Break

We have a variety of workstations here. For instance, we have an IBM-based Soundscape for doing backgrounds. Up until now, however, the majority of workstations available were not equipped to facilitate some of the tricks that I was able to do on the Emulator IV. Another workhorse workstation, one that I've used for many years, is the AMS Audiophile. The AMS is like a Jeep that can climb any hill. So for the last ten years we've been able to do some really interesting things outside of the workstation, in the sound design world, where we've been making sounds that nobody has ever heard before.

Actually, Emulator is even going further now; there's so many things we can do because of the special effects that are built into the system. We find that the Emulator is a superior workstation when it comes to special effects for actual sound creation and design. The whole workstation attitude is more clinical and scientific, which you need to have if you're editing down to the frame. I need to be able to perform to match what I'm seeing and I sometimes go for some really wild-sounding effects. The only way you can do that is by bending existing samples, doing weird frequency shifts, and dopplering certain things. We also use Hyperprism, which is kind of like an Etch-a-Sketch in that you can draw Doppler or EQ into the sounds, and you get an actual visual representation of what you're doing with the sound. Hyperprisim is a plug-in to Pro Tools and a standalone sound effects processing system. It allows you to move the sound around in space, and you can even do all kinds of surround sound things using it.

We also use the KYMA, a sound design tool from Symbolic Sound, which I refer to as the morphing synthesizer. It actually allows you to take two different sound sources and digitally morph them together. We did a lot of experimenting with the KYMA with the movie *Virtuosity*, when we were creating the special effects for the villain's voice. Every time he went into morph mode, we'd morph his voice as well. The effect was really great. The KYMA is a whole new way of processing. All of our sounds are then stored on 650 MB 3M magneto-optical cartridges. For me, though, I find this the most creative part of the job — the actual recording of the sound effect. I love the whole process but I particularly like this aspect. It gets me out of the studio and out exploring the world.

After this, everything is transferred to DA-88's and brought to the dub stage where we start mixing. The beauty of these DA-88's is if more tracks are needed, my editors can slide those DA-88's in. When we were using 24-track, you had to have one 24-track in every room. You had to be a Todd-A-O or some major company in order to be able to afford all the equipment to facilitate the kinds of projects that we're doing on this scale right now. It's amazing how the technology in the last ten years has allowed really *anyone* to get into this now.

So now the mixing is in the final process and all the elements are put together. Everything is mixed on my Otari customized 54P console with moving fader automation and PEC Direct. PEC is for motion picture dubbing only. It's used to balance in your sound before you actually record, so you're matching your levels from the repro head to your record head in order to seamlessly punch in dialogue anywhere in the movie. The PEC Direct is part of the console as well as part of the tape recorder — it's an interface between the two. We mix every track from all the DA-88's down to a Sony 24-track into what we call "stems," which are manageable predubs of all the different effects — the background, the Foley, the music, and the dialogue. These stems are mixed down to separate tracks on the 24-track machine so that if we ever need to come back and pull just one element out, we can. So we have total control right down to the "print master," which is the final dub of the movie. In the end, we combine all the stems down to that final print master and that's it...it's a wrap!

Pure Digital

Sticking with ones and zeros from start to finish

By Phil Ramone

Originally appeared in September 1996

Recently, Phil Ramone went into Capitol's Studio A to record the song "Mistakes I Made" with artist Fran Lucci. The track was completely recorded and mixed on a Yamaha 02R digital recording console using no outside effect processors. Phil describes how this unique session progressed to completion.

While a lot of recordings claim to be "digital recordings," the term is often misused. Recently my engineer, John Patterson, and I completed a project with singer/songwriter Fran Lucci that truly was a "digital recording." We used a Yamaha 02R digital console and recorded the audio directly onto TASCAM DA-88's. Throughout the process, the audio signals never returned to the analog domain (except for monitoring the session) until after the final mix was put onto DAT. We even used only the digital reverbs found in the board.

When Peter Chaikin, pro audio recording products manager for Yamaha, first told me about the new Yamaha 02R digital console, I was intrigued by its possibilities. But to be to really sure of what it could do, the board had to be tested in a demanding setting. With a group of musicians concentrating on getting the music right, the last thing a producer wants to hear is technical glitches. So, for me, recording a rhythm section cutting a new tune was the perfect situation for this test, because if the board was going to act up, we'd know it right away. I chose Capitol's Studio A because I am very familiar with how it sounds and because it would provide a nice, open acoustical environment.

It was important to see if the 02R could faithfully reproduce this wonderful room. I also chose to work at the studio because of the great people there. Everyone was helpful and

The Story Behind the Story

OK, I know — doing a recording entirely in the digital domain is not a big deal anymore. In fact, nowadays it takes incorporating some analog techniques into the process to raise a few eyebrows. That was not the case in 1996, and Yamaha's 02R promised to do a lot of things in the digital domain, and, in this story, Phil Ramone sets out to see if it lives up to its hype.

Phil offers some good techniques here, and there are still plenty of this boards still in use.

enthusiastic — from Michael Frondelli and Paula Salvatore on the administrative side to chief engineer Jeff Minnich and engineer Leslie Ann Jones.

The band was to be made up of Mark Portmann on keyboards, Steve Schaffer on drums, Paul Jackson Jr. on guitar, and Abe Laboriel on bass. Fran would sing a vocal with the band as a reference, but I'm always aware that there is a possibility that the performance could be a keeper. It turned out that quite a bit of what she sang with the band was used in the final mix.

You can see from the accompanying input and track-assignment list that the 02R was going to be pretty full. We wanted to do this with just one 02R, so we had to limit ourselves to just 16 tracks for the basics. It took a little bit of thinking to fit all of this stuff onto two machines; we grouped the four toms to a stereo pair of tracks and Mark gave us left and right outputs from his rack's mixer for his keyboard sounds (his sound for the basic track was a stereo Rhodes-type sound). He also sent us a second pair of inputs (19 and 20), which were playing a loop.

Input List

Input section

1 click direct
2 bass DI direct
3 snare bottom ø5
4 kick direct
5 snare top5
6 hi-hat direct
7 OH Left direct
8 OH right direct
9 tom 1/2
10 tom 1/2
11 tom 1/2
12 tom 1/2
13 vocal direct
14 ac. gtr direct
15 el. gtr direct
16 el. gtr direct
17 keys left 3
18 keys right 4
19 keys/loop 6
20 keys/loop 6
21 gtr efx (unused) 7
22 gtr efx (unused) 8
23 talkback mic stereo bus only
24 talkback micstereo bus only

Monitor section

1 click
2 bass
3
4 kick
5 snare
6 hi-hat
7 OH left
8 OH right
9 toms left
10 toms right
11 keys left
12 keys right
13 vocal
14 loop
15 el. guitar left
16 el. guitar right

Though we brought the console with us, we used the studio's existing wiring. Microphone inputs came from the studio into the control room and then were patched into the 02R. Though only the first eight inputs have XLR connections, all of inputs 1 through 16 have the same controls, including a variable gain control and a 20 dB pad (there is no mic/line switch). Inputs 1 through 8 also give you phantom power and the kind of insert typically found on many project boards: one ¼-inch connector with the send at the tip and the return on the ring. Since channels 1 through 8 have the two types of connectors, they also have a switch that toggles between input A (the XLR) and input B (the ¼-inch). The external phantom power supplied for the condenser mics on the toms (inputs 9 through 12) and guitar (inputs 15 & 16) was our only use of any external gear for the session.

Although 9 through 16 are on ¼-inch connectors, those channels still have enough gain to accept a mic level signal. During some initial testing at Capitol, the gain structure on these inputs seemed different, and we thought that there would not be enough gain for a mic signal in channels 9 through 16. But it turned out that we were using a snake with some military-style connectors, and we found that these plugs will not work with the 02R. The 02R wants to see consumer-type ¼-inch TRS plugs like you'd find at the end of a headphone cable.

Cue It Up

Capitol has a headphone system with several 8-channel mix stations that allow musicians to adjust their own headphone mixes, so we decided to feed that system with the sends from the 02R, which are easily linked in stereo pairs. This makes them great for cue sends. We linked sends 1 and 2 as a pair and used them to make a keyboard-heavy mix of all the instruments. We also linked sends 3 and 4 and made that a drum-heavy mix. Send 5 was guitar-only, and send 6 was vocal-only. The click, the bass, and the stereo bus were patched directly from tape into the Capitol system. The last two sends of the 02R, 7 and 8, were dedicated for use with the 02R's two internal effect processors. John set send 7 to feed a short-to-medium-sized room reverb (for the instruments) and 8 a longer plate reverb (for the vocals and strings).

The 02R has a great feature that allows you to see quickly and easily what channels are being sent to which effect send. For example, let's say you are wondering, "Did I send the guitar to send 7, which is my plate reverb?" If you press the master button labeled "Send 7," the channel faders snap to show the level of each channel going to send 7. The channel faders act as send controls normally would, so you can make any changes right there. If you press the master "Send 1" button, the faders snap to show you which channels are turned up on send 1. If you hit "View," then the faders snap back to represent the tape return level in the mix.

After we got a basic track that the musicians and I felt was good, we gathered in the control room for a playback. Musicians are very quick to notice if anything is messing with the sound of their instrument. But without question, everyone was excited by what they were hearing through the speakers. So with the basic track out of the way, we were ready to move on and do a few overdubs. There would be some synth string sweetening, a quick drum overdub, and a few vocal fixes. Paul wanted to shoot another guitar track as well. Though the entire console was full, I still needed to add a third DA-88 for the overdubs. But I knew that interfacing this third machine was going to be a piece of cake. We had put a third TDIF (TASCAM Digital Interface) card in the slot of the 02R, which corresponds to channel faders 9 through 16. In the digital I/O page of the 02R, you can change these faders to accept digital input instead of analog sources, so they can become tape monitor inputs. Once we knew that we had the basic track down and didn't need those analog inputs anymore, we made the change. No patching was needed.

In addition, before we actually started overdubbing, we used the 02R's scene memory to save the tracking setup so that we would be able to recall bussing, EQ, send levels, panning, and dynamics for every channel, just in case we needed to come back to that setup.

Anyway, the first overdub we did was a mallet-cymbal track. We made the switch so we could hear all three DA-88's. The cymbal mics were on inputs 7 and 8, so we didn't have to do anything special with them. Once this overdub was done, we saved the overdub scene to memory and then went back to the tracking setup to redo the guitar. Since Paul didn't really need to hear the cymbal overdub to do his part, it was easier to do this switch back instead of repatching his guitar inputs down to a pair of inputs between 1 through 8. Though we still had to do the software toggle to switch channels 9 through 16 between analog and

Maintaining Digital Gain Structure

Toward the end of the recording session at Capitol Studios, I had one experience that is definitely worth relating. Upon hearing some intermittent distortion in the stereo mix (hey, it happens), we realized that the meters on the stereo output bus were showing "overs." Normally to cure something like this in the heat of battle, you might think of just pulling back the master fader and then the output would be fine. Maybe that works in the analog world, but that doesn't work on a digital console because it doesn't address the fact that the overs are occurring before the master fader. It's not like an analog board where you have headroom above a nominal 0 level. For example, say you have 20 dB of headroom on the stereo bus of the board you're using. Pulling down the master to trim your mix isn't a problem unless you have already trimmed it 20 dB and are still over zero on your meters. When you are over on a digital board, you are over, and while pulling the master fader down might make the output level lower, it does nothing to change the internal gain structure of the console, causing the digital distortion.

To solve this problem quickly without interrupting the session, I used the attenuators on each channel of the 02R to trim all of the inputs down by 2 or 3 dB. This gave me back a bit of headroom so that there wouldn't be this problem. If the gain structure coming into the board is fine, then you can use a different method of grouping all of the monitor sources (faders or pots) together and pulling them all down simultaneously.

The 02R's View page helps with this since there is a readout in dB next to the diagram of the fader. This eliminates the guesswork on how much you are trimming. (Remember the all-too-familiar step of patching an oscillator into a channel to establish a fader trim reference?)

You can also run into this sort of gain structure problem on the input side of things. Let's say you have a signal coming into a digital board and are using an on-board compressor to give you a nice "0" output. To get this nice 0 output, you have attenuated the compressor's output by 2 dB. Now let's say that in some spots where you have this nice 0 output, the compressor is compressing 6 dB. Not nice! The input to the compressor is distorting, and I'll leave it to you to do the math! You need to be especially cognizant about gain structure on a digital board. You simply cannot think of using a digital console as you would an analog one.

—*John Patterson*

Beat the Clock

For monitoring DAT playback, the Yamaha 02R provides three digital 2-track inputs: one AES and two S/PDIF. They correspond on the monitor section to digital 2-tracks one, two, and three, respectively — a digital version of the normal 2-track returns that an analog console would have. But here's something to consider: Most DAT players do not have a separate word clock input. When using a normal DAT player to record from a digital console, it would receive word clock through the AES or S/PDIF data stream during recording and lock onto that. That's easy enough. But playing back a DAT is another story.

If the DAT machine had a word clock connection, you could use the 02R's clock output as a reference for the DAT machine. But since most DAT machines do not have word clock inputs, the AES output from the DAT machine has to "drive" the 02R during DAT playback. Since the clock being sent from the DAT is not the same as the clock being used by the 02R (the DA-88's word output), you might sometimes hear a very slight click during the start of a DAT playback as the clock rates settle in. This is a minor inconvenience, but is nothing serious.

One of the nice features in the 02R is that the AES input for digital 2-track one can be assigned (via the digital I/O page) to stereo fader 17 and 18. This would be useful when, for instance, you have a SMPTE DAT or a Pro Tools session that you want to return digitally to inputs 17 and 18 and treat just like any other pair of tracks. Again, if you have such an input to the AES port assigned to 17 and 18 and you want to use it in your session, you have to address the question of clocking — and, of course, all of the digital signal sources must be at the same sample rate.

When running DA-88's, Yamaha suggests that the 02R slave its clock to the master DA-88. If the source coming into the AES input doesn't have a clock input, you may run into a few problems. We ran into this situation when trying to do some DSP'ing with an Eventide DSP4000, which has AES ins and outs, but no facility to receive an external clock. I tried to bring the DSP4000 up on inputs 17 and 18, but I couldn't get the whole system to run smoothly. I kept getting a prompt from the 02R that said "Reject AES 2-track digital input one?" One possible way to get around the problem is to figure out which clock you can't change (like the one coming into the AES input) and try to get the other units in your setup to lock to that clock.

—John Patterson

digital inputs, the scene memory recalled everything else we had going. It was literally done in a matter of seconds. When Paul was happy with his take, we recalled the overdub scene and all of those parameters came back for us to do the string sweetening.

We all know how important getting that killer lead vocal is in pop music. Any distraction on the technical side can blow the vibe and make it difficult for the engineer to keep their concentration level up. As we switched gears and went to record Fran's vocal, the scene memory feature and the 02R's "libraries" made it easy for me to make the switch without missing a beat. The lead vocal mic (a Neumann tube U 47) had to be moved from channel

13 for overdubbing since channel 13 was now being used to monitor track 5 from the third DA-88. It was very easy to match the gain structure and settings of channel 13 and use them for this new input channel. Although the channel's gain pot setting is not saved in scene memory (the pot is a conventional audio potentiometer), the control is detented. It's easy to count the number of clicks from "zero" and reset the pot. For the basic tracking, John had used a compressor preset from the 02R's library and modified it for Fran. He also saved this new compressor into the library. When we switched the vocal input, we went into the library and assigned Fran's compressor setting and EQ to the new channel. Again, all this was done in a matter of seconds without disrupting the flow of the session.

Back to New York

Once the recording had been finished, we used a Yamaha MDF-1 MIDI Data Filer to dump scene memories and dynamic automation moves from the 02R onto a floppy disk. Back at The Shire (my studio in New York), the MDF-1 was used to load this data into our 02R. We could have picked up the mix where we left off in Capitol, but for creative reasons we started a new mix with fresh ears. Had we done the session using Capitol's board, we would not have had the same flexibility to take the mix on disk and recall it exactly as we left it at the touch of a few buttons. Don't get me wrong, Capitol's board is a good one, and I have gotten some great-sounding music using it, but the recall process is considerably more complicated.

Since we wanted to do the remix at The Shire using the main channel faders, we used the 02R's "flip" function to swap the tape monitor and channel fader paths. Mixing on the 02R works like it does with most big-ticket digital consoles: You start with a scene memory (snapshot) and your automation proceeds with events (like channel on/off or dynamic moves) relative to that scene memory.

As you would expect, the automation runs via SMPTE. It so happens that the 02R's SMPTE input is an RCA connector, and the DA-88's SMPTE output (via the SY-88 sync card) is also an RCA connector, so patching the two was easy. If we had been doing a session with our sequencer running virtual tracks, the 02R could also accept MIDI timecode and lock to that.

Knowing that the recording is going to wind up on a CD, you have to select a sample rate for the project with that in mind. It doesn't make any sense to do the normal trick of recording at 48 kHz and then mixing at 44.1 kHz. If you go through an analog console, you are coming out of the multitrack via analog outputs to an Apogee converter and maybe laying the mix to DAT or PCM 9000 at 44.1 kHz. But in our case, once the audio is on tape, it is never going to leave the digital domain — it's just like on a hard-disk editing session. Your session sample rate determines what the output is going to be. We did the original multitrack session at 44.1 kHz so that we wouldn't have to do any sample-rate conversion to mix for CD.

Because the 02R's signal path is all digital, it allows you to automate changes in EQ and panning, as well as channel on/off and fader moves. In fact, we used this ability to fix a pop on the lead vocal by briefly changing the EQ at a specific point in the song. By inserting different scene memory changes in your mix, you can also automate changes to other parameters (such as dynamics) as well. Your imagination is your only limit. The effects used in the final mixdown came from the 02R's two internal processors, so the recorded signals were never converted to analog for routing to and from an external processor. For those of you keeping score at home, the final mix at The Shire was put down to a TASCAM DA-20 Mk II DAT machine via the AES input.

Listening to the final mix, I am very happy with the result. While the musicians and Fran were focusing on the music and striving to get the most out of their performances, the board never once got in their way nor was there any downtime of any kind in either the recording or mixing of the track. The console retained the warmth of the instruments, and the technology gave us the flexibility to walk out of the room with a floppy disk and some tapes and recall our work thousands of miles away.

I should point out that if I had been called on to do a large orchestra date, another 02R or more would have been needed. But I think it's clear that the board does have its applications. And what this board says it will do, it does.

No Limits

When dealing with guitar sounds, try anything — you might just like what you hear

By Jack Joseph Puig

Originally appeared in April 1998

Working with artists such as Eric Clapton, the Black Crowes, Jellyfish, Semisonic, Talk Show, Tonic, and You Am I, producer/engineer Jack Joseph Puig has recorded his share of guitarists. Jack Joseph spent some time with EQ, *sharing his views on recording guitar, and offers some insight for getting good guitar tones on tape.*

It's difficult to discuss recording guitar tones because you really can't narrow it down to one particular aspect, such as the microphone. When I worked with Eric Clapton, I recall arriving at the studio where he was diddling around through an old tweed Fender amp. I stood there in astonishment at the tone that was coming out of the amp and thought, "I have to capture that."

All guitar tones start at the musician's hand, and you have to realize this. From there, each part of the chain contributes to the end result, and that chain includes the way the musician plays, the guitar itself, the pick, the voicings, the cable, amp, room, position of the amp in the room, and even the way the musician holds the instrument. You really need to look at the picture as a whole. It would be impossible to address all of the aspects of what makes a guitar sound, but we can look at a few.

Watch and Learn

The object is to find the weakest link and get around it quickly without drawing attention to it. A good place to start is to watch the musician play his instrument. An inexperienced guitar player might hug the guitar and sort of wrap his body around it. He is choking the instrument by not allowing it to vibrate. If he can allow the instrument to breathe, it will sound more open. If the guitarist wants the sound to be a little more bright or aggressive, you can suggest that he move his picking hand a little farther toward the bridge, or maybe turn the pick sideways so the string catches the side of the pick a bit. These are simple things that can make for a better tone. By watching a person play, you can notice little things like that and make adjustments before even dealing with any gear.

For instance, if you are working with a musician who has a very light touch but wants to get an edgy sound, a simple MXR Dyna Comp can make a big difference. It's not a good idea to say anything about the playing style — you don't want him to start thinking about the way he's playing. Put the Dyna Comp in the chain after the guitar cable and whack it up. All of a sudden — even though he's still playing lightly — the amp is getting a stronger signal and it sounds like he's playing more aggressively. Or you might try suggesting a heavier pick, which puts more weight on the strings, adding a bit of edge to the sound. Players get used to certain picks and the way they feel; always show respect to the player. I generally have a pack of picks with me that range from medium to thick, metal, wood, plastic, felt, and smooth and jagged edges. This part of the equation is as important as selecting the proper amp.

When You Assume...

Equally as important in the chain is the guitar cable. Don't assume that any cable will work. My favorite is from Matchless, but keep in mind what kind of guitar it is. If it's a (Gibson) Chet Atkins acoustic, it has electronics built in and puts out so much signal that the cord is not nearly as important as if you are using a guitar with less output (for example, a vintage guitar with weaker pickups). In that case, the guitar will be very sensitive to the cable. For every band I have worked with, I've gone through every one of their cables and checked them out. We'll get myriad cords, try them all, and figure out which cable works best with a particular guitar player's setup. I have even outfitted bands with guitar cables because they make such a big difference.

I like to record with the guitar player in the control room, but if you use a cable longer than about 12 feet, the pickups will have trouble driving the line. I had a box built to drive the line so that the pickups will not be affected much, but you can use a Matchless Cool Box (pedal) to drive the line. The Cool Box (which is one of my favorite pedals) is a tube buffer with a tone-shaping knob on it. What is brilliant about it is that you can take many guitars or amps that might be satisfactory at best and, by using that box alone, you can change the world — really warm up a tone, or make it brighter or darker. As an alternative, other guitar pedals can be used to buffer the guitar from a long line, though maximum length for me is about 12 feet if a buffer is not used. Choose an alternate to the Cool Box at your discretion, depending upon what you'd like to hear.

An important thing to consider is the relationship between the amplifier and the room. If I walk into a huge room and see a guitarist playing a small amp, I immediately know that I am not going to put that amp in the center of the room because it will sound too small. I need to put that amp in an area that will give it more body, or perhaps change to a smaller room. Placing the amp in a corner makes the walls behind the amp act as a horn to project the sound and make it seem bigger. Listen to the way the amp sounds in the room and make adjustments. If the sound is a little bright, place the amp on a piece of carpet. If the amp sounds muddy, place it on a chair (or better yet a riser) and it will add clarity to the sound because the amp is no longer coupling to the floor and reinforcing the bass frequencies.

Lost on a Desert Island

I wish I could say that there was another mic besides a Shure SM57 that pretty much works almost every time — but I can't. Without a doubt, that microphone is a desert island mic. But I still try different mics all the time, and I have had great success with different dynamic or condenser microphones. The SM57 has been used on every possible amplifier, by a million engineers in a million situations. And every record sounds different. So it's really not just about the mic, but the way you listen to the amp and your attitude about the recording.

I could make a bunch of suggestions for microphones that you could try as an alternate to the SM57, but that's kind of ridiculous because every situation is different. That's why I chose the SM57 as my desert island mic. As an experiment, I once told an assistant, "Go into the mic locker, pick whatever mics are on the immediate left when you walk in, and put them up on the various instruments." The outcome was a couple of tracks from Tonic's *Lemon Parade*, one of which was a big hit.

If the sound is too thin in the control room, move the mic around to get what you need. You don't necessarily need to add another mic or change the mic. An old trick is to put on headphones, whack them up really loud, and listen to the amp so you'll hear what that mic is picking up. Try this with the guitar plugged in and turned up, but no one playing it. It acts like an antenna and provides a sound to the amp. Put the mic up close and you'll hear hum and buzz because no one is holding the guitar. As you move the mic toward the center of the speaker, you get more highs, detail, and fret noise. As you move the mic away from the center of the cone, you get more woofy-ness.

You may need to use two mics: one focused to pick up every little detail and another off-axis to pick up the low end (a lot of times I'll use a dynamic and a condenser to cover different aspects of the sound, using each to fill in what the other is missing). When you add those together, they may add in a good way or in a weird way, but that weird way might be very cool for the song.

If someone brings in a 4 x 12 cabinet, it doesn't mean that all four speakers sound good. Listen to them through the headphones to find the good sounding one(s). This gives you a way of assessing what's happening in the chain. Something to keep in mind when using condenser mics (such as a U 67 or U 47) is that they do pick up sound at their head. If the mic is hanging upside down with the head toward the floor, it's picking up sound bounced off the floor, which could make it brighter. But if the head is up, it doesn't pick up the same reflection. Take the time to listen both ways until you've learned the difference.

Seeing Red

The Hughes and Kettner Red Box is a cool device to use as part of the sound along with the mics. A speaker level output from the amp is plugged into the Red Box and the Red Box puts out two signals — an output to the speaker and a mic level feed to the console. There's definitely a phase issue between the Red Box and the mics because the sounds arrive at two different speeds (the speaker-to-microphone path takes longer). Sometimes you'll get amazing cancellations that sound great. An interesting thing to do is to use the mics on one side of the mix and the Red Box on the other to give it a "false stereo" feel. That technique is all over the Black Crowes' *Three Snakes and a Charm*.

Use the Force

To me, getting a guitar sound is not just in the mics and placement. It's equally in the signal chain. Everybody always says "there are no rules," and it's really true. You can try all sorts of things like using a DI or miking the front of an electric guitar. I have even taped a telephone pickup from Radio Shack onto the guitar body and added that in to the sound. Don't limit yourself artistically. The mic selection and placement really comes in only when you hear a tone in the room and say, "I have to capture that," as opposed to manipulating the tone. It's a great day when you reach the point when you learn all these things and the process becomes more like walking — you no longer think about it. You listen to the amp in the studio and instinctively know what to do. As your career goes on, you have a larger variety of solutions because you have learned more tricks.

Share these experiences with other engineers and they'll share theirs with you, allowing you both to grow and make better recordings for you and your artist. The point is that the human touch is an important part of the equation!

SECTION IV

SURROUND SOUND

Martin Porter, *EQ*'s Executive Editor at the time, saw surround sound as the future of recording *waaaay* back in 1993. Then there were only a handful of producers, engineers, and artists doing it, but they were the top guys in the business. Each of these studio veterans loved the challenges mixing in surround sound gave them, and embraced it rapidly.

Unfortunately, the public wasn't as enthusiastic as the audio trailblazers, and surround sound for music didn't catch on as fast as we had hoped, but it has caught on, and is now on the verge of gaining mass market acceptance.

Join us for the earliest days of mixing surround sound for music, and let the best in the biz tell you what to do and, more important, what not to do.

Creating Surround Sound Mixes

Enough theorizing — here's how to get into surround sound mixing and, more important, why

By Robert Margouleff and Brant Biles with Steve La Cerra

Originally appeared in October 1997

Since its introduction in the 1960s, stereo (2-channel sound) has dominated our industry. During the early 1970s, the record industry marketed recordings in quadraphonic (4-channel sound), but quad never really caught on for several reasons. One: Groove geometry couldn't support four discrete channels of sound on a vinyl record. Two: The music business didn't involve the artist enough. And three: There were too many encoding schemes and no one could agree on a standard. While the various companies involved argued, the whole thing fell by the wayside.

Well, it's more than 20 years later and audio technology has grown by leaps and bounds. Motion pictures are routinely mixed in surround sound and encoded into film soundtracks using formats such as Dolby Pro Logic Surround, Dolby Digital, DTS (Digital Theater Systems), and SDDS (Sony Digital Dynamic Sound). Anytime that you start mentioning something with three initials — whether it's DTS, AC-3, THX (which is *not* a codec), DVD, or the like — people tend to get a glazed look in their eyes due to the information overload caused by all this new technology. Since we are professionals working in the audio industry, we think it's a very good idea to define the parameters of what's going on in surround, and why it's important.

Why Surround?

The first thing you're probably asking yourself is, "Why would I want to mix a record in surround sound?" And given the checkered history of surround audio, it's a legitimate question. Here's a story to help you understand why: Last summer, we were mixing the *Pavarotti and Friends for War Child* concert in 5.1 surround, for release by HDS Records in DTS (we'll get to what "5.1" means later). Originally produced by Phil Ramone and recorded by John Pellowe, it had been recorded live with a full orchestra. We were given only six stereo pairs of premixed stems, thus making our job kind of a cross between mixing and mastering.

There were a few problems initially, but when we dug into it and got it sounding good, a few people came in for a listen. Upon doing so, they would slip out of the control room in tears because they were so struck with emotion. It happened to us as well, and we had to actually stop, step back for a minute, and then continue mixing. Surround greatly intensifies the emotional energy of the music — that is the bottom line.

Over the course of the last few years, people have left music behind for other electronic stimuli. Our industry needs to bring them back through the true power of music. Millions of people already have surround systems installed in their homes to play back movies on video and laserdisc, so why not share the same platform for music reproduction? It seems we're at the beginning of a convergence of new technologies, where music, film/video, and computing will all come from (and be accessed by) the same system. Surround allows us to communicate in a whole new way (with a much larger canvas) and with many new colors of paint for our creative palates.

First Thing's First

For starters, let's make clear what we're talking about — *discrete* multichannel audio. We're not talking about psychoacoustic surround systems, which all use two speakers to create the illusion of sound coming from all around you. This technology is called transaural audio, an example of which is QSound. Transaural audio is now being developed for the delivery of surround for multimedia computers. Sometimes referred to as "Fifty-Yard-Line" surround, it's good for only one person, and you have to be positioned on the center line of the two speakers to be able to hear the phantom surround images. If you're at exactly the right angle and the listening geometry is perfect, then one person will get 3D audio. What we are concerned with is digital, discrete, 5.1 surround sound. Some people in the industry refer to an audio-only surround mix as a "6-channel mix" to distinguish it from multichannel audio-for-video. For this article, we'll refer to it as "5.1."

In and of itself, 5.1 is *not* a specific surround format, owing its allegiance to any particular company or codec. It is a listening platform and hardware concept for a surround monitoring system. If you want to listen to music in 5.1, you need six discrete audio channels in your listening room. These channels are Left Front, Center, Right Front, Left Surround, Right Surround, and Subwoofer — that's the ".1." Since the Subwoofer, or LFE (Low Frequency Effect in the film industry/Low Frequency Enhancement in the music industry), channel isn't full frequency, the powers that be didn't feel it was worthy of its own number when naming this format "5.1." It's important, though, to note that 5.1 audio-only mixes can be played using the same amps and loudspeakers used for home theater surround.

As audio professionals, it's also important to remember that the philosophies of mixing audio-only surround and surround for video are completely different. Video requires a "front-loaded" mix to support a picture. In audio-only mixing, the constraints of film/video mixing can be broken. By regarding all channels as equals, the possibilities become endless. In the motion-picture world, the two most popular 5.1 formats are Dolby Digital and DTS, with Sony's SDDS trailing as a distant third. All three store data digitally and are delivered by varying methodologies. (It's worth mentioning that the HDTV standard also includes 5.1 audio.)

Six Mix

Within the 5.1 platform are several formats that use encoders to form a new bitstream from the six channels of digital information included in the mix. This encoded bitstream is then burned onto a CD, laserdisc, DVD, or other storage medium. Upon playback, the listener needs a complementary decoder to translate data from within that new bitstream back into the six channels of digital audio. This process of encode-decode is called a codec.

Now you're probably thinking, "Here we go again with different decoders and no standard," but the truth is that the 5.1 setup and hardware are the same for these systems except for the codec. Fortunately for the consumer market, the same DSP chip from one of several manufacturers can decode both the DTS and Dolby Digital formats. Soon, the discs themselves will have an ID flag to let the decoder know which codec was used. Once this is known, the decoder will automatically switch modes and process the incoming signal appropriately. This will overcome the main reason that quad failed, because it will be possible to have a single decoder unit that recognizes all incoming bit streams.

As previously mentioned, there are two major 5.1 surround formats already in the marketplace. Both call for five full-range speakers (preferably all the same) plus a subwoofer. Let's take a brief look at them:

Dolby Digital

Previously known as AC-3, Dolby Digital is well-entrenched in the motion picture industry with roughly 10,700 Dolby Digital-equipped screens worldwide. For home use, Dolby has developed a data compression ratio of (typically) 11:1, originally developed to fit 5.1 audio onto the same disc with the video data for movies on DVD. The data rates for 5.1-channel Dolby Digital are designated as 320 kilobits per second (kbps) for film, 384 kbps for laserdisc, and 384 or 448 kbps for DVD. Dolby's current encoder can accept incoming data at 32-, 44.1-, or 48-kHz sample rates, with word lengths of 16, 18, or 20 bits (this can be extended to 24-bit word length in the future).

DTS

In 1993, *Jurassic Park* became the first motion picture to be released in DTS. Since that time, DTS has become firmly established in the motion picture industry. DTS is now currently installed in over 12,000 theaters worldwide. For home video, the DTS codec is scalable from

256 kbps to 1,536 kbps, and DTS is focusing on 1,411 kbps as the optimum for transparent sound quality. Even though DTS began exclusively in the movie business, its emphasis on optimum sound quality stems from a corporate commitment to bring 5.1 to the forefront of the music industry.

A DTS compact disc carries six channels of digital audio (5.1) in 20-bit words at a 44.1 kHz sample rate. To fit this information onto a CD, DTS compresses the data at a ratio of about 3:1. As of this writing, there are around 10,000 DTS decoders in homes across the U.S., and that number is expected to grow to 50,000 by the end of this year. DTS was the first company to jump into the 5.1 CD and DVD-audio-only pool. Right now, only DTS-encoded 5.1 mixes are being released on standard CD. Although an additional decoder is needed, you can play a DTS CD on a standard CD or laserdisc combination player (and DVD player as well), provided that the player has a digital output for connecting to the decoder.

Jumping In

Artistically speaking, mixing in surround opens up a whole new world of creativity to an artist. Surround interacts with listeners by putting them in the performance. Instead of being observers, they are participants. For example, if you listen to a CD, the music sits in front of you as an object. One can then choose to regard it or not — sort of like looking at a painting hung on the wall. In surround though, the listener moves from that objective experience into a subjective experience, where the music and listener occupy the same space — you are now an element in the painting and not just an outside observer. This is a very different world, which will determine how people write, perform, and record music in the future. It's not just, "Let's take a stereo recording and make it into surround." We're talking about many new artistic production decisions like, "Are we going to put the congas in the rear and the rhythm guitar in the left front? Should the lead vocal move to the center channel while the background vocals move in rhythm around the room?"

In traditional mixing, we use all kinds of devices, such as reverberation, echo, doubling, spacial processing, compression, and pitch-shifting — every trick in the book — to create the illusion of space and depth. In conventional stereo recordings, a person might double a part and pan one left and one right. In surround, artists might think along the lines of recording four (or five) different performances or orchestrations of the same part, and have one come from each loudspeaker. It's the same part, but you'd get this overwhelming immersion in the sound because it's being delivered from multiple locations instead of just two.

A lot of recorded performances (especially in pop music) are not documentary reports of reality. For example, most symphony orchestra recordings are made in the documentary style. You put a dummy microphone head in an auditorium, the orchestra plays, and that's the whole recording (which is totally valid). This is not to say that orchestral recordings in surround aren't phenomenal, because they are! A pop record (on the other hand) is done in a more serial way, with lots of overdubs. Many pop records will never be (and never were intended to be) performed live. It's not a real-time event. So what happens is that you move into this realm where the medium is part of the performance. When you suddenly have six channels of audio to put the performance into (instead of two), the listening experience is incredible.

As producers and engineers, we can now think in terms of six busses. Earlier this past year, we remixed Boyz II Men *II* for DTS. This was a major project that had been recorded on 24-track analog. Some songs had multiple slave reels for ganging up background vocal and percussion performances into submixed stereo pairs for the final stereo mix. One particular song, "Water Runs Dry" (originally produced by Babyface), had a total of 18 individual tracks of background vocals. Instead of using the available stereo submix, we set them up so that you sit in the center of the room and get this massive blend of the quartet. If you want to hear a little more of Nate you can move over to the left rear speaker. If you want to hear a little more of Sean, you can walk over to the right front. In this way, the mix becomes interactive and you actually change the mix depending upon your position in the room. The mix takes place in the room — not in the loudspeakers.

Also worth mentioning is that there seems to be a lack of hearing fatigue when mixing in surround. We're all familiar with the fact that when mixing in stereo, the ears get fatigued over the course of the day. But, to our surprise, with surround mixing, fatigue seems greatly reduced. We believe this is due to the nature of human hearing. When a sound is generated from two locations, there are phase peaks and valleys at different frequencies, at different places in a room. This phenomenon is more apparent if the two sources are located front and rear as opposed to left and right. So, as you move while working (nobody keeps perfectly still with their teeth on a bite bar), your ears get more of a variance in SPL at different frequencies. Also, with music in 5.1, the ratio of average SPL to perceived loudness is lower than that of stereo.

The Politics of Surround

In the past, surround has not been a very democratic medium because it has been expensive for both pros and consumers. But as audio professionals, we have to recognize two important things: First, 5.1 lives in what is now known as the home theater — which is the largest-selling segment of the hi-fi business. In fact, it's the only area of home entertainment that isn't depressed. Second: Technological advances in recording equipment are making surround attainable in any home studio (there's the democracy).

Tools of the Trade

We have been mixing and mastering projects digitally at The Enterprise (Los Angeles, CA) using a Neve Capricorn that has an all-digital signal path and dynamic memory. Other producers and engineers have been using consoles such as those from Euphonix (digital control of an analog signal path with dynamic memory), SSL, and older Neves. Though the older analog desks lack dynamic memory, it is still possible to do surround mixes on them. So where does this surround mix end up?

Mostly on a TASCAM DA-88. In the case of mixing for the DTS codec, all six output busses must be digital (AES), 20-bit, and at 44.1 kHz. In the case of an analog console, the analog busses must go to six A/D converters, that can put out a 20-bit word length. Once in the digital domain, all six channels get routed to a Prism MR-2024T. The Prism unit takes these six 20-bit channels and converts them to eight channels of 16-bit TDIF (TASCAM Digital Interface) information. The MR-2024T achieves this by storing the upper 16-bits of all six channels on the first six tracks of the DA-88, respectively. The remaining 4 bits per channel are then combined and stored on tracks 7 and 8. On playback, the Prism recombines the first six tracks of 16-bit information with its respective bottom four bits and spits back out the original 20-bit information sent to it. Thus, we store a 20-bit, 5.1 mix on a 16-bit DA-88 tape.

Although we use a Neve Capricorn, there is great news for you, the thrifty audio equipment buyer: The Yamaha 03D and revised 02R can output six digital busses. Both have dynamic memory and panning — just like the Capricorn and Euphonix — but cost under 12 grand (under five for the 03D). That, combined with the DA-88, means that a project studio can mix in discrete 6-channel surround with automated faders, panning, equalization, and dynamics (though the mix would still have to be mastered and encoded). As a matter of fact, you can set up a standard 8-bus analog mixer for 5.1. We recently mastered the Eagles' *Hell Freezes Over,* which was mixed by Elliot Scheiner at Capitol on a Neve VR with an analog film bus. The point is, with a little forethought and creativity, it can be done.

To maximize panning flexibility, you might want a joystick panner, but the Capricorn doesn't have one, and we've used that console to do many surround mixes (the tips of our fingers have calluses on them from twisting the knobs all over the place). If not a joystick, then certainly a console that can memorize panning moves in automation. If you were using an analog console and needed to move a sound from the Left Front to the Rear Right, you might try returning the track to two faders. Then assign each fader to its intended output bus and crossfade between them. You do it once and, like magic, you've got automated surround panning. Simplifying matters further is the fact that there are a lot of high-quality, self-powered loudspeaker designs available, which decrease the wiring headaches. We've been using Genelec 1032A's with a pair of M&K's M5000 subwoofers.

In our monitoring situations, we try to set all of the speakers equidistant (90 to 100 inches) from the listening position. This places the Left-Front, Center, and Right-Front speakers in an arc. If that cannot be done, then a compensation of level for the Center channel is in order. We want to make sure that there are symmetrical and equal front and rear soundstages.

One of the nicest tools we have found for surround mixing is the EMT 250 reverb, which — originally designed in the 1970s for quad — is single input, four output. We've also used Lexicon 480L's and two PCM80's with one machine returning to the front and the other returning to the rear.

Generally you'll find that you use less effects in surround than in stereo, and the front-to-back assignment of sound is more dramatic than left-to-right panning. We have taken to mixing into either Sonic Solutions or Pro Tools, eliminating the need for tape, and this obviously makes assembling an album, level-matching, and mastering much easier. These masters really need to be prepared in some sort of standardized room, though. In fact, A&M and Abbey Road studios are currently building control rooms dedicated and equipped for surround mixing.

It's all at the "bloody cutting edge" right now, and we don't have all the answers yet, but we're working hard to get as many as we can. We're in the lab right now and quite honestly, we haven't had this much fun in years! The surround bell has rung and it can't be unrung!

The Near Future

While we're writing this, the RIAA is working with the DVD Alliance to evaluate a proposed software/hardware standard for a high-density audio-only DVD. Among other features, it would store a discrete 6-channel mix (bit depth and sample rate to be determined) along with a high-resolution stereo mix. A DVD can hold all of this information because of its high storage capacity. The RIAA is also recommending that this disc be dual-layer composed of the high-density layer plus a standard-density "Red Book" layer to provide your standard 16-bit PCM stereo mix (which would ensure backward compatibility). Under consideration for inclusion in the software/hardware standard are codecs from Sony/Philips, Toshiba/Warner, DTS, and Dolby.

*Both Robert Margouleff (known for his Grammy-award winning work with Stevie Wonder) and Brant Biles are independent producer/engineers who have worked together in varying capacities over the last ten years. In addition to the recordings mentioned in this article, their most recent projects include surround remastering for Paul McCartney (*Band on the Run*) and Alan Parsons (*On Air*), surround 5.1 remixing/restoration of the Marvin Gaye anthology* Forever Yours, *and broadcast mixing for* Carlos Santana Live at the Universal Amphitheatre *and* Sheryl Crow Live at the House of Blues.

Mixing with the Big Bands

Capturing the music of Duke Ellington in surround requires some creative thinking and a really big shell

By Tom Jung

Originally appeared in October 1997

I just completed a discrete 5.1 mix of the *DMP Big Band Salutes Duke Ellington*, and the artistic goal of the process was for me to try and put the listener in the room with the band, to re-create the room in which the performance took place. What that means is that, in addition to miking the band differently, we also miked the room differently.

At the recording session, we monitored in stereo, but experimented with different room recording techniques. This particular project was recorded live in the studio and I actually had an RPG Performance Shell inside the studio. This is an acoustic shell that one might put over a stage area to form a conventional bandshell. It's quite large, and I set up the band so that they were at the opposite end of the room, blowing toward the shell — the reverse of its conventional purpose. I used a hot-rodded Shure VP88 stereo microphone pointed toward the inside of the shell to record the very diffusive reflections from it. I didn't want hard or early reflections, and the inside of the shell is full of RPG diffusers, so it produces a very diffuse soundfield. To capture as much of that aspect as possible, I pointed the microphone toward the inside middle of the shell.

While we were recording for 5.1, we were simultaneously recording the session for a matrix surround release in Circle Surround, and one of the main reasons that I used the Shure stereo mic was that it creates an almost perfect mono — no worry about phasing problems in the matrix. (A quick side note: People with regular CD players can play the disc in the normal manner. If they have a Circle Surround decoder, they have the option to decode the surround information that is embedded in the data stream.)

Now Hear This

I use the same monitor system for both discrete and matrix surround mixes; recently, the new powered Paradigm monitors. I have three Active 20 two-way monitors for the Front Left, Center, and Front Right. I had been using the same monitors for the rear channels and was adamant about having five matched speakers — and I think that for some types of music that's a necessity. But my artistic goal is to put the listener in the room with the performance, rather than have the performance surrounding the listener. I am not against having the instruments behind the listener, because, when it's appropriate, it can be very effective, such as on Alan Parsons's *On Air*, where it is tastefully done. [*Editor's note: Parsons has released both stereo and DTS 5.1 surround versions of* On Air.] But since I'm doing mostly acoustic music, it makes more sense to get the listener involved by building the venue around the listener as opposed to building the *band* around the listener.

Because of that, I went to another powered speaker from Paradigm, called the Active 450-ADP, which is an interesting speaker. It is dipolar (out of phase) down to about 200 Hz, and then becomes bipolar below 200 Hz. The mids and highs are more diffusive than with a conventional loudspeaker, and the sweet spot tends to be wider. I do feel it's important for the front and rear speakers to have at least a family resemblance.

For a subwoofer, I'm using the Paradigm Servo 15, though I'm not totally convinced a subwoofer is necessary for acoustic music. For pop and synth-type music and cinema purposes it is. But when used on recordings containing acoustic bass, it gives the instrument an unnatural color and can exaggerate it. I have used it in the past and regretted it. And you don't know if people at home have their subwoofers set too loud, so there's a danger of possible errors in the listening environment. For example, what if there's *no* Center channel? That's why I use the subwoofer and Center channel sparingly. (I learned this the hard way with a recording of the Glenn Miller Orchestra that I heard at a tradeshow in Las Vegas. Their system had no center speaker, and when they played my disc there was no bass.)

I also have been experimenting with an extra microphone to add the height factor into recordings. At one point I had an overhead monitor speaker, but then I came back to reality and recognized that no one has an overhead speaker in their listening rooms! However, I do use a height mic as a signal send into a pair of stereo digital reverbs. I use two Sony DPS-V77's, one of which is used for the Front Left and Front Right, the other is returned to the Rear Left and Rear Right. This helps me approach the height goal, but does not totally accomplish it. What I really want is a 5-channel reverb.

Tree Mics

DMP Big Band Salutes Duke Ellington was recorded onto a Yamaha (20-bit) DRU8. When it came to miking, we had the horns miked with a quasi-Decca "tree" arrangement. This mic technique was (and, I believe, still is) used by Decca to make orchestral recordings. Three mics are arranged into a triangle, separated equally by a few feet. The distance between the mics can vary depending on the width of what you want to record (*e.g.*, for a symphony orchestra, you'd space them farther apart). There's a left mic, a center mic, and a right mic all set to cardioid, though I believe Decca engineers also used Neumann M 50's, which become more omnidirectional in the low frequencies. The center mic is placed slightly closer to the performers than the left and right mics. For 5.1, these mics go to the Left, Center, and Right (Front) channels. In this case, I used two Soundelux U95's and an AKG C12VR to capture the overall sound of the band.

There were also a few "spot" mics on certain instruments. Drums were recorded with two mics: a beyerdynamic M160 ribbon for overhead and a Shure Beta 52 on the kick drum. Both were bussed to one track of the DRU8. We also used two Shure SM80's (no longer manufactured, the SM80 was an omni version of the SM81). One was placed on the bass and another was placed on the piano — just for highlighting the sound. To maintain phase integrity between the spot mics and the tree mics, we tweaked the delays on the SM80's via our Yamaha 02R console. As mentioned, the Shure VP88 was used for the RPG Performance Shell surround signal.

Pots and Pans

For the discrete 5.1 mix, I used a Yamaha 02R-V2, which has the ability to pan across five busses. The Decca tree mics were panned to the Left, Center, and Right, and then I moved them slightly toward the listener, which placed the horns slightly up front and created the depth of the live orchestra. Drums were panned between the Center and the Right Front; piano was panned between the Left Front and the Center.

Panning on the bass was rather interesting. The 02R-V2 allows you to vary the center pan between two sort of modes. In one mode, the control sends the signal to the phantom Center channel derived from the Left and Right channels — just like a conventional stereo mix. At the other extreme, the control discretely feeds the Center channel. I didn't want to route the bass exclusively to the Center channel because of the previously mentioned reasons. So this control allowed me to bleed a bit of bass in the discrete Center channel and the phantom Center channel — just in case.

Don't underestimate the power of the Center channel, because, as you move around the listening room, the center channel really helps to maintain a solid image. Also, having a center channel with the bass is constructive, acoustically speaking. Most front speakers are in corners that can excite ugly room modes; a center speaker is usually not in a corner and, as such, is not subject to severe acoustic problems. So I try to strike a balance between the discrete Center channel and the phantom Center. Or you can shoot for an average between the Center and the subwoofer channel.

The signal from the VP88 was panned to the Rear channels and pulled in toward the listener a bit. That information was also sent to the rear Sony 'V77. Over half of the information going to the rear was just that mic. Stereo 'verbs front and rear help add a sense of spaciousness and I have even experimented with a mono reverb routed to the Center channel.

This discrete 5.1 mix was sent to a Prism MR2024T converter that arranges the six channels of 20-bit data across eight tracks of 16-bit, which were then recorded on a DA-88. This DA-88 tape was then sent to DTS for encoding, so that the 20-bit data stream could be transferred to disc and mastered for release — keeping the signal 20-bit from the DRU8 through the 02R, and down to the final product.

Tom Jung is the engineer, producer, and president of Digital Music Products, Inc. For more information on surround sound and other DMP projects, you can visit their Web site at www.dmprecords.com.

Surround Gets *Road Tested*

Mixing Bonnie Raitt's album in surround puts you in with the crowd

By Ed Cherney

Originally appeared in October 1997

About a year and a half ago, I recorded and mixed Bonnie Raitt's *Road Tested*, a live double-CD. At that time, I didn't know that it'd be remixed for surround. But several weeks ago, Brant Biles and I were approached by DTS to do a 5.1 remix. Maybe I had some premonitions (or got lucky) because in addition to recording the instruments on 48-track digital (using David Hewitt's remote truck), I also recorded audience mics in stereo pairs onto a TASCAM DA-88. I had pairs of mics way back in the balcony and running up and down the hall. There was also a pair of shotgun mics located on the sides of the stage, pointing into the audience. I miked these various locations because we were recording in two different halls (three shows in Portland, OR and three shows in Oakland, CA), and I knew that the halls would sound different. I figured that by using the DA-88 to record the room mics, I could advance- or retard-offset them to the 48-track tape, allowing me to adjust any time anomalies between them and match the ambience of the two rooms.

When I mixed the album for stereo, it was a major piece of work to get all of that information coming out of two speakers, but even then I really tried to get a surround thing going with just two speakers. I've been a proponent of Spatializer, so on the stereo album I used it a lot to try and get the listener (through two speakers) to feel like they were in the hall — that there were some things going on behind and to the sides. Obviously I'd be able to get more depth using six speakers.

Square One

Brant Biles and I started the surround mix process by going back into the studio and recalling the stereo mix. When I had mixed for stereo, we marked down all the EQ settings, delays, reverbs, compression — all of the processing. In addition, we had the floppy from the GML automation done at Brooklyn Recording Studio (Los Angeles, CA) on a Neve 8078 — which, by the way, was tricky to configure for mixing in surround (more on that coming). After doing the recall, we began to tweak the mix until it sounded like the stereo album. From there we started moving sounds out of the left and right speakers, into the other speakers.

Getting Panned

Instruments were basically panned to where the musicians were standing on stage. We weren't sending instruments into the Rear channels just to show you how dramatic the surround was (I didn't go for the gimmicky thing). But I did take some of the reverb and ambience to the rear so you'd get the feeling of reflections from the back wall. For example, the stage setup had keyboards on stage left, B3's on stage right, guitar slightly to the right, percussion more toward the left, and Bonnie in the middle.

Ed Cherney, shown here with Jann Arden at Hollywood's Record Plant, found mixing a live album in surround challenging.

Over the course of the six shows, various guests appeared with Bonnie and we tried to re-create their positioning on the stage. At the same time, we used ambient signals for these instruments to create the effect of reflections from the rear. Glenn Clark (in Bonnie's band) played B3 on some songs, and we'd have him panned right with some ambience from the room mics coming from behind and to the sides. His sound source was coming from the stage, but the reflections came from different parts of the room, arriving at your ear at different times. Using short delays of around 20 milliseconds, we played some games by panning the delay to the opposite speaker location from where Glenn was. If he was coming out of the Right Front, there'd be a little delay on the opposite side over your left shoulder.

The original, realistic positions of the ambient mics were used as a guide for their position in the surround mix. We literally felt like we were in the fifth row when we were mixing. There were people behind me talking, people five rows back whom you could hear over your shoulder, and even somebody yelling out something to Bonnie (there's one in every crowd). That added a lot of excitement, and the mixes sound as if you're sitting in the middle of all of those people.

Console-ing Thoughts

As I mentioned earlier, we mixed the 5.1 version on a Neve 8078. This was a challenge. The 8078 had 40 inputs and 32 tape monitor returns, but remember that I had a 48-track DASH tape plus eight tracks on DA-88 — so there weren't enough line inputs for all of the tracks. To solve this we brought the remaining tape tracks up on the monitor side of the console. Unfortunately, the tape monitor returns could only hit the L/R master bus, and not the multitrack busses. (The quad busses had been bypassed years ago for stereo mixing.) The L/R master bus fed the Front Right and Front Left channels. So, to be able to route the monitor returns to the Rear channels as well, we decided to use two cue sends in the monitor section of the console and feed them to the rear busses. That gave us four of the six busses that we needed, with the subwoofer and Center channel busses remaining. All the effects returned to the monitor section and went to the Rears via the cue sends.

For the subwoofer and Center feed, we used two of the multitrack busses on the input side of the console, which meant that the monitor section couldn't access the sub or Center. We tried to configure the console so that we didn't need to send anything from the monitor section to the subwoofer. If we did need to route a tape return to the subwoofer, the solution was to mult the tape machine output, patch one output of the mult to the monitor return, and patch another out from the mult to an empty channel on the input side of the console. Then we'd have the same signal on both sides of the console with one fader (on the monitor side) feeding the L/R or Rear busses and another fader (on the input side) feeding the sub and Center. Basically we only used the subwoofer for things like bass guitar, kick drum, and some synth sounds that had low pads. That was about it, but what was assigned to the subwoofer was really effective.

In a stereo mix, without the subwoofer channel, you have to work hard to create the shape of the low end, plus get it to pop but still be clear. The subwoofer alleviated a lot of those problems because now I could get an octave or two lower on the instrument — which I could never put into a stereo mix without muddying the whole thing up. That helped maintain the clarity more so than in a stereo recording. Bonnie's vocal was typically routed to the center. Any effects that I used on Bonnie would go to the sides and any kind of longer ambience for her voice went to the rears.

In terms of clearing out space, the ability to pan reverbs to the surround channels was a definite help. We used longer-than-normal reverb times for the plate and room programs we had going. A lot of times when you try to put reverbs into a stereo mix, it just gets muddy, but by putting them in the rear channels you could hear them decay more clearly. We also sent some slightly delayed signals from the instruments (like solos) to the rear to emulate the slap in the hall.

In the stereo mix, the balances were often a moving target. In the surround mix, we established a level for an instrument and pretty much stayed with it. A lot of the automated moves from the stereo mix weren't needed. Take for example, the rhythm guitar. In the stereo mix, it would be moved around to accommodate a keyboard part coming in, or a solo, or background vocals. We didn't have to do much of that in surround. There was more space, and the parts were easier to hear.

As you might notice from reading other 5.1-related articles, the amount of compression required in a 5.1 mix is usually much less than that for a stereo mix. I often play the compression game in stereo mixing, but I didn't have to do that this time around. Although there were compressors warmed-up and ready to go, we ended up not compressing any of the six busses. I also backed off the compression on individual instruments. When instruments have to be "there" and you're packing them into two channels, sometimes you have to limit the dynamics just to make them appear loud. It's tough to place the vocal on top of that, and sometimes you can run out of headroom in a stereo mix. With 5.1 you can clear things out of the way and place the vocal more easily.

Monitoring in the Pink

In the control room, we matched the levels for all of the speakers using pink noise and an SPL meter. Measurements were made at the listening position and each speaker was adjusted to produce an SPL of 85 dB. Then we could mix accordingly. Bus outs from the console went into three 20-bit Prism A/D converters, then off to a Prism MR-2024T 20-bit TDIF converter that sent a bit stream to the DA-88 (the MR-2024T maintains 20-bit resolution on a DA-88 by printing six channels of 20-bit data across eight tracks). The output from the DA-88 was routed back through the MR-2024T and to three D/A-converters. Analog outputs from the converters went to six patchable GML faders in a roll around side-cart, which then fed the individual speakers. (We didn't need amps because we had Genelecs).

By monitoring through the converters and the DA-88 for the entire time, playing back a mix was as easy as rewinding the DA-88 and hitting "Play." Using a group master, we were able to set levels on the six channels and then use the group master for the control room level. Setting all of this up took about a day and a half, but once the system was up and running, everything worked fine.

In addition to Bonnie Raitt, engineer/producer Ed Cherney has also worked with Little Feat, Eric Clapton, Bob Dylan, Jackson Browne, Jann Arden, the Manhattan Transfer, and the Rolling Stones. If you haven't heard any of his recordings, smarten up!

The Joy of Six

Proper mixing in 6-channel surround sound can bring out parts of the music you barely heard before

By David Tickle

Originally appeared in October 1997

When you set up a 5.1 system for mixing, there are many variables, so it's critical to ensure that your monitor system is balanced. It's very difficult to second-guess what kind of system a person might have in their home and then compensate for that. They might have a good set of (left and right) stereo speakers, but the Center channel or the surround speakers might be inferior. Due to that, my approach to mixing 5.1 for audio (which is different from my approach to mixing 5.1 for film) is that every speaker should be identical except for the subwoofer.

While you first experiment with mixing in 5.1, choose a speaker system that you're really comfortable with, because you'll find variables that never existed before in stereo and it's best to at least have a grounding with familiar monitors. I often use Yamaha NS10M's for mixing in stereo and — after trying many different types of speakers — I decided (for the time being) to stay with those because I was so accustomed to them. I use three NS10M's in front and two in the back, with Yamaha 2002 amplifiers.

The distance from the monitors to the listening position will depend upon the size of your control room and the size of the monitors. Using the NS10M's as an example, I would typically place the monitors approximately eight feet from my ears. If I were using larger monitors, I'd place them about 12 feet from the listening position. It is very important that all of the speakers are at equal distances from the listening position; this forms an arc between the three front speakers. You can use a piece of string (or a tape measure) from the center of the listening position to each speaker to make certain that they are equidistant. The subwoofer can be located approximately the same distance from the listening position as the other monitors, though its placement is less critical than that of the other five monitors. I have actually been using two subwoofers, one placed to either side of the center speaker.

Tuning Up

Once you have established the type of speaker, the next important aspect is calibration. It is imperative that you have the exact same sonic quality coming from each individual speaker and, using a dB meter, you need to make sure that the amplifiers are balanced to produce the same SPL from each speaker. I tend to place the meter only a foot in front of the nearfield monitor, rather than at the listening position. I set up a tone, white noise or pink noise (whatever seems more relevant at the time), and get my SPL to 85 dB. But whatever the dB level you decide upon, make sure that every speaker produces that same level.

Once that is done, you must check your phase. When you go to 5.1 (as opposed to stereo), the possibilities for phase error increase exponentially. I'm amazed that almost every time I set up a 5.1 rig to do a mix, when I test phase coherency through the system, I'll find a few faults — even though everything looks like it's plugged in correctly. There's a lot of wiring involved (between the console, converters, recording medium, and back again) and it's six cables for every stage. That creates many possibilities for mis-wiring. When you think you have everything in phase (which includes making sure that each speaker is in phase with every other speaker in the system), then you can be certain that your signals will be phase coherent.

Next, choose a "main" instrument for the mix. It could be anything: a vocal or a classical guitar, etc. I'll use a vocal for my analogy here. I'll put a simple processing chain on the voice — whatever I need to make it sound the way I normally want it to sound — maybe a Pultec or Neve EQ, or a little bit of compression. The point is to achieve a quality timbre on the main instrument. I take that instrument and place it so that it's coming out of the Left-Front and Right-Front speakers.

At this stage, I'm just monitoring in stereo and I've got a sound that I'd be familiar with if I was mixing stereo (check it in mono as well). I pan that to the right side and then swivel my chair so that I'm facing the Front-Right and Rear-Right speakers, as if *that* was now my mix plane. I check to be sure that I have the exact same quality of the vocal coming from that plane as I would coming from the front plane.

Which Bus?

Depending on what console you're using, discrepancies may show up in your mix busses. I use the Euphonix CS2000 with Hyper-Surround because I am really fond of what it can do as a computer, as well as the sonic quality. Every single output on this console is of the highest quality, master-grade. Echo sends all have the same electronics as the master stereo bus, so you can actually use an echo send to get exactly the same sonic quality and characteristics as your main stereo bus.

If you go to other consoles, you might run into problems when mixing records for 5.1 because they are not designed with that kind of output quality on six busses. Your stereo bus sounds great, but to get signal to the Center, subwoofer, and Rear surround channels, you'll need a combination of either additional busses and/or echo sends. If the electronics on an echo send are different from those of the stereo master bus, the sonic quality of the echo send is not going to be the same (though it may be good). That's why you want to listen to the lead vocal in these various stereo planes — so that you can hear any sonic inconsistencies in the console.

I try to make sure that when I place my main instrument in any of the four stereo planes I have now created that the sonic quality is identical. After that's been done, you can be confident that the system is playing back coherently.

Getting to the Bottom of It All

One of the things I find exciting about 5.1 is the discrete subwoofer channel. Subwoofers vary tremendously in quality — some producing an analytical quality where you can actually hear the shape and defining line of the bass, some sounding woolly and fuzzy. In any case, you will have to decide upon a crossover point. If (for instance) you use Genelec speakers, the crossover requirements are different from NS10M's because the Genelecs actually do produce some low frequencies on their own. If you crossover at 100 cycles between the Genelecs and a subwoofer, you may get a buildup of bass. To prevent that, some people using Genelecs are setting a crossover point of 85 Hz. For my system, I crossover at 100 cycles because from that point down, the NS10M's drop off pretty rapidly. I find that by placing it there (rather than 85 Hz), the transition from the subwoofer to the NS10M's is pretty smooth. (As a quick side note, there's a lot of discussion going on right now about setting a standard for the crossover point. But because this is so new, it's still subject to experimentation.) More about the subwoofer later.

The Final Frontier

Because you have so much space to explore when presenting a 5.1 mix, a bit of careful planning is required. Depending on what tracks you have throughout the album, I think you have to create some kind of dynamic. In some tracks, you'll have a lot of information coming from all of the speakers, and it's going to be a busy, exciting kind of mix. There will be other tracks where you may use the surround channels for more ambient sounds and less of the "whiz-bang" stuff. You'll find that when you end up with an album of ten or more tracks mixed in 5.1, and sounds shoot all over the place, it can be very wearing to the listener if it's not done gracefully. It's a dynamic tool presented in 5.1 that we didn't have for a stereo record.

Having said that, you can proceed by putting up the faders and getting a basic stereo rough mix of the program material — just like for a regular mix — no subwoofer, center, or surrounds. Get familiar with the music. It's very important to maintain the feel and emotional values of the music when you go to 5.1 because sometimes the whiz-bang elements can produce an effect that might not be the original emotional intent for the material. I prefer to use 5.1 to *enhance* whatever that emotional quality was, to actually exaggerate it more and pull it out, rather than just to change it.

With a basic stereo balance done, now you can go through individual channels of the mix and see where they work best, placement-wise, in the surround field. Get the bass, drums, and rhythm section happening. You'll find that there are certain things you like in the center, such as the bass guitar, bass drum, snare drum, and vocal — the main things that generally appear in the center of a stereo mix. In the 5.1 front stereo plane you have two different ways of creating mono (since I'm most familiar with the Euphonix console, I'll use that as an example).

A bass drum can be in mono by coming from the left and right speaker equally (that's what we're used to), or just from the center. The CS2000 has a completely variable "focus" control where you can send an instrument into the Center channel. As it feeds the Center channel, the focus control also starts to take the signal away from the (Front) Left and Right channels at the same rate. When it's fully assigned to the center, that signal is removed from the left and right. So you could make the drum a lot wider and bigger by having it coming from the front three speakers.

We are not used to that in normal stereo. It adds this extra depth that — when you actually build the mix — becomes a fantastic tool. Instruments sound a lot more natural and real. If you have too many signals coming from only the center, there's a good chance of overloading your Center channel before you've even got most of your mix going (because you're not dividing that energy between two channels). I might push the Center signal into the Left- and Right-Front a little, not so much to get the width of the instrument, but to share the energy of the instrument across the three channels, so that I don't overload the Center channel.

Regarding the snare drum, once I have set the amount of snare energy going to the Center (as well as the Left-Front and Right-Front), I can actually bring the snare in front of the center speaker by introducing it slightly into the surround plane.

Step to the Rear

From that point I continue to build my mix while maintaining the feel of the music. Certain sounds seem more appropriate for the surround channels, others for the front. If a sound is too percussive, it can be a real distraction in the rear — where you're always turning your head. That's the "exit-syndrome" — you're looking for the exit sign, which can be quite distracting. But at the same time I think that everyone should thoroughly explore using the surround channels because who says you can't have a sound coming from over there, anyway?

Other instruments lend themselves more to being placed in the surround plane. I love placing keyboard pads to the rear and also harmony vocals that enter during certain sections of a song. Here's a really creative use of the surround channels, where I think it works best of all: Take a song that has a verse, chorus, verse, chorus, bridge structure. In the production of the song you may have some kind of dynamic shift in the bridge, where the bridge becomes more airy, spacey, or bigger-sounding, and then goes back to a more driving thing when it returns to the verse or chorus. That's a normal thing for a lot of records. In 5.1, when you get to the bridge you can suddenly make the surround channels a lot fuller than they have been for the other sections of the song. This takes you into a larger dimension and gives you an incredible dynamic tool.

One of the problems we deal with when mixing in stereo is fitting everything into those two VUs, so that the mix jumps out at you. In our stereo mixes, we use compression and filtering to make the bass drum and bass fit together, and the sum of the two becomes the impact. We then filter and compress the vocal and piano so that they don't step on each other and so on, until all of the instruments are jumping toward you.

In 5.1, you have six channels to put these instruments into, instead of two. You don't need to compress in the same way that you would in a stereo mix because there's so much more room and you don't have to force everything through two channels. You also have to do very minimal filtering. Consequently, a drum kit sounds *way* more like a drum kit than ever before — like it's in the room with you. I still use compression and filtering, but I tend to use the compression just on individual instruments (e.g., I might put a compressor on a guitar and then place that sound in the mix). I probably wouldn't use overall compression on the entire mix, whereas on a stereo mix I typically *would* use overall compression to make it dance and jump out at you (of course, it depends on the program material).

Big Bottom?

There are some interesting, unusual things you can do with the subwoofer. On the Freddy Revel record that I mixed, *Sol to Soul*, I put the low end of the piano into the subwoofer and the left speaker. All of a sudden, you could hear the foot pedal, the resonance of the sound board, and the hammers letting go of the strings — very high-definition. On another project, I put some of the lead vocal into the subwoofer, which made the voice enormous without being bassy and produced a distinct aura around the voice. It's not the type of thing where you'd recognize that the voice is coming from the sub; it's more a feeling of increased presence and size.

Compressing the Budget

I've been mixing in 5.1 for DTS, who employ 20-bit resolution on their CDs. To me, 20-bit certainly sounds way more advanced than 16-bit stereo. But there's going to be another big jump when we go to 96 kHz/24-bit, and that's coming fairly soon (I believe it is already available in some instances, like Sonic Solutions). Because of that, I was thinking about what will happen to my 20-bit mixes when we have 24-bit available. On *Sol to Soul*, I decided that, rather than renting three stereo A/D converters and three stereo D/A's to record this digitally (on a DA-88 at 20-bit), I could use six channels on my analog 24-track, which has Dolby SR. Since all of my program material was digital, the analog 24-track wasn't being used, and we printed the 5.1 mix on six tracks of the 2-inch machine. I didn't have to rent anything to do the mix — it's straight in and out of the machine. At the end of the record, we rented the digital hardware to convert to 20-bit, and dumped the whole album in one day. When 96 kHz/24-bit becomes available, we can *easily* remaster from the 2-inch tape without having to remix it.

Surround is a great creative tool, and I think consumers will love it once it catches on. But the biggest thing will be when musicians start to figure out what to do with 5.1 — it will be a phenomenal new arena within which to create. It makes me wonder what Hendrix would have done in surround....

David Tickle is an independent engineer/producer who has worked with artists such as Rod Stewart, Jackson Browne, Prince, Peter Gabriel, U2, Joe Cocker, George Michael, and the Clash.

Are You Experienced?

Welcome to the brave new world of surround sound

By Ed Cherney

Originally appeared in August 1998

The Music Producer's Guild of the Americas (MPGA) was founded in September 1997 to support the creative and professional needs of music industry producers and recording engineers. It was simply time for us to address those matters that concern us as a professional group, and I encourage many of you to join the 150 members who are currently onboard.

The following pages are the proceedings from a rather historical event that the MPGA conducted under the sponsorship of *Pro Sound News* and Solid State Logic. The MPGA Conference on Multichannel Music Mixing, held at the Doubletree Hotel in New York in May '98, was the first event where leading music producers and engineers voiced their ideas, interests, questions, and concerns about this emerging technical challenge. About 250 attendees were witness to the information that unfolded throughout the day. And with the publication of the proceedings, we will be reaching many tens of thousands more with some of the most insightful ideas I have ever heard about harnessing the emotional power of 5.1 channels of sound for a music recording.

The following 11,000+ words (the longest article *EQ* has ever published) documents the morning session from our event, which brought together some of the leading minds and ears in our business to discuss the creative and technical challenges of going surround.

Let the tape begin...

Host: Ed Cherney, President MPGA

Guests: Al Schmitt, Larry Hamby, Michael Bishop, Alan Parsons, Phil Ramone, Nile Rodgers, Chuck Ainlay, and Elliot Scheiner

Ed Cherney: First of all, let's discuss what 5.1 is. It doesn't matter what format, what manufacturer, or what encoder you're using now — 5.1 is a system where you can discretely mix six channels of music: a Left, Center, Right, two surrounds, and a subwoofer. You can send any part of any instrument to any part of it, and you can sit in this array of speakers and the sky is the limit. You can do anything. I just heard something that Alan Parsons has been working on, and even though he didn't use the center speaker much, musically this thing surrounded you and pounded you. You knew something really special was happening. So we're entering into a new age, and we want to be at the forefront of it. We want to be involved in it. As music-makers, it's really fun to make 5.1 surround records. It's a lot more fun than trying to cram a whole bunch of stuff down a stereo bus.

I'd like to start with Alan Parsons, who's been involved in quad and has been on the cutting edge of this for a long time. Then we'll go around to our panelists and talk about the experiences they've had doing it. As a recording engineer, producer, or a composer, what's the way you might want to approach this?

Alan Parsons: Quad is where it all started, isn't it? I, and probably most of the people here, have had some bad experience with quad. I think it was the fact that it was an analog format and destined for viny — destined for a system that basically just didn't work. I cannot tell you how disappointing it was mixing a discrete tape, coming away with a 4-track analog 1-inch tape, and saying there's my piece of work. It sounded brilliant — then when you got the pressing back from the factory, it was just like listening to stereo on four speakers. It was really no better than that. It was great to get back, in the last 18 months, to the notion of not just a field in front of you, but a field that is all-enveloping, all around you.

You mentioned my not having a center speaker, but I really did approach the album that I'm doing pretty much from a quad standpoint, just the four channels — Left-Front, Right-Front, and the two surrounds — and I actually derived the subbass and center information. There was one exception — one tune where I felt getting the center speaker to leap into life would be an appropriate thing to do, which was actually just a spoken word thing. Just from personal preferences, I tend to work on the outside of the soundfield. If you have joysticks, if you have genuine 5.1 panning, you can bring things into the room, the field, so you have a sound right in front of your nose. But, somehow, the taste of most of the product I've heard tends to be to take a front stage image, to put the vocals directly in front of you in the center, and also the drums. It's things like horn parts and backing vocals, stuff like that, that really work well coming at you from behind.

One of the things I would like to see discussed this morning is loudspeaker positioning. There are all kinds of different ways of handling this. There are standards that come from Europe where the surround speakers are farther apart, the front speakers are angled differently, and so on. But I'm a firm believer that all five main speakers should be the same — full-blown, full-frequency loudspeakers. I could talk all day about the actual process of mixing. One other little confession to make. I did this last thing on a 24-track desk not designed for surround at all, so all my track routing, all my panning around, was done with regular pan pots. I actually had a track where a singer and guitar player was a wandering minstrel, wandering around the outside of the room. The way of achieving that without any kind of joystick was to use a regular pan pot patched to the mixer, stop when he gets to one corner, punch in, repatch, and have him walk to the next stage. It can be done. You can do a lot with surround without necessarily having a state-of-the-art console.

I think another thing that needs to be discussed is the importance — if, indeed, there is an importance — of the Center channel. The Center channel came from film circles.

Ed Cherney: The film mixers are really the pioneers. We owe it to them. This Center channel may be a throwback to them, but it was about hearing the dialog. We've come to an era now where they actually mix music louder in films, but originally it was about the dialog, hearing what was going on. We must convert and use that in making music and making interesting-sounding mixes. Working in this context, people do it differently.

I was just in a studio in Los Angeles to listen to a master of a 5.1 Bonnie Raitt live recording that I did, which I think lends itself to this format. For me, it was being able to create side walls and back walls — depth so experiential that you hear the music moving around the room. But before that I was listening to what Alan had done, and this was a dynamic, living thing that seemed like it was composed and conceived and arranged to be in this surround format. I just happened to notice there was nothing really coming out of the center channel, but it was awesome. You were

Who's Who

Ed Cherney, chairman of the board and president of MPGA, has been an Emmy Award nominee, is a six-time TEC Award nominee and twice a TEC Award winner. His recording, producing, and mixing credits include artists such as the Rolling Stones, Bonnie Raitt, Bob Dylan, Jackson Browne, Roy Orbison, George Harrison, Ringo Starr, Bob Seger, and Elton John.

Alan Parsons began his career at Abbey Road Studios, where he rose in the ranks from assistant engineer to engineer, and later to producer. Along the way he worked on albums like *Abbey Road* by the Beatles and *Dark Side of the Moon* by Pink Floyd. The Alan Parsons Project first brought his name to the front cover of an album, and his compositions and productions are legend. He is also a major mover in record production organizations, being a founding light of the British producers' guild Re-Pro.

Larry Hamby is vice president of Windham Hill Records, and former vice president of A&R at A&M Records and Epic Records.

Phil Ramone is known to all as outspoken producer extraordinaire of the likes of Billy Joel, Paul McCartney, Frank Sinatra, Natalie Cole, BB King, Luciano Pavarotti, and Gloria Estefan. He pioneered satellite links for recording, Dolby 4-track discrete sound, Dolby optical surround sound, digital live recordings, and fiber-optic systems to record in real time from different locations. He is currently president of N2K (Need To Know) Encoded Music, which, via its sister company, Music Boulevard, uses "e_mod" in what is reputed to be the first secure and commercially viable digital online music delivery system.

Introduced into the TEC Hall of Fame in 1997, **Al Schmitt** has a string of Grammy Awards and nominations to go with a list of artists he's produced and recorded including David Grusin, Melissa Manchester, Luther Vandross, DeeDee Bridgewater, Paul Anka, Vanessa Williams, Madonna, Anita Baker, Frank Sinatra, Natalie Cole, Quincy Jones, Henry Mancini, George Benson, Steely Dan, Toto, and Dr. John.

just surrounded by this music — it just pulled you inside — and I didn't want to hear the Bonnie Raitt record after listening to that!

Alan Parsons: The Center channel can be derived if, like me, you don't feel that the Center channel has a great contribution to make in an average-size room. You could argue that if we were to do a demonstration in this room, it would probably be a very useful thing to have, because the center imaging would be improved. But if you're in a home environment or a decent control room environment, your phantom center is going to be just as good as a dedicated center.

Ed Cherney: Moving ahead. Michael Bishop started out doing rock & roll, but he's been working in the classical realm lately. Maybe we want to touch on that style of music, because classical music is another genre that really lends itself to this format, where you're re-creating something

Known as part of the engineering and production team of Telarc Records, **Michael Bishop** has been engineering award-winning recordings for 25 years, including a 1998 Grammy Award for Best-Engineered Classical Album. In addition to the many orchestral, jazz, blues, and pop recordings he has recorded, Michael's sound effects design and production is equally noteworthy, having helped earn a record-setting four consecutive Grammys for Peter Schickele (PDQ Bach). Recording credits include the James Gang, Dizzy Gillespie, Gerry Mulligan, Joe Williams & the Count Basie Orchestra, Bobby Short, Junior Wells w/Sonny Landreth, Derek Trucks, John Mooney, Alvin Hart, Oscar Peterson, Dave Brubeck Quartet, Robert Shaw/Atlanta Symphony Orchestra & Chorus, Maria Muldaur, Mel Torme, Erich Kunzel/Cincinnati Pops, Jesus Lopez-Cobos/Cincinnati Symphony Orchestra, Yoel Levi/ Atlanta Symphony Orchestra & Chorus, and Wendy Varner.

Nile Rodgers has produced a list of artists as long as your arm, including Madonna, David Bowie, Mick Jagger, Diana Ross, Stray Cats, the B-52's, Debbie Harry, Duran Duran, INXS, Sister Sledge, Sheena Easton, Thompson Twins, Jeff Beck, Al Jarreau, David Lee Roth, Eric Clapton, Ashford & Simpson, Maya Angelou, Bob Dylan, Peter Gabriel, and Eddie Murphy. In addition to gold and platinum sales awards for his work, Nile also sports an array of Grammys, *Billboard* awards, and other industry accolades.

Chuck Ainlay was '96 and '97 winner of the Nashville Music Award for Recording Engineer of the Year and Grammy nominee for Best Engineered Recording Non-Classical in '94. Recent production/ engineering artist credits include Dire Straits, Mark Knopfler, Vince Gill, George Strait, Trisha Yearwood, Wynonna, Lyle Lovett, Steve Earle, Junior Brown, Nanci Griffith, Todd Snider, Patty Loveless, Marty Stuart, and George Jones.

Two Grammys and ten Grammy nominations, among other forms of kudos, have long been putting **Elliot Scheiner** on the recording map as both producer and engineer for artists like the Eagles, Steely Dan, Fleetwood Mac, Bonnie Raitt, Van Morrison, Jimmy Buffett, Bruce Hornsby, Glenn Frey, Toto, Billy Joel, George Benson, Chaka Khan, David Sanborn, and Smokey Robinson.

—John Townley

and you can put the listener right in the concert hall at home. Michael?

Michael Bishop: Like Ed said, I started out in rock 'n' roll back in the quad days, back in the '70s, and one of the first quad things I did was a 4-channel mix of the James Gang. That quad mix never saw the light of day because nobody had any confidence that it could ever be played at home properly. Quad was one of those things we built a console for — we had quad joysticks all across it — and it never got used since we had nothing to put it out on. Since companies like Dolby Digital and DTS came along and gave us a format, we're now finally able to dig up some of those old things that we've been thinking about for years. By the mid-'80s I was working for Telarc International, and our focus with that label was classical, and now jazz and blues.

Of course in classical, with large orchestras, we've always been trying to give a large acoustic image of a large symphony orchestra, but on only two channels. All these years we've been trying to develop techniques to push everything beyond those two channels. 5.1 has made it possible for us to envelop the listener with the whole orchestral experience. But we learned something in the bad old quad days: One of the things that we were doing with the Cleveland Orchestra, for instance, was to take the orchestra, put it in a circle, and surround the conductor, and thus surround the listener. It was probably one of the worst disasters in classical music. Orchestras were not meant to be heard in a circle. Not only was it horrible for the listener, it was even worse for the musicians, because you took them out of their familiar performing environment and had them play in a completely unfamiliar place. The conductor was waving over his back and going crazy. It was a total disaster, but believe it or not, we get letters from people now asking us when are we going to be recording orchestras in a circle again. Never!

My goal in recording an orchestra is to put the listener in the best seat in the house — to wrap that acoustic environment around the listener and spread the orchestra out in somewhat of a horseshoe. I only recently started using the Center channel for orchestra recordings. I was ignoring it for a while, sort of a throwback to having perfected a really good stereo image. I was working so carefully on a phantom Center that I really didn't feel the need for a Center channel. That is, until our marketing people started getting complaints from consumers that there was nothing on the Center channel. They'd paid for it, so what was happening? Now I put up a center microphone that doesn't go to our stereo version but only to the 5.1 recorder. I should add that our specialty is recording direct to 2-track with very large symphony orchestras and also symphony orchestras combined with rhythm sections, soloists, and choruses — particularly with our Cincinnati Pops line, which has been a very popular line of classical crossover.

Ed Cherney: Are you doing the 5.1 and the stereo at the same time?

Michael Bishop: Yes. We're doing it live to 2-track and live to 5.1 at the same time.

Ed Cherney: When you're monitoring, are you switching back and forth from 5.1 to stereo? How are you deriving your stereo from this 5.1?

Michael Bishop: During the session, we're monitoring in stereo. We have a 5.1 setup in the control room, but we unfortunately have to stick with the stereo monitor the majority of the time, because the conductor is listening for performance mistakes and is focusing as much as possible on what the orchestra is doing. It's actually distracting to the producer to turn on the surround parts during the session. This is what makes it a little interesting. I have to record the 5.1 without listening to it, except two channels at a time on headphones, and then on a playback break we might get a chance to check it out.

This is something I've been developing one session at a time, with very small moves of the microphones, trying a lot of different setups out in the hall. The hardest thing, besides not being able to monitor during the actual session and only check it out on playbacks, is to re-create that acoustic environment. Many of the producers and engineers in this room are working with multitrack tapes and are panning things around, but what I'm doing is working with just microphone placement and hard-bus scanning in order to achieve the surround. So I've been working a lot on just where to go in the hall — or in the studio — because we also do a lot of jazz and blues recordings, so I'm miking the studio for 5.1 as well.

I'm making a lot of use of the Neumann K 100 binaural head for the surround pickup. Ideally I like to be able to put the binaural head across the front channels and the surrounds, a double set of them, but more often than not I'm working with that and a combination of spaced omnis to go with an orchestra. On a recent Mahler 3 recording that we did, which will be out on CD and in a 5.1 version a little later this year, I think we're finally starting to hit a good combination on a surround pickup. I'm putting microphones in places I never really thought I would have to, rethinking what I'm having to do in stereo and in 5.1.

Ed Cherney: You're trying to make stereo and 5.1 compatible with each other at the same time?

Michael Bishop: They have to be musically compatible for me. The 5.1 version will never collapse down to the stereo version properly, by the way, which has been a concern of mine with talk on the DVD standards of automatically folding down 5.1 into stereo. I haven't done a 5.1 recording in pop, classical, jazz, or anything that will fold down properly into two channels. But maybe this isn't the time to get into that...

Alan Parsons: May I mention something that has nothing to do with fold-down in particular? Just as a matter of interest, my album was mixed the same way as Michael was just saying. I was doing the stereo mix at the same time as the surround. I set up all my pans and placements in surround, getting it to the point where I was close to a decent 5.1 mix, and then it's time to get depressed and go back to stereo, to the rest of the real world. Then using the placement, and actually folding down effectively — but only from four, not from all the 5.1 sources, which made it a little bit easier — I got my stereo mix as I wanted it. There's the mix that, let's face it, 97 percent of the world is going to hear. Then I switch back to the same mix, which thank heaven is automated, and tweak that one up. Studio owners will not want to hear this. They will want to think they can book in a client for a stereo mix and then come back and do a surround mix on another occasion, but in my experience the two processes can be combined.

Michael Bishop: That musical balance that you're achieving during the stereo mix session — you want to be able to convey with the same feel to the 5.1. Even with automation and instant recall, there are just those times when you've made a little tweak and you want to be able to repeat that for the 5.1 experience, too.

Alan Parsons: Another thing you would probably do is switch off the surround reverbs, because what's the point of having two reverbs going when you only need one? That would be another small change you might make.

Michael Bishop: One thing that I failed to mention is the use of the LFE channel — the "point one." In orchestral music it can be really effective to selectively feed things to that channel. I mix assuming there are five equal speakers plus a subwoofer, and five equal full-range speakers. Often, however, I have to keep in mind that there are home theater systems that have little mini-Bose monitors with a subwoofer, and if you don't pay any attention to what's happening on that low-frequency track, you may deprive the home listener of any low end at all — or you'll give the wrong impression of what's supposed to be happening on the low end and have just the mid and top coming out on the rest of your mix. So I've got to maintain five full channels, and then I'll have the low-frequency information of whatever recording I'm working on go onto the LFE. Then I'll sometimes feed some extra things to the LFE just for dramatic effect, to kick them in the behind at certain times and to make the subwoofers dance across the floor.

Ed Cherney: Michael, what are you mixing down to — two tracks of stereo and then six more tracks? Into what format are you doing that?

Michael Bishop: Typically, all the 20-bit stuff is going through some custom converters and the Apogee 88000, which is going through a Prism interface to DA-88's or PCM 800's in a 20-bit format. Ideally, it would be nice to be recording all this at 96k, 6-channel, 24-bit, because if we start to do any mixing after the fact, in any postproduction, we start degrading those bits right away.

Ed Cherney: You could be mixing to analog if you wanted to.

Michael Bishop: We could be, but, particularly for classical, it doesn't go over. Even just the smallest amount of wow in the best of tape machines destroys any orchestral sounds that you have. I have done that for some of our blues things, recording from analog multitrack and then doing a digital mix. We have a Schubert project that was recorded recently in Scotland that was done in a combination of 96k/24 and 48k/24, simply because there weren't enough 96k A-to-D's. Now we've got to deal with having to edit a combination 96k/48k master and boil it down to 44.1 for CD 5.1 release, in addition to the stereo, which was done in DSD. So it's getting a little bit complicated.

Nile Rodgers: I want to break the format here for a second, because when Alan was saying maybe this isn't the time to discuss this problem, I think in a way it is. About a year and a half ago we did a live concert in Japan, and we were fortunate enough to do the mix to DVD and 5.1 — and with my style of music and the particular performance, it really felt like an appropriate situation.

All my life I've liked to see bands live and to hear them perform live, and I've always wanted to have that kind of dream recording. I grew up with *Frampton Comes Alive* and then found out that maybe Frampton didn't really "come alive"; he started off alive and then was overdubbed. But this performance we did really is live, there is no overdubbing, there is no extra stuff.

I just want to bring my engineer up and talk about this, because while we were doing this live he was out in a truck — usually he can watch us perform, but this time he's out in a truck — recording to 5.1. I'm thinking, what the hell is he doing, is he listening to the mix that he normally puts up? It's exactly the same sort of situation that you were talking about. Are you listening in the stereo environment, or are you listening in 5.1? Was he actually listening in stereo the way that he normally listens, and then we would go and mix the DVD versions?

The other thing I was thinking about when we were making the record was knowing that we're going to be looking at pictures at the same time on this particular project. I know that I'm sort of an old-fashioned guy — when I'm looking at pictures, I want to hear the music....

Alan Parsons: ...when you don't have pictures, when you don't have a live band, when it's re-creating a soundstage that's imaginary, it's a different story. You start spreading the pictures out on the walls...

Nile Rodgers: I think about this constantly. I get bogged down. I just want to hear the music happening. I agree with what you said at the beginning. I'm looking for those performances now where I feel magically pulled into the recording. All of my favorite old records were records where I could imagine myself being on the date — like, what the hell was Jimmy doing when he was playing this stuff? — and lately I don't hear records like that. When I hear records I say, "Oh yeah, he got the bass sound from this record, he took the loop from that," but it's not that passion I've always grown up with. I find that missing from my life.

Larry Hamby: During the live recording, most important to me at the time was a monitored stereo [mix] in the mobile, because the most important thing was to get it on tape correctly — knowing that when we got to the studio to mix it I could monitor for 5.1 at that point and mix that way. I wasn't mixing in the mobile to 2-track, I was just trying to get it on tape as best I could, knowing that I could worry about it later. Just getting it on tape cleanly was the most important thing at that point.

When we got to the mixing stage, we had to do a lot of bouncing back and forth between a stereo monitoring situation and a surround monitoring situation just to make sure it was all going to even out. At that point stereo was more important, since we didn't know when the DVD was coming out.

Chuck Ainlay: I think a lot of what's coming up here is that this format can provide lots of different situations. For film, the use of the center speaker really tends to pull your attention to the screen, which is great.

Ed Cherney: This is Chuck Ainlay, from Nashville, Tennessee. Chuck works with Tony Brown and engineers Vince Gill, the Mavericks, and has mixed a lot of great records, country, rock, and pop, that you've heard. He's been working a lot on stereo records that were really designed to be played on country radio, remixing these for DVD 5.1 audio, and approaching it in a different way. It's kind of tough with just a drummer, three guitar players, a bass player, and a keyboard player. How do you portray that in a 5.1 format?

Chuck Ainlay: The question is how do you approach this, and I think everybody has to realize it can be approached in a lot of different ways, depending on the intent of the recording. In a classical recording, you can put the orchestra in front of you and use rear speakers primarily as ambience. A pop recording that's not actually focused by video or film or live presentation can be something that does envelop you all the way around and evoke a lot of emotion from the music. In fact, it's the way I grew up listening to music — putting a pair of speakers in the front of the room and a pair of speakers in the back of the room because it sounded better to me. I think this can be approached in a number of different ways, and I don't think we're here to tell people how they're supposed to go at it.

Ed Cherney: That's it. There aren't any rules with this, and if you sat in a system surrounded by speakers — and hopefully people at home are going to have these systems — you can just make it up as you go. It's a whole different battle. And, typically, making stereo records, a lot of times you're trying to cram ten pounds worth of sausage into two pounds of sausage-casing. Now this thing opens up and it's a whole new adventure, and that's really what we're exploring. Do you foresee the day when stereo won't be around and everything we're going to be doing is in a 5.1 context? Phil, do you think we're ever going to come to that?

Phil Ramone: No. There are some members of this panel who made records when it was mono, when it became stereo, and when it became a CD. Some things got phased out, but the most important part of it, obviously, is putting the music first. I have to please myself. Part of the fun of making music is always to understand how underachieved we were. I remember screaming about the CD — and people arguing about the quality, the high end, the lack of warmth — and all the stuff we were losing. But I don't want to get into a Beta-vs.-VHS type argument.

When challenged, there are two things you want to do. You obviously want to make a great stereo product. For those that don't know, I've been a big proponent for ten years of making stereo pairs for remixing and have been doing it when there weren't even [TASCAM] DA-88 [digital multitrack recorders]. Now suddenly it looms as a very important achievement, because if you think about not trying to do a live concert, but a recording where your final mix needs to be in the same budget as the stereo mix, it works by running stereo pairs. Engineers hate me for it because they have to stand around while we do these things in discrete formats and with discrete echoes. What it does bring at the end of the day is that you can run the 2-track.

An example is the Dave Grusin *West Side Story* I did. On our DVD, I learned really fast. I didn't allow any fold-down; the actual 2-track stereo is in sync with the 5.1. The 5.1 is in its discrete form, but when I ran it, I made sure that the 2-track appears as it does in the regular CD, because we have to put out a regular CD and a DVD.

My encouraging learning process was to find out we could create a moment in the studio that was a live recording of a rhythm section, with horns and saxes coming around Dave Grusin, who was the centerpiece. It was a big advantage that the drums were in a booth, the bass player was in a booth, and percussion was in a booth. It gave me more of a treatment of ambience without trying to perform it straight ahead with surround coming around us. That was a creative choice, and I think that's what we're talking about here.

I also tried to decide if there needed to be any lip-sync'ing, because then it becomes a different animal. When you're watching it and you see something to the side of you, the whole panning becomes a question. My theory was to try to make us experience it as a musical event only. Then I added picture, because I didn't have the budget to go out and make a million-dollar production of just the visuals, as much as I would have liked to. I took still pictures because I thought that the music with a minimal amount of pictures was interesting — you would get bored after two or three times or never want to watch it again, unless it was a concert piece.

So I think we're headed into an incredibly important phase of what one would call the DVD audio experience and CDs in that format. What we need to consider in the next two years is the sale of the DVD and the player, forgetting about all the quality problems, as you're never going to tell that audience to buy five equal expensive speakers. I think it would be delicious if you could, but we have to assume we're going to have to go through the same fight we used to when people bought those little, itty-bitty, so-called left and right speakers.

The advantage we have is ten or 15 years of great CD quality and a real audience, an audience that's now driving a car that sounds better than most homes. We're in a great place — I truly think we'll be talking 5.1 in the car next year with no problems. I also think we'll be talking about home theater as a way of life. The common TV room of when I was growing up doesn't exist, but what does exist is a place for the kids or yourself or your friends to watch a DVD movie. And why wouldn't you want to hear your music on that system?

We're headed into a high-class format, 24-bit/96 kHz. Elliot Scheiner has made some great demos for DTS. I'm not here to discuss format as much as concept — and our audience is our concept. We only made one DVD this year, but in '98 we will make two, maybe three. The one we've made sold in the respectable 5,000 range. That's not enough to make anybody a lot of money, but it puts the music business in a place where we can say that next year, hopefully, the audience will come back because we're giving them high quality, worrying about resolution for them, not trying to be cute by worrying about formats and radio, but trying to make music that is palatable, reissuable.

There are so many great records. I just got called up to hear the Billy Joel collection, going back to the original analog tapes, and had to remind Ted Jensen that we had some screwy things we had to do with the Dolbys in those days. In less than 20 years, we have made a change again, and traditionally ten to 15 years is the run of a specific cycle, so I think we are headed for an incredible change.

Ed Cherney: Phil, do you think, from a record company perspective, you want to be able to have one package and one CD disc that has your stereo mix and your 5.1 mix on it? Should you sell just this one thing and be able to put it in any player, in your car or at home, and have it figure out what it is and play a stereo mix or a 5.1 — or should you have to go to the store and get a whole separate DVD audio-only disc?

Larry Hamby: I just wanted to comment briefly on your question. It's very unwieldy to put that much stock into the marketplace. The record industry is manufacturing more music than retail can absorb now, and the number of retail outlets is shrinking all the time. So the marketplace will determine that. We had the same problem, those of you who can remember, when we had mono and stereo in the marketplace at the same time. Most of us remember as consumers how complicated that was, which bin do you look in.

Phil Ramone: Thank God nobody asked me about delivery systems on the Internet — they are going to be a proportionate share in the next five years of some form of this music. I don't suspect that people will be buying 5.1 in a direct download, but we are talking about where our living is. When the stores shrink and the airplay shrinks, there are only certain places you can find out about this new format. The DVD is a natural to be bought as one format with the CD music right on it. It's just a question of what we decide and how much picture we want with it, or if we want any picture with it. But that's not as important as information. It could be credits, pictures, and stills. The session stills are pretty interesting, I think. What you get back with the DVD, for those that mourn the loss of that nice 12-inch format, is the lost book, the old-fashioned cover, the pictures, the liner notes, the biography...

Alan Parsons: I've been saying for years, Phil, that it was a disaster that we ever went to a 5¼-inch disc. DVD, for all its wonderfulness, and the fact that it's got eight times the capacity of a CD, is still not enough. If we want to do a stereo mix and a 5.1 and have pictures and full-length movies, 12-inch was the way to go. I've always been disappointed that DVD is the same size as CD.

Ed Cherney: Getting away from the audio, there's room on there to put liner notes and musical facts and pictures...

Alan Parsons: But you're short of memory, still.

Larry Hamby: On that, it was an interesting experience with enhanced CD (ECD) — when we experimented with that over the last couple of years, we had the same notion. Here was a wonderful opportunity for people to see all these things they used to get with the 12-inch package, and it was rejected.

Michael Bishop: The consumer won't pay for it, they won't pay any extra, and you're going to extra expense to produce it.

Larry Hamby: The problem may just have been that you had to go to a computer as opposed to your home theater.

Phil Ramone: The reason I did this [holding up a tall package] is because I felt very insecure about who would buy this at the standard CD price, so we put it out at that price, but we had to remake the book. The booklet that's in here is twice the size of the booklet that's on the CD that you buy of the same album. As an expense for a record company — the sleeve and the package — it killed us. I was determined not to let us fall into the trap of the old-fashioned cheap, throwaway package, but you are talking about whether this will fit in a bin and will the stores allow you to have this high size. They did for the first one, they won't for the next. I think that the key to this thing is what people get used to.

People said the computer was a pain in the butt to watch an ECD, and it was. I don't know your failure rate, but we had quite a bit, whereas Web TV was a lot more interesting to gather that information. I think we have to realize we are a multiformatted group of people, and the key to it is the highest quality audio. We have always been the stepchild. This is our chance to be the leader for the first time, because we know they know how to make great pictures and effects. We have the ability to take those effects and put them in the DVD and make far more interesting music than we've ever made, even if it's just a standard, interesting recording with a five-piece band.

Ed Cherney: I'd like to move over to Elliot Scheiner, Grammy Award-winning engineer and producer. Elliot had a lot of experience, especially doing live 5.1 projects. Right now he's just done Fleetwood Mac, Hell Freezes Over *for the Eagles, and the new John Fogerty, and I wanted him to talk a little bit about his experiences with that. I know he's done them on different formats. And I'd also like to hear some talk about mastering this stuff, what it takes to actually finish the project and deliver it to the consumer and what steps you have to take, where do you go? How do you finish this thing off?*

Elliot Scheiner: Before that, I want to agree with Chuck that in mixing in 5.1, anything goes. You can do anything you want; there are no rules. What works for one person doesn't necessarily work for another. I had an incident the other day. I mixed *Gaucho* in 5.1 a few months ago. Recently, I had to get the tires replaced on my car, and there was an audio place next door. I ran in and was looking at a 5.1 amplifier, and the guy said, "Let me put this up for you." He puts up *Gaucho*. So I'm sitting here and he says I don't really like this record, because you don't hear the horns and vocals coming out of the back...well, I loved it that way. Donald and Walter loved it that way. This guy hated it. You're not going to please everybody. You've got to go for what you want to hear. I didn't tell him I mixed it — I was embarrassed. So you can do whatever you want. I've made my mistakes.

The first thing that I did was the Eagles record. I used the center speaker, and I paid for it in the end, because all the focus on some things came right to the center, and when it was done, I hated it. The biggest issue for me right now is fold-down. What I've experienced so far is that record companies are taking the final product away from us. They're taking the mixes, and instead of bringing them to a mastering facility, they bring them to a video post-production facility. So now there's a guy who has really no audio experience with records, and he's taking a 5.1 recording and saying, "Gee, the strings are a little loud in the back, I think I'll bring them down." I had this experience with Fleetwood. It turned out this engineer decided he didn't agree with the mix. So my integrity was in trouble, and when I heard the fold-down, it was horrible. One of the main issues is that we need to be able to have the mastering facilities do the 5.1, and if there is going to be a fold-down, then either we have to be there or trust our mastering guy.

Phil Ramone: If you run your 2-track, which you've approved, do not allow them under any conditions to take your 5.1 and try to fold it. It does not fold. Even if you use center information or you don't, it doesn't matter, because the build-up is incredibly stupid.

Ed Cherney: How do you prevent that? Even on a stereo record you have to fight with record companies not to make a digital clone, make a DAT, and start manufacturing all over the world with that. Doug Sachs is here from The Mastering Lab, as is Steven Markeson and Bob Ludwig. We rely on you guys all the time — maybe I could prevail upon you to stand up and talk about what kind of plans you have to deal with this 5.1; to be able to master and give the music producers a place to go, to be able to do our final tweaks, EQ, and compression. In addition, mastering guys typically are our last line of quality control before the manufacturers get their hands on it. They're the ones who can alert you when the record company isn't ordering 1630's and they are ordering a DAT or some other thing that they're going to put into a funky editor.

Stephen Markeson: Obviously, we're all concerned about this. It's really in its infancy, and nobody knows what to do with five identical channels, processing, and what not. It's going to be a challenge — we're going to worry about how we're going to store this, ship it, and how our plant's going to handle it. These are all big issues. How is this all going to work together, how are we going to set standards? These are things I think we should talk about.

I just set up a 5.1 system in my house with limited capabilities and small speakers. It works, it really works. The problem is, how do you know where your center channel goes? At what level? And the subwoofer? Good luck. This is all really important stuff, I think. Once we can set an MRL playback standard, I think that we can proceed.

Ed Cherney: Then comes the issue of educating the public, the people who have these systems at home, in order for them to be able to set the levels between the speakers, placing them somewhere, in some way, that works.

Larry Hamby: You were talking about an excitement and a passion in records that you haven't felt over the last ten or 15 years. Part of the fun with stereo, that era and some of the greatest music, was that nobody knew what was going on. The consumer didn't know what to do, the engineers didn't know what to do, the artist didn't know what to do. It was just there, and you messed with it. Every record had a different approach. There were no standards, it was wacky, most speakers were out of phase, or one behind the other. It was so much fun. Now everybody's gotten so good, and it's not as much fun anymore.

Alan Parsons: You've got six speakers now, any one of which, or a combination, could be out of phase!

Stephen Markeson: And the other thing is, when you guys are delicately balancing this stuff, somebody's got their center channel way up, and they're going, "Hey check *that* out!"

Ed Cherney: I don't think we've heard from Al Schmitt. Primarily you've been working with jazz in this media, haven't you?

Al Schmitt: A lot of jazz, a lot of movie scores, large orchestra things. Whenever I go into the studio to set up, my thoughts are with 5.1. I use additional microphones that I didn't use before. I mix in stereo, but I want to have those microphones that I can add when I'm mixing to 5.1. There are no rules. Some guys like a lot of things coming from the back. I'm not particularly fond of that — I like to hear the orchestra in front, I like to set up as if I were conducting, so I can hear it around me and have the ambience behind me, to make it as if someone were sitting at a concert. You can do this with five pieces or you can do this with 95 pieces. Again, the music is what counts, not what's coming from where. It's the emotional thing that's happening.

I'm going through the exact same thing with mastering where the mastering engineer didn't like my mix in the 5.1 and wanted to change things around. We all have to think about it. It's the wave of the future, but I think that we really must consider how we record at this point and what microphones we use and how we set up for 5.1. If I'm doing a film score or something on a huge soundstage, I'll set up my tree and my microphones out with the orchestra, but I'll also set up the orchestra deeper into the studio. I'll set up some ambient mics back, maybe 15 feet from the conductor, which will give an ambient sound. There are no rules.

I've heard a lot of the quad records where stuff was spinning around — you got seasick in 20 minutes listening to this music. So I think we'll all learn from it. I did a lot of Dave Mason mixes for Columbia Records in quad that never came out. The first one had a lot of stuff going on in back, and as we got into it and learned more, it was less and less. Again, trying to educate the consumers is one thing, but they're going to put their speakers wherever they want to, to make it sound however they want, whatever's going to make them happy. That's what we're going to have to deal with.

Larry Hamby: I think you also have to realize the end consumer isn't really as worried about getting the exact surround placement, they just want music.

Al Schmitt: Things that are important to us are not always what blows the consumer away. We're getting into the mix and we're hearing certain things that knock us out, but maybe the consumer is not knocked out by that. They're maybe more knocked out by hearing somebody's mouth open, or a loop sound.

Alan Parsons: Especially college kids. I've been listening to the quad version of *Dark Side of the Moon* I did way back in 1973, and the first reaction is to switch everything off except one channel to see what's going on. If you've got a vocal in one channel, you're listening for the coughs and all. The kids will do that.

Elliot Scheiner: That is a problem. Most of the stuff I've mixed has been live stuff, except for *Gaucho*, and, in making a studio record, you've got punches, you're hiding stuff — in a stereo image you hide everything you can. Now everything's exposed, so how do you hide this? All of a sudden I've got horns coming out of the rear and, well, that could be a problem — you don't feel any ambience on the horns the rest of the time, so how do you hide that stuff?

Alan Parsons: One interesting point to make, though I don't know if I speak for everybody here, is I found that mixing for surround is actually easier. You are more tolerant to misgivings in the balance when it's coming out of five speakers than when it's coming out of two. You put the same problem in a stereo scenario, and you need to tweak it up.

Ed Cherney: You can make it louder, too — 90 dB in 5.1 is a lot louder than 120 dB coming out of stereo.

Michael Bishop: And you can discover dynamic range again. You don't have to compress the heck out of everything because now you can let things percolate all around the room.

Ed Cherney: There's room for dynamics, pulling compressors, pulling equalizers off things, which is really fine, hearing dynamics in music again. Before, sometimes you'd get into these volume wars where it's either full on or it's gone. Music is about dynamics.

Nile Rodgers: What was amazing for me, when we were doing our project, was when I was watching the thing at home. I was impressed. I was sitting there listening to my own music going, "Boy that stuff sounds good!" I hadn't felt like that for a long time. After making as many records as I have, I'm highly critical of everything that I'm hearing. So I agree with Alan totally. For the first time the dynamics were cool, and I loved the mistakes. My trumpet player's a madman, a lunatic, and I could feel his vibe, I could feel that lunacy happening on my right side, and it was great. I thought, "If I could do every record like this, it would be really cool."

Ed Cherney: How can the audience know if they're hearing what you want them to? Can they know, or do they even want to know?

Phil Ramone: People do want to know. Recently, I went to buy a standard, whatever's-in-the-store system. I bought two different amplifiers and two different systems — one was a Panasonic and one was a Bose system. Well, the Bose system didn't play the low end. It didn't know where it was, and I realized how crazy this was because I went back to the manufacturing and back to the mastering to find out what happened to my subwoofer. Then I played it on a Panasonic, and I actually had to take the subwoofer down. So there are things like that the audience doesn't know, including us.

Ed Cherney: Do you think what's going to happen with the record labels is that you're going to produce a record and you're going to get a call saying, "Give me a stereo mix and also a 5.1 mix while you're at it?" Will it be within the same budget? Will we have to start budgeting differently? Do we do it at the same time?

Larry Hamby: Yes, it's cost-efficient. There may be situations where we're going to want to go into the marketplace at different times — to lead with the stereo and then follow with 5.1 to create some kind of demand — but nonetheless it's a lot easier to get guys like you, when we can get you, in one shot. It's probably easier for you, too. I'm talking about within the same space of time, not two mixes at once.

Ed Cherney: With some pop records, doing it at the same time would be a royal pain. Just to deliver an album that a record company accepts, no matter what you turn in, you're going to get the calls from the vice president of A&R or the president of the company saying, "Well, we like this mix but we need a more 'vulnerable' mix." [Laughter from crowd.]

Larry Hamby: You are always going to have those people in your life — that's the way it works. But it will be like now, when you'll do a stereo mix and then a TV mix, that kind of process.

Elliot Scheiner: You're saying stay all day mixing this one song and do all the versions?

Larry Hamby: No, before you've got to leave — and say you're working on three different records — I'll call you and say, "Can you come back and do the 5.1 mix?" I'm saying, while you're employed for the project, during that space of time, however it fits your creative process, at the end of the day when we're done, we shake hands — and thanks for that vulnerable mix!

Ed Cherney: Do you see a time in the next five years when it's going to be a matter of course that you deliver a DVD 5.1 audio program for every artist that you do?

Larry Hamby: I would like to envision that time — I hope so. I love it. Everybody who hears this loves it. So, absolutely.

Ed Cherney: Does all the music lend itself to that, the way it's going?

Phil Ramone: Just to join in with Larry, if we don't budget and start to predict what's coming, we are going to lose control. The last thing you want to do is to hand it in to another place for a 5.1 mix. The sensitivity is so important to the way you made the music, and you and the artist, whether you produced it or are co-producer, are all part of the texture, the timbre. I've seen some reissues of records I've made, it's shameful.

Ed Cherney: Sure, when they were being reissued for CD, and they were making them off EQ'd safety copies, you didn't know what they were made of.

Phil Ramone: There are so many great mixers at this table, and all of you are there for a major purpose. People like myself hire you for your instinct and all of the rest. It's the quality of time that you spend to go two points further that's really going to be critical. I think for Larry and myself, and anyone who's trying to sell this in the next two to four years, it's critical to make provision for a format — even if you make it in stereo pairs and leave it to come back to. At the time you're making the mix, it's not hard to subdivide the board. It does mean your assistant stays for another couple of hours, but it is the only way to preserve what you've done. Otherwise, your attempt to re-create the mix for 5.1 is going to be a disaster, especially in someone else's hands. As a producer myself, I'd like to think that what I worked on with the engineer came out the way we wanted it in all formats. We have to think the future, and the budgets will have to adjust.

Al Schmitt: You know, again I think that we get hired to do mixing and engineering for our personality that we put into our mixes. We all do things a little bit differently, and that's what's going to happen with 5.1. We're all going to find our own little way of doing things, and someone will say, "Oh that's an Elliot Scheiner style." People will pick up from that, other engineers who are learning. We all put our personalities into it. We all have different ideas of how it should be laid out, where the echoes should go, and where the ambience should go — and that's what's going to separate the men from the boys.

Ed Cherney: You'll see the danger when you start seeing a CD in stores that is something that you did a while ago, and somehow it got rechanneled for 5.1

Phil Ramone: It's happening now. There are lots of fake DVDs, and I'm appalled that people are doing it. They just put it through an encoder like any of the surround sound systems — and it's a real drag for a musical person, because things get thrown back there that you have no control over. It may sound pretty good, but it's not the record, not the record you know. Al, you remember the days at Capitol Records in New York where there was a guy sitting upstairs doing stereo, and all the rock & roll records were downstairs. Elliot worked with me at A&R, where we finally devised a system by which we could actually make a stereo and mono at the same time that did have a center build-up control.

We're talking about the art, and I think that one of the reasons I was attracted to be a part of MPGA was that we've never had a platform to stand on that controlled the finished product. I think no artist or painter lets a painting go out in a reproduction that he doesn't look at and approve. I really pray that we put our own standards in, because in the long term, there will be a person in the year 2010 who will buy *Gaucho* again. I remember *The Alan Parsons Project.* I'd love to hear it now in 5.1, re-engineered by you. Well, *The Wall* will be done for the revised version, and I can't wait for that record. I think that the next generation of musical person is your audience and is insanely interested in this. When record companies understand that, that the stamp of approval should come only from the people who work on it, it will be so much nicer for us. It's more respectful. Look at Francis Ford Coppola's films, or any of George Lucas's people's productions — without their personal stamp, their movies are not the same. Look at the work they did redoing the *Star Wars* series. We are in a perfect place to demand it. An accountant from a record company can learn that the numbers will work for him in the long picture.

Ed Cherney: Now we'd like to open up the floor to questions.

Steve Trainman [from Billboard*]:* I think that MPGA is in a position to bring the artists, the producers, the record companies, the hardware guys, the studio equipment people, and the studios into a DVD audio group that can really take the lead in getting the right product out — and also getting product out there the consumer will know how to use effectively to maximize their enjoyment.

Ed Cherney: You know we're definitely going to try to do that. We're only six months old. We just hit 125 members, and that's definitely on the agenda. I do want to say that there is so much bad information about what DVD and 5.1 audio are, that you can't tell what is going on, and we're in the middle of it. It's like that for all of us. That's why we're having this meeting, so we can clear up some things and move together. The ultimate thing we want to do is make great music, great sound, and great product.

Alan Parsons: I think one point that needs to be made is that surround audio is deliverable in formats other than DVD at the moment. DTS has a CD format, there are laserdiscs, and Sony is working on a format as well.

Ed Cherney: Robert Margouleff. Robert's done about 35 5.1 projects.

Robert Margouleff: I think there are a couple of things to understand. First, 5.1 is going to live on different formats. The DVD world is still very much up in the air. There are standards issues that are not settled yet — not settled by the RIAA, not settled by the International Steering Committee.

Everyone is coming up with different formats right now. There are compatibility issues that need to be settled. What is out there right now is DTS. I've been working in that medium for about 2½ or 3 years. There are standards in DTS. We've just finished the second standards disc, which does define level, direction, channels, and so forth and has become probably one of the most popular discs we have.

We're putting out DTS decoders, a large quantity of them, and they should be used. Yes, we do share a platform with movies and with laserdiscs. Home theater is a platform that sloshed in from the movie side of things. When we put on a laserdisc of a movie and then we switch to a DTS-encoded CD or a Dolby 5.1 CD we want to make sure that all the levels are the same for everybody; that they're not wildly out of whack. We also have an electrical standard in the studio where all the channels are the same.

As for downmixing, for me as a mixer it is very important that we have a co-existent mix in stereo on the same disc. I don't think it's going to be a real issue with the DVD world when that happens. Right now, for me, the DVD world as far as audio is concerned is vaporware. But whether it's the CD that's out there now or when we deliver on DVD, it's going to be truly a situation in which we're going to be able to deliver both a real stereo mix and a real 5.1 mix on the same disc. I think that's going to really answer the question about double-stocking.

Ed Cherney: Leslie Ann Saunders has just been elected as part of the Board of Directors of the MPGA and we're very happy to have her involved. Leslie?

Leslie Ann Saunders: I just wanted to point out that on the laserdisc, at the end of the format, there is usually pink noise isolated on all the channels with proper level for testing. That should be something that would be simple to do on the DVD, to be part of every release that comes out. It's the last index, so you can go to it right away and check things when you want and know at least that your speakers are in the right order for the consumers.

Ed Cherney: Who would we bring that up with — the labels, manufacturers, or mastering houses?

Leslie Ann Saunders: The mastering houses — doing it that way would automatically add it to the end, and it would just become the last index, along with the song title.

David Pico: About mixing 5.1 and going back and remixing old masters and putting them out: It suddenly occurred to me that in the contracts originally, when we produced these records, there were definitions of what we get paid for — there's the royalty rate for CDs, royalty rate for cassettes, and so on. There's nothing for 5.1. What do we do about that?

Ed Cherney: Typically, as a producer, your deal is piggybacked with the artist's. If the artist isn't seeing a royalty from that, you're getting screwed the same way the artist is.

Alan Parsons: I think David has a point there. I think most contracts would say the producer or the artist will deliver a stereo master of a format suitable for manufacture of phonographic records or whatever. Maybe anything other than a stereo mix might be excluded from that contract.

Doug Sachs: Mastering's going to come down to formats that are unknown — what's going to survive in DVD audio. We're talking about 96k, 24-bit, and all of us mastering engineers, when we talk about it, may say why is my DVD audio disc 50 dB quieter than his DVD audio disc? We're getting ready for the possibility for wide dynamic range. Until the format is decided, it's going to be pretty interesting in the mastering world. One thing for sure, if the industry needs mastering for two channels, I think they're going to need mastering for five channels more than ever.

Doug Mann: How do you feel or what are your perceptions on doing the DVD mix while you still have your stereo mix up on the board? Do you think it should be done then, or at a later date?

Elliot Scheiner: I think the opinion is mixed up here. Some of us feel it can be done at the same time, others don't.

Ed Cherney: I think it depends on the style of the music you're doing. Obviously, Michael Bishop, who is doing classical and jazz things, feels that his part of his job is doing it at the same time. But I'm telling you, working on a pop record, the last thing I want to do is start patchkeying with another mix after I've been beaten up and wrestled to the ground to please an artist and a label. When I've got a stereo mix that's happening, the last thing I want to do is sit there all night and start messing with a 5.1 surround mix.

Chuck Ainlay: What I've been successful doing is taking recalls from the original mix and going back and recalling and splitting out the mix. Basically using all the automation data, the same EQ and compression settings, and then just having to add some reverbs and delays to enhance the rear channels. I find that I can probably do about two songs a day that way, but that's really pushing it.

Ed Cherney: That works for me, too. I thought it was going to take a long time, but it was two, three, four mixes a day.

Elliot Scheiner: I think the other thing to think about, too, is that this is a purely digital medium that this will be released on. In the future, we might be seeing more digital desks used to mix this on, where you will have instant reset and the capability of doing some sort of template from one mix to another. Say you do your stereo mix, then you do your surround mix following that — perhaps you could bounce back and forth, kind of holding on to bits of previous songs, so it would possibly enhance the speed at which you could do this. I don't know, there are a lot of things that can happen in the future.

Phil Ramone: I know that you don't agree with me, but the key that I'm trying to get everybody to see, and the reason I'm asking that people think about the multitrack format of storage, is because when you go back to recall a mix two weeks later in the same recording studio, it's very unlikely that all of the gear is digital. How do you get back to those settings? I know what it takes when you tweak to get that little finesse, and you've got that little slap going on the lead vocal, and it's perfect. I just feel that your textures are why we pay you to be there, and I feel that the key to a great mixer is really to store this — because if you don't, someone else will do it.

Nile Rodgers: The thing about a 5.1 mix to me — and this may be really out of whack — is I think that in a strange way it's a new project. Even though the artistic content is the same, this is a new medium where I can experience the music in a different way. If all I'm trying to do is copy my stereo mix, somehow distribute it in a way where it's sympathetic to the original mix, that doesn't feel like a new artistic adventure to me. I like to think of my 5.1 mix as its own mix.

Al Schmitt: I feel when I recall a mix and bring it back up on the board, I'm getting what I originally started with, at least in quality of sound. When I bring up the stems back through the board, it doesn't sound the same to me; I just don't get the same quality. It's a generation away — it's gone through the board again.

Phil Ramone: I don't disagree with that. I'm only bringing it up. It's my fear, and it's probably unfounded in some ways, that record companies in the future won't be dealing with this aesthetic that we all think we're going to get, to call you back to do that. My fear is that you won't get the time and the money, in some cases, to do it. And if some young intern is going to be doing this in some "DVD room," I'd just like to ask us to protect it, that's all.

Nile Rodgers: What Larry said originally is the correct thing. When a producer is hired to turn in a project, this just becomes one of the mixes that you have to turn in. If the label believes that their artist is going to come out on this format, then you're contracted to do that. You've got to turn in a 5.1 mix.

Ed Cherney: One more question.

Jim Base: Where in the creative process would you like to see the 5.1 concept introduced? In the mixing or when you're sitting down to write the song?

Ed Cherney: I think where it's going to go is written, conceived, arranged, and created for 5.1. I think we'll see that at some point, and then we'll get to see how clever writers, arrangers, and producers really are.

Al Schmitt: When stereo first came in, guys like Juan Garcia Escovil did things where the arrangements were specifically for stereo. I think we're going to find arrangers and composers doing the same thing for 5.1.

Ed Cherney: I just want to wrap up. What are we being left here with today, Chris?

Chris Stone: So far we have attempted to fill half the mind, and half the mind is the creative process. Now we're going to look forward and we're going to listen to what our minds, with what we've seen and heard, can add to it.

ACKNOWLEDGMENTS

Important people you should know about.

While the expression "this book would not have been possible without [insert name here]" may be overused, it has probably never been more true than in this case, with the missing name belonging to **Martin Porter.** I mean that in the most literal sense, as it was Marty, my boss during my tenure at *EQ* and still my boss today, who called me into his office and said, "You should pull together all those great first-person *EQ* stories and print them as a book."

Of course, he also made this book possible by his actions as Executive Editor all those years. It was Marty's vision that had us chase after recording's big guns, and his ideas that made for some of the best stories (e.g., "We should get Joey Ramone to interview Phil Ramone…").

Another key component in the *EQ* mix was Editorial Director **Hector La Torre**. An experienced audio engineer himself, Hector reviewed the edit for technical accuracy and made sure we were covering the products and topics that our readers wanted to hear about.

EQ never had a person who held the title "editor" until **Mitch Gallagher** joined the crew in 1999. Mitch was an *EQ* fan through the years, and took the ball and ran with it — keeping it fresh, current, and successful to this day. Today, Mitch and long-time Technical Editor (not to mention writer, performer, engineer, and really good guy) **Craig Anderton** continue to drive *EQ*'s audience where they need to be — and make sure they're prepared when they get there.

Of course, there wouldn't have been an *EQ* as we know it if it weren't for publisher **Paul Gallo**, who took the title over from another publisher and gave us the direction and freedom to create the magazine that wound up defining the project studio movement.

That takes care of the top of the masthead, but there are many more players here. Senior Editor **Steve La Cerra** deserves special mention. For over a decade, Steve tracked down the most interesting people in the business and got them to reveal their most intriguing techniques. Steve is also a respected studio and live sound engineer, and brought many of his own experiences into *EQ*'s pages — much to the readers' delight.

Robert Granger worked with me for years on *EQ*, and continues to do so today on various other projects. In addition to contributing some killer stories to the magazine, he also proved to be a valuable "creative backboard," as I constantly threw things at him to see if they would (or should) fly.

As you can imagine, over the ten-plus years I have worked with a number of writers and editors, each one leaving their mark on the pages. With that, I would like to thank **JT Way, Jon Ruzan**, **Jon Varman**, **Greg Collins**, **Roger Nichols**, **David Jacobs**, **Al Kooper**, **Liana Jonas**, **Rich Tozzoli**, **Janice Brown**, **David Frangioni**, and **Michael Sanchez**.

And a special thanks to **Edward Colver** for his indelible photographs that defined *EQ* as much as the editorial did.

Outside of the office and the pages of *EQ*, I'd like to thank my family — **Marianne, Brian**, **Kevin**, and **Emily** — for their ongoing support and for just being them. And of course Mom and Dad for starting me off right.

INDEX

C

D

E

I

J

K

L

M

N

O

P

Q

R

S

T

U

V

W

Y

Z